# plant sciences

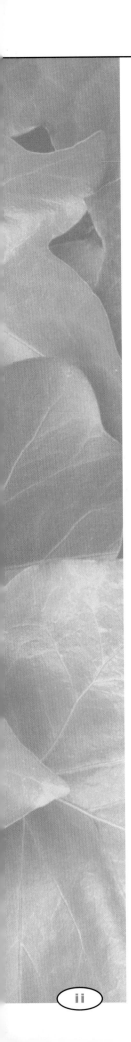

# plant sciences

VOLUME **3**
Ha–Qu

**Richard Robinson, Editor in Chief**

**Macmillan Reference USA**
*an imprint of the Gale Group*
troit • San Francisco • London • Boston • Woodbridge, CT

Macmillan Reference USA
1633 Broadway
New York, NY 10019

Gale Group
27500 Drake Rd.
Farmington Hills, MI 48331-3535

Printed in Canada
1 2 3 4 5 6 7 8 9 10

**Library of Congress Cataloging-in-Publication Data**
Plant sciences / Richard Robinson, editor in chief.
    p.  cm.
Includes bibliographical references (p. ).
ISBN 0-02-865434–X (hardcover : set) — ISBN 0-02-865430-7 (vol. 1) —
ISBN 0-02-865431-5 (vol. 2) — ISBN 0-02-865432-3 (vol. 3) —
ISBN 0-02-865433-1 (vol. 4)
   1.  Botany—Juvenile literature.   2.  Plants—Juvenile literature. [1.
    Botany—Encyclopedias.] I. Robinson, Richard, 1956-
QK49.P52 2000
580—dc21
00—046064

# Preface

Someone once said that if you want to find an alien life form, just go into your backyard and grab the first green thing you see. Although plants evolved on Earth along with the rest of us, they really are about as different and strange and wonderful a group of creatures as one is likely to find anywhere in the universe.

## The World of Plants

Consider for a minute just how different plants are. They have no mouths, no eyes or ears, no brain, no muscles. They stand still for their entire lives, planted in the soil like enormous drinking straws wicking gallon after gallon of water from the earth to the atmosphere. Plants live on little more than water, air, and sunshine and have mastered the trick of transmuting these simple things into almost everything they (and we) need. In this encyclopedia, readers will find out how plants accomplish this photosynthetic alchemy and learn about the extraordinary variety of form and function within the plant kingdom. In addition, readers will be able to trace their 450-million-year history and diversification, from the very first primitive land plants to the more than 250,000 species living today.

✳Explore further in Photosynthesis, Light Reactions and Evolution of Plants

All animals ultimately depend on photosynthesis for their food, and humans are no exception. Over the past ten thousand years, we have cultivated such an intimate relationship with a few species of grains that it is hardly an exaggeration to say, in the words of one scientist, that "humans domesticated wheat, and vice versa." With the help of agriculture, humans were transformed from a nomadic, hunting and gathering species numbering in the low millions, into the most dominant species on the planet, with a population that currently exceeds six billion. Agriculture has shaped human culture profoundly, and together the two have reshaped the planet. In this encyclopedia, readers can explore the history of agriculture, learn how it is practiced today, both conventionally and organically, and what the impact of it and other human activities has been on the land, the atmosphere, and the other creatures who share the planet with us.

✳Explore further in Agriculture, Modern and Human Impacts

Throughout history—even before the development of the modern scientific method—humans experimented with plants, finding the ones that provided the best meal, the strongest fiber, or the sweetest wine. Naming a thing is such a basic and powerful way of knowing it that all cultures have created some type of taxonomy for the plants they use. The scientific understanding of plants through experimentation, and the development of ra-

tional classification schemes based on evolution, has a rich history that is explored in detail in this encyclopedia. There are biographies of more than two dozen botanists who shaped our modern understanding, and essays on the history of physiology, ecology, taxonomy, and evolution. Across the spectrum of the botanical sciences, progress has accelerated in the last two decades, and a range of entries describe the still-changing understanding of evolutionary relationships, genetic control, and biodiversity.

✳Explore further in Ecology, History of; Biodiversity; and Phylogeny

With the development of our modern scientific society, a wide range of new careers has opened up for people interested in plant sciences, many of which are described in this encyclopedia. Most of these jobs require a college degree, and the better-paying ones often require advanced training. While all are centered around plants, they draw on skills that range from envisioning a landscape in one's imagination (landscape architect) to solving differential equations (an ecological modeler) to budgeting and personnel management (curator of a botanical garden).

✳Explore further in Curator of a Botanical Garden and Landscape Architect

## Organization of the Material

Each of the 280 entries in *Plant Sciences* has been newly commissioned for this work. Our contributors are drawn from academic and research institutions, industry, and nonprofit organizations throughout North America. In many cases, the authors literally "wrote the book" on their subject, and all have brought their expertise to bear in writing authoritative, up-to-date entries that are nonetheless accessible to high school students. Almost every entry is illustrated and there are numerous photos, tables, boxes, and sidebars to enhance understanding. Unfamiliar terms are highlighted and defined in the margin. Most entries are followed by a list of related articles and a short reading list for readers seeking more information. Front and back matter include a geologic timescale, a topic outline that groups entries thematically, and a glossary. Each volume has its own index, and volume 4 contains a cumulative index covering the entire encyclopedia.

## Acknowledgments and Thanks

I wish to thank the many people at Macmillan Reference USA and the Gale Group for their leadership in bringing this work to fruition, and their assiduous attention to the many details that make such a work possible. In particular, thanks to Hélène Potter, Brian Kinsey, Betz Des Chenes, and Diane Sawinski. The editorial board members—Robert Evans, Wendy Mechaber, and Robert Wallace—were outstanding, providing invaluable expertise and extraordinary hard work. Wendy is also my wife, and I wish to thank her for her support and encouragement throughout this project. My own love of plants began with three outstanding biology teachers, Marjorie Holland, James Howell, and Walt Tulecke, and I am in their debt. My many students at the Commonwealth School in Boston were also great teachers— their enthusiastic questions over the years deepened my own understanding and appreciation of the mysteries of the plant world. I hope that a new generation of students can discover some of the excitement and mystery of this world in *Plant Sciences*.

*Richard Robinson*
Editor in Chief

# Geologic Timescale

| ERA | PERIOD | | EPOCH | STARTED (millions of years ago) |
|---|---|---|---|---|
| **Cenozoic:** 66.4 millions of years ago–present time | **Quaternary** | | Holocene | 0.01 |
| | | | Pleistocene | 1.6 |
| | Tertiary | **Neogene** | Pliocene | 5.3 |
| | | | Miocene | 23.7 |
| | | **Paleogene** | Oligocene | 36.6 |
| | | | Eocene | 57.8 |
| | | | Paleocene | 66.4 |
| **Mesozoic:** 245–66.4 millions of years ago | **Cretaceous** | | Late | 97.5 |
| | | | Early | 144 |
| | **Jurassic** | | Late | 163 |
| | | | Middle | 187 |
| | | | Early | 208 |
| | **Triassic** | | Late | 230 |
| | | | Middle | 240 |
| | | | Early | 245 |
| **Paleozoic:** 570–245 millions of years ago | **Permian** | | Late | 258 |
| | | | Early | 286 |
| | Carboniferous | **Pennsylvanian** | Late | 320 |
| | | **Mississippian** | Early | 360 |
| | **Devonian** | | Late | 374 |
| | | | Middle | 387 |
| | | | Early | 408 |
| | **Silurian** | | Late | 421 |
| | | | Early | 438 |
| | **Ordovician** | | Late | 458 |
| | | | Middle | 478 |
| | | | Early | 505 |
| | **Cambrian** | | Late | 523 |
| | | | Middle | 540 |
| | | | Early | 570 |
| **Precambrian time:** 4500–570 millions of years ago | | | | 4500 |

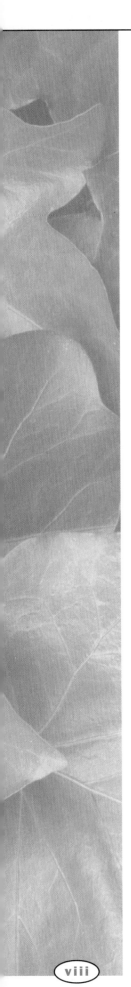

# Contributors

Miguel Altieri
*University of California, Berkeley*

Sherwin Toshio Amimoto
*Redondo Beach, CA*

Edward F. Anderson
*Desert Botanical Garden, Phoenix, AZ*

Gregory J. Anderson
*University of Connecticut*

Mary Anne Andrei
*Minneapolis, MN*

Wendy L. Applequist
*Iowa State University*

Rebecca Baker
*Cotati, CA*

Peter S. Bakwin
*National Oceanic and Atmospheric Administration*

Jo Ann Banks
*Purdue University*

Theodore M. Barkley
*Botanical Research Institute of Texas*

Ronald D. Barnett
*University of Florida*

Patricia A. Batchelor
*Milwaukee Public Museum*

Hank W. Bass
*Florida State University*

Yves Basset
*Smithsonian Tropical Research Institute*

Stuart F. Baum
*University of California, Davis*

Gabriel Bernardello
*University of Connecticut*

Paul E. Berry
*University of Wisconsin-Madison*

Paul C. Bethke
*University of California, Berkeley*

J. Derek Bewley
*University of Guelph*

Christopher J. Biermann
*Philomath, OR*

Franco Biondi
*University of Nevada*

Richard E. Bir
*North Carolina State University*

Jane H. Bock
*University of Colorado*

Hans Bohnert
*Nara Institute of Science and Technology*

Brian M. Boom
*New York Botanical Garden*

David E. Boufford
*Harvard University Herbaria*

John L. Bowman
*University of California, Davis*

James R. Boyle
*Oregon State University*

James M. Bradeen
*University of Wisconsin-Madison*

Irwin M. Brodo
*Canadian Museum of Nature*

Robert C. Brown
*Iowa State University*

Leo P. Bruederle
*University of Colorado, Denver*

Robert Buchsbaum
*Massachusetts Audubon Society*

Stephen C. Bunting
*University of Idaho*

John M. Burke
*Indiana University*

Charles A. Butterworth
*Iowa State University*

Christian E. Butzke
*University of California, Davis*

Kenneth M. Cameron
*New York Botanical Garden*

Deborah K. Canington
*University of California, Davis*

Vernon B. Cardwell
*American Society of Agronomy*

Don Cawthon
*Texas A & M University*

Russell L. Chapman
*Louisiana State University*

Arthur H. Chappelka
*Auburn University*

Lynn G. Clark
*Iowa State University*

W. Dean Cocking
*James Madison University*

James T. Colbert
*Iowa State University*

Daniel J. Cosgrove
*Pennsylvania State University*

Barbara Crandall-Stotler
*Southern Illinois University*

Donald L. Crawford
*University of Idaho*

Thomas B. Croat
*Missouri Botanical Garden*

Lawrence J. Crockett
*Pace University*

Sunburst Shell Crockett
*Society of American Foresters*

Richard Cronn
*Iowa State University*

Anne Fernald Cross
*Oklahoma State University*

Rodney Croteau
*Washington State University*

Judith G. Croxdale
*University of Wisconsin*

Peter J. Davies
*Cornell University*

Jerrold I. Davis
*Cornell University*

Elizabeth L. Davison
*University of Arizona*

Ira W. Deep
*Ohio State University*

Nancy G. Dengler
*University of Toronto*

Steven L. Dickie
*Iowa State University*

David L. Dilcher
*University of Florida*

Rebecca W. Doerge
*Purdue University*

Susan A. Dunford
*University of Cincinnati*

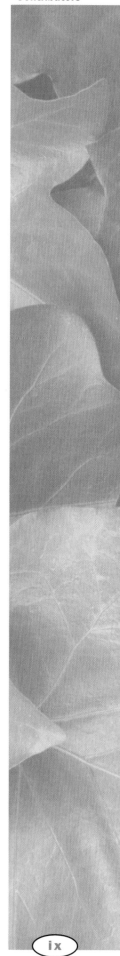

Frank A. Einhellig
*Southwest Missouri State University*

George S. Ellmore
*Tufts University*

Roland Ennos
*University of Manchester*

Emanuel Epstein
*University of California, Davis*

M. Susan Erich
*University of Maine*

Robert C. Evans
*Rutgers University*

Donald R. Farrar
*Iowa State University*

Charles B. Fenster
*Botanisk Institutt*

Manfred A. Fischer
*University of Vienna, Austria*

Theodore H. Fleming
*Tuscon, AZ*

Dennis Francis
*Cardiff University*

Arthur W. Galston
*Yale University*

Grace Gershuny
*St. Johnsbury, VT*

Peter Gerstenberger
*National Arborist Association, Inc.*

Stephen R. Gliessman
*University of California, Santa Cruz*

J. Peter Gogarten
*University of Connecticut*

Govindjee
*University of Illinois, Urbana-Champaign*

Linda E. Graham
*University of Wisconsin, Madison*

Peter H. Graham
*University of Minnesota*

Michael A. Grusak
*U.S. Department of Agriculture, Children's Nutrition Research Center*

Gerald F. Guala
*Fairchild Tropical Garden, Miami*

Robert Gutman
*Athens, GA*

Charles J. Gwo
*University of New Mexico*

Ardell D. Halvorson
*U.S. Department of Agriculture, Agricultural Research Service*

Earl G. Hammond
*Iowa State University*

Jeffrey B. Harborne
*University of Reading*

Elizabeth M. Harris
*Ohio State University Herbarium*

Frederick V. Hebard
*American Chestnut Foundation*

Steven R. Hill
*Center for Biodiversity*

J. Kenneth Hoober
*Arizona State University*

Roger F. Horton
*University of Guelph*

D. Michael Jackson
*U.S. Department of Agriculture, Agricultural Research Service*

William P. Jacobs
*Princeton, NJ*

David M. Jarzen
*University of Florida*

Roger V. Jean
*University of Quebec*

Philip D. Jenkins
*University of Arizona*

Russell L. Jones
*University of California, Berkeley*

Lee B. Kass
*Cornell University*

George B. Kauffman
*California State University, Fresno*

Jon E. Keeley
*National Park Service*

Dean G. Kelch
*University of California, Berkeley*

Nancy M. Kerk
*Yale University*

Alan K. Knapp
*Kansas State University*

Erich Kombrink
*Max-Planck-Institut für Züchtungsforschung*

Ross E. Koning
*Eastern Connecticut State University*

Thomas G. Lammers
*University of Wisconsin, Oshkosh*

Mark A. Largent
*University of Minnesota*

Donald W. Larson
*Columbus, OH*

Matthew Lavin
*Montana State University*

Roger H. Lawson
*Columbia, MD*

Michael Lee
*Iowa State University*

Michael J. Lewis
*University of California, Davis*

Walter H. Lewis
*Washington University*

Douglas T. Linde
*Delaware Valley College*

Bradford Carlton Lister
*Rensselaer Polytechnic Institute*

Margaret D. Lowman
*Marie Selby Botanical Gardens, Sarasota, FL*

Peter J. Lumsden
*University of Central Lancashire*

Lynn Margulis
*University of Massachusetts, Amherst*

Wendy Mechaber
*University of Arizona*

Alan W. Meerow
*U.S. Department of Agriculture, Agricultural Research Service*

T. Lawrence Mellichamp
*University of North Carolina, Charlotte*

Scott Merkle
*University of Georgia*

Jan E. Mikesell
*Gettysburg College*

Orson K. Miller Jr.
*Virginia Polytechnic Institute*

Thomas Minney
*The New Forests Project*

Thomas S. Moore
*Louisiana State University*

David R. Morgan
*Western Washington University*

Gisèle Muller-Parker
*Western Washington University*

Suzanne C. Nelson
*Native Seeds/SEARCH*

Robert Newgarden
*Brooklyn Botanic Gardens*

Daniel L. Nickrent
*Southern Illinois University*

John S. Niederhauser
*Tucson, AZ*

David O. Norris
*University of Colorado*

Lorraine Olendzenski
*University of Connecticut*

Micheal D. K. Owen
*Iowa State University*

James C. Parks
*Millersville University*

Wayne Parrott
*University of Georgia*

Andrew H. Paterson
*University of Georgia*

Jessica P. Penney
*Allston, MA*

Terry L. Peppard
*Warren, NJ*

John H. Perkins
*The Evergreen State College*

Kim Moreau Peterson
*University of Alaska, Anchorage*

Peter A. Peterson
*Iowa State University*

Richard B. Peterson
*Connecticut Agricultural Experiment Station*

D. Mason Pharr
*North Carolina State University*

Bobby J. Phipps
*Delta Research Center*

Janet M. Pine
*Iowa State University*

Ghillean T. Prance
*The Old Vicarage, Dorset, UK*

Robert A. Price
*University of Georgia*

Richard B. Primack
*Boston University*

V. Raghavan
*Ohio State University*

James A. Rasmussen
*Southern Arkansas University*

Linda A. Raubeson
*Central Washington University*

A. S. N. Reddy
*Colorado State University*

Robert A. Rice
*Smithsonian Migratory Bird Center*

Loren H. Rieseberg
*Indiana University*

Richard Robinson
*Tuscon, AZ*

Curt R. Rom
*University of Arkansas*

Thomas L. Rost
*University of California, Davis*

Sabine J. Rundle
*Western Carolina University*

Scott D. Russell
*University of Oklahoma*

J. Neil Rutger
*U.S. Department of Agriculture,
Dale Bumpers National Rice
Research Center*

Fred D. Sack
*Ohio State University*

Dorion Sagan
*Amherst, MA*

Ann K. Sakai
*University of California-Irvine*

Frank B. Salisbury
*Utah State University*

Mark A. Schneegurt
*Witchita State University*

Randy Scholl
*Ohio State University*

Jack C. Schultz
*Pennsylvania State University*

Hanna Rose Shell
*New Haven, CT*

Timothy W. Short
*Queens College of the City
University of New York*

Philipp W. Simon
*University of Wisconsin-Madison*

Garry A. Smith
*Canon City, CO*

James F. Smith
*Boise State University*

Vassiliki Betty Smocovitis
*University of Florida*

Doug Soltis
*Washington State University*

Pam Soltis
*Washington State University*

Paul C. Spector
*The Holden Arboretum, Kirtland,
OH*

David M. Spooner
*University of Wisconsin*

Helen A. Stafford
*Reed College*

Craig Steely
*Elm Research Institute*

Taylor A. Steeves
*University of Saskatchewan*

Hans K. Stenoien
*Botanisk Institutt*

Peter F. Stevens
*University of Missouri, St. Louis*

Ian M. Sussex
*Yale University*

Charlotte A. Tancin
*Carnegie Mellon University*

Edith L. Taylor
*University of Kansas*

Thomas N. Taylor
*University of Kansas*

W. Carl Taylor
*Milwaukee Public Museum*

Mark Tebbitt
*Brooklyn Botanical Gardens*

Barbara M. Thiers
*New York Botanical Garden*

Sean C. Thomas
*University of Toronto*

Sue A. Thompson
*Pittsburgh, PA*

Barbara N. Timmermann
*University of Arizona*

Ward M. Tingey
*Cornell University*

Alyson K. Tobin
*University of St. Andrews*

Dwight T. Tomes
*Johnston, IA*

Nancy J. Turner
*University of Victoria*

Sarah E. Turner
*University of Victoria*

Miguel L. Vasquez
*Northern Arizona University*

Robert S. Wallace
*Iowa State University*

Debra A. Waters
*Louisiana State University*

Elizabeth Fortson Wells
*George Washington University*

Molly M. Welsh
*U.S. Department of Agriculture,
Agricultural Research Service*

James J. White
*Carnegie Mellon University*

Michael A. White
*University of Montana*

John Whitmarsh
*University of Illinois, Urbana-
Champaign*

Garrison Wilkes
*University of Massachusetts, Boston*

John D. Williamson
*North Carolina State University*

Thomas Wirth
*Thomas Wirth Associates, Inc.,
Sherborn, MA*

Jianguo Wu
*Arizona State University*

# Table of Contents

# plant sciences

# Hales, Stephen

**English Physiologist**
**1677–1761**

Stephen Hales was a preeminent scientist of the late eighteenth century and the founder of plant **physiology**. Born in Kent, England, in 1677, Hales grew up in an upper-class Kent family and was educated at Cambridge University. Though he received no formal training in botany during college, Hales obtained a solid background in science, including physics and mechanics. Upon graduation from Cambridge, Hales moved to Teddington, a town on the Thames River in England, where he lived the rest of his life.

**physiology** the biochemical processes carried out by an organism

Hales has been called the first fully **deductive** and **quantitative** plant scientist. He made many significant discoveries concerning both animal and plant circulation. Crucially, Hales measured plant growth and devised innovative methods for the analysis and interpretation of these measurements.

**deductive** reasoning from facts to conclusion

**quantitative** numerical, especially as derived from measurement

Hales's most original contribution was his transfer of application of the so-called statical method he and others had used on animals to plant **specimens**. The basis behind the statical method was the belief that the comprehension of living organisms was possible only through the precise measurements of their inputs and outputs. Thus the way to understand a human being would be to measure the fluids and other materials that had entered and left it. In the case of a tree, a statistician would measure changes in the amount and quality of the water it consumed and the sap it contained.

**specimen** object or organism under consideration

In 1706, under the influence of Isaac Newton's new mechanics, Hales tried to figure out the mechanism that controlled animal blood pressure by experimenting on dog specimens. At the same time, Hales had the idea that the circulation of sap in plants might well be similar to the circulation of the blood in humans and other animals. As he was exploring animal circulation, Hales grew increasingly interested in plant circulation. He wrote later in his book *Vegetable Staticks* of his first circulation experiments: "I wished I could have made the like experiments to discover the force of the sap in vegetables."

After a decade of quiet research and study, Hales did indeed devise such experiments on plants. He attached glass tubes to the cut ends of vine plants. He then watched sap rise through these tubes, and he monitored how the sap flow varied with changing climate and light conditions. In 1724, Hales

Stephen Hales.

completed *Vegetable Staticks* (quoted above), wherein he distinguished three different aspects of water movement in plants. These he called imbibition, root pressure, and leaf suction.

The prevalent notion among Hales's contemporaries was that the movement of plant sap was similar to the circulation of human blood, which was discovered by William Harvey in 1628. Crucially, Hales demonstrated that this theory was false. Instead, he demonstrated the constant uptake (absorption) of water by plants and water's constant loss through transpiration (evaporation into the air). Drawing on this principle, Hales made many exact and careful experiments using weights and measures. All of these he repeated using different types of plants (willows and creepers, for example) in order to verify his conclusions. Thus, from his beginnings as a physiologist, Hales went on to create a mechanics of water movement. SEE ALSO DE SAUSSURE, NICHOLAS; PHYSIOLOGIST; PHYSIOLOGY, HISTORY OF; WATER MOVEMENT.

*Hanna Rose Shell*

**Bibliography**

Isley, Duane. "Hales." *One Hundred and One Botanists*. Ames, IA: Iowa State University Press, 1994.

Morton, Alan G. "Hales." *History of Botanical Science*. London: Academic Press, 1981.

# Halophytes

**ions** charged particles

**ecosystem** an ecological community together with its environment

**vacuole** the large fluid-filled sac that occupies most of the space in a plant cell. Use for storage and maintaining internal pressure

Halophytes (salt plants) are organisms that require elevated amounts of sodium up to or exceeding seawater strength (approximately 33 parts of sodium per thousand) for optimal growth. In contrast, most crops cease to produce with sodium at 1 to 3 ppt. Halophytes are found worldwide, including in deserts where infrequent rainfall leaches **ions** to the surface. They encroach into irrigated lands as ion concentrations increase over time. They are best known as mangroves, a term for a number of unrelated tree species, which in tropical **ecosystems** stabilize coastlines in species-rich habitats threatened by development. Halophytism characterizes species in many plant families, indicating adaptive evolution from nontolerant ancestors. Typical adaptations are succulence, water-conserving mechanisms, and specialized surface morphology (e.g., trichomes and waxes). Resistance to salinity is costly, explaining the slow growth of halophytes. Energy expenditure for ion pumping is required for sodium export (from glands), partitioning (movement of sodium away from growing tissues) or storage (in **vacuoles**, specialized cells, or senescing leaves). Another source of energy expenditure is for absorption of essential ions and nutrients from the soil. This active transport process is made more difficult by high levels of sodium in the surrounding soil. Valued for their ecological importance, few halophytes are economically significant, while species such as *Salicornia* have potential utility as oil crops. SEE ALSO COASTAL ECOSYSTEMS; DESERTS; TRICHOMES.

*Hans Bohnert*

**Bibliography**

National Research Council. *Saline Agriculture: Salt-Tolerant Plants for Developing Countries*. Washington, DC: National Academy Press, 1990.

Ungar, I. A. *Ecophysiology of Vascular Halophytes*. Boca Raton, FL: CRC Press, 1991.

## Herbals and Herbalists

For most of human history, people have relied on herbalism for at least some of their medicinal needs, and this remains true for more than half of the world's population in the twenty-first century. Much of our modern **pharmacopeia** also has its roots in the historical knowledge of medicinal plants.

### What Are Herbs, Herbals, and Herbalists?

To botanists, herbs are plants that die back to the ground after flowering, but more generally, herbs are thought of as plants with medicinal, culinary (especially seasoning), or aromatic uses.

Traditional herbals are compilations of information about medicinal plants, typically including plant names, descriptions, and illustrations, and information on medicinal uses. Herbals have been written for thousands of years and form an important historical record and scientific resource. Many plant medicines listed in older herbals are still used in some form, but some herbals, especially earlier ones, also contain much inaccurate information and plant lore.

Herbalists follow a long tradition in using plants and plant-based medicines for healing purposes. Some gather medicinal plants locally, while others use both local and foreign plant material. Some rely on age-old knowledge and lore, while others also consult the findings of new research.

Red mangroves on a Florida coastline.

**pharmacopeia** a group of medicines

An engraving, circa 1713, showing various plants and corresponding body parts thought to benefit through some use of the plant.

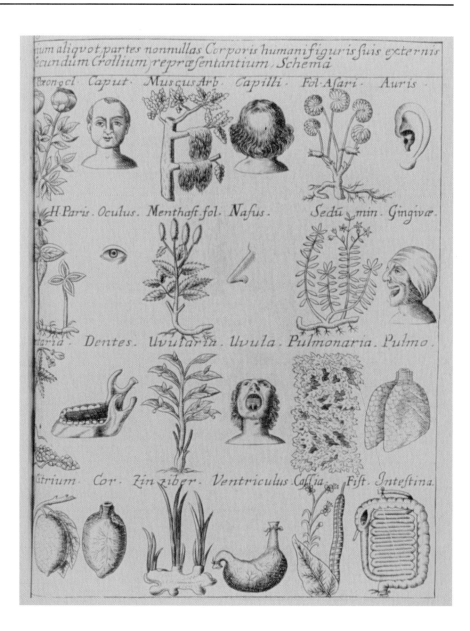

## Herbalism in History

There are herbalist traditions going back centuries or millennia in most parts of the world, and lists of medicinal plants survive from antiquity, such as Shen Nung's *Pen Ts'ao* (2800 B.C.E.) and the Egyptian *Papyrus Ebers* (1500 B.C.E.).

European herbal medicine is rooted in the works of classical writers such as Dioscorides, whose *De Materia Medica* (78 C.E.) formed the basis of herbals in Europe for 1,500 years. Then, as voyages of exploration began to bring new plants from faraway lands, European herbal authors expanded their coverage. This also led to a heightened interest in naming and classifying plants, contributing to the development of botanical science.

Significant European herbals include those by Otto Brunfels (c. 1488–1534), Leonhart Fuchs (1501–1566), Pier Andrea Mattioli (1500–1577), and John Gerard (1545–1612), among others. Reports from the New World include the Badianus manuscript (1552), an Aztec herbal by Martín de la Cruz and Juan Badiano, and works by Nicholas Monardes (1493–1588) and John Josselyn (fl. 1630–1675). Herbals were published in Europe into the eighteenth century but declined as modern medicine took new forms.

## Herbal Medicine Today

Today, traditional herbalist healers continue to use knowledge passed down for generations. Some **ethnobotanists** are studying with traditional healers to save such knowledge before it disappears.

**ethnobotanist** a scientist who interacts with native peoples to learn more about the plants of a region

Due to a growing interest in alternative medicine, herbalism is also attracting new practitioners, and herbal research is constantly underway. Critics note that dosages can be difficult to control, even among plants of the same species, and side effects can be unpredictable.

A number of essential modern drugs derive from plants, and scientists generally agree that only a fraction of the world's plants have been studied for their medicinal potential. However, threats to the environment, particularly in tropical forests where the highest numbers of species (many still unknown to science) reside, may reduce the possibility of identifying new plant-derived drugs. SEE ALSO ETHNOBOTANY; HERBS AND SPICES; MEDICINAL PLANTS; TAXONOMY, HISTORY OF.

*Charlotte A. Tancin*

### Bibliography

Anderson, Frank J. *An Illustrated History of the Herbals.* New York: Columbia University Press, 1977.

Arber, Agnes. *Herbals: Their Origin and Evolution. A Chapter in the History of Botany, 1470–1670,* 3rd ed. Cambridge: Cambridge University Press, 1986, reprinted 1988.

Arvigo, Rosita, Nadine Epstein, Marilyn Yaquinto, and Michael Balick. *Sastun: My Apprenticeship with a Maya Healer.* San Francisco: HarperSanFrancisco, 1994.

Balick, Michael J., and Paul A. Cox. *Plants, People, and Culture: The Science of Ethnobotany.* New York: Scientific American Library, 1996.

Duke, James A. *The Green Pharmacy: New Discoveries in Herbal Remedies for Common Diseases and Conditions from the World's Foremost Authority on Healing Herbs.* Emmaus, PA: Rodale Press, 1997.

Foster, Steven. *Herbal Renaissance: Growing, Using, and Understanding Herbs in the Modern World.* Salt Lake City, UT: Gibbs-Smith Publisher, 1993.

Schultes, Richard E., and Robert F. Raffauf. *The Healing Forest: Medicinal and Toxic Plants of the Northwest Amazonia.* Portland, OR: Dioscorides Press, 1990.

Thomson, William A. R., ed. *Medicines from the Earth: A Guide to Healing Plants.* New York: Alfred van der Marck Eds., 1983.

# Herbaria

An herbarium is a collection of dried plants or fungi used for scientific study. Herbaria are the main source of data for the field of botany called taxonomy. Plant taxonomists study the **biodiversity** of a particular region of the world (**floristic** research) or the relationships among members of a particular group of organisms (monographic research). Although a plant looks different when it is dried compared to when it is growing in nature, most of the key features needed for taxonomic studies can be found in a well-

**biodiversity** degree of variety of life

**floristic** related to plants

**LARGEST HERBARIA IN THE WORLD**

| Name | Location | Date Established | Number of Specimens (approximate) |
|---|---|---|---|
| Museum National d'Histoire Naturelle | Paris, France | 1635 | 8,877,300 |
| Royal Botanic Gardens | Kew, England | 1841 | 6,000,000 |
| New York Botanical Garden | New York, New York, U.S.A. | 1891 | 6,000,000 |
| Komarov Botanical Institute | St. Petersburg, Russia | 1823 | 5,770,000 |
| Swedish Museum of Natural History | Stockholm, Sweden | 1739 | 5,600,000 |
| The Natural History Museum | London, England | 1753 | 5,300,000 |
| Conservatoire et Jardin Botaniques | Geneva, Switzerland | 1824 | 5,200,000 |
| Harvard University | Cambridge, Massachusetts, U.S.A. | 1864 | 5,000,000 |
| Smithsonian Institution | Washington, D.C., U.S.A. | 1848 | 4,858,000 |
| Institut de Botanique | Montpellier, France | 1845 | 4,368,000 |

**SOURCE:** Data from P. N. Holmgren, *Index Herbariorum*, 8th ed. (New York: New York Botanical Garden, 1990), Index.

**specimen** object or organism under consideration

prepared herbarium **specimen**. These features include the size and shape of the various parts of the organism, as well as surface texture, cellular structure, and color reactions with certain chemical solutions. From the investigation of these features, the taxonomist prepares a detailed description of the organism, which can be compared to descriptions of other organisms. Today it is possible to extract genetic material (deoxyribonucleic acid; DNA) from herbarium specimens. Gene sequences provide many data points for comparison between organisms.

## Herbaria of the World

If prepared and maintained properly, herbarium specimens hold their scientific value for hundreds of years and therefore serve as a repository of information about Earth's current and past biodiversity. The oldest herbaria in the world, found in Europe, are more than three hundred years old. Traditionally all colleges or universities that offer training in plant science create and maintain herbaria, as do most botanical gardens and natural history museums.

There are approximately 2,639 herbaria in 147 countries around the world. Typically herbaria associated with smaller institutions concentrate on the plants and fungi of their regional flora, and perhaps additionally hold specimens representing the research interest of the faculty and graduate students. Larger herbaria strive to represent the plants and fungi from a wider geographic area and a greater diversity of organisms. Such herbaria may be housed in large natural history museums (the Field Museum of Natural History in Chicago, for example) or botanical gardens (such as the New York Botanical Garden), major research universities (such as Harvard University), or may be maintained by a governmental agency (such as the Smithsonian Institution).

When taxonomists publish a monograph or flora, they must provide a list of all the specimens examined in the course of the study, indicating the name of the herbarium where the specimens were deposited. Because the scientific method dictates that studies be replicable, anyone wanting to repeat a taxonomist's study has to begin by reexamining the specimens that were used.

## OTHER U.S. HERBARIA

Major herbaria in the United States are the Missouri Botanical Garden in St. Louis, established in 1859 and holding 3.7 million specimens; the Field Museum of Natural History in Chicago, established in 1893 and holding 2.5 million specimens; and the University of California at Berkeley, established in 1872 and holding 1.7 million specimens.

## Collecting and Preparing Specimens

Taxonomists not only examine specimens already deposited in herbaria, but also collect new herbarium specimens in the course of their research. When taxonomists go on collecting trips, they are equipped with tools such as plastic or waxed paper bags in which to place the individual specimens, clippers, knives, trowels, and perhaps a saw. Long poles with clippers attached to the ends or tree-climbing equipment may be used to collect flowers or leaves from tall trees. Collecting underwater plants such as algae may require hip boots, snorkel and face mask, or even scuba gear. Whatever the group of organisms, a good collection consists of just enough material to contain the important features for identification, such as leaves, roots, flowers, fruits, or other reproductive parts.

A collector always takes a field notebook on a collecting trip, because it is critical to record information about the organism as it is collected. The exact locality of a collected specimen is recorded using maps, compasses, or geo-positioning devices, which enables another collector to return to the same site if more material is needed. The collector also details the surroundings of the collected specimens, including the habitat (forest, meadow, or mountainside, for example), elevation, and what other types of plants or animals are found nearby. Also recorded are features that will change when the plant dries—such as its color, size, or odor—and a photograph of the organism or collection site may be taken.

It is necessary to remove as much of the moisture as possible from collected specimens to prevent decomposition by fungi or bacteria. For flowering plants, this is done by pressing the plant in absorbent paper and placing it between rigid boards (forming what's known as a plant press), and then placing the press over a source of heat. For fungi such as mushrooms, the specimen is instead placed whole (or sliced in half) on a drying apparatus that uses low heat and a fan to remove the water. Organisms such as lichens or mosses are air-dried for several days to remove moisture. Plants that contain a large amount of water are challenging to prepare as specimens. Cactus stems or large fruits such as pumpkins must be thinly sliced before pressing, and the absorbent material around the specimen must be replaced frequently.

When the specimen is dry, it is prepared for insertion in the herbarium. Preparing the specimen at this stage involves two steps: packaging and labeling. The typical pressed plant specimen is glued to a sheet of heavyweight paper, typically 27.5 x 43 centimeters in size. Specimens such as bryophytes, lichens, fungi, or very bulky plants are loosely placed in paper packets or boxes. Boxes are also used for specimens of very hard material such as coconut fruits or pine cones. Some plants and fungi are very tiny, consisting of a single cell, and therefore too small to see without a microscope. An herbarium specimen of such an organism is stored on a microscope slide. Whatever the size of the specimen, each is accompanied by a paper label, which includes the name of the plant and all of the information the collector recorded in his or her field book. In the past these labels were written by hand or manually typed. Today the collection data are more commonly entered into a computerized database and then formatted to print on a specimen label.

## Preserving and Accessing Specimens

After an herbarium specimen is prepared, it is ready to be inserted in the herbarium. A modern herbarium holds its specimens in specially designed, air- and water-tight, sealed steel cases, which are divided internally into shelves or cubbyholes. When stored in such a case, herbarium specimens are protected from the greatest threats to their long-term maintenance, namely damage by water, insects, and fungi. Within an herbarium case, individual specimens are usually grouped by name or geographical region into folders or boxes.

An herbarium is usually maintained by a curator, a scientist responsible for overseeing the processing of new herbarium specimens, maintaining order within the collection, and guarding the specimens against damage. The curator is usually a taxonomist, chosen for the position because of his or her knowledge of the types of plants, fungi, or area that is the specialty of the herbarium. Large herbaria with important collections in many regions or groups of plants have many curators, each responsible for a particular part of the herbarium. In smaller university herbaria, the curator may also be a professor.

A curator is also responsible for overseeing the use of the herbarium by other scientists. Herbaria make their specimens available for study by visiting scientists and most also loan specimens to other herbaria when requested to do so. Herbarium curators want to make the specimens in their care available to all serious scientific studies. In addition to loaning specimens and welcoming other scientists into their herbaria, curators today often share searchable indices or catalogs, or even images of their collection through the World Wide Web. Scientists use the Internet for quick access to information about a specimen but generally still need to see the actual specimen to study it fully.

Although taxonomists are the most frequent users of herbaria, there are many other users. A forester might examine collections made over the years to see how biodiversity of the forest has changed over time. A conservation biologist might use an herbarium to see how the distribution of a rare or a weedy species has changed due to alterations in the environment. A government agency might use an herbarium to determine where to place roads or dams to cause the least disturbance to a biologically diverse area. A plant pathologist might use an herbarium to examine specimens that are the cause of plant diseases or to examine the distribution of the plant hosts of diseases to predict future areas of infection. Occasionally historians consult herbaria to learn more about the people who have collected plants over the years. For example, it is not well known that historical figures such as General George A. Custer, inventor George Washington Carver, or musician John Cage collected herbarium specimens, but collections made by all three have been found in the New York Botanical Garden herbarium, and other long-established herbaria probably contain equally surprising finds. SEE ALSO CURATOR OF AN HERBARIUM; FLORA; PLANT IDENTIFICATION; SYSTEMATICS, MOLECULAR; SYSTEMATICS, PLANT; TAXONOMY.

*Barbara M. Thiers*

**Bibliography**

Holmgren, Patricia. *Index Herbariorum*, 8th ed. New York: New York Botanical Garden, 1990.

# Herbicides

Herbicides are chemicals that kill plants. Herbicides are widely used in modern agriculture to control weeds, reduce competition, and increase productivity of crop plants. They are also used by homeowners to control lawn weeds and by turf grass managers, foresters, and other professionals. Herbicides are used not only on land, but also in lakes, rivers, and other aquatic environments to control aquatic weeds.

The modern use of herbicides began in the 1940s, with the development of 2,4-D (2, 4-dichlorophenelyacetic acid). By the end of that decade, herbicide use had grown from a few thousand acres to several million. There are now approximately four hundred different herbicides registered for use in the United States. While the rates of application vary by crop, the vast majority of commercial agricultural crop acreage receives at least one application of herbicide every year.

Herbicides may be applied directly to the soil or to the leaves of the target plant. Soil applications may be targeted at preventing seed germination, to affect root growth, or to be absorbed and to work systemically (within the whole plant body). Foliar (leaf) applications may target the leaves or be absorbed. In addition to directly killing the target weed, herbicides can, over time, reduce the number of weed seeds in the soil, decreasing the need for continued intensive applications in the future.

A row of Worcester Pearmain apple trees in an English orchard. Seven weeks after the trees were treated with an herbicide, the grass beneath turned brown and died.

**auxin** a plant hormone

**compound** a substance formed from two or more elements

**chloroplast** the photosynthetic organelle of plants and algae

**reaction center** a protein complex that uses light energy to create a stable charge separation by transferring a single electron energetically uphill from a donor molecule to an acceptor molecule, both of which are located in the reaction center

**free radicals** toxic molecular fragments

Herbicides kill plants by interfering with a fundamental process within their cells. 2,4-D is a synthetic **auxin**. It promotes cell elongation (rather than cell division), and in effective concentrations kills the target plant by causing unregulated growth. Plants treated with 2,4-D display misshapen stems, inappropriate adventitious root growth, and other aberrant effects (growing in an unusual location on the plant). The excessive growth exhausts food reserves, and the combination of effects eventually causes the death of the plant. 2,4-D is often used to kill dicot weeds growing among monocot crops, since monocots are more resistant to its effects. 2,4-D and a related **compound**, 2,4,5-T were combined in Agent Orange, the defoliant used in the Vietnam War. Health effects from exposure to Agent Orange are believed to be due to contamination with dioxin, and not to the herbicides themselves.

Glyphosphate (marketed as Roundup®) interferes with an enzyme involved in amino acid synthesis, thereby disrupting plant metabolism in a variety of ways. It is one of the most common herbicides and is available for homeowner use as well as for commercial operators. Glyphosphate is a nonselective herbicide, killing most plants that it contacts. However, it is fairly harmless to animals, including humans, since amino acid metabolism is very different in animals. A gene for glyphosphate resistance has now been introduced into a number of important crop plants, allowing increased use of glyphosphate to control weeds on these crops.

Atrazine interferes with photosynthesis. Atrazine is taken up by roots and transported to **chloroplasts**, where it binds to a protein in the Photosystem II **reaction center**. This prevents the normal flow of electrons during photosynthesis and causes chloroplast swelling and rupture.

Paraquat also interferes with photosynthesis, but through a different mechanism. This herbicide accepts electrons from photosystem I and then donates them to molecular oxygen. This forms highly reactive oxygen **free radicals**, which are immediately toxic to the surrounding tissue. Paraquat is also toxic to humans and other animals.

As with any agent that causes death in a group of organisms, herbicides cause natural selection among weed species. Evolution of herbicide resistance is a serious problem and has spurred research on new herbicide development and a deeper understanding of mechanisms of action. These concerns have joined with environmental and health concerns to promote a more integrated approach to weed management, combining tillage practices, selection for weed-tolerant varieties, better understanding of weed biology, and better timing of herbicide application. This integrated approach requires more time and attention from the farmer but can also offer significant benefits. SEE ALSO AGRICULTURE, MODERN; DICOTS; HORMONES; MONOCOTS; PHOTOSYNTHESIS, LIGHT REACTIONS AND.

*Richard Robinson*

**Bibliography**

Aldrich, R. J., and R. J. Kremer. *Principles in Weed Management*, 2nd ed. Ames, IA: Iowa State University Press, 1997.

Devine, Malcolm D., Stephen O. Duke, and Carl Fedtke. *Physiology of Herbicide Action*. Englewood Cliffs, NJ: Prentice-Hall, 1993.

# Herbs and Spices

The terms *herb* and *spice* are popular terms for plants or plant products that are used as flavorings or scents (e.g., spices and culinary herbs), drugs (e.g., medicinal herbs), and less frequently as perfumes, dyes, and stimulants.

Many herbs and spices are edible but may be distinguished from fruits and vegetables by their lack of food value, as measured in calories. Unlike fruits and vegetables, their usefulness has less to do with their primary metabolites (e.g., sugars and proteins) than with their secondary metabolites (**compounds** commonly produced to discourage **pathogens** and predators). The distinct flavors and smells of spices and culinary herbs are usually due to essential oils, while the active components of medicinal herbs also include many kinds of steroids, alkaloids, and glycosides. Most plants referred to as herbs or spices contain many different secondary compounds.

## Spices

Spices are pungent, aromatic plant products used for flavoring or scent. The derivation of the word spice from the Latin *species*, meaning articles of commerce, suggests that these were plants that early Europeans could not grow, but instead had to trade for via Asia or Africa. Consistent with this, people tend to limit the word spice to durable products such as seeds, bark, and resinous **exudations**, especially those from subtropical and tropical climates, and use the word herb when the useful part is the perishable leaf. Commercially important spices include black pepper, the fruit of *Piper nigrum*, and cinnamon, the inner bark of two closely related tree species from the laurel family.

## Culinary Herbs

The word herb is popularly used to refer to a plant product that has culinary value as a flavoring, while scientifically an herb is a plant that lacks permanent woody stems. Most of our well-known culinary herbs are obtained from the leaves or seeds of herbaceous plants, many of which originated in the Mediterranean region of Europe. Many of the best known belong to the mint family, such as peppermint (*Mentha* x *piperita*), or the carrot family, such as coriander (*Coriandrum sativum*).

## Herbal Medicines

Medicinal herbs were once the mainstays of all medicine and include plants that range from edible to extremely toxic. Every culture has developed its own herbal **pharmacopeia,** with herbs taken as teas or tinctures, smoked, or applied to the body as poultices or powders. While much of the world still depends on herbal-based medicine, western medical practitioners rely mainly on synthetic drugs. Some of these are synthetic copies of the active compounds found in older herbal remedies, while others are more effective chemicals modeled on these naturally occurring compounds. At least thirty herbal drugs still remain important in western medicine. Some are obtained directly from plants, such as digitoxin from the woolly foxglove (*Digitalis lanata*), which is used to treat congestive heart failure, while others are the result of refinement and manipulation of plant products, including oral contraceptives from yams (*Dioscorea* species). Recent years have seen

The bark of cinnamon, a commercially important spice.

**compound** a substance formed from two or more elements

**pathogen** disease-causing organism

**exudation** releasing of a liquid substance; oozing

**pharmacopeia** a group of medicines

some resurgence in the use of traditional herbal medicines in many western cultures. SEE ALSO ALKALOIDS; CULTIVAR; DIOSCOREA; ECONOMIC IMPORTANCE OF PLANTS; FLAVOR AND FRAGRANCE CHEMIST; HERBALS AND HERBALISTS; MEDICINAL PLANTS; OILS, PLANT-DERIVED; TEA.

*Robert Newgarden and Mark Tebbitt*

**Bibliography**

Brown, Deni. *Encyclopedia of Herbs and Their Uses.* New York: Dorling Kindersley Publishing Inc., 1995.

Tyler, Varro E. *The Honest Herbal: A Sensible Guide to the Use of Herbs and Related Remedies.* New York: Pharmaceutical Products Press, 1993.

**History of Plant Sciences**   *See Ecology, History of; Evolution of Plants, History of; Physiology, History of; Taxonomy, History of.*

# Hooker, Joseph Dalton

### British Botanist
### 1817–1911

Joseph Dalton Hooker.

Joseph Dalton Hooker was one of the leading British botanists of the late nineteenth century. He was born in Halesworth, Sussex, and was the son of another great British botanist, Sir William Jackson Hooker (1785–1865). Hooker graduated with a degree in medicine from Glasgow University, where his father was a professor of botany. His father eventually held the position of Director of Kew Gardens in London and, through his leadership, made it one of the finest botanical gardens in the world, with an extensive collection of plants from the British colonies. In 1855 Joseph Hooker became assistant director of Kew Garden and became director when his father died in 1865.

Hooker is best known for his work in taxonomy, the science of classification, and plant geography, the science of plant distribution. These primary interests were shaped by his participation in a famous four-year scientific expedition under the command of Captain James Clark Ross that sought to determine the position of the south magnetic pole. Hooker was aboard the H.M.S. *Erebus,* one of the two expeditionary ships that left England in 1839. Although he was appointed the ship's assistant surgeon, Hooker made extensive collections of botanical material from geographic regions not previously explored, including the Great Ice Barrier and several oceanic islands such as Tasmania, the Falklands, and New Zealand. Hooker was struck by the similarity of the floras of these regions. He explained these similarities by adopting a land-bridge theory, one that postulated the existence of a lost circumpolar continent. It was on the basis of these observations that Hooker began to adopt an evolutionary explanation for the similarities. His work was summarized in a collection known as *The Botany of the Antarctic Voyage of H.M. Discovery Ships Erebus and Terror.* The publication of its six quarto volumes between 1853 and 1855 established Hooker as one of the great botanists of the nineteenth century.

Hooker continued to travel and explore through much of his life, and in the process compiled many floras. He also collected many plant specimens, which he introduced to England. He is especially well known for his stunning, previously unknown species of *Rhododendron* that he discovered in the Sikkim region of the Himalayas. Many of these are still grown in Kew Gardens. He also made notable contributions in pure morphology, including classic studies on the unusual plant *Welwitschia* (1863).

Hooker is also known for his close friendship with the most famous naturalist of his day, Charles Darwin (1809–1882). In fact, Darwin trusted Hooker enough to confide his radical new theory of descent with modification by means of natural selection (later called evolution by means of natural selection) in 1844, some fifteen years before Darwin wrote *On the Origin of Species* (1859). Although Hooker knew of this theory well in advance of its publication, he was not convinced of its importance until his own observations of the distribution of plants were completed. Darwin and Hooker remained close friends until Darwin's death. Hooker led a long and productive life and was knighted in 1877. He died in Sunningdale, England, in 1911.

SEE ALSO BIOGEOGRAPHY; BOTANICAL GARDENS AND ARBORETA; CURATOR OF A BOTANICAL GARDEN; DARWIN, CHARLES; TAXONOMIST; TAXONOMY.

*Vassiliki Betty Smocovitis*

**Bibliography**

Allen, M. *The Hookers of Kew, 1785–1911*. London: Michael Joseph, 1967.

Desmond, R. "Joseph Hooker." In *Dictionary of Scientific Biography*, Vol. 6. New York: Scribner's Sons, 1970.

Huxley, Leonard. *Life and Letters of Sir Joseph Dalton Hooker*. London: John Murray, 1918.

Turrill, William Bertram. *Joseph Dalton Hooker*. London: Thomas Nelson and Sons Ltd., 1964.

# Hormonal Control and Development

Plant hormones are a group of naturally occurring organic substances that, at low concentrations, influence physiological processes such as growth, differentiation, and development. Many plant hormones are transported from one place in the plant to another, thus coordinating growth throughout the plant, while others act in the tissues in which they are produced.

For a hormone to have an effect it must be synthesized, reach the site of action, be detected, and have that detection transferred into a final biochemical action. The steps following detection are called signal transduction, while the components of the signal transduction chain are referred to as second messengers. Because the concentration of hormone molecules affects the intensity of the response, the level of the hormone is also significant. The level is determined by the **biosynthesis** of the active hormone molecule and its removal by metabolism to inactive byproducts, or its binding to molecules like sugars, which also has an inactivating effect. Plant scientists have investigated these phenomena by analyzing the levels and biochemical forms of the hormones present in relation to differences in development. Recently the use of mutants and bioengineered plants in which growth or development is abnormal has enabled us to start understanding how hormones work. This research has been coupled with the isolation of the genes and proteins that are needed for the normal functioning of the hormone.

**biosynthesis** creation through biological pathways

13

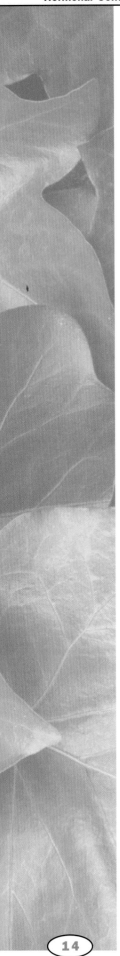

Generalized signal transduction scheme, which may or may not proceed via a membrane G-protein and/or the production of a protein gene regulator (transcription factor). The final effect is the activation of transcription of a gene producing one or more proteins that brings about the effect on growth or development.

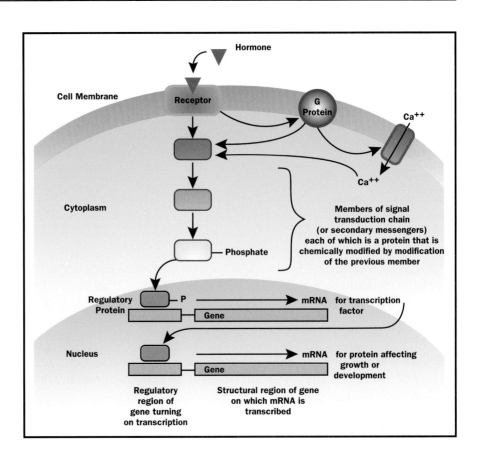

**auxin** a plant hormone

**precursor** a substance from which another is made

**carotenoid** a colored molecule made by plants

**vascular** related to transport of nutrients

**Biosynthesis. Auxin** (indoleacetic acid, IAA) is synthesized from indoleglycerophosphate, the **precursor** to the amino acid tryptophan, and, in some plants, from tryptophan itself. GA$_1$, the principal active gibberellin in most plants, is synthesized via the isoprenoid pathway, followed by a series of many other gibberellin intermediates. The level of GA$_1$ is very tightly regulated. The genes for the enzymatic conversions have been isolated, and the transcription of these genes have been shown to be under both feedback and environmental control. Gregor Mendel's tallness gene encodes a step in the gibberellin biosynthesis pathway just before GA$_1$. Cytokinins are synthesized by the attachment of an isopentenyl side chain to adenosine phosphate. The enzyme for this process, isopentenyl transferase, is the main regulating step in cytokinin biosynthesis, and its gene has been used in the genetic transformation of plants to enhance cytokinin levels. Abscisic acid is synthesized via **carotenoid** molecules. Ethylene is derived from methionine via the nonprotein amino acid ACC (1-amino-cyclopropane-1-carboxylic acid). The transcription of the genes for the enzymes making ACC and its conversion into ethylene is under precise developmental control, notably during fruit ripening.

**Transport.** Most hormones simply travel along with the contents of the xylem or phloem by a combination of diffusion and bulk transport. Auxin is special in that it is transported primarily in the cells of the **vascular** cambium or its initials and is moved away from the tip of the stem or root where it is synthesized (termed *polar transport*). Auxin enters the cell from the cell wall above as an un-ionized molecule (because the wall has an acidic pH) that can cross the cell membrane. At the neutral pH inside the cell it becomes ionized, preventing its outward diffusion through the cell membrane. Outward transport is on special carrier proteins located only at the base of the cell, so movement is downward. (In roots, the situation is reversed.) When a stem is placed on its side the carriers most likely migrate to the side of the lower cell so that the auxin is transported to the lower side of the stem, causing increased growth on that side and a bending upwards. This is thought to account at least in part for gravitropism, or growth away from the ground. The genes for the transport proteins have been isolated.

**Detection.** For a hormone molecule to have an effect it must bind to a receptor protein. *Arabidopsis* mutants that do not respond to ethylene have been used to study the ethylene receptor. It is located in the cell membrane with parts that react with the next signaling compound exposed on the inside of the cell. Copper has been shown to coordinate the binding of ethylene to the receptor site. The auxin binding protein is located in the **endoplasmic reticulum**, from which it also migrates to the cell membrane. Its gene has also been isolated.

**endoplasmic reticulum** membrane network inside a cell

**Signal Transduction.** Following detection, the signal from the presence of the hormone molecule has to be translated into action. There are usually many steps in this process, although a general pattern can be seen. Often the hormone triggers the phosphorylation of an activator protein, which then binds to the regulatory region of a gene, thus turning on gene transcription. This gene may produce the final product, or may itself produce a gene regulator (or **transcription factor**). Steps prior to the phosphorylation of the regulatory protein may include an interaction with a membrane G protein that in turn releases other factors and the opening of calcium channels in the membrane permitting an increase in the cytoplasmic level of calcium. Some aspects of action appear, however, to be more direct, not needing gene transcription per se, although some signal transduction is always involved. The mode of action varies from hormone to hormone, and even between different hormone actions, as described below.

**transcription factors** proteins that bind to a specific DNA sequence called the promoter to regulate the expression of a nearby gene

**Auxin in Cell Elongation.** Cell elongation is a vital part of growth. Auxin causes cell elongation within ten minutes by making the cell walls more extensible. This occurs through a series of steps: Auxin stimulates the pumping of hydrogen **ions** out of the protoplast via proton pumps driven by adenosine triphosphate (**ATP**), so acidifying the wall; this activates an enzyme called expansin, which is activated by acid conditions (about pH 4.5); expansin breaks the hydrogen bonds between the cellulose **microfibrils** of the wall and the other sugar-chain molecules that cross-link the microfibrils; the cell walls are made more extensible; and the cell then elongates because of the **turgor pressure** inside the cell.

**ions** charged particles

**ATP** adenosine triphosphate, a small, water-soluble molecule that acts as an energy currency in cells

**microfibrils** microscopic fibers

**turgor pressure** the outward pressure exerted on the cell wall by the fluid within

Auxin also has a rapid action on promoting the transcription of a number of auxin-specific genes, whose exact function is currently unknown. It is uncertain whether auxin activates preexisting proton pumps in the cell membrane or whether it induces synthesis of new proton pumps. Auxin also stimulates the transcription of genes for other enzymes that act on other cell wall polymers.

**Gibberellin in Alpha-Amylase Production in Cereal Grains.** Germinating seeds need to mobilize their stored carbohydrates to grow. In germinating cereal grains, gibberellin promotes the synthesis of the enzyme alpha-

**endosperm** the nutritive tissue in a seed, formed by fertilization of a diploid egg tissue by a sperm from pollen

amylase in cells of the aleurone surrounding the **endosperm**. The alpha-amylase breaks down the starch of the endosperm into sugars for transport to the growing seedling. Gibberellin acts through second messengers to promote transcription of the gene for alpha-amylase. Gibberellin first binds at the surface of the aleurone cell. The initial steps in the transduction chain are unknown, but gibberellin rapidly promotes the biosynthesis of a transcription-promoting factor named GA-myb. GA-myb binds to specific regulatory regions of the alpha-amylase gene, so turning on the transcription of the alpha-amylase mRNA, which is translated to produce alpha-amylase.

**Gibberellin in Stem Elongation.** The presence of gibberellin is normally needed for stems to elongate, and gibberellin-deficient mutants are usually dwarf. This has been explained by the idea that a protein factor in the signal transduction chain has the effect of preventing growth, but in the presence of gibberellin this factor is negated, allowing growth to proceed. However, a further mutation of a dwarf *Arabidopsis* has produced a tall plant, even though the level of gibberellin is still deficient. In the double mutant the inhibitory protein factor is negated because of a mutation in its structure, allowing growth to proceed. There is also genetic evidence of a second negative regulator in the signal transduction chain. At the present time we do not know the end product that actually promotes or inhibits the elongation of the cell.

**solute** a substance dissolved in a solution

**Abscisic Acid (ABA) and Stomatal Closure.** Stomata are leaf surface pores surrounded by guard cells. ABA promotes stomatal closure by causing the exit of potassium ions from the guard cells. $K^+$ is the main **solute** causing turgor in the guard cells and opening the stoma. ABA binds to a cell-surface receptor on the surface of the guard cells. This causes a calcium ion influx and an increase in the level of inositol triphosphate, a signaling molecule, which causes a release of calcium from internal stores. The $Ca^{++}$ brings about a membrane depolarization, triggering the outward $K^+$ ion channels to open. Calcium also has a direct effect on the potassium ion channels via the phosphorylation of a specific protein in guard cell protoplasts.

**Ethylene and Seedling Stem Growth.** Exposure of *Arabidopsis* seedlings to ethylene usually causes stunted growth. However, some mutants are insensitive to ethylene. Other mutants grow stunted, as if they were exposed to ethylene, even when they are not. These mutants have helped the investigation of ethylene signal transduction. Ethylene's receptor interacts with a protein that blocks an ion channel. In the presence of ethylene, the receptor causes the protein to unblock the channel. The entry of (unknown) ions then activates other second messengers. Activation results in the synthesis of a transcription factor, finally triggering the synthesis of specific enzymes that can cause stunted growth. In ripening fruit, ethylene promotes the transcription of the mRNAs that encode for many enzymes that produce the chemical changes, including color, taste, and softening, which we know as ripening. This presumably occurs via a similar transduction chain, but the paucity of mutants makes it more difficult to investigate than in *Arabidopsis*. SEE ALSO GENETIC MECHANISMS AND DEVELOPMENT; HORMONES.

*Peter J. Davies*

**Bibliography**

Davies, Peter J. *Plant Hormones: Physiology, Biochemistry, and Molecular Biology.* Dordrecht, The Netherlands: Kluwer Academic Publishers, 1995.

Taiz, Lincoln, and Zeiger, Eduardo. *Plant Physiology*, 2nd ed. Sunderland, MA: Sinauer Associates, 1998.

# Hormones

Hormones are small molecules that are released by one part of a plant to influence another part. The principal plant growth hormones are the auxins, gibberellins, cytokinins, abscisic acid, and ethylene. Plants use these hormones to cause cells to elongate, divide, become specialized, and separate from each other, and help coordinate the development of the entire plant. Not only are the plant hormones small in molecular weight, they are also active in the plant in very small amounts, a fact that made their isolation and identification difficult.

The first plant growth hormones discovered were the auxins. (The term *auxin* is derived from a Greek word meaning "to grow.") The best known and most widely distributed hormone in this class is indole-3-acetic acid. Fritz W. Went, whose pioneering and ingenious research in 1928 opened the field of plant hormones, reported that auxins were involved in the control of the growth movements that orient shoots toward the light, and that they had the additional, striking quality of moving only from the shoot tip toward the shoot base. This polarity of auxin movement was an inherent property of the plant tissue, only slightly influenced by gravity. Other less-investigated auxins include phenyl-acetic acid and indole-butyric acid, the latter long used as a synthetic auxin but found to exist in plants only in 1985.

The gibberellins are a family of more than seventy related chemicals, some active as growth hormones and many inactive. They are designated by number (e.g., $GA_1$ and $GAL_{20}$). $GA_3$ (also called gibberellic acid) is one of the most active gibberellins when added to plants. Slight modifications in the basic structure are associated with an increase, decrease, or cessation of biological activity: each such modified chemical is considered a different gibberellin.

Cytokinins are a class of chemical **compounds** derived from adenine that cause cells to divide when an auxin is also present. Of the cytokinins found in plants, zeatin is one of the most active.

Abscisic acid helps protect the plant from too much loss of water by closing the small holes (stomata) in the surfaces of leaves when wilting begins.

**compound** a substance formed from two or more elements

| PLANT HORMONES AND THEIR FUNCTIONS | |
|---|---|
| **Hormone** | **Functions** |
| Auxins (indoleacetic acid; IAA) | Stimulates shoot and root growth; involved in tropisms; prevents abscission; controls differentiation of xylem cells and, with other hormones, controls sieve-tube cells and fibers |
| Gibberellins | Stimulates stem elongation, seed germination, and enzyme production in seeds |
| Cytokinins | Stimulates bud development; delays senescence; increases cell division |
| Abscisic acid | Speeds abscission; counters leaf wilting by closing stomates; prevents premature germination of seeds; decreases IAA movement |
| Ethylene (gas) | Produced in response to stresses and by many ripening fruits; speeds seed germination and the ripening of fruit, senescence, and abscission; decreases IAA movement |

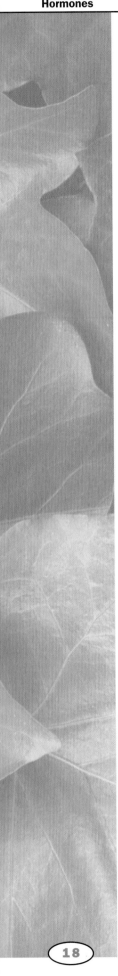

The only known gas that functions as a plant growth hormone is the small $C_2H_2$ molecule called ethylene. Various stresses, such as wounding or waterlogging, lead to ethylene production.

## Major Effects of the Principal Plant Growth Hormones

**Auxins.** Indoleacetic acid (IAA), produced primarily in seeds and young leaves, moves out of the leaf stalk and down the stem, controlling various aspects of development on the way. IAA stimulates growth both in leaf stalks and in stems. In moving down the leaf stalk, IAA prevents the cells at the base of the leaf from separating from each other and thus causing the leaf to drop (called leaf abscission). The speed of IAA polar movement through shoot tissues ranges from 5 to 20 millimeters per hour, faster than speeds for the other major hormones.

The growth responses of plants to directional stimuli from the environment are called tropisms. Gravitropism (also called geotropism) refers to a growth response toward or away from gravity. Phototropism is the growth response toward or away from light. These tropisms are of obvious value to plants in facilitating the downward growth of roots into the soil (by positive gravitropism) and the upward growth of shoots into the light (by positive phototropism, aided by negative gravitropism).

The role of auxin in controlling tropisms was suggested by Went and N. Cholodny in 1928. Their theory was that auxin moves laterally in the shoot or root under the influence of gravity or one-sided light. Greater concentration on one side causes either greater growth (in the case of the shoot) or inhibited growth (in roots). This Cholodny-Went theory of tropisms has been subject to refinement and question for decades. Evidence exists, for instance, that in some plants tropism toward one-sided light results not from **lateral** movement of auxin to the shaded side, but rather from production of a growth inhibitor on the illuminated side.

**lateral** away from the center

A widespread, though not universal, effect of IAA moving down from the young leaves of the **apical** bud is the suppression of the outgrowth of the side buds on the stem. This type of developmental control is called apical dominance: if the apical bud is cut off, the side buds start to grow out (released from apical dominance). If IAA is applied to the cut stem, the side buds remain suppressed in many plants.

**apical** at the tip

In addition to enhancing organ growth, IAA also plays a major part in cell differentiation, controlling the formation of xylem cells and being involved in phloem differentiation. In its progress down the stem, IAA stimulates the development of the two main **vascular** channels for the movement of substances within the plant: xylem, through which water, mineral salts, and other hormones move from the roots; and phloem, through which various organic compounds such as sugars move from the leaves. In plants that develop a cambium (the layer of dividing cells whose activity allows trees to increase in girth), the polarly moving IAA stimulates the division of the cambial cells. Cut-off pieces of stem or root usually initiate new roots near their bases. As a result of its polar movement, IAA accumulates at the base of such excised pieces and touches off such root regeneration. In the intact plant, the shoot-tip toward shoot-base polar movement of IAA con-

**vascular** related to transport of nutrients

tinues on into the root, where IAA moves toward the root tip primarily in the stele (the inner column of cells in the root).

Interesting effects of IAA have been found in a more limited number of plant species. Plants of the Bromeliad family, which includes pineapples, start to flower if treated with IAA. Some other plants typically produce flowers that can develop as either solely male or solely female flowers depending on various environmental factors: In several such species IAA stimulates femaleness.

**Gibberellins (GAs).** Produced in young leaves, developing seeds, and probably in root tips, the biologically active GAs, such as $GA_1$ and $GA_3$, move in shoots without polarity and at a slower rate than IAA down the stems where they cause elongation. In roots they show root-tip toward root-base polar movement—the opposite of IAA. Their effect on stem elongation is particularly striking in some plants that require exposure to long days in order to flower. In such plants the stem elongation that precedes flowering is caused by either long days or active GAs and is so fast that it is called bolting. A similar association of light effects and active GAs is found in seeds that normally require light or cold treatment to germinate. GAs can substitute for these environmental treatments. In cereal seeds, GA, produced by the embryos, moves into the parts of the seeds containing starch and other storage products. There the GA triggers the production of various specific **enzymes** such as alpha-amylase, which breaks down starch into smaller compounds usable by the growing embryos. In the flowers that can develop as either male or female, active GAs cause maleness (the opposite effect to that of auxin). Not surprisingly, in view of the relatively large amounts of GAs in seeds, spraying GAs on such seedless grape varieties as Thompson produces bigger and more elongated grapes on the vines.

**enzyme** a protein that controls a reaction in a cell

**Cytokinins.** Produced in roots and seeds, the cytokinins' often-reported presence in leaves apparently results from accumulation of cytokinins produced by roots and moved to the shoot through the xylem cells. Research using pieces of plant tissue growing in test tubes revealed that adding cytokinins increased cell divisions and subsequently the number of shoot buds that regenerated, while increasing the amount of added IAA increased the number of roots formed. The test-tube cultures could be pushed toward bud or root formation by changing the ratio of cytokinin to IAA. The growth of already-formed lateral buds on stems could be stimulated in some plants by treating the lateral buds directly with cytokinins. With IAA from the apex of the main shoot inhibiting outgrowth of the lateral buds and with cytokinins stimulating their outgrowth, the effects of the two hormones on lateral buds suggests a balancing effect like that seen in root/shoot regeneration in the tissue cultures. Treatment with cytokinins retards the senescence of leaves, and naturally occurring leaf senescence is accompanied by a decrease in native cytokinins. When the movement of cytokinins such as zeatin through excised **petioles** was tested in the same sort of experiment that showed IAA moving with polarity at 5 to 10 millimeters per hour, cytokinins showed the slower rate of movement and the lack of polarity characteristic of GAs. However, through root sections, zeatin movement was **nonpolar**, unlike the movement of GAs.

**petiole** the stalk of a leaf, by which it attaches to the stem

**nonpolar** not directed along the root-shoot axis

**Abscisic Acid.** Abscisic acid is found in leaves, roots, fruits, and seeds. In leaves that are not wilting, the hormone is mostly in the **chloroplasts**. When wilting starts the abscisic acid is released for movement to the guard cells

**chloroplast** the photosynthetic organelle of plants and algae

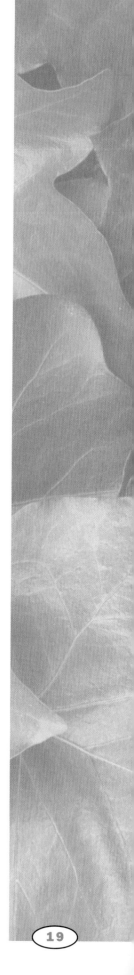

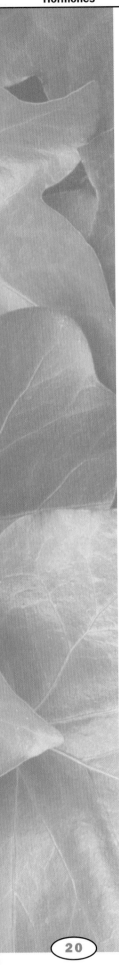

of the stomates. Abscisic acid moves without polarity through stem sections and at the slower rate typical of GAs and cytokinins.

**abscission** the separation of a leaf or fruit from a stem

As its name implies, abscisic acid stimulates leaf or fruit **abscission** in many species, as evidenced by faster abscission from treating with the hormone and by increases in the amount of native abscisic acid in cotton fruits just prior to their natural abscission. Abscisic acid's most investigated effect, however, is its protection of plants from too much water loss (wilting) by closing the stomates in leaves when wilting starts. The onset of wilting is accompanied by fast increases in the abscisic acid levels in the leaves and subsequent closure of the stomates. Spraying the leaves with abscisic acid causes stomate closure even if the leaves are not wilting. In seeds, abscisic acid prevents premature germination of the seed.

**Ethylene Gas.** Ethylene gas is produced by many parts of plants when they are stressed. Also, normally ripening fruits are often rich producers of ethylene. Among ethylene's many effects are speeding the ripening of fruits and the senescence and abscission of leaves and flower parts; indeed, it is used commercially to coordinate ripening of crops to make harvesting more efficient. Ethylene gas releases seeds from dormancy. If given as a pretreatment, it inhibits the polar movement of auxin in stems of land plants (but, surprisingly, increases auxin movement in some plants that normally grow in fresh water). Ethylene moves readily through and out of the plant. The stimulation of flowering in pineapple and other bromeliads by spraying with IAA, mentioned earlier, is due to ethylene produced by the doses of auxin applied. Despite its frequent production by plants, ethylene is apparently not essential for plant development. Mutations or chemicals that block ethylene production do not prevent normal development.

## Interactions of Hormones

In addition to the many effects on development of individual plant growth hormones, a sizeable number of effects of one hormone on another have been found. For example, IAA alone can restore the full number of normal tracheary cells in the xylem, but to restore the full number of sieve-tube cells in the phloem zeatin is needed in addition to IAA. Similarly, to restore the full number of fibers in the phloem, GA must be added along with IAA.

**basipetal** toward the base

Hormones affect each other's movement, too. Mentioned above was the decrease in IAA movement from pretreatment with ethylene. Similarly, abscisic acid decreases the **basipetal** polar movement of IAA in stems and petioles. Therefore, in view of IAA's role as the primary inhibitor of abscission in plants, the abscisic acid-induced decrease in IAA movement down the leaf stalk toward the abscision zone probably explains at least part of abscisic acid's role as an accelerator of abscission. In other cases, increases in IAA basipetal movement have resulted from GA or cytokinin treatment. The nonpolar movement typical of cytokinins was changed to polar movement when IAA was added, too. SEE ALSO DIFFERENTIATION AND DEVELOPMENT; EMBRYOGENESIS; GENETIC MECHANISMS AND DEVELOPMENT; GERMINATION AND GROWTH; HORMONAL GROWTH AND DEVELOPMENT; PHOTOPERIODISM; SEEDLESS VASCULAR PLANTS; SENESCENCE; TROPISMS.

*William P. Jacobs*

**Bibliography**

Abeles, Frederick B., Page W. Morgan, and Mikal E. Saltveit, Jr. *Ethylene in Plant Biology*, 2nd ed. San Diego, CA: Academic Press, 1992.

Addicott, Fredrick T., ed. *Abscisic Acid.* New York: Praeger Publishers, 1983.

Davies, Peter J., ed. *Plant Hormones: Physiology, Biochemistry, and Molecular Biology.* Boston: Kluwer Academic Pulishers, 1995.

Jacobs, William P. *Plant Hormones and Plant Development.* Cambridge, England: Cambridge University Press, 1979.

# Horticulture

The word *horticulture* translates as "garden cultivation," or to cultivate garden plants. It was first used in publication in 1631 and was an entry in *The New World of English Words* in 1678. Today horticulture means the science, technology, art, business, and hobby of producing and managing fruits, vegetables, flowers and ornamental plants, landscapes, interior plantscapes, and grasses and turfgrasses. Although horticulture has been practiced for several millennia, it became a recognized academic and scientific discipline as it emerged from botany and medicinal botany in the late nineteenth century. Liberty Hyde Bailey, professor of horticulture at both Michigan State and Cornell Universities, is credited as the father of American horticulture, as he founded the first academic departments of horticulture.

Modern horticulture encompasses plant production (both commercial and gardening) and science, both practical and applied. Horticulture and the associated green industries are a rapidly developing professional field with increasing importance to society. The direct "farm-gate" value of horticultural crop production in the United States exceeds $40 billion; the overall value to the economy is much higher due to value added in preparation and preservation, or installation, and use and maintenance of horticultural plants and products.

Horticultural plants include fresh fruits and vegetables, herbaceous annual and perennial flowering plants, flowers produced as cut flowers for vase display, woody shrubs and trees, ornamental grasses, and turfgrasses used for landscapes and sports facilities. The crops encompass plants from tropical areas (fruits, vegetables, and tropical foliage plants) to those from the temperate zone. Horticulture crops are typically consumed or used as freshly harvested products and therefore are short-lived after harvest. Product quality, nutrition, flavor, and aesthetic appearance are important attributes of horticultural crops and are the goal of production and management. The production of horticultural plants is typified by intense management, high management cost, environmental control, significant technology use, and high risk. However, the plants, because of their high value as crops, result in very high economic returns. Horticultural crop plant production and maintenance requires extensive use of soil manipulation (including use of artificial or synthetic soil mixes), irrigation, fertilization, plant growth regulation, pruning/pinching/trimming, and environmental control. Plants can be grown in natural environments, such as orchards, vineyards, or groves for fruits, grapes, nuts, and citrus, or as row crops for vegetables. Plants can also be produced in very confined environments, such as in nurseries, greenhouses, growth rooms, or in pots. Horticultural plants exhibit wide varia-

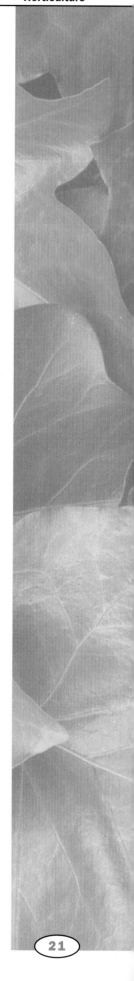

tion and diversity in their cultivated varieties (cultivars) with differences in flower or fruit color and plant shape, form, size, color, or flavor and aroma adding to that diversity and to the plants' value.

Horticultural plants are very important to human health and well being and are critical to the environment of homes, communities, and the world. Horticulture food crops play an important role in human nutrition. The U.S. Department of Agriculture (USDA) recommends five to nine servings of fruits and vegetables be consumed daily to provide important nutrients and vitamins and to maintain overall good health. The use of landscape plants has been demonstrated to increase the property value of homes and improve communities and the attitudes of those owning or using the property. Use of plants in the landscape, development of public parks and greenbelts, and planting trees all help remediate pollution and contribute to production of oxygen in the air. Plants used indoors, whether flowers or house plants or interior plant scaping, improve the indoor environment by purifying air, removing some pollutants and dusts, and adding beauty, thereby improving the attitude and well being of those who occupy or use the inside areas.

A number of techniques are used in horticulture. New plant cultivars are developed through plant **hybridization** and genetic engineering. The number of plants is increased through plant propagation by seeds, cuttings, grafting, and plant tissue and cell culture. Plant growth can be controlled by pinching, pruning, bending, and training. Plant growth, flowering, and fruiting can also be controlled or modified by light and temperature variation. Further, growth and flowering can be altered by the use of growth-regulating chemicals and/or plant hormones. The rate of plant growth and quality of plant products are controlled by managing fertilizer and nutrient application through **fertigation** or **hydroponic** solution culture. Postharvest product longevity is controlled by manipulating plant or product hormone **physiology** or by controlling respiration by lowering temperature or modifying environmental gas content.

The scientific and technological disciplines of horticulture include plant genetics, plant breeding, genetic engineering and molecular biology, variety development, propagation and tissue culture, crop and environmental physiology, plant nutrition, hormone physiology and growth regulation, plant physical manipulation (pruning and training), and environmental control. The crop disciplines of horticulture include pomology (fruit and nut culture), viticulture (grape production), enology (wine production), olericulture (vegetable culture), floriculture (flower culture) and greenhouse management, ornamental horticulture and nursery production, arboriculture (tree maintenance), landscape horticulture, interior plant scaping, turf management, and postharvest physiology, preservation, and storage. SEE ALSO AGRICULTURE, MODERN; BOTANICAL GARDENS AND ARBORETA; HORTICULTURIST; HYDROPONICS; ORNAMENTAL PLANTS; PROPAGATION.

*Curt R. Rom*

**hybridization** formation of a new individual from parents of different species or varieties

**fertigation** application of small amounts of fertilizer while irrigating

**hydroponic** growing without soil, in a watery medium

**physiology** the biochemical processes carried out by an organism

**Bibliography**

Acquaah, George. *Horticulture Principles and Practices*. Upper Saddle River, NJ: Prentice-Hall, 1999.

American Society for Horticultural Science. [Online] Available at http:ashs.org.

Janick, Jules. *Horticultural Science*. New York: W. H. Freeman and Company, 1986.

Harlan, Jack R. *The Living Fields: Our Agricultural Heritage.* Cambridge: Cambridge University Press, 1998.

Lohr, Virginia I., and Diane Relf. "An Overview of the Current State of Human Issues in Horticulture in the United States." *HortTechnology* 10 (2000): 27–33.

# Horticulturist

A horticulturist practices the scientific or practical aspects of horticulture—growing, producing, utilizing, and studying horticultural crop plants and plant products. Careers in horticulture range from the scientific to the applied.

Careers in horticulture can be found in government (both state and national) agricultural research agencies, public and private universities, small companies, and multinational corporations. Jobs may entail laboratory work, greenhouse crop production and/or management, and field production. Research may involve developing and testing new products or technologies to improve the quality, appearance, handling, storage, or research and development of new plants or plant-derived products. Additional fundamental research is done to gain understanding of plant function, **physiology**, biochemistry, and genetics at the organismal, cellular, enzymatic, or molecular levels.

Horticulturists interested in teaching find employment at the high school, community school, vocational school, community college, or university levels. Emerging careers in horticulture include the study of plant-people interactions (the effects plants have on people), and horticulture therapy—the use of horticulture and gardening as a means of rehabilitation for those with physical, mental, or emotional limitations or challenges.

The practical or applied horticulturist is trained to utilize or manage plants and to design and maintain landscapes appropriately. Field horticulturists may be involved in the production of fruits and nuts (pomology), grapes (viticulture), and flowers and greenhouse crops (floriculture). They may also handle the arrangement, display, and marketing of cut flowers and

**physiology** the biochemical processes carried out by an organism

A horticulturist checks long-stemmed roses in a greenhouse.

greenery (floristry). Other possible areas of responsibility include the production of ornamental plants, trees, and shrubs (nursery production); landscape design, installation, and management; public or private garden installation and care; the design, installation, and maintenance of plants in indoor environments (interior plantscaping); turfgrass production, installation, and upkeep; and the handling, storage, and shipping of horticulture crops or plant products. The practical field horticulturist handles plant nutrition by fertilization, water status by irrigation, and plant size and shape by pinching, pruning, training, and mowing. Plant growth, development, and flowering is managed by the use of regulating chemicals or environmental management (temperature and light intensity and duration). The horticulturist is often the person primarily responsible for pest (both insects and disease) control and prevention management. Ultimately, the horticulturist is responsible for producing plants or plant products of the highest quality, value, and appearance.

Exciting developments in horticulture include the exploration of new plants as landscape greenery or for their potential medicinal contents and the discovery of wild types of cultivated crop plants such as strawberry, onion, tomato, or apple, which may contain genes for disease resistance or improved nutritional quality. Crops are being bioengineered for improved pest resistance, thereby requiring less pesticide in production, and being modified for increased storage life. Molecular biology and genetic engineering may result in the development of entirely new crops and/or the production of plants containing phyto-pharmaceuticals—plant-produced chemicals for use as beneficial drugs. Molecular biology and biochemistry are shedding new light on how plants grow and function, which will lead to new developments in crop production systems and management.

The level of employment and responsibility of a horticulturist relates to one's amount of training, education, and experience. Horticultural training at the high school and vocational level typically involves work in plant management, production, and maintenance operations. At the college level, horticulturists receive fundamental education in plant science and biology as a foundation to understanding plant growth, development, and management. Typically, college curricula include strong training in science, including botany and plant anatomy/morphology, chemistry and biochemistry, genetics, physics, soil science, pest management, and plant physiology. Additionally, students receive training in the science and technology of horticulture, including greenhouse operations, nursery production, landscape design, landscape installation and management, fruit and vegetable production, and plant propagation. Students interested in pursuing scientific/technology development careers or those who wish to teach horticulture may continue college studies in a master's or Ph.D. program.

Beginning horticulturists are typically responsible for plant management operations. Increased education, training, and experience result in increased decision-making and responsibility for operations and crew management. Entry-level positions with no training or experience begin at minimum wage, but with higher levels of training, experience, and increased ownership of an operation, salaries exceeded $100,000 per year. In 1999, students with a college degree found employment in the range of $25,000 to $40,000 for entry-level management positions. Salaries increase with experience gained through internships, fellowships, special research projects, travel, and part-time employment.

Horticulture production, education, and science careers can be found throughout the world. In the United States, primary horticulture production occurs in California, Florida, Texas, Georgia, Michigan, New York, Ohio, Pennsylvania, and New Jersey. However, landscape horticulture, retail garden center production, florist operations, public and private gardening, park landscape management, and landscaping design, installation, and maintenance operations flourish in all towns, cities, and metropolitan areas. International careers can be found through government and nongovernment agencies such as the Peace Corps, or with large multinational horticultural companies.

A commonality of horticulturists is, simply, that they enjoy working with plants. Horticulturists typically have a strong environmental ethic and enjoy contributing to beautifying and improving the environment and conserving natural resources. SEE ALSO ARBORIST; COLLEGE PROFESSOR; CURATOR OF A BOTANICAL GARDEN; CURATOR OF AN HERBARIUM; HORTICULTURE; LANDSCAPE ARCHITECT.

*Curt R. Rom*

**Bibliography**

Acquaah, George. *Horticulture Principles and Practices.* Upper Saddle River, NJ: Prentice-Hall, 1999.

Aggie Horticulture (Texas A&M University). [Online] Available at http://aggie-horticulture.tamu.edu/introhtml/internet.html.

American Society for Horticultural Science. [Online] Available at www.ashs.org.

Janick, Jules. *Horticultural Science.* New York: W. H. Freeman and Company, 1986.

Ohio State University Horticulture in Virtual Perspective. [Online] Available at http://www.hcs.ohio-state.edu/webgarden.html.

Virtual Garden. [Online] Available at http://www.vg.com/.

# Human Impacts

The human species has had a greater impact on the **biosphere** than any other single species. It is now poised to cause more changes in the future of the biosphere than even photosynthetic bacteria caused when they first filled the atmosphere with oxygen. While human impacts are as old as the human species itself, their pace and extent have grown rapidly, and recent changes have begun to dwarf the consequences of even the most profound change ever brought about by our species, the development of agriculture.

**biosphere** the region of the Earth in which life exists

## The Coming of Agriculture

Until the development of agriculture, the human species did not affect the biosphere any more significantly than other highly efficient predators. While small nomadic groups could, and did, deplete local game populations, and could, and did, drive some species to the edge of extinction through over-hunting, human impacts were for the most part small, local, and short-lived.

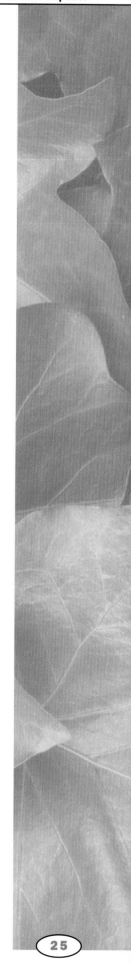

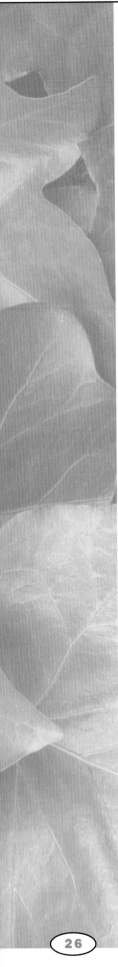

A Kansas wheat field being harvested. The ancient grasslands of the Midwest with the food chains they sustained have been replaced by agriculture

Agriculture changed all that. By cultivating and harvesting grains, humans set in motion a series of changes with deep effects on both the natural world and their own culture that have continued, and intensified, to this day. First and most profoundly, grains gave humans a source of surplus food that allowed population growth. While a surplus of meat would rot, a surplus of grain could be stored for months, even years, without losing its nutritional value. With a steady source of food supplied by plants, the human population began the extraordinary growth that continues exponentially in the twenty-first century.

## Changes in the Landscape

The inexorable growth of the human population has caused significant impacts on the landscape everywhere humans have settled. For instance, before the coming of the Europeans in America, it is said that the eastern forests were so thick that a squirrel could travel from the Atlantic coast to the Mississippi River without ever setting foot on the ground. Less than two centuries later—a blink of the eye in evolutionary time—more than two-thirds of that forest had been cleared for pasture or plowing. While the earliest settlers feared the bears and the wolves that haunted their forests, by the nineteenth century, not even deer or beavers were found in central Massachusetts. (Remarkably, much of this has changed yet again. With the western movement of agriculture in the late 1800s and the general decline of farming in the northeast, much of the forest has returned, and that squirrel has a better chance of making its journey now than it did at any time in the last 150 years.)

But while part of the country has reverted somewhat to its forested past, much of the rest remains significantly altered by agriculture, especially in the Midwest. Here, the flat terrain and deep, rich soils combine to form an ideal region for growing grain. The ancient grasslands have mostly long since disappeared, and with them went the herds of bison and other animals that formed the food chain of the prairie. While eastern forests may have returned with the shift of agriculture to the Midwest, it is unlikely that the prairie will ever regain its predominance in turn—there simply is nowhere else for agriculture to move to in this country.

## For Better or Worse

The Midwest is not the only region in which ancient food chains have been altered. In fact, it is estimated that almost 50 percent of the terrestrial net primary productivity of the Earth—almost one-half of all the photosynthesis carried out over the entire surface of the land—is consumed, wasted, or diverted by humans. In a very real sense, our species farms the entire planet. As the population expands in the twenty-first century, this number is expected to grow.

This harnessing of Earth's potential for our own purposes is not necessarily a bad thing, and how we view such transformations depends quite a lot on our own preconceptions about nature and the place of humans in it. Are buffalo better than cows? Are forests better than pastures? Throughout much of our history, most people have decided, consciously or not, that human need, and sometimes greed, is sufficient reason for wreaking change on the natural world. It is unarguably true that more people live in better conditions as a result of agriculture and all it has brought. Agricultural changes are, in any event, a fait accompli—the human species is simply not going to return to its hunting and gathering ways.

## The Industrial Revolution

While agriculture has wrought slow, pervasive changes on human culture and the landscape over more than ten millennia, other human endeavors have had much faster impacts on Earth and its **biota**. The greatest of them all, and second only to agriculture in its overall impact, has been the Industrial Revolution. Beginning in the late 1700s with the invention of the steam engine and continuing through the twenty-first century, humans have harnessed increasing amounts of stored energy to drive larger, faster, and more powerful machines.

**biota** the sum total of living organisms in a region of a given size

The effects on the biosphere have been pervasive. Fuel-powered machines have allowed humans to cultivate more land, consume more resources, and sustain larger populations than was conceivable before the beginnings of this most important revolution. In addition to these effects, the use of fuel has had far-reaching consequences by itself. Wood-fired boilers soon gave way to coal, but not before deforestation of thousands of acres of virgin forests in the rapidly industrializing regions of Europe. Coal mining is a dirty business, and leaves in its wake scars on the landscape that can take generations to heal. More significantly, coal and its replacement, oil, are fossil fuels, the geologic remains of ancient plants that contain carbon removed from the carbon cycle millions of years ago. Burning fossil fuels releases carbon dioxide into the atmosphere, and records show the atmospheric level of $CO_2$ has risen steadily since the beginning of the Industrial Revolution. Carbon dioxide is a greenhouse gas, which traps heat in the atmosphere, preventing it from escaping into space. (Other greenhouse gases include methane and water vapor.) Deforestation raises $CO_2$ levels even more, since forests remove $CO_2$ from the air and lock it up in their woody tissues.

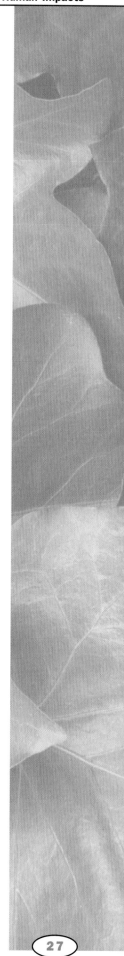

A piece of a Peruvian rain forest being converted for agricultural use by the slash-and-burn method.

## Global Climate Change

While the chemistry and physics of the atmosphere are highly complex, and although there is still some debate about the pace and ultimate extent of global warming, most atmospheric scientists agree that the average temperature of the planet is likely to rise by at least a few degrees over the next several centuries. What portion of this effect is attributable to human activity is still under debate, although many scientists think the human contribution is very significant.

The scope of the possible effects of global warming is hard to forecast accurately, but some examples may provide a glimpse of potential outcomes. The current distribution of plant species is determined in large part by their climatic requirements. Boreal forest, or taiga, circles the Earth just below the arctic circle. Its coniferous trees require cold winters and mild summers, with moderate but not excessive rainfall. As surface temperatures rise, as much as 40 percent of the world's boreal forests could be lost, according to estimates published by the Intergovernmental Panel on Climate Change. At the same time, deserts and other arid lands may experience more water stress, increasing the rate of desertification in these regions. In contrast, some areas will become milder and wetter. All of these changes will shift plant geographic distribution, and with this, alter wildlife and plant predator distributions.

## Invasive Species

Changes in climate are likely to accelerate another trend, one already begun by humans in their global travels. The distribution of plants changes over time, but in most natural migrations, predators move along with the plant, providing checks on the potential for otherwise explosive growth into a new habitat. When humans deliberately introduce a foreign plant into a new habitat, however, the system of ecological controls is not often transplanted at the same time. In these situations, a new species may have a significant impact on local **ecosystems**, driving out indigenous species and altering balances in place for many years. Such has been the case, for instance, with purple loosestrife in eastern wetlands, melaleuca in the Everglades, and kudzu throughout the southern United States.

**ecosystem** an ecological community together with its environment

As temperature and rainfall patterns change, global climate change is likely to provoke the large-scale introduction of new species into ecosystems where they have never existed before. A significant unanswered question is whether these changes are likely to be slow, allowing time for species to migrate gradually and for communities to slowly adapt to new constellations of species, or whether change will come rapidly, causing extinction of some species too slow to migrate, and population explosions of others that outpace their predators in a new environment. The rate of climate change, as well as its extent, will have a significant impact on the characteristics of plant communities in the twenty-first century.

## The Sixth Extinction

While species have become extinct at a small, steady rate throughout evolutionary time, the three-and-a-half-billion-year history of life has been punctuated by only five great extinction events, most caused by heavenly cataclysms, such as an asteroid colliding with Earth. We are now in the early stages of the sixth great extinction, but one with a difference—this cataclysm is entirely of human origins.

This wave of extinction is perhaps the most alarming, and most grim, of the impact humans have had on the biosphere. By some estimates, one in eight species of plants is on the edge of extinction, and most of these were not expected to survive into the twenty-first century. Similar predictions have been made for other life forms. Human activities have increased the extinction rate by a thousand-fold, so that for every new species created by evolution, one thousand become extinct through the effects of human activities. Expanding populations, pollution, and atmospheric ozone depletion all have played their part, but the most dramatic effect has come from the clearing of tropical rain forests for agricultural and lumber activities. Forest clearing in tropical areas destroys 86,000 acres of forest per day, and an area the size of Kansas every year. With this land go thousands of species, many of them never identified.

The loss of these species is significant for practical as well as bioethical reasons—the unique biochemistry of each species makes each a potential source for new drugs or raw materials with unique and valuable properties. Plants are especially valuable in this regard, since their inability to run away from predators has led to the evolution of many types of bioactive **compounds**, only now being discovered by plant prospectors and

**compound** a substance formed from two or more elements

**ethnobotanist** a scientist who interacts with native peoples to learn more about the plants of a region

**biodiversity** degree of variety of life

**ethnobotanists**. Destroying this inventory before even cataloging potentially throws away our future.

## Future Prospects

The enormity of human impacts on the biosphere—increasing global temperatures, decreasing **biodiversity**, higher populations—is sometimes enough to make one despair of changing anything. While it is true that the major outlines of the future are unlikely to be reversed in the next several decades, it is most definitely not true that inaction is the only sensible course. Many important steps have already been taken to steer a course toward a more sustainable environmental future. While political differences and short-sighted economic interests will continue to prevent the full range of international actions needed, heartening agreements are already in place to decrease ozone destruction, limit greenhouse gas emissions, and protect biodiversity. The world's people and its political leaders are slowly understanding that the future health and prosperity of the human species depends critically on the health of the world's environments.

Despite these promising beginnings, a great deal remains to be done, and the doing of it will depend on the commitment and foresight of people like the readers of this book, who are willing to learn, get involved, and try to make a difference. In the twenty-first century, that commitment to make a difference may have the greatest impact of all. SEE ALSO ACID RAIN; AGRICULTURE, HISTORY OF; AGRICULTURE, MODERN; ATMOSPHERE AND PLANTS; BIOGEOCHEMICAL CYCLES; BIOREMEDIATION; BOREAL FOREST; CARBON CYCLE; DEFORESTATION; ECOLOGY, FIRE; GENETIC ENGINEERING; GLOBAL WARMING; GRASSLANDS; GREEN REVOLUTION; INVASIVE SPECIES; RAIN FORESTS.

*Richard Robinson*

**Bibliography**

Eldridge, Niles. *Life in the Balance: Humanity and the Biodiversity Crisis.* Princeton, NJ: Princeton University Press, 1998.

Erlich, Paul R., and Anne H. Erlich. *The Population Explosion.* New York: Simon & Schuster, 1990.

Primack, Richard. *A Primer of Conservation Biology.* Sunderland, MA: Sinauer Associates, 2000.

Terborgh, John. *Requiem for Nature.* Washington, DC: Island Press, 1999.

**continental drift** the movement of continental land masses due to plate tectonics

# Humboldt, Alexander von

### German Explorer and Scientist
### 1769–1859

Alexander von Humboldt was the greatest explorer-scientist of the eighteenth and early nineteenth centuries. Humboldt's contributions to science were remarkably diverse. He was the first person to map areas of equal air temperature and pressure, a technique now used in every weather forecast around the world. By measuring the magnetism of rocks in the Alps, he found that Earth's magnetic field reverses its polarity. This fundamental discovery allowed geologists in the twentieth century to prove the theory of **continental drift**. Humboldt also developed the idea of seismic waves that

Alexander von Humboldt.

travel through Earth's surface after an earthquake. In physics, he conducted more than four thousand experiments on electricity and magnetism. Perhaps his most important research, however, concerned the distribution and environmental relationships of plants.

Humboldt's interest in botany developed early on. While a teenager he spent many hours with Karl Willdenow, one of the leading botanists in Europe, collecting and classifying plants in the woods around Berlin. In 1789, while studying at the University of Gottingen, Humboldt met Johann Forster. Forster had accompanied James Cook on a voyage around the world and was one of the best naturalists of his day. On expeditions with Forster to France, England, and the Netherlands, Humboldt learned the techniques of scientific observation, plant classification, and precise measurement that he would employ throughout his long and incredibly productive career.

In 1790, Humboldt began work in plant geography that would revolutionize botany. Humboldt's botanical work was greatly influenced by German natural philosophers such as Immanuel Kant. Kant believed that there was an underlying causal unity in nature and that Earth should be viewed as a single, interconnected whole. Extending these ideas to the study of plants, Humboldt sought to create a universal, **holistic** science of botany that encompassed both the diversity and connectedness of the natural world. In his words: "Science can only progress . . . by bringing together all of the phenomena and creations that the earth has to offer . . . nothing can be considered in isolation . . . . Nature, despite her seeming diversity, is always a unity."

**holistic** including all the parts or factors that relate to an object or idea

By 1797 Humboldt had become bored with his work in geology at the German Ministry of Mines. "I was spurred by an uncertain longing for the distant and unknown," he wrote. "For . . . danger at sea . . . the desire for adventures." On June 5, 1799, accompanied by his colleague, the botanist Aimé Bonpland, Humboldt embarked on an expedition to South America to "find out how the geographic environment influences plant and animal life." Landing in Cumana, Venezuela, Humboldt spent the next five years exploring uncharted regions of the Oronoco River, Colombia, Peru, and Ecuador.

During this journey, Humboldt survived attacks by Native Americans, tropical disease, starvation, near drowning in capsized canoes, and shocks from electric eels. Despite incredible hardships, he carried out meticulous observations on South American plants, geography, geology, climate, Aztec art, and native languages. In Ecuador, he mapped the **zonation** of vegetation on mountain sides and correlated this zonation with climatic changes. In Venezuela, anticipating the field of conservation biology, he analyzed complex relationships between logging, river ecology, and erosion. These fundamental studies of the relationships between plants and their environment laid the foundation for the emergence of the science of ecology during the nineteenth century. SEE ALSO BIOGEOGRAPHY; ECOLOGY, HISTORY OF; PLANT COMMUNITY PROCESSES.

**zonation** division into zones having different properties

*Bradford Carlton Lister*

**Bibliography**

Adams, Alexander B. *Eternal Quest: The Story of the Great Naturalists.* New York: G. P. Putnam's Sons, 1969.

Botting, Douglas. *Humboldt and the Cosmos.* New York: Harper and Row, 1973.

Von Humboldt, Alexander. *Personal Narrative of a Journey to the Equinoctial Regions of the New Continent.* New York: Penguin Books, 1995.

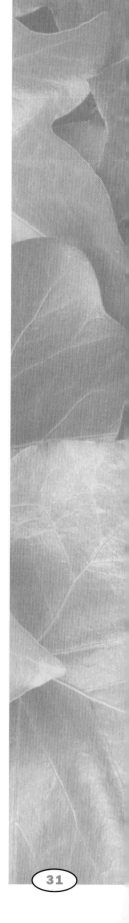

Three varieties of grain: rye, triticale, and wheat.

**taxa** a type of organism, or a level of classification of organisms

**sterile** unable to reproduce

# Hybrids and Hybridization

Hybridization is generally defined as the interbreeding of individuals from two populations or groups of populations that are distinguishable on the basis of one or more heritable characters. By extension, a hybrid is an individual resulting from such interbreeding. Hybrid zone refers to a region in which hybridization is occurring. Artificial hybridization refers to instances in which these crosses occur under controlled conditions, often under the direction of plant or animal breeders. In contrast, natural hybridization involves matings that occur in a natural setting.

## Factors Limiting Natural Hybridization

A variety of factors serve as reproductive barriers among plant **taxa**. These barriers, which can be subdivided into those acting prior to fertilization (prezygotic) or following fertilization (postzygotic), restrict natural hybridization and help maintain species boundaries.

**Prezygotic Barriers.** The potential for natural hybridization is largely determined by the proximity of potential mates in both space and time. The likelihood of hybridization is therefore governed, to a large extent, by differences in the ecology (spatial isolation) and/or phenology (temporal isolation) of the individuals of interest. Even if ecological and temporal differentiation are absent, pollen transfer may be limited by differences in floral morphology (form). Differences in traits such as floral color, fragrance, and nectar chemistry can influence pollinator behavior and may discourage the transfer of pollen among different species (ethological isolation). Alternatively, the structure of the flower may preclude or limit pollination of one taxon by the pollinator(s) of others (mechanical isolation). Finally, even if pollen transfer is successful, the pollen may not germinate on a foreign stigma; if it does, the pollen tubes may fail to effect fertilization due to slow growth or arrest prior to reaching the ovule (cross-incompatibility).

**Postzygotic Barriers.** Assuming that fertilization occurs, the resulting hybrid progeny (offspring) may fail to survive to reproductive maturity due to developmental aberrations (hybrid inviability). If the hybrids do survive, their flowers may be unattractive to pollinators, thereby restricting further hybridization (floral isolation). Alternatively, the hybrids may be attractive to pollinators but partially or completely **sterile** (hybrid sterility). Finally, even if first generation hybrids are viable and fertile, later-generation hybrids may exhibit decreased levels of viability and/or fertility (hybrid breakdown).

## History of Investigations

The scientific study of hybridization dates back to Carolus Linnaeus (1707–1778). In 1757, as part of an investigation as to whether or not plants reproduce sexually, Linnaeus produced hybrids between two species of goats-beard (*Tragopogon porrifolius* and *T. pratensis*). Although this work served primarily as proof of the sexual nature of reproduction in flowering plants, Linnaeus argued that "it is impossible to doubt that there are new species produced by hybridization generation." Shortly thereafter, Joseph Gottlieb Kölreuter (1733–1806) revealed two important flaws in Linnaeus's conclusions. Kölreuter first showed that hybrids from interspecific crosses are often sterile "botanical mules," a result that led him to conclude that hybrids are difficult to produce and unlikely to occur in nature without human intervention or habitat disturbance. He went on to demonstrate that, although early generation hybrids are often **morphologically** intermediate to their parents, later generation hybrids tend to revert back to the parental forms. This finding apparently refuted Linnaeus's earlier suggestion that hybrids were constant or true-breeding and represented new species.

In the latter part of the eighteenth century through the nineteenth century, hybridization techniques were widely applied to plant and animal breeding, a focus that continues today. The utility of hybridization for breeding programs lies in the fact that first-generation hybrids often exceed their parents in vegetative vigor or robustness. This phenomenon, known as hybrid vigor or heterosis, has been used to maximize yields in crop plants. Early botanists were also interested in the validity of hybrid sterility as a species criterion. This work was accompanied by increasingly frequent reports of natural hybrids between wild plant species. There was, however, little discussion of an evolutionary role for hybridization during this period, although sporadic reports of true-breeding hybrids continued to surface.

In the mid-nineteenth century, Gregor Johann Mendel (1822–1884) used hybridization to solve the problem of heredity. By analyzing the hybrid progeny of crosses between distinct varieties of garden pea (*Pisum sativum*), Mendel was able to demonstrate that genetic information is passed from one generation to the next in discrete units, and that these units (later known as genes) exist in pairs (later known as **alleles**). This work, which went largely undiscovered until 1900, provided a framework for the development of modern genetics.

## Importance of Hybridization

In the early twentieth century, three key discoveries laid the foundation for modern evolutionary studies of hybridization. The first discovery was by Øjwind Winge (1886–1964), who showed that new, true-breeding hybrid species could be derived by the duplication of a hybrid's chromosome complement (i.e., allopolyploidy). A second important discovery resulted from the work of Arne Müntzing (1903–1984), G. Ledyard Stebbins (1906–2000), and Verne Grant (1917–) on the possible origin of a new species via hybridization without a change in chromosome number (i.e., homoploid hybrid **speciation**). A third key advance resulted from studies of natural hybrid populations by Edgar Anderson (1897–1969) and coworkers. Anderson suggested that interspecific hybrids might be favored by natural selection and thus contribute to the formation of **intraspecific taxa** such as varieties or subspecies.

### Allopolyploid Hybrid Speciation.
Polyploidy refers to the situation in which an organism carries more than two full chromosomal complements. When the chromosome complements come from different species, these individuals are referred to as allopolyploids. **Allopolyploidy** is without a doubt the most frequent solution to the problems of hybrid sterility and segregation. In its simplest form, **genome** duplication in hybrids leads to the formation of fertile allopolyploids. This most commonly occurs via the fusion of unreduced (**diploid**) gametes.

**morphologically** related to shape or form

**allele(s)** one form of a gene

**speciation** creation of new species

**intraspecific taxa** levels of classification below the species level

**allopolyploidy** a polyploid organism formed by hybridization between two different species or varieties (*allo* = other)

**genome** the genetic material of an organism

**diploid** having two sets of chromosomes, versus having one (haploid)

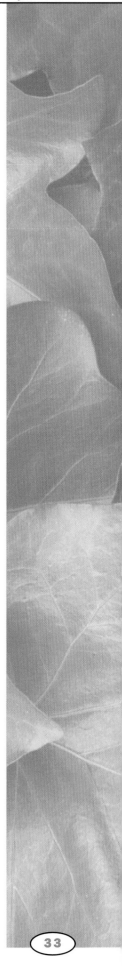

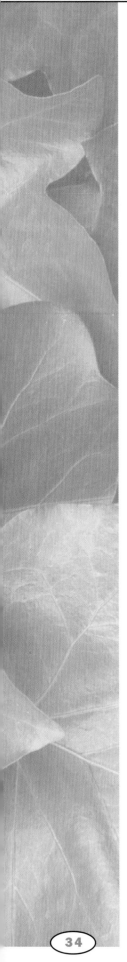

**tetraploid** having four sets of chromosomes; a form of polyploidy

**progenitor** parent or ancestor

**genotype** the genetic makeup of an organism

**interspecific hybridization** hybridization between two species

Allopolyploidy has several consequences that are relevant to hybrid speciation. First, it may lead to instantaneous reproductive isolation between the new allopolyploid species and its diploid parents. Crosses between **tetraploid** and diploid individuals, for example, will produce triploid offspring that are partly or completely sterile due to the presence of unpaired chromosomes in meiosis. Second, genome duplication can generate biochemical, physiological, and developmental changes, giving polyploids ecological tolerances that are quite different from those of their diploid **progenitors**. Altered ecological preferences increase the likelihood of successful establishment of an allopolyploid because it need not compete directly with its diploid parents. Third, genome duplication provides a means for stabilizing the hybrid vigor often associated with first-generation hybrids. This also contributes to the evolutionary potential of a newly arisen allopolyploid species. Finally, genome duplication promotes a series of genetic and chromosomal changes that increases the differences between the polyploid species and its diploid progenitors. These include the loss of deoxyribonucleic acid (DNA), the silencing or divergence of duplicated genes, and the increase in frequency of alleles that perform best in a polyploid genetic background.

**Homoploid Hybrid Speciation.** The evolutionary conditions required for homoploid hybrid speciation are much more stringent than for allopolyploidy. Unlike allopolyploids, homoploid hybrids are not instantaneously reproductively isolated from their parents (because the chromosome number remains the same), and new hybrid **genotypes** are likely to be lost though matings with their parents. Thus, models for homoploid hybrid speciation must explain how a new hybrid genotype can become reproductively isolated from its progenitor species.

The most widely accepted model of homoploid hybrid speciation is the recombinational model of Stebbins and Grant. In this model, the genes or chromosomal rearrangements responsible for hybrid sterility are assumed to assort in later generation hybrids to form lineages characterized by a new combination of sterility factors. The new hybrid lineages would be fertile and stable yet partially reproductively isolated from their parents by a sterility barrier. Although early authors focused on evolution of sterility barriers, naturally occurring hybrid species appear to have become isolated from their parental species by both ecological divergence and sterility barriers. Thus, models of this process now incorporate both ecological and genetic isolation. Modern contributions to the study of this process include rigorous experimental and theoretical tests of the model, as well as the gradual accumulation of well-documented case studies from nature.

**Introgressive Hybridization.** As discussed above, the development of reproductive isolation represents a major challenge for the origin of homoploid hybrid species. Thus, it is perhaps not surprising that intraspecific taxa such as varieties, ecotypes, or subspecies more commonly arise via **interspecific hybridization** than do fully isolated hybrid species. The process by which intraspecific taxa arise via hybridization is straightforward. In natural hybrid zones, interspecific hybridization is often followed by backcrossing to one or both parental species. This process is referred to as introgression, and it produces hybrid offspring that largely resemble one of the parental species, but also possess certain traits from the other parental species. If the hybrid gene combinations become fixed, the resulting hybrid products are referred to as stabilized introgressants. As with allo- and homoploid hybrid species, most stabilized introgressants are ecologically divergent with respect to their parental species. Thus, ecological divergence appears critical to successful establishment; otherwise, new introgressants are likely to be eliminated by competition and/or gene flow with parental populations. Although molecular markers have been used since the 1970s to document introgressive races and subspecies in many groups of plants and animals, the overall contribution of introgression to adaptive evolution remains poorly understood. SEE ALSO BREEDING; BURBANK, LUTHER; CULTIVAR; EVOLUTION OF PLANTS; PHYLOGENY; POLYPLOIDY; SPECIATION; SPECIES; TAXONOMY.

*John M. Burke and Loren H. Rieseberg*

**Bibliography**

Anderson, Edgar. *Introgressive Hybridization.* New York: John Wiley & Sons, 1949.

Grant, Verne. *Plant Speciation.* New York: Columbia University Press, 1981.

Levin, Donald A. "The Origin of Isolating Mechanisms in Flowering Plants." In *Evolutionary Biology*, Vol. 11, eds. M. H. Hecht, W. C. Steere, and B. Wallace. New York: Appleton Century Crofts, 1978.

Rieseberg, Loren H. "Hybrid Origins of Plant Species." *Annual Review of Ecology and Systematics* 28 (1997): 359–89.

# Hydroponics

Hydroponics is the practice of growing plants without soil. Plants may be suspended in water or grown in a variety of solid, **inert** media, including vermiculite (a mineral), sand, and rock wool (fiberglass insulation). In these cases, water that permeates the medium provides the nutrients, while the medium provides support for root structures. Hydroponics allows precise control of nutrient levels and oxygenation of the roots. Many plants grow faster in hydroponic media than in soil, in part because less root growth is needed to find nutrients. However, the precise conditions for each plant differ, and the entire set up must be in a greenhouse, with considerable investment required for lights, tubing, pumps, and other equipment.

**inert** incapable of reaction

Sprouts growing in a hydroponic hot house in Japan.

While hydroponics is as old as the hanging gardens of Babylon, modern hydroponics was pioneered by Julius von Sachs (1832–1897), a researcher in plant nutrition, and hydroponics is still used for this purpose. It is also used commercially for production of cut flowers, lettuce, tomatoes, and other high-value crops, although it still represents a very small portion of the commercial market. SEE ALSO AGRICULTURE, MODERN; ROOTS; SACHS, JULIUS VON.

*Richard Robinson*

**Bibliography**

Mason, John. *Commerical Hydroponics.* New York: Simon & Schuster, 2000.

# Identification of Plants

All known plant species have names. Unfortunately, outside of flower shops and botanical gardens, they do not come with nametags. Therefore, it is often necessary to identify an unknown plant, that is, to determine the species to which it belongs and thus its name. Identification assumes that the plants have already been classified and named. When you identify a plant, you are basically asking: "Of all known species, which one most closely resembles this individual in my hand?"

Professionals and serious amateurs identify plants by keying. This is a stepwise process of elimination that uses a series of paired contrasting statements, known as a dichotomous key. Keying is like a trip down a repeatedly forking road: If at the first fork you turn right, you cannot possibly reach any of the towns that lie along the left fork. Each successive fork in the road eliminates other towns, until you finally reach your destination.

When keying, the user begins by reading the first pair of statements (called a couplet). For example, a key may begin by asking the user to decide between "plants woody" and "plants not woody." If the unknown is woody, all nonwoody species are immediately eliminated from consideration. Successive couplets will eliminate further possibilities until only one remains, which is the species to which the unknown must belong. The advantage of this procedure is that the user must only make one decision at a time, rather than mentally juggling long lists of features of many possible candidates.

**specimen** object or organism under consideration

Once the plant has been keyed, it is necessary to confirm the identification. Most books that include keys also include detailed descriptions; some also include illustrations of all or selected species. If the **specimen** that was keyed matches the appropriate description and/or illustration, the identification may be assumed to be correct. If one has access to an herbarium, the specimen that was keyed can be compared to previously identified specimens of the species as a further check of the identification.

Although plant classifications are based upon information from many disciplines, including genetics, chemistry, and molecular biology, identification almost always relies on readily observed structural features, both vegetative and reproductive. For this reason, it is essential that specimens for identification be as complete as possible. Those of small plants should include not only all aboveground portions but also the roots. For large woody plants, a fully expanded twig of the current season will suffice. In all cases, specimens must include reproductive structures (i.e., flowers, fruits, seeds). Features that are not represented in the physical specimen (e.g., height or girth of trees, features of the bark, colors or odors that fade in drying) should be noted at the time of collection.

Equipment requirements to identify plants are few: a magnifying lens of 10 to 300 power, a 10-centimeter ruler, simple dissecting tools (forceps, teasing needles, razor blades), and a key. An excellent bibliography of appropriate keys for plants of all parts of Earth is provided by Frodin (1983). As for personal requirements, the most important is a critical eye, that is, the ability to observe carefully and to correctly interpret what is observed. This requires some familiarity with both plant structures and the terminology used to describe them. A comprehensive resource for this topic is Radford's introductory textbook (1986). Above all, as with most skills, there is no substitute for plenty of practice. SEE ALSO FLORA; FLOWERS; HERBARIA; INFLORESCENCE; SYSTEMATICS, MOLECULAR; SYSTEMATICS, PLANT; TAXONOMIC KEYS; TAXONOMY.

*Thomas G. Lammers*

**Bibliography**

Frodin, D. G. *Guide to Standard Floras of the World.* Cambridge, England: Cambridge University Press, 1983.

Jones, Samuel B., Jr., and Arlene E. Luchsinger. *Plant Systematics.* New York: McGraw-Hill, 1979.

Judd, Walter S., C. S. Campbell, Elizabeth A. Kellogg, and Peter F. Stevens. *Plant Systematics: A Phylogenetic Approach.* Sunderland, MA: Sinauer, 1999.

Radford, Albert E. *Fundamentals of Plant Systematics.* New York: Harper & Row, 1986.

# Inflorescence

An inflorescence is a collection of flowers in a particular branching pattern that does not contain full-size leaves among the flowers. While there are many kinds of inflorescences to be found in flowering plants (angiosperms), each species has its own form of inflorescence, which varies only minimally in individual plants. However, if a plant bears only a single flower, or makes many single flowers scattered on a tree with interspersed leaves, no inflorescences are said to be present.

Inflorescences (sometimes called flower stalks) can be divided into two main categories, with many types within each. These two categories are determinate and indeterminate, and can be distinguished by the order in which the flowers mature and open. Determinate inflorescences mature from the top down (or the inside out, depending on the overall shape of the inflorescence). In other words, the oldest and therefore largest flowers (or flower buds) on a determinate inflorescence are located at the top (or center) while the youngest flowers can be found at the bottom (or outside edge). Thus, the flowers mature from the top down (or the inside out). The situation is reversed for indeterminate inflorescences: the youngest flowers are at the top and the oldest flowers are found at the bottom. Flowers in an indeterminate inflorescence mature from the bottom up (or the outside in). The terms determinate and indeterminate refer to the potential number of flow-

A flowering rush (*Butomus umbellatus*) displays its umbel of pink to red flowers.

ers produced by each inflorescence. In a determinate inflorescence, the number of flowers produced is determined by the manner in which the inflorescence is put together. An indeterminate inflorescence can continue to produce more flowers at its tip if conditions are favorable and are thus more flexible in flower number.

Each of the two broad categories of inflorescences can be divided into specific types. For the indeterminate inflorescences, the simplest types are the spike, raceme, umbel, panicle, and head. The spike has a single unbranched stem with the flowers attached directly to the stem. A raceme is similar, but the flowers each have their own short stems, which are attached to the main stem. An umbel has flowers with stems that all attach out in the same point on the main stem, resulting in an umbrella-like appearance that can be flat-topped or rounded. Panicles are highly branched with small individual flowers. A head typically has very small individual flowers that are collected in a densely arranged structure; sunflowers and daisies are good examples. Determinate inflorescences tend to be more branched and include the cyme, dichasium, and corymb. A cyme is a branched inflorescence where all flower **pedicels** and branches originate at the same point. A dichasium is more elongated and a corymb is flat-topped. All of these basic types can be further modified in shape and/or reiterated, resulting in complex inflorescences that can be very difficult to identify.

Inflorescences serve as a way for a plant to maximize its reproductive success. Flowers are collected into showy structures to better attract pollinators, to increase seed production, or aid in seed dispersal. Inflorescences can result in platforms suitable for insects or birds to land upon. Some inflorescences are tough and protect the floral parts from damage from the elements or from pollinating mammals. SEE ALSO ANATOMY OF PLANTS; FLOWERS.

*Elizabeth M. Harris*

**pedicel** a plant stalk that supports a fruiting or spore-bearing organ

**Bibliography**

Gifford, Ernest M., and Adriance S. Foster. *Morphology and Evolution of Vascular Plants*, 3rd ed. New York: W. H. Freeman and Company, 1989.

Harris, James G., and Melinda W. Harris. *Plant Identification Terminology; An Illustrated Guide.* Spring Lake, UT: Spring Lake Publishing, 1994.

Heywood, V. H., ed. *Flowering Plants of the World.* Englewood Cliffs, NJ: Prentice-Hall, Inc., 1985.

# Ingenhousz, Jan

### *Dutch Physician*
### *1730–1799*

Jan Ingenhousz made major contributions to plant **physiology** as well as human medicine. He was born in the Netherlands, received a medical degree in 1753, and went on to further study in Leiden, Paris, and Edinburgh, finally aiding in the discovery of a new smallpox inoculation procedure. For a time he lived in England, where he befriended Benjamin Franklin and Joseph Priestley. After his success with the smallpox vaccine, however, Empress Maria Theresa of Austria called Ingenhousz to the Austrian court. There he served as personal physician to the empress for twenty years. He returned to in England in 1778.

Ingenhousz had an early interest in gases, which led to his interest in photosynthesis. The results of his work demonstrated both the disappearance of gas and the production of oxygen during photosynthesis. Ingenhousz disproved the belief that carbon comes from the soil by establishing a relationship between photosynthesis and plant respiration, claiming that the carbon used by plants came from the carbon dioxide in the air. In addition, he showed that only green leaves have the ability to purify the air through photosynthesis.

In 1778 Ingenhousz conducted experiments on plant production of oxygen. He showed that the green leaves of plants must be exposed to substantial daylight for oxygen production to occur. From this result, he was able to counter the arguments and statements of his contemporary chemists regarding the source of oxygen. Ingenhousz began applying many of the techniques pioneered by Priestley to the study of plant respiration. Priestley had designed a mechanism for measuring oxygen called a eudiometer. Nitric oxide was injected into a closed vessel in which there was already water. A reaction would then occur between nitric oxide and the oxygen in water, producing nitrous dioxide, which is soluble in water. Therefore, the amount of oxygen in the water could be measured by watching the water in the vessel rise.

Using this technique, Ingenhousz showed that plants need the presence of light in order to purify air. In the presence of light, he concluded that "all plants possess a power of correcting, in a few hours, foul air, unfit for respiration; but only in clear light, or in the sunshine."

After he had made this conclusion (what we now call carbon fixation), Ingenhousz began thinking about ways in which oxygen might help respiratory patients; he built some equipment for this purpose but never got terribly far.

In addition to his work on carbon fixation, Ingenhousz performed substantial particle research using algae **specimens**. His research on algae led to his preliminary observations of what would later be called Brownian

Jan Ingenhousz.

**physiology** the biochemical processes carried out by an organism

**specimen** object or organism under consideration

39

Motion and illustrated that lifeless particles show motion. Notably, Ingenhousz was also the first to use thin glass coverslips for liquid preparations viewed under microscopic lenses. SEE ALSO ATMOSPHERE AND PLANTS PHOTOSYNTHESIS, CARBON FIXATION AND; PHOTOSYNTHESIS, LIGHT REACTIONS AND; PHYSIOLOGIST; PHYSIOLOGY; PHYSIOLOGY, HISTORY OF.

*Hanna Rose Shell*

### Bibliography

Isley, Duane. "Jan Ingenhousz." In *One Hundred and One Botanists*. Ames, IA: Iowa State University Press, 1994.

Morton, Alan G. "Jan Ingenhousz." In *History of Botanical Science*. London: Academic Press, 1981.

Van der Pas, P. W. "J. B. Van Helmont." *Dictionary of Scientific Biography* 6 (1972): 11–16.

# Interactions, Plant-Fungal

Fungi are the most common parasites of plants, causing many kinds of diseases. Nonetheless, a fungus often parasitizes a plant without causing harm, and it may even be beneficial. Two well-known examples of beneficial fungi are the mycorrhizae and fescue endophytes.

A mycorrhiza is a fungus-root association in which the fungus infects the root without causing harm. In fact, the plant often benefits because the fungal **hyphae** in the soil obtain mineral nutrients that are some distance from the root. Ectomycorrhizae are commonly found on both hardwood and coniferous trees in the forest or yard. A fungal mantle covers the root, and a network of hyphae can be found between cells in the root cortex. A special benefit of this mycorrhiza is that **pathogens** cannot penetrate the root. Many different fungi may serve as the fungal **symbiont**. A mushroom or puffball in the forest may be evidence of an ectomycorrhizal association.

Vesicular-arbuscular (VA) mycorrhizae are common in crop plants all over the world. These endomycorrhizae have no fungal mantle but have extensive hyphae in the root cortex. Many branched hyphal structures called arbuscules invade cells and obtain food. The vesicles, ball-like structures found between **cortical** cells, seem to serve in food storage. The VA mycorrhizal fungi are all closely related and obligate parasites.

The tall fescue **endophyte** *Acremonium* is a parasite that does not harm the plant. However, the infected grass is toxic to cattle. Endophyte-infected plants benefit by having greater stress tolerance and resistance to attack by insects. Endophyte-infected fescue is already being used as turfgrass, where the benefits can be realized without fear of toxicity to cattle. This character is readily maintained since the endophyte fungus is transmitted through the seed. SEE ALSO CHESTNUT BLIGHT; DUTCH ELM DISEASE; INTERACTIONS, PLANT-INSECT; MYCORRHIZAE; PATHOGENS; POTATO BLIGHT.

*Ira W. Deep*

**hyphae** the threadlike body mass of a fungus

**pathogen** disease-causing organism

**symbiont** one member of a symbiotic association

**cortical** relating to the cortex of a plant

**endophyte** a fungus that lives within a plant

### Bibliography

Smith, Sally E., and David J. Read. *Mycorrhizal Symbiosis*, 2nd ed. San Diego, CA: Academic Press, 1997.

Stuedemann, John A., and Carl S. Hoveland. "Fescue Endophyte: History and Impact on Animal Agriculture." *Journal of Production Agriculture* 1 (1988): 39–44.

Budded hyphae magnified two hundred times.

# Interactions, Plant-Insect

Insect-plant interaction refers to the activities of two types of organisms: insects that seek out and utilize plants for food, shelter, and/or egg-laying sites, and the plants that provide those resources. These interactions are often examined from the plant's perspective, and a principal broad research question is: "How do the activities of the insect affect plant growth and development?"

The interactions can be beneficial to both the plant and the insect, as illustrated by pollination. During pollination, an insect moving within a flower to obtain nectar may transfer pollen either within that flower or among other flowers on that plant. Other relationships between insects and plants can be detrimental to the plant but beneficial to the insect (e.g., herbivory, or feeding upon the plant). Plant-feeding insect species are numerous, constituting more than one-quarter of all **macroscopic** organisms. Although most plant parts are fed upon by insect **herbivores**, the majority of insect herbivores are specific in terms of the plant species and the plant part on which they will feed. Some examples of significant insect herbivores

**macroscopic** large, visible

**herbivore** an organism that feeds on plant parts

Tent caterpillars crawl across a silken web that covers a tree branch and its leaves.

worldwide on cultivated crops include: aphids on cereal crops, diamondback moth larvae (immatures) on members of the cabbage family, and larvae of the moth genus *Heliothis* on a broad range of plants, including cotton. In addition to the direct effects of herbivory, insects can be damaging to plants by acting as vectors (carriers) of pathological microorganisms, transmitting the organisms when the insects feed on the plants.

## Interactions in Agricultural Settings

In order to prevent significant losses of agricultural crops to herbivory, both in the field and following harvest, some form of insect population control is often required; some crops may require protection from more than one insect herbivore. Under conventional farming methods in the industrialized world, insecticides are applied to agricultural fields to control insect pests. Often, more than one type of insecticide and/or more than one treatment will be applied in a single crop cycle. The type of control method used for a particular insect/crop combination in part depends upon the understanding of the insect and its use of a particular crop plant. Research into novel aspects of insect-plant interaction may provide improved alternatives for controlling insect pest populations. For instance, recent research examining the effects of moth larvae feeding on corn has demonstrated that after herbivore damage, corn plants release a new complex of **odorants** into the air, and that some of these molecules are attractive to parasitic wasps. The parasitic wasps then seek out and parasitize the larvae feeding on the

**odorant** a molecule with an odor

corn plants. These odorants have the potential to be used to help control moth damage on corn.

A very different view of insect-plant interaction focuses on the use of insects as biological control agents for weeds and takes advantage of the fact that insects can feed destructively on plants. A well-known example of insect control of weeds occurred in Australia when prickly pear cacti were controlled by the cactus moth from Argentina, *Cactoblástis cactòrum* (Berg), an insect herbivore imported for that purpose.

### Areas of Inquiry

Some insect-plant relationships can be traced through the fossil record, as some fossilized leaves show evidence of ancient herbivory that occurred prior to the fossilization of the plant material. Other insect-plant relationships continue to develop as insect species incorporate novel host plants into their diets and plants evolve new defensive compounds. The dynamic nature and variety of these interactions provides much opportunity to increase our understanding of the **physiology** of both types of organisms, interactions between them, and ecological and evolutionary processes.

*Wendy Mechaber*

**physiology** the biochemical processes carried out by an organism

### Bibliography

Bernays, Elizabeth A., and Reginald F. Chapman. *Host-Plant Selection by Phytophagous Insects.* New York: Chapman & Hall, 1994.

Tumlinson, James H., W. Joe Lewis, and Louise E. M. Vet. "How Parasitic Wasps Find Their Hosts." *Scientific American*, March 1993.

# Interactions, Plant-Plant

In plant communities each plant might interact in a positive, negative, or neutral manner. Plants often directly or indirectly alter the availability of resources and the physical habitat around them. Trees cast shade, moderate temperature and humidity, alter penetration of rain, aerate soil, and modify soil texture. Plant neighbors may buffer one another from stressful conditions, such as strong wind. Some plants make contributions to others even after they die. Trees in old-growth forests that fall and decompose ("nurse" logs) make ideal habitat for seeds to sprout, and such a log may be covered with thousands of seedlings. While effects on the physical habitat are consistent aspects of communities, plant-to-plant competition to preempt resources also takes place, and in some instances chemical interactions occur between species.

**Commensalism** occurs as one species lives in a direct association with another (the host), gaining shelter or some other environment requisite for survival and not causing harm or benefit to the host. Orchids and bromeliads (*Neoregelia* spp.) live on the trunk or branches of their host, gaining water and nutrients from the air or bark surface without penetrating host tissue. Stocky roots and **xeromorphic** leaves that help gain and retain water are characteristic of **vascular** epiphytes (*epiphyte* means to live upon another). Bryophyte, lichen, and fern epiphytes are so abundant in the tropical rain forest that they often embody more plant material than their host trees. Another facilitation is illustrated by seedling growth of the Saguaro cactus (*Cereus giganteus*), which typically occurs in the shade of paloverde trees or

**commensalism** a symbiotic association in which one organism benefits while the other is unaffected

**xeromorphic** a form adapted for dry conditions

**vascular** related to transport of nutrients

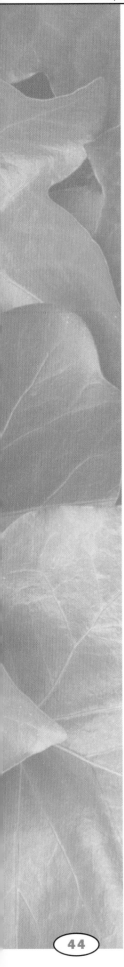

A strangler fig tree, an example of a parasitic plant-plant interaction harmful to the host.

**legumes** beans and other members of the Fabaceae family

other plants, which create a better water-relationship environment for the cactus and protect it from the negative effects of the intense sun. Farming practices often use "nurse" plants to create a temporary improvement in the environment for the main crop. For example, oat and alfalfa may be seeded together so that oat shades and maintains better soil surface moisture for the emerging alfalfa seedlings.

Direct plant-plant contacts that benefit both organisms are termed mutualism. Taking the broader view of plants to include microorganisms, a good example of this arrangement is the association of **legumes** and nitrogen-fixing bacteria that live within legume root nodules. The legume benefits by obtaining nitrogen from the bacteria, while the bacteria gain necessary carbohydrate energy from legume photosynthesis. The free-living bacteria actually change and become bacteroids, no longer able to live outside the roots. The vast majority of higher plants have fungal-root associations called mycorrhizae. The vascular plants benefit because the fungus is much better at absorbing and concentrating phosphorus (and perhaps other mineral nutrients) than the root tissue, while the fungus gains a source of carbon compounds from the plant.

Parasitic plant-plant interactions are harmful to the host. A number of plants (e.g., dodders, broomrakes, and pinedrops) do not contain chlorophyll and cannot photosynthesize. They parasitize green plants by penetrating the outer tissue of the host plant with haustoria (rootlike projections), which eventually tap the water and food-conducting tissue. Mistletoe also form haustoria but the primary function of these structures is obtaining water, as this partially parasitic plant is capable of manufacturing its own food by photosynthesis. Witchweed (*Striga* spp.) has green leaves but is an **obligate** parasitic weed that causes tremendous crop losses to tropical-origin cereal grain crops and legumes. Witchweed has evolved so that chemicals from the host plant have become signals for witchweed seed to germinate and attach to the host. Subsequently, witchweed penetrates the host roots and steals water, minerals, and hormones. Strangler fig is a tree that germinates high in the host tree and sends roots to the ground, eventually killing the host when the fig roots and vines surround and strangle the flow of sugars in the host.

**obligate** required, without another option

It is rare that plants are unaffected by neighboring plants. Negative effects on one of the neighbors are referred to as interference, and they include competition and **allelopathy**. Competition, the situation in which one plant depletes the resources of the environment required for growth and reproduction of the other plant, is the most common plant-plant phenomenon in nature. Members of plant associations that are more successful at gaining major resources—water, nutrients, light, and space—have the advantage and typically dominate the community. Competitive advantage may result from a plant's season of growth, growth habit, or **morphological** features such as depth of rooting, and special physiological capabilities like differences in rate of photosynthesis. In contrast to competition, allelopathic interference is the result of a plant adding toxic chemicals to the environment that inhibit the growth and reproduction of associated species or those that may later grow in the area. Many negative effects on target species probably occur from a combination of competition and allelopathy. Chemicals released from one plant may also be a communication to other plants, causing germination (e.g., *Striga*) or signaling defense responses to insect attack. SEE ALSO Allelopathy; Defenses, Chemical; Ecosystem; Interactions, Plant-Fungal; Interactions, Plant-Insect; Interactions, Plant-Vertebrate; Invasive Species; Mycorrhizae; Nitrogen Fixation; Parasitic Plants; Plant Community Processes; Symbiosis.

**allelopathy** harmful action by one plant against another

**morphological** related to shape

*Frank A. Einhellig and James A. Rasmussen*

**Bibliography**

Kareiva, Peter M., and Mark D. Bertness, eds. "Special Feature: Re-Examining the Role of Positive Interactions in Communities." *Ecology* 78, vol. 7 (1997).

Raven, Peter H., Ray F. Evert, and Susan E. Eichhorn. *Biology of Plants*, 6th ed. New York: W. H. Freeman and Company, 1999.

# Interactions, Plant-Vertebrate

Because plants can photosynthesize, they form the base of food chains in most **ecosystems**. During the past five hundred million years, vertebrates have evolved many methods of extracting energy from plants, which can have positive or negative impacts on individual plants and their populations.

**ecosystem** an ecological community together with its environment

A bronzy hermit hummingbird (*Glaucis aenea*) sips from a red passion flower (*Passiflora vitifolia*).

**frugivory** eating of fruits

**herbivore** an organism that feeds on plant parts

**avian** related to birds

Positive interactions between plants and animals are called mutualisms. Familiar examples include pollination and **frugivory**, in which plants provide flowers containing nectar, pollen, and fruits with a fleshy pulp as food for animals, while animals disperse plant's pollen and seeds. Major vertebrate pollinators include a wide variety of birds (e.g., hummingbirds, orioles, and sunbirds) and many plant-visiting bats. Similarly, frugivorous vertebrates, including many kinds of birds, bats, and primates (and even certain fish in the Amazon River), consume fleshy fruits and move seeds to new locations. Many species of tropical trees and shrubs rely exclusively on vertebrates for pollination and/or seed dispersal.

In contrast, many vertebrates interact negatively with plants as **herbivores** and seed-eaters. Herbivory, which involves the consumption of leaves, roots, and stems, can reduce plant growth rates and seed production if it does not kill plants outright. Seed predation, in which animals destroy plant embryos, is a specialized form of herbivory. Herbivory is much more common in mammals than in birds. Ptarmigan and grouse are **avian** herbivores; rodents, rabbits, cows and their relatives, and horses and their relatives are mammalian herbivores. Seed-eating is much more common than herbivory in birds. (Examples include parrots, pigeons, finches, and sparrows.) Major mammalian seed-eaters are squirrels, rats, and mice. Whereas vertebrate mutualists are beneficial for certain economically important plants, vertebrate herbivores and seed-eaters can cause millions of dollars of damage annually to many economically important crops. Humans, too, are vertebrates, and the interactions of plants and humans, especially through agriculture, has had profound consequences for each. SEE ALSO COEVOLUTION; POLLI-NATION BIOLOGY.

*Theodore H. Fleming*

**Bibliography**

Howe, H. F., and L. C. Westley. *Ecological Relationships of Plants and Animals.* New York: Oxford University Press, 1988.

# Invasive Species

Plants that grow aggressively and outcompete other species are called invasive species. Invasive plants are usually those that were introduced, either intentionally or unintentionally, into a locality where they previously did not grow. Introduced plants, also called exotics or alien species, form an important part of our environment, contributing immensely to agriculture, horticulture, landscaping, and soil stabilization. But among the thousands of plant species introduced to North America, approximately 10 percent display the aggressive growth tendencies of invasive species. Although the terms *exotic*, *alien*, and *invasive* are sometimes used interchangeably, not all exotic plants are invasive. In addition, some native species, those plants that grew in an area prior to European settlement, can be invasive, especially as natural landscapes are altered.

## Characteristics of Invasive Species

Invasive species are not a separate biological category, and all types of plants, including vines, trees, shrubs, ferns, and herbs, are represented by invasive species. They do, however, share certain characteristics that help them rapidly grow and invade new areas. Invasive plants typically exhibit at least some of the following:

- production of many seeds
- highly successful seed dispersal
- no special seed germination requirements
- grow in disturbed ground
- high photosynthetic rates
- thrive in high-nutrient conditions
- rapid growth and maturity
- early maturation
- reproduction by both seeds and vegetative means
- long flowering and fruiting periods

Most exotic plants do not pose an obvious threat to native plants when they are first introduced, but we do not fully understand the dynamics of what makes plants invasive. The same plant species can be invasive in one habitat or area and not aggressive in another. Sometimes many years separate the first introduction of a plant and its later spread as an invasive species. For example, Atlantic cord grass (*Spartina alterniflora*) was present in small areas on the Pacific coast for more than fifty years before it became invasive.

Often by the time a plant is recognized as being a major problem it has become so well established that eradication is difficult or impossible. Even

when plants are recognized as a potential problem, finding the money and manpower needed to eliminate them may not be easy. For example, leafy spurge (*Euphorbia esula*), which forms dense stands that cattle refuse to graze, was seen as a potential problem in Ward County, North Dakota, in the 1950s. By the time funding was available to deal with the problem on both public and private lands, leafy spurge was present in all townships in the county and had increased from one small patch to about 12,000 acres.

## Spread of Invasive Species

People have been the major factor in the spread of invasive species. Humans have always carried plants with them for food, medicine, fiber, ornament, or just curiosity. As human population has increased, so has the demand for food, housing, transportation, and other necessities of life. More and more land is disturbed to provide people with what they need and want, and disturbed land is where invasive species get their footholds. Increased international travel and global world trade also contribute to the problem. Invasive species have arrived in North America in the cargo holds of airplanes, as seeds in grain shipments, in the soil of ornamental plants, and as ship ballast. Improvements in transportation technology allow both people and plants to travel thousands of miles in just a few hours.

New environments provide an ideal place for invasive plants. These species leave behind the natural controls (usually insects) that kept them under control in their native habitats and can often spread unchecked. Some, such as the common dandelion (*Taraxacum officinale*), ox-eye daisy (*Chrysanthemum leucanthemum*) or tree-of-heaven (*Ailanthus altissima*), have become integrated over time into the flora of urban areas and are the dominant and familiar vegetation.

Most of the invasive species in North America are originally from Europe or Asia, areas with very similar climate. Many of these species were first introduced as ornamental plants. An excellent example is honeysuckle (*Lonicera* spp.), which was introduced in the late 1890s as horticultural shrubs and vines and for wildlife habitat improvement. Honeysuckle often outcompetes native plants due to earlier leaf expansion and later fall leaf retention. Large thickets of honeysuckle interfere with the life cycles of many native shrubs and herbs. These stands alter habitats by decreasing light and depleting soil moisture and nutrients. Some honeysuckle species also release chemicals into the soil that inhibit the growth of other plants. Fruits are consumed and passed by birds, which makes effective control difficult.

Another ornamental that turned invasive is kudzu (*Pueraria lobata*), a vine with attractive purple flowers that was first exhibited in the United States at the Philadelphia Centennial Exposition in 1876. It is now listed as a noxious weed in many states, especially in the South, where it smothers large trees as it clambers for light.

Accidental introduction is also a common way for invasive species to become established. Mile-a-minute weed (*Polygonum perfoliatum*), an Asian vine named for its fast growth rate, appeared in rhododendron nurseries in Pennsylvania in 1946, presumably the result of seeds mixed with imported plants. Since then it has spread to other areas in Pennsylvania as well as to surrounding states and is rapidly becoming a major problem along roadsides and other disturbed areas.

Purple loosestrife spreading in a wetland.

## Impact and Eradication

The economic impact of invasive plants is staggering. They affect agriculture, the environment, and health. Invasive plants cause reductions in crop harvests as well as increased production costs. Farmers worldwide spend billions of dollars annually on chemicals and other methods to control weeds. The toll in human time is enormous, as hand-weeding of crops is the number one work task of 80 percent of people in the world. Some invasive species that contaminate harvested crops or pastures are toxic and pose a threat to both people and animals ingesting that food or milk.

Invasive plants are also a major threat to native plants and animals, including rare and endangered species. In fact, alien species are considered by some experts to be second only to habitat destruction as a threat to **biodiversity**. In the United States, for every acre of federal land destroyed by fire in 1995, two acres were lost to invasive plants. Two-thirds of all endangered species are impacted by invasive plants. Wetlands, home to many endangered plants, are especially susceptible to invasive species, such as purple loosestrife (*Lythrum salicaria*), which has taken over thousands of acres in at least forty-two states.

**biodiversity** degree of variety of life

The problem of invasive species affects all fifty states. Introduced species make up 8 to more than 50 percent of the total plant species of most states. Nowhere is the problem more serious than in Hawaii, where exotic species now outnumber native species. In Florida, at least 1.5 million acres of natural areas are infested with nonnative plants. Of mainland states, New York and Pennsylvania have the highest ratio of introduced-to-native species.

Methods for eradicating invasive plants range from hand-pulling to chemical controls. When weeding plants, it is important to disturb the soil as little as possible because disturbed areas are where invasive species can grow well. Other mechanical means include mulching soil to prevent or reduce seed germination, applying heat to seedlings, mowing, and girdling trees (pulling a strip of bark off all the way around the trunk to prevent the flow of nutrients). As more and more noxious weeds become resistant to chemical treatments, attempts at biocontrol (using natural predators) are

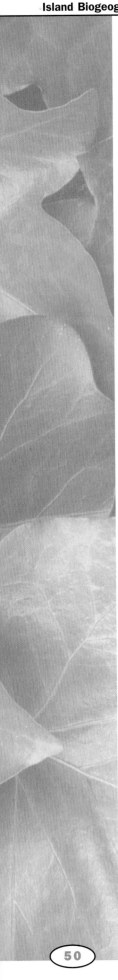

increasing. Researchers have identified thirteen different insect species that may potentially control leafy spurge, and a beetle that eats the leaves of purple loosestrife has already been released in some areas.

Perhaps most important is public awareness and participation in the problem. People should avoid using invasive plants in their yards and gardens. This can be a complicated task as some invasive species, such as purple loosestrife, are sold in garden stores and catalogs. Beware of any plants described as "spreading rapidly." Another important defense is being on the lookout for alien plants and removing them before they become a problem. Organized efforts at invasive plant removal are a major weapon in preventing their spread. In Utah, middle and high school students who participate in a Scotch Thistle Day each spring have significantly reduced the amount of this noxious weed in their area.

Although most invasive species have been introduced from other areas of the world, native plants can become aggressive, especially as habitats are altered or destroyed. Boxelder (*Acer negundo*) and wild grapes (*Vitis* spp.) as well as other native species can form fairly exclusive **monocultures** that thrive in disturbed environments. On the other hand, some otherwise invasive species can be useful in heavily disturbed sites. For example, tree-of-heaven grows where other plants cannot, thus providing just the foothold needed by other species to **colonize**.

The problem of invasive species is a costly one in terms of time, money, and loss of native habitats and species. Since the 1950s, weed-associated losses and costs worldwide have increased exponentially and are continuing to spiral upward. Of the more than sixty-seven hundred plants worldwide that are considered to be invasive, only about two thousand presently occur in North America. This leaves more than four thousand invasive plants now growing in other countries that could in the future become a problem in the United States. SEE ALSO ENDANGERED SPECIES; HUMAN IMPACTS; KUDZU; SEED DISPERSAL; WETLANDS.

*Sue A. Thompson*

**monoculture** a large stand of a single crop species

**colonize** to inhabit a new area

**Bibliography**

Collins, Tim, David Dzomback, John E. Rawlins, Ken Tamminga, and Sue A. Thompson. *Nine Mile Run Watershed Rivers Conservation and Natural Resources.* Harrisburg, PA: Pennsylvania Department of Conservation and Natural Resources, 1998.

Randall, John M., and Janet Marinelli, eds. *Invasive Plants: Weeds of the Global Garden.* Brooklyn, NY: Brooklyn Botanic Garden, 1996.

Westbrooks, R. *Invasive Plants, Changing the Landscape of America: Fact Book.* Washington, DC: Federal Interagency Committee for the Management of Noxious and Exotic Weeds, 1998.

## Island Biogeography  *See Biogeography.*

## Jasmonates  *See Senescence.*

# Kudzu

Kudzu (*Pueraria lobata*, Fabaceae) is a woody vine whose extremely rapid and aggressive growth has made it a highly successful and widely disliked invasive species throughout much of the southern United States.

Kudzu overgrowing a forest in Georgia.

A native of Asia, kudzu was imported in the late 1800s as a shade-giving ornamental, and was widely planted in the 1930s to control erosion from cotton fields. In the mild and moist climate it prefers, and without its natural predators, kudzu spreads rapidly. In the United States, it covers more than three million acres across twenty-one southern states, blanketing an area nearly the size of Connecticut.

A kudzu vine can grow as much sixty feet in a growing season. It sets new roots at each **node**, thus forming a potential new plant every two or three feet. A five-acre field abandoned to kudzu may contain one hundred thousand plants, and the foliage may be two or more feet thick. The tap roots are massive, measuring up to seven inches across and six feet deep, and weighing up to two hundred pounds or more. Kudzu vines grow up and over almost anything, including trees, barns, and telephone wires. They can starve even full-grown trees of light, water, and nutrients.

**node** branching site on a stem

While kudzu has some nutritional value as livestock forage, it is too difficult to control to make it a valuable crop. Current eradication efforts use

either repeated applications of herbicide or continuous, intensive grazing. SEE ALSO FABACEAE; INVASIVE SPECIES.

*Richard Robinson*

**Bibliography**

Hoots, Diane, and Juanitta Baldwin. *Kudzu: The Vine to Love or Hate.* Kodak, TN: Suntop, 1996.

# Landscape Architect

A landscape architect is an environmental design professional who applies the art and science of land planning and design on many scales, ranging from entire regions to cities, towns, neighborhoods, and residences. The profession is quite diverse, and students may attend more than sixty undergraduate and graduate programs in the United States and Canada, many of which offer comprehensive and/or individualized training in the following areas:

- **Landscape Design:** Outdoor space designing for residential, commercial, industrial, institutional, and public spaces

- **Site Planning:** Designing and arranging built and natural elements on the land

- **Urban/Town Planning:** Designing and planning layout and organization of urban areas, including urban design, and the development of public spaces such as plazas and streetscapes

- **Regional Landscape Planning:** Merging landscape architecture with environmental planning, including land and water resource management and environmental impact analysis

- **Park and Recreational Planning:** Creating or redesigning parks and recreational areas in cities, suburban and rural areas, and larger natural areas as part of national park, forest, and wildlife refuge systems

A landscape architect and his assistant work on a map in Raleigh, North Carolina.

- **Land Development Planning:** Working with real estate development projects, balancing the capability of the land to accommodate quality environments

- **Ecological Planning and Design:** Studying the interaction between people and the natural environment, focusing on flexibility for development, including highway design and planning

- **Historic Preservation and Reclamation:** Preserving, conserving, or restoring existing sites for ongoing and new use

- **Social and Behavioral Aspects of Landscape Design:** Designing for the special needs of the elderly or physically challenged

The study of plant sciences is often an integral part of the above specialties. Increased focus on ecological planning and natural systems design includes the study of native plant materials and **ecosystems**. The development of public and private gardens and recreation destinations places specific focus on ornamental horticulture using cultivated plant materials.

**ecosystem** an ecological community together with its environment

Opportunities abound for landscape architects working for residential and commercial real estate developers, federal and state agencies, city planning commissions, and individual property owners. Salaries vary widely depending on experience and whether one works for a private or public organization, but it equals or exceeds those of architects and civil engineers.

Future opportunities for landscape architects are extremely promising. The increasing complexity of projects requires interdisciplinary communication and commitment to improving the quality of life through the best design and management of places for people and other flora and fauna. SEE ALSO ARBORIST; HORTICULTURIST; ORNAMENTAL PLANTS.

*Thomas Wirth*

### Bibliography

American Association of Landscape Architects. [Online] Available at http://www.asla.org.

Simonds, John O. *Landscape Architecture*, 3rd ed. New York: McGraw-Hill, 1997.

Wirth, Thomas. *The Victory Garden Landscape Guide*. Boston: Little, Brown, and Company, 1984.

# Leaves

Leaves are often the most conspicuous part of any plant. Leaves vary tremendously in shape and in size: from the tiny leaves (less than 1 millimeter across) of the floating aquatic plant duckweed to the giant leaves (more than 10 meters in length) of the raffia palm. Nevertheless, all leaves share certain features of construction and development and carry out the same basic function: photosynthesis.

## Leaf Types

Leaves are designed to optimize the capture of light for photosynthesis. In dicots, leaves typically have a broad, flattened blade attached to a stalk or **petiole**. The flat shape of the blade facilitates the penetration of light

**petiole** the stalk of a leaf, by which it attaches to the stem

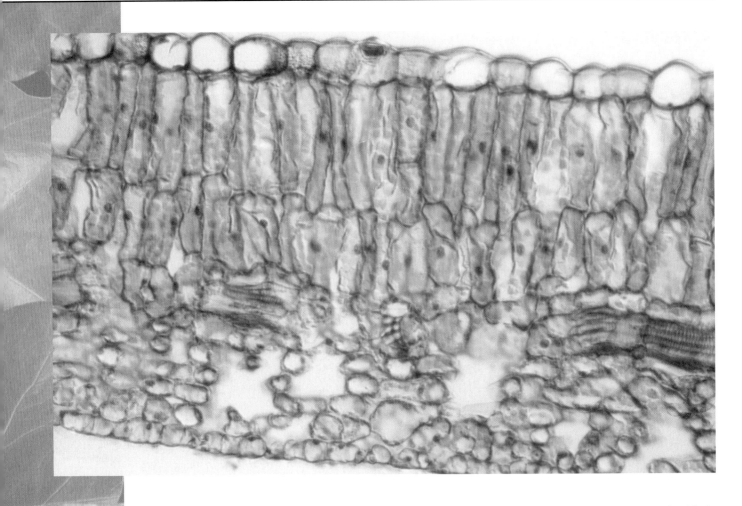

A micrograph of a transverse section of a leaf.

into the photosynthetic tissues within, while the petiole positions the blade so that it is shaded as little as possible by neighboring leaves. Leaf blades are referred to as simple when they are undivided and as compound when they are subdivided into individual leaflets. Compound leaves are either pinnately compound (like a rose leaf) or palmately compound (like a horse chestnut leaf). Simple leaves may also have complex shapes: In plants such as the maple or oak, leaves are highly lobed. The lobing of simple leaves and dissection of compound leaves are thought to serve the same function: The leaf maintains a large photosynthetic surface, but the complex outline allows the leaf to radiate heat energy to the surrounding atmosphere, thus maintaining photosynthetic tissues at optimum temperatures.

The leaves of monocots are designed along a different ground plan. The base of the leaf typically surrounds the stem, forming a leaf sheath. The leaf blade is borne at the tip of the sheath. In grasses, sedges, lilies, and orchids, the leaf blade is simple, long, and strap-shaped. In other monocots, such as palms, the blade is typically compound, and, like compound-leaved dicots, leaves may be pinnately compound (like a date palm) or palmately compound (like a fan palm). In palms and some other monocots, the junction of the sheath and blade forms a petiole-like structure.

Plant species are often recognized by their distinctive leaf shapes. Some species, however, are distinguished by producing more than one leaf shape on the same plant, a phenomenon known as heterophylly. Heteroblasty is the most common subtype of heterophylly and typifies plants such as ivy or eucalyptus, which produce one leaf shape early during the juvenile phase and another leaf shape later during the adult or reproductive stage. Another type of heteroblasty is environmentally induced heterophylly, in which specific environmental cues cause an immature leaf to develop along one of two or more alternate pathways. This type of heterophylly commonly results in the formation of sun and shade leaves on the same plant: Leaves that develop on the exposed edge of the canopy are narrow and thick, while those produced in the shaded interior are broad and thin.

## Anatomy of Leaves

Despite tremendous variation in size and shape, leaves generally possess the same cell types and arrangement of internal tissues. Leaf veins form a transport system that extends throughout the leaf. Major veins are the large veins that can be seen with the naked eye. The xylem of major veins functions to import water and dissolved mineral nutrients from the rest of the plant to the leaf, while the phloem of major veins exports carbohydrates produced by leaf photosynthesis. The **vascular** tissues of major veins are associated with **collenchyma** and **sclerenchyma** tissues and so contribute to the support of the leaf. Smaller veins are called minor veins. They lack associated supporting tissue and are embedded in the ground photosynthetic tissue. Minor veins form a network that acts as a distribution system: They supply leaf cells with water and **solutes** from the xylem and load photosynthetic products into the phloem. Whether the arrangement of minor veins forms a netlike reticulate pattern (typical of dicots) or a gridlike pattern (typical of monocots), adjacent veins are usually no more than 200 micrometers apart. Thus water and solutes rarely have to diffuse more than 100 micrometers between vascular tissues and photosynthetic cells.

**vascular** related to transport of nutrients

**collenchyma** one of three plant cell types

**sclerenchyma** one of three plant cell types

**solute** a substance dissolved in a solution

The photosynthetic tissue of the leaf is called mesophyll. Mesophyll tissue contains **chloroplast**-packed cells of two distinct shapes: palisade **parenchyma** cells that are elongated and spongy parenchyma cells that are spherical or lobed. In leaves with a horizontal orientation, palisade cells form one or two layers toward the upper side of the leaf. Palisade parenchyma cells have dense chloroplasts and, in fact, capture most of the light energy penetrating the leaf. Up to 90 percent of total leaf photosynthesis may occur within palisade parenchyma cells. Spongy parenchyma cells are arrayed in several layers below the palisade. They are exposed to more diffused light and tend to have fewer chloroplasts. Both palisade and spongy parenchyma cells have a relatively high surface-to-volume ratio: this gives a large surface area for the diffusion of carbon dioxide from the intercellular air space of the leaf into the cell where photosynthesis takes place.

**chloroplast** the photosynthetic organelle of plants and algae

**parenchyma** one of three plant cell types

Cells of the leaf **epidermis** typically are shaped like jigsaw puzzle pieces, which is thought to lend structural support to the leaf blade. **Stomata** usually occur on both the upper and lower surfaces of the leaf. The thinness of most leaf blades ensures that carbon dioxide diffusing inward through the stomatal pores will rapidly reach the mesophyll cells. While leaves are designed to maximize the uptake of $CO_2$ through the stomatal pores, they lose water vapor through those same pores while the stomates are open. Some plant species reduce such water loss by restricting the stomates to the lower, shaded side of the leaf blade where temperatures are lower and the diffusive loss of water vapor is slower.

**epidermis** outer layer of cells

**stomata** openings between guard cells on the underside of leaves that allow gas exchange

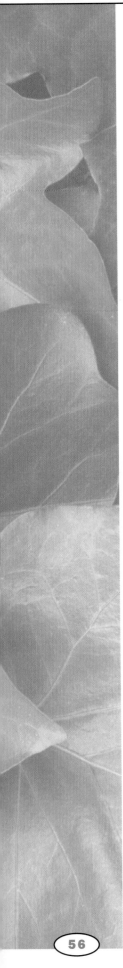

## Development of Leaves

**apical meristem** the growing tip of a plant

**primordium** the earliest and most primitive form of a leaf

Leaves are formed on the flanks of the shoot **apical meristem**. Leaf formation involves four overlapping stages: leaf initiation, morphogenesis, histogenesis, and expansion. Initiation occurs when an alteration of growth pattern within the shoot apical meristem results in a definite protuberance on the surface of the meristem, the leaf **primordium.** The leaf primordium is produced in a precise location on the meristem according to the phyllotaxis (leaf arrangement) of that particular species. In most dicots, leaf arrangement is helical, and each new leaf primordium is produced in the location that will continue the helix, 137.5 degrees from the last formed leaf. In most monocots, leaf arrangement is distichous, meaning each new leaf primordium is produced at 180 degrees from the previous leaf.

Morphogenesis is the development of the leaf's shape. In dicots, the primordium grows perpendicular to the meristem to form a fingerlike projection. Once the projection is formed, the primordium alters its growth direction to form a ledge around the margin of the protuberance. This ledge becomes the leaf blade, while the thicker original protuberance forms the petiole-midrib axis. At this stage of development, the distribution of growth is diffused, with the whole blade and petiole-midrib axis growing at an even rate. In species with a complex leaf shape, such as a lobed or compound blade, the distribution of growth becomes uneven: growth is enhanced where a lobe or a leaflet will be formed and suppressed between the lobes or leaflets. These events occur very early, so that a leaf often displays its mature shape when it is less than 1 millimeter in length.

In monocots, the original leaf primordium is formed in the same way, but its pattern of growth differs almost from the start. The zone of leaf initiation extends around the flanks of the shoot apical meristem, giving a crescent-shaped primordium. The crescent-shaped primordium then grows vertically. The "wrap-around" base becomes the leaf sheath, and the apical end becomes the strap-shaped blade. Monocots with more complex leaf shapes, such as palms, have a highly specialized pattern of morphogenesis.

Histogenesis is the process of tissue development. While the leaf is expanding and acquiring its final shape, precursor cells of all the tissue systems are undergoing cell proliferation. Cell proliferation is at first distributed throughout the leaf, but as expansion continues, cell division gradually ceases beginning near the tip of the leaf until it finally becomes restricted to the leaf base. In most dicots, this period is brief: the full complement of leaf cells may be already present when the leaf is only 10 percent of its final size.

**intercalary** inserted; between

In many monocots, cells near the base of the leaf continue to divide throughout the life of the leaf, forming an **intercalary** meristem. When you cut the grass of your lawn, cells in the intercalary meristem are induced to divide, producing more leaf tissue toward the leaf tip.

As leaf cells cease dividing, they first enlarge and then complete differentiation, acquiring the distinctive characteristics of specialized cell types. As with cell proliferation, cell differentiation occurs in a tip-to-base, or basipetal, direction.

Leaf expansion overlaps the morphogenesis and histogenesis stages. Usually all parts of the leaf expand the same amount so that the shape of the young leaf is preserved at maturity; this pattern is called isometric growth. In some species, however, different parts of the leaf expand at different rates, called allometric growth. Allometric growth can either enhance or minimize the degree of lobing in a leaf: if the lobes grow more than the interlobe region (the sinus), they will become more pronounced. In contrast, a leaf such as that of the nasturtium actually starts out with a lobed shape but becomes smooth and round in outline through increased growth of the sinus.

## Leaf Modifications

Although leaves tend to share the same ground plan, species that have adapted to extreme environmental conditions often have highly modified leaves. Two well-known examples are the leaves of xerophytes, plants adapted to arid environments, and leaves of hydrophytes, plants adapted to wet environments. Xerophytes are desert plants that must carry out photosynthesis and conserve water at the same time. Xerophytes reduce water loss by having small, but thick, leaves, thus reducing the surface area for evaporative water loss. Light intensity is usually high in the desert, so sufficient light penetrates to all photosynthetic mesophyll cells, even in a thick leaf. Xerophytes have a thick **cuticle** and waxes on the leaf surface, further reducing water loss. Their leaves often have a thick covering of trichomes that both trap a layer of moister air next to the leaf and reflect heat energy away from photosynthetic tissues. Some xerophytes, such as the oleander, have their stomates restricted to pits called stomatal crypts that further reduce evaporation of water vapor. A few specialized desert plants such as the clock plant hold their leaf blades parallel to the sun's rays throughout the day, using a specialized region of the leaf petiole called a pulvinus. The leaf photosynthetic tissue is exposed to sufficient light but absorbs less heat energy, thus keeping internal tissue temperatures cooler.

Hydrophytes face the opposite challenge to xerophytes. Their leaves are submerged, so there is no shortage of water, but they must photosynthesize under conditions of low light and low availability of carbon dioxide. Hydrophyte leaves are typically very thin, both to absorb the low, diffused light available underwater and to allow for the diffusion of dissolved carbon dioxide and minerals into leaf tissue. Hydrophytes lack stomata and have only a thin cuticle. They also have reduced vascular tissue. (Xylem is missing altogether in the leaves of some hydrophytes.) As hydrophyte leaves are buoyed by water, there is little need for supporting sclerenchyma tissue.

Many other examples of highly modified leaves occur as specialized adaptations among the flowering plants. Insectivorous plants have leaves that serve as traps for their insect prey. Cacti and many other desert plants have leaves that are modified as spines that serve to protect the plant from herbivores while the stems carry out photosynthesis. Some monocots have leaves modified for storage: the leaf sheaths of an onion bulb are thickened, and the mesophyll parenchyma cells are filled with stored sugars.

## Evolution of Leaves

The fossil record shows that the first land plants lacked leaves—or rather the stem functioned in both photosynthesis and support. Only toward the end of the Devonian period, about 350 million years ago, did plants begin

Detail of a cabbage leaf.

**cuticle** the waxy outer coating of a leaf or other structure, providing protection against predators, infection, and water loss

to bear distinct leaves borne on stems. Leaves of some of these early land plants were huge. Tree club mosses and primitive conifers called Cordaites had meter-long strap-shaped leaves where their modern relatives have highly reduced scale or needle leaves. Fossils of some of the earliest flowering plants from the beginning of the Cretaceous period, about 125 million years ago, show that leaves were of medium size and simple in shape. During the evolutionary diversification of the flowering plants, some groups have developed large, highly elaborate leaves, while others form small, reduced leaves. The early evolutionary divergence of the dicot and monocot lines is reflected in the different basic construction and mode of development of leaves in these two groups. SEE ALSO ANATOMY OF PLANTS; AQUATIC PLANTS; CACTI; CARNIVOROUS PLANTS; PHOTOSYNTHESIS, CARBON FIXATION AND; PHOTOSYNTHESIS, LIGHT REACTIONS AND; PHYLLOTAXIS; TISSUES; TRICHOMES.

*Nancy G. Dengler*

**Bibliography**

Esau, Katherine *Anatomy of Seed Plants.* New York: John Wiley & Sons, 1977.

Gifford, Ernest M., and Adriance Foster. *Morphology and Evolution of Vascular Plants,* 3rd ed. New York: W. H. Freeman, 1988.

Prance, Ghillean T. P. *Leaves.* New York: Crown, 1985.

Raven, Peter H., Ray F. Evert, and Susan E. Eichhorn. *Biology of Plants,* 6th ed. New York: W. H. Freeman and Company, 1999.

Taiz, L., and E. Zeiger. *Plant Physiology,* 2nd ed. Sunderland, MA: Sinauer Associates, 1998.

## Leguminosae    *See Fabaceae.*

# Lichens

**cyanobacteria** photosynthetic prokaryotic bacteria formerly known as blue-green algae

Lichens are the "dynamic duo" of the plant world. They consist of a fungus and a photosynthetic partner (green algae or **cyanobacteria**, or sometimes both) that live and grow so intimately interconnected that they appear to be a single organism. The fungus surrounds its green partner and shares in the sugars and other carbohydrates that the alga or cyanobacterium produces by photosynthesis. At the same time the fungus provides a protected environment for its food-producing partner and expands its potential habitats. Lichen fungi have a range of nutritional relationships with their associated algae or cyanobacteria from almost pure parasitism to a very benign association called symbiosis, or, more specifically, mutualistic symbiosis, wherein both partners benefit equally from the partnership. Lichens are an extremely successful life form, with thousands of species throughout the world. Some are extremely tiny and inconspicuous, little more than a black or gray smudge, but others can form broad, brightly colored patches or grow to be up to 3 meters long.

## Fungal and Algal Components of Lichens

The fungi that form lichens mainly belong to the sac fungi or Ascomycetes, although a few are mushroom-forming fungi, the Basidiomycetes. Each recognizable lichen (with a few interesting exceptions) represents a separate species of fungus; about fourteen thousand are known. The name

The curly edged frondose (foliose) lichen *Parmelia caperata* in Taynish Woods in Scotland.

we give to each lichen is actually the name of its fungal component. There are, however, only a few hundred species of photosynthetic **symbionts** (photobionts for short) that are involved in lichen partnerships. Lichen fungi are very choosy about their photobionts, and so each recognizable lichen generally contains a specific photobiont. Any given photobiont may, however, be found in many different lichens. A number of lichens associate with a green alga as their main photosynthetic partner but also produce small warts or gall-like bumps containing cyanobacteria, which contribute to the lichen's nutrition and survival.

**symbiont** one member of a symbiotic association

## Lichen Types and Reproduction

Lichens come in many shapes and sizes. They can be roughly grouped into four growth types: crustose, foliose, squamulose, and fruticose. Crustose lichens form a thin or thick crust so tightly attached to the material on which it grows (the substrate) that one has to remove the substrate together with the lichen to make a collection. A foliose lichen is leaflike; it is flat and has a clearly distinguishable upper and lower surface. Foliose lichens are attached to the substrate directly by the lower surface or by means of tiny

hairlike structures called rhizines. Squamulose lichens are scalelike with flat lobes as in foliose lichens but more like crustose lichens in size and stature. Fruticose lichens are clearly three dimensional, growing vertically as stalks or shrubby cushions or hanging down from branches or rock faces with hair- or strap-shaped branches.

The arrangement of tissues within most lichens follows the same basic plan. In a typical foliose lichen, a relatively tough upper cortex functions as a protective layer. Below the cortex is a green layer formed by the photobiont, then comes a cottony **medulla**, and, finally, on the lower surface, there is usually a protective lower cortex. The rhizines develop from the lower cortex.

**medulla** middle part

Lichen reproduction is rather complex because at least two organisms are involved. The lichen fungus can produce sexual fruiting bodies and spores, but the photobionts reproduce only by cell division within the lichen. When a fungal spore is dispersed by wind or water, it can germinate almost anywhere, but it will form a new lichen only if it encounters the right kind of photobiont. This is a chancy business, and the vast majority of spores perish without forming new lichens.

There is, however, a less perilous way for lichens to reproduce. Any fragment of a lichen containing both the fungus and photobiont has the potential of developing into a new lichen. Many lichens have, in fact, evolved special, easily dispersed fragments in the form of powdery particles (soredia) or spherical to elongated granules or outgrowths (isidia).

## Ecology of Lichens

Although lichens as a whole can be found growing on a wide variety of surfaces including rock, bark, wood, leaves, peat, and soil, individual species are more or less confined to specific substrates. Lichens are most conspicuous where other forms of vegetation are sparse, such as the bark of roadside trees or the surface of granitic boulders. They are usually the first organisms to invade entirely bare rock, contributing to the first particles of soil on the rock surface. Lichens carpet the ground in the vast boreal forests of the north, drape the trees and shrubs of foggy coastal regions and tropical cloud forests, and cover the exposed rocks on mountaintops and in the Arctic. They occur from the tropics to the polar regions and from lake edges and seashores to the desert. In general, however, lichens do best where there is much light, moist air, and cool temperatures. Lichens are notoriously sensitive to even small amounts of air pollution, especially the sulfur dioxide so common in cities and near factories, and large cities often have no lichens at all. Their disappearance from an area is an early sign of deteriorating air quality.

## Importance and Economic Uses of Lichens

The importance of lichens to the natural world and to humans is not well appreciated except, perhaps, for their role in soil formation. Lichens containing cyanobacteria are important sources of nitrogen in certain forest and desert **ecosystems**. The ground-dwelling boreal lichens preserve the ground's moisture. Lichens growing in the dry soils of the interior prairies and foothills prevent erosion.

**ecosystem** an ecological community together with its environment

Although lichens have usually been used as human food only in times of emergency (they are unpalatable and have very little nutritional value), a few lichen delicacies are enjoyed by native people of western North America and by the Japanese. Reindeer lichens in the boreal forest, however, are essential as winter forage for caribou herds, which are, in turn, basic to the survival and culture of northern native people. Some lichens yield a chemical called usnic acid, which is an effective antibiotic against certain types of bacteria. Other chemicals produced only by lichens have been used as a source of rusty red, yellow, and purple dyes for coloring wool and silk. Extracts of oakmoss lichens have been used for generations in the perfume industry. The litmus used to determine the acidity of solutions comes from a lichen. The most important use of lichens today, however, is for detecting and monitoring air pollution.
SEE ALSO ALGAE; BOREAL FOREST; FUNGI; PLANT COMMUNITY PROCESSES.

*Irwin M. Brodo*

### Bibliography

Casselman, Karen L. *Craft of the Dyer: Colour from Plants and Lichens*, 2nd ed. New York: Dover Publications Inc., 1993.

Hale, Mason E. *How to Know the Lichens*, 2nd ed. Dubuque, IA: W. C. Brown Co., 1979.

McCune, Bruce, Linda Geiser, Alexander Mikulin, and Sylvia D. Sharnoff. *Macrolichens of the Pacific Northwest.* Corvallis, OR: Oregon State University Press, 1997.

Nash, Thomas H., III, ed. *Lichen Biology.* Cambridge: Cambridge University Press, 1996.

Richardson, D. H. S. "Pollution Monitoring with Lichens." *Naturalists' Handbook 19.* Slough, England: Richmond Publishing Co., 1992.

Sharnoff, Sylvia D., and Stephen Sharnoff. "Lichens of North America Project" [Online] 1997. Available at http://www.lichen.com.

# Linnaeus, Carolus

### Swedish Botanist
### 1707–1778

Swedish botanist Carolus Linnaeus is best remembered for his classification system and binomial system of nomenclature. He brought order to the chaotic state of biological knowledge in the eighteenth century, introducing a systematic means of processing and organizing information on plants and animals. His particular interest was in plants, especially flowering plants, and the bulk of his efforts and publications focused on botanical studies. His most lasting contribution to biology is his binomial nomenclatural system, which grew out of what was for him a more primary focus: the development of a comprehensive system for classifying plants and animals.

Also known as Carl Linnaeus or Carl von Linné, he was born in Småland, Sweden, and even in his early years displayed an unusual interest in plants. His father, a curate in the Lutheran church, taught him many plant names. In adolescence Linnaeus learned about the doctrine of sexual reproduction in plants, which at that time was still a relatively recent concept. While still a medical student at universities in Lund and Uppsala, he began to develop a classification system based on the reproductive organs of plants. Faculty recognized his abilities and asked him to conduct lectures on botany. In 1732 he received support from the Swedish Royal Academy of Science

Carolus Linnaeus.

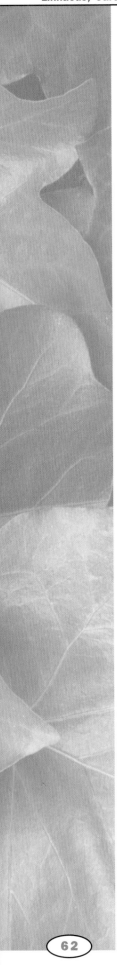

A plate from Linnaeus's 1737 work *Genera Plantarum* showing the twenty-four classes of Linnaeus's sexual system.

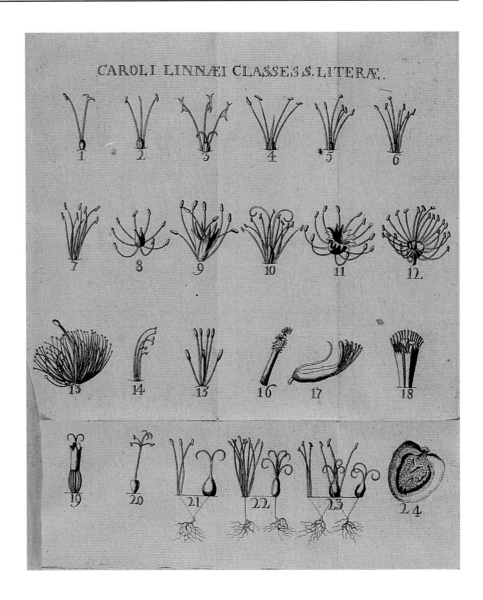

specimen object or organism under consideration

to travel to Lapland to observe the plants and animals there and how people lived and supported themselves. This trip made a lasting impression on young Linnaeus. He wrote about the plants he observed in *Flora Lapponica* (1737), and the **specimens** he collected in Lapland are now at the Institut de France, Paris.

In 1735 Linnaeus traveled to Holland to get a medical degree at Harderwijk. While in Holland he met prominent naturalists and was able to publish some of his own research. He made short trips to England, Germany, and France, again meeting important naturalists. In Holland he worked for George Clifford, a wealthy merchant with an extensive private botanical garden, which Linnaeus worked on and catalogued. This opportunity exposed Linnaeus to a wide range of plants that he would not have seen in his native Sweden, an experience that aided him in developing his ideas about classification. A catalogue of plants in Clifford's garden was published as *Hortus Cliffortianus* (1738).

Among the ten manuscripts Linnaeus published while in Holland were *Systema Naturae* (1735) and *Genera Plantarum* (1737). The former contained the first appearance of his classification scheme, while the latter contained his natural definitions of **genera**, building on work previously done by Joseph Pitton de Tournefort (1656–1708) and others.

Linnaeus returned to Sweden in 1738, was married, and practiced medicine in Stockholm for three years. In 1741 he was appointed a professor at the university in Uppsala, where he remained for the rest of his life, teaching, collecting and studying plants, and publishing. He was popular with his students and trained among them many enthusiastic naturalists. Early in his university career he traveled around Sweden, but after 1749 he stayed in Uppsala, sending a number of his students out on plant exploration journeys to many parts of the world. His landmark *Species Plantarum* (1753) and many other publications trace the development of his thought through the course of his career.

Linnaeus received many honors during his lifetime and was famous in Sweden and abroad for his ideas about classification and nomenclature. The eighteenth century was marked by a collective desire to gather and organize the whole of knowledge in encyclopedic schemes, and certainly Linnaeus's efforts were in harmony with the spirit of his times. His unusual talents for systematic organization and for **intuiting** the relationships among plants allowed him to accomplish a methodical review and theoretical organization of the natural world on a massive scale at a time when such work was desperately needed. His precise terminology, use of an international language, and global scope ensured widespread applicability and usability of his system. Modern systematic biology began with his mid-eighteenth-century publications. Historians of science recognize this by referring to earlier publications in the life sciences as "pre-Linnaean literature." Linnaeus's main collections are held by the Linnean Society of London, and other collections that he made throughout his lifetime are scattered at various institutions.

## Classification of Organisms

Naturalists in eighteenth-century Europe were faced with a bewildering and ever-growing number of previously unencountered plants and animals, the result of European voyages of exploration. Many sought to develop some sort of natural classification system that would organize plants and animals according to the true relationships among things in the natural world. Such a system would necessarily be based on a complex assessment of numerous characteristics of the things being classified. This goal proved very difficult to attain, and some began to devise more artificial systems, sacrificing a broad focus on natural affinities for an easier-to-apply method using one or a few characteristics by which to sort and organize living organisms.

Linnaeus too saw the desirability of a natural system, and he published some basic principles for attaining one, but there were still not enough plants and animals known to allow for a sufficiently broad synthesis. Thus, for plants, he worked out an extremely simple system based on counting stamens and **pistils**, which provided an easy, practical, and usable means for sorting and identifying plants. The scheme was first published in *Systema Naturae* (1735), which contained tables in which the "three kingdoms of nature"—animal, vegetable, and mineral—were comprehensively classified.

**genera** plural of genus; a taxonomic level above species

**intuiting** using intuition

**pistil** the female reproductive organ

For plants Linnaeus defined a genus (plural: genera) as a group of species with similar flowers and fruits. Genera were grouped into twenty-three classes of flowering plants by the number and disposition of stamens, with a twenty-fourth class for apparently nonflowering plants. Within classes they were arranged into smaller groups or orders according to the number and disposition of pistils. This scheme was called the "sexual system" because of its focus on the reproductive organs of plants. It was simple enough that even amateurs could use it to sort plants and ascertain whether they were already known to science.

The eighteenth century saw an information explosion in the natural sciences, and the utility and practicality of Linnaeus's classification scheme lay in the way it facilitated processing of information about the natural world. His sexual system of classification, although controversial and not widely accepted at first, was in general use in many countries for nearly a century, after which it was supplanted by more natural systems. Although it fell from use, in its time it reduced confusion in the study of organisms and facilitated the advancement of botany and zoology by providing a stopgap measure until a natural classification system could be developed.

### Naming of Organisms

nomenclatural related to naming or naming conventions

polynomial "many-named"; a name composed of several parts

The **nomenclatural** system that Linnaeus developed in the process of classifying nature proved to be of greater and more lasting benefit to biological science. In the century before Linnaeus, plants and animals were given long, descriptive names (known as **polynomials**) to differentiate them. For example, the polynomial name of catnip was "Nepeta floribus interrupte spicatus pendunculatis" (Nepeta with flowers in an interrupted pedunculated spike). There were no universally applied rules for constructing these names, however, resulting in considerable confusion in naming and referring to living things.

Linnaeus's solution to this problem, which was first applied to the plant world, was to group plants by genus and provide genus names (retaining many already in familiar use, or coining new ones), and then to give each species within a genus a "trivial" name, or what is known now as a specific epithet, so that each would have a unique two-part name, thereby unequivocally identifying that species. These trivial names, often in the form of Latin adjectives, were not necessarily descriptive, but they were linked to descriptive information, diagnoses, and references to previous descriptions in botanical literature. For example, he named catnip *Nepeta cataria* (cat-associated Nepeta). This enabled scientists to identify organisms with greater certainty, and provided a solid means for expanding and advancing knowledge. All in all, Linnaeus named approximately forty-four hundred species of animals and seventy-seven hundred species of plants.

The use of shorter names did not originate with Linnaeus. Folk names for plants and animals are typically short, and some scientists, notably Caspar Bauhin (1560–1624), used one- or two-word names when possible. However, pre-Linnaean names were often longer, using more adjectives in order to differentiate species within genera. Linnaeus was the first to construct a methodical and consistent nomenclatural system and to apply it to all living organisms then known to European science. His system was so comprehensive and so conducive to an integrated view of past and contemporary botanical studies that it won widespread acceptance and continues in current usage.

The nomenclatural system for plants was first published in his landmark work, *Species Plantarum* (1753). For animals, a similar system was published in the tenth edition of *Systema Naturae* (1758). These two works form the baseline for current nomenclatural practice in botany and zoology. Taxonomists in both disciplines still refer to Linnaeus's works when checking names of organisms, as mandated by international codes of nomenclature in both disciplines. SEE ALSO HERBARIA; TAXONOMIST; TAXONOMY; TAXONOMY, HISTORY OF.

*Charlotte A. Tancin*

**Bibliography**

Blunt, Wilfrid. *The Compleat Naturalist: A Life of Linnaeus.* London: Collins, 1971.

Dickinson, A. *Carl Linnaeus: Pioneer of Modern Botany.* New York: Franklin Watts, 1967.

Frangsmyr, Tore, ed. *Linnaeus: The Man and His Work.* Berkeley, CA: University of California Press, 1983.

Goerke, H. *Linnaeus,* tr. Denver Lindley. New York: Charles Scribner's Sons, 1973.

Gourlie, N. *The Prince of Botanists: Carl Linnaeus.* London: H. F. & G. Witherby Ltd., 1953.

Isely, Duane. *One Hundred and One Botanists.* Ames, IA: Iowa State University Press, 1994.

Kastner, Joseph. *A Species of Eternity.* New York: Alfred A. Knopf, 1977.

Morton, Alan. G. *History of Botanical Science: An Account of the Development of Botany from Ancient Times to the Present Day.* London: Academic Press, 1981.

Reed, H. S. *A Short History of the Plant Sciences.* New York: Ronald Press Co., 1942.

Stafleu, Frans A. *Linnaeus and the Linnaeans: The Spreading of Their Ideas in Systematic Botany, 1735–1789.* Utrecht: A. Oosthoek's Uitgeversmaatschappij J.V. for the International Association for Plant Taxonomy, 1971.

Stearn, W. T. "The Background of Linnaeus's Contributions to the Nomenclature and Methods of Systematic Biology." *Systematic Zoology* 8, 1 (1959): 4–22.

# Lipids

Lipids are a group of **compounds** that are rich in carbon-hydrogen bonds and are generally insoluble in water. The main categories are glycerolipids, sterols, and waxes.

Glycerolipids have fatty acids attached to one or more of the three carbons of glycerol. If three fatty acids are attached, the molecule is triacylglycerol, which is a primary storage form of carbon and energy in plants. Triacylglycerol is concentrated in many seeds for use during germination, and so seeds are of commercial importance as sources of fats and oils for cooking and industry. Diacylglycerol (DAG), which has two fatty acids, plays a role in cell signaling. Glycerolipids without any attached charged groups are known as neutral lipids.

If a polar molecule is added as a headgroup to DAG, the complex becomes a polar glycerolipid. The most common are phospholipids, the primary lipid component of higher plant membranes outside the plastids. Phospholipids are named after the headgroup, so if choline is present along with

**compound** a substance formed from two or more elements

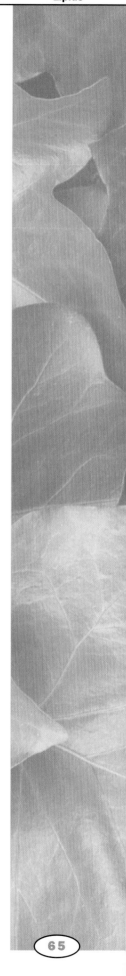

phosphate, the lipid is phosphatidylcholine. Several other headgroups exist. Polar lipids without phosphate also are important membrane molecules; for example, digalactosyldiacylglycerol, with two sugars as a headgroup, is a major component of **chloroplast** membranes.

Sterols are complex ring structures that are also major components of membranes. Some, such as brassinosteroids, also serve hormonal functions.

Waxes are elongated and modified fatty acids. They are found on the surfaces of plants, are highly impervious to water, and play a protective role. SEE ALSO ANATOMY OF PLANTS; HORMONES; OILS, PLANT-DERIVED.

*Thomas S. Moore*

**chloroplast** the photosynthetic organelle of plants and algae

## Lycopods  *See Seedless Vascular Plants.*

## Maize  *See Corn.*

# M

# McClintock, Barbara

### American Botanical Geneticist
### 1902–1992

Barbara McClintock, a pioneering botanical geneticist, was awarded the Nobel Prize in physiology or medicine in 1983 for her investigations on transposable genetic elements. She was born on June 16, 1902, in Hartford, Connecticut, and with her family soon moved to Brooklyn, New York, where she attended public schools. After graduating high school at age sixteen, McClintock attended the New York State College of Agriculture at Cornell, where she excelled in the field of plant genetics and graduated, in 1923, with a Bachelor of Science (B.S.) in Agriculture, having concentrated in plant breeding and botany.

## Career at Cornell

Awarded Cornell's graduate scholarship in botany for 1923–24, which supported her during the first year of her graduate studies, McClintock concentrated on **cytology,** genetics, and zoology. She received her master's degree (A.M.) in 1925 and a doctoral degree (Ph.D.) in 1927. Her master's thesis was a literature review of cytological investigations in cereals, with particular attention paid to wheat. In the summer of 1925, as a research assistant in botany, she discovered a corn plant that had three complete sets of chromosomes (a triploid). Then she independently applied a new technique for studying the chromosomes in the pollen of this plant and published these findings the following year. McClintock investigated the cytology and genetics of this unusual triploid plant for her dissertation.

Upon completing her doctorate in June 1927, McClintock became an instructor at Cornell and continued to pursue her studies on the triploid corn plant and its offspring. When triploid plants are crossed to plants with

Barbara McClintock.

**cytology** the microscopic study of cells

two normal sets of chromosomes, called diploids, they can produce offspring known as trisomics. Trisomics have a diploid set of chromosomes plus one extra chromosome. Plants with extra chromomes could be used for correlating genes with their chromosomes if one could distinguish the extra chromosome in the microscope. McClintock's continued investigations on the chromosomes of corn led her to devise a technique for distinguishing the plants' ten individual chromosomes.

In 1929, in the journal *Science*, McClintock published the first description of the chromosomes in corn. She knew that having the ability to recognize each chromosome individually would now permit researchers to identify genes with their chromosomes. Using a technique of observing genetic ratios in her trisomic plants and comparing the ratios with plants having extra chromosomes, McClintock cooperated with and guided graduate students to determine the location of many genes grouped together (linkage groups) on six of the ten chromosomes in corn.

Around the same time McClintock devised a way to cytologically observe pieces of one chromosome attached to another chromosome. These translocation or interchange chromosomes stained darkly in the microscope and could be easily observed during cell division (meiosis) to produce pollen grains. The interchange chromosomes were then used to locate the remaining four linkage groups with their chromosomes. They were also used to explain how some corn plants become **sterile**. In 1931 McClintock guided graduate student Harriet Creighton in demonstrating cytological "crossing over," in which chromosomes break and recombine to create genetic changes. It was the first cytological proof that demonstrated the genetic theory that linked genes on paired chromosomes (homologues) did exchange places from one paired chromosome to another. It confirmed the chromosomal theory of inheritance for which Thomas Hunt Morgan would be awarded a Nobel prize in 1933.

**sterile** unable to reproduce

McClintock hoped for a research appointment commensurate with her qualifications. By 1931, however, the country was suffering from the Great Depression and research jobs at universities were not abundant, particularly for women. However, because of McClintock's excellent work and reputation, in 1931 she was awarded a National Research Council (NRC) fellowship to perform research with two leading corn geneticists, Ernest Gustof Anderson at the California Insititue of Technology (Caltech) and Lewis Stadler of the University of Missouri. Stadler, who was studying the physical changes (mutations) in plants caused by X rays, invited McClintock to study the chromosomes of his irridiated plants. She discovered that observable changes in the plant were due to missing pieces of chromosomes in the cell. At Caltech she employed interchange chromosomes to investigate the **nucleolar** organizer region in cells.

**nucleolar** related to the nucleolus

After a short period in Germany in 1933 studying on a Guggenheim fellowship, McClintock returned to Cornell, where she continued her research of the cytology of X-rayed plants that she had first examined at Missouri. This research led her to clarify and explain how some chromosomes became ring shaped, were lost during cell replication, or resulted in physical differences in plant tissues. These investigations led to her studies of the breakage-fusion-bridge cycle in corn chromosomes and would eventually lead, in 1950, to her revolutionary proposal that genes on chromosomes

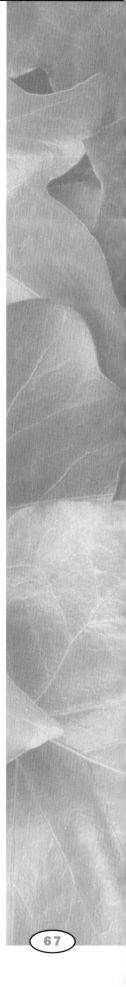

moved (transposed) from one place to another on the same chromosome and that they could also move to different chromosomes.

## Career at Cold Spring Harbor

In 1936 McClintock, at Stadler's urging, accepted a genetics research and teaching position at the University of Missouri, which she held for five years, until she seized an opportunity to be a visiting professor at Columbia University and a visiting investigator in the genetics department of the Carnegie Institution of Washington (CIW), working at Cold Spring Harbor on Long Island in New York. She was offered a permanent job at Cold Spring Harbor in 1943 and spent the rest of her life working there with brief visiting professor appointments at Stanford University, Caltech, and Cornell.

In the winter of 1944 McClintock was invited by a former Cornell colleague, George Beadle, to go to Stanford to study the chromosomes of the pink bread mold *Neurospora*. Within ten weeks she was able to describe the fungal chromosomes and demonstrate their movement during cell division. This work was important to an understanding of the life history of the organism, and the fungus would be employed by Beadle and his colleagues to illucidate how genes control cell metablolism. In 1958 Beadle shared a Nobel Prize for that work.

Returning to Cold Spring Harbor in 1945, McClintock traced genes through the changes in colored kernels of corn. In that same year she was elected president of the Genetics Society of America. Over the next few years, using genetic and cytological experiments in the corn plant (*Zea mays*), she concluded that genetic elements (transposable elements, or transposons) can move from place to place in the **genome** and may control expression of other genes (hence called controlling elements). She published her findings in the 1950s, and more than thirty years later, in 1983, she was honored with the Nobel Prize for her remarkable discovery.

**genome** the genetic material of an organism

Many have wondered why it took so long for McClintock's work in transposition to be recognized by the leaders in the scientific community. One reason could be that although she studied corn chromosomes employing cytogenetic techniques, other researchers studied simpler organisms (bacteria and their viruses) and used molecular techniques. McClintock's experiments were complex and laborious, taking months or even years to yield results. Molecular studies in simpler organisms gave almost immediate answers, thus providing their researchers with instant celebrity. Additionally, McClintock's findings contradicted the prevailing view that all genes were permanently in a linear sequence on chromosomes.

Further, although McClintock's conclusion that genes could move from place to place in the corn genome was accepted, the idea was considered peculiar to corn, probably not universally relevant to all organisms. It was not until the 1970s when transposons were found in a number of other organisms, first in bacteria and then in most organisms studied by geneticists, that the value of McClintock's initial studies realized. Research on transposable elements, or transposons, led to the revolution in modern recombinant deoxyribonucleic acid (DNA) technology that has played a significant role in medicine and agriculture. When McClintock's work was

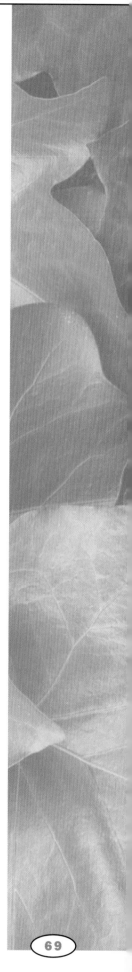

rediscovered, she was recognized and rewarded with the Nobel Prize for her great insights. McClintock died on September 2, 1992, in Huntington on Long Island, New York. SEE ALSO CHROMOSOMES; GENETIC MECHANISMS AND DEVELOPMENT; POLYPLOIDY.

*Lee B. Kass*

## Bibliography

Creighton, Harriet B., and Barbara McClintock. "A Correlation of Cytological and Genetical Crossing-over in *Zea mays.*" *Proceedings of the National Academy of Sciences* 17 (1931): 492–97.

Dunn, L. C. *A Short History of Genetics: The Development of Some of the Main Lines of Thought, 1864–1939.* New York: McGraw-Hill, 1965.

Fedoroff, N. V. "Barbara McClintock (1902–1992)." *Genetics* 136 (1994): 1–10.

Keller, Evelyn Fox. *A Feeling for the Organism: The Life and Work of Barbara McClintock.* San Francisco: W. H. Freeman and Co., 1983.

McClintock, Barbara. *The Discovery and Characterization of Transposable Elements: The Collected Papers of Barbara McClintock*, ed. John A. Moore. New York: Garland Publishing, 1987.

# Medicinal Plants

Plants can not run away from their enemies nor get rid of troublesome pests as humans or other animals do, so what have they evolved to protect themselves? Whatever this protection is it must be successful, for the diversity and richness of green plants is extraordinary, and their dominance in most **ecosystems** of the world is unquestioned. Plant successes are closely intertwined with the evolution and production of highly diverse **compounds** known as secondary metabolites, compounds that are not essential for growth and reproduction, but rather, through interaction with their environment, enhance plant prospects of survival. These metabolites are therefore plant agents for chemical warfare, allowing plants to ward off microorganisms, insects, and other animals acting as predators and **pathogens**. Such compounds may also be valuable to humans for the same purposes, and therefore may be used as medicines.

**ecosystem** an ecological community together with its environment

**compound** a substance formed from two or more elements

**pathogen** disease-causing organism

## What Characterizes Medicinal Plants

There are twenty thousand known secondary plant metabolites, all exhibiting a remarkable array of organic compounds that clearly provide a selective advantage to the producer, which outweighs their cost of production. Humans benefit from their production by using many of them for medicinal purposes to fight infections and diseases. An estimated two-fifths of all modern pharmaceutical products in the United States contain one or more naturally derived ingredients, the majority of which are secondary metabolites, such as alkaloids, glycosides, terpenes, steroids, and other classes grouped according to their physiological activity in humans or chemical structure. To illustrate the breadth of human reliance on medicinal plants, the accompanying table provides a list of the most significant plants, their uses in modern medicine, and the major secondary metabolites responsible for their activities. This list grows annually as new plants are found with desired activities and remedies to become pharmaceuticals for use in medicine.

## COMMON MEDICINAL PLANTS AND THEIR USES

| Scientific Name | Common Name | Family | Compounds | Compound Class | Uses |
|---|---|---|---|---|---|
| *Atropa belladonna, Duboisia myoporoides* | Belladonna | Solanaceae | Atropine, scopolamine | Alkaloid | Anticholinergic, motion sickness, mydriatic |
| *Cassia/Senna* species | Senna | Fabaceae | Sennoside | Glycoside, anthraquinone | Laxative |
| *Catharanthus roseus* | Madagascar periwinkle | Apocynaceae | Vincristine, vinblastine | Alkaloid | Anticancer (antileukemia) |
| *Chondrodendron tomentosa, Curarea toxicofera* | Curare | Menispermaceae | (+)–Tubocurarine | Alkaloid | Reversible muscle relaxant |
| *Cinchona calisaya, Cinchona officinalis* | Jesuits' bark | Rubiaceae | Quinine, quinidine | Alkaloid | Antimalaria (quinine), antiarrhythmia (quinidine) |
| *Colchicum autumnale* | Autumn crocus | Liliaceae | Colchicine | Alkaloid | Gout |
| *Digitalis lanata, Digitalis purpurea* | Foxglove | Scrophulariaceae | Digoxin, digitoxin, lanatosides | Cardiac glycoside (steroidal) | Heart failure and irregularity |
| *Dioscorea* species | Yam | Dioscoreaceae | Diosgenin, precursor of human hormones and cortisone | Saponin glycoside (steroidal) | Female oral contraceptives, topical creams |
| *Ephedra sinica* | Ephedra, Ma huang | Ephedraceae | Ephedrine | Alkaloid | Bronchodilator, stimulant |
| *Pilocarpus* species | Jaborandi | Rutaceae | Pilocarpine | Alkaloid | Glaucoma |
| *Podophyllum peltatum* | May-apple | Berberidaceae | Podophyllotoxin, etoposide | Resin | Anticancer |
| *Rauwolfia serpentina* | | Apocynaceae | Reserpine | Alkaloid | Antihypertensive, tranquilizer |
| *Taxus brevifolia* | Pacific yew | Taxaceae | Taxol | Diterpene | Anticancer (ovarian, breast) |

## How Plant Pharmaceuticals Are Discovered

The search for new pharmaceuticals from plants is possible using a number of distinct strategies. Random collecting of plants by field gathering is the simplest but least efficient way. The chances are much greater that new compounds of medicinal value will be discovered if there is some degree of selectivity employed by collecting those plants that a botanist knows are related to others already having useful or abundant classes of secondary metabolites. Even more relevant is to collect plants already targeted for specific medicinal purposes, possibly among indigenous or ethnic peoples who use traditional, plant-derived medicines often with great success to provide for their well-being. Such data are part of **ethnobotany**, when researchers often obtain detailed information on the plants people use to treat illnesses, such as the species, specific disease being treated, plant part preferred, and how that part is prepared and used for treatment. This strategy can provide rapid access to plants already identified by traditional practitioners as having value for curing diseases, and this shortcut often sets the researcher rapidly on the road to the discovery of new drugs.

Taking the ethnobotanical approach, a specific part of the targeted ethnomedicinal plant is extracted, usually in a solvent like ethanol, and then studied in **biodirected assays** or tests to determine its value using, for instance, tissue cultured cells impregnated with the organism known to cause the disease. For example, to assay for malaria the procedure could involve culturing red blood cells infected with the malarial-causing protozoan *Plasmodium falciparum*, placing a few drops of extract into the culture, and ex-

**ethnobotany** the study of traditional uses of plants within a culture

**biodirected assays** tests that examine some biological property

amining after a few days what effect, if any, the addition of the extract had on the protozoa. One final step in this process leading to the discovery of a new drug is to establish the mechanism of action of the compound, reactions in the body, and side effects or toxicity of taking it. The whole process from field discovery to a new pharmaceutical takes up to ten years and requires a multidisciplinary-interactive approach involving **ethnobotanists**, natural products chemists, pharmacognosists (those who study the biochemistry of natural products), and cell and molecular biologists.

## Medically Important Compounds Derived From Plants

About ninety species of plants contribute the most important drugs currently used globally, and of these about 75 percent have the same or related uses as the plant from which each was discovered. Two examples provide additional details of their discovery and development as drugs.

**May-apple.** Eastern North American Indians long used the roots and rhizomes (underground stems) of the native May-apple (*Podophyllum peltatum*, Berberidaceae) as a drastic laxative. By the nineteenth century, white "Indian Doctors" used extracts of these parts to treat cancerous tumors and skin ulcers, perhaps learned from Indians or by direct observation of its corrosive and irritating nature. The plant's main secondary metabolite is podophyllotoxin, a resin responsible for May-apple's antitumor effects. It is a mitotic poison that inhibits cell division and thus prevents unregulated growth leading to cancerous cells and tumors. However, in clinical trials podophyllotoxin proved too toxic for use as a cancer chemotherapeutic agent, although it remains the drug of choice as a caustic in removing venereal warts and other benign tumors.

Attempts to find safer compounds led chemists to manipulate the molecule, and by trial and error they discovered a semisynthetic derivative that proved at least as effective as the original compound without the same level of toxicity. (Semisynthetics are products of chemical manipulation using the naturally occurring plant compound as a base.) A compound called etoposide was eventually found most valuable in treating a type (non-small cell) of lung cancer, testicular cancer, and lymphomas (cancer of lymphoid tissue), and particular (monocytic) leukemias (cancer of blood-forming organs) by preventing target cells from entering cell division. Etoposide was approved for use in the United States in 1983, twelve years after its discovery. Peak annual sales of the compound reached approximately $300 million in the late 1980s and early 1990s, and thousands of lives have been prolonged or saved during nearly two decades of its use as a leading anticancer drug derived from plants. It is possibly the most important pharmaceutical originating from a plant species native to eastern North America.

**Foxgloves.** Heart and **vascular** disease is the number one killer in the United States, a position held virtually every year in the twentieth century. Fluid accumulation or edema (dropsy) and subsequent congestive heart failure have been treated by European farmers and housewives as part of European folk medicine for a long time. Their remedy consisted of a concoction of numerous herbs that always contained leaves of foxglove (*Digitalis* species, Scrophulariaceae). In the 1700s William Withering, an English botanist and physician, observed in the countryside the successful use of this herbal mixture to treat dropsy and associated diseases. He eventually se-

A May-apple (*Podophyllum peltatum*).

**ethnobotanist** a scientist who interacts with native peoples to learn more about the plants of a region

**vascular** related to blood vessels

A foxglove (*Digitalis purpurea*).

**cardiotonic** changing the contraction properties of the heart

**systematists** scientists who study systematics, the classification of species to reflect evolutionary relationships

lected one plant from the mixture as the probable source of activity, and in 1785 Withering published his landmark book *An Account of the Foxglove, and Some of Its Medicinal Uses* in which he described how to determine the correct dosage (for foxglove was considered a potent poison that was ineffective medicinally unless used at near toxic levels) and how to prepare foxglove, favoring the use of powdered leaves.

Withering's discovery revolutionized therapy associated with heart and vascular disease, and even today, powdered foxglove leaves are still prescribed and used much as they were more than two centuries ago. The active leaf metabolites are **cardiotonic** glycosides obtained mostly from two European species, *Digitalis lanata* and *D. purpurea*. They provide the most widely used compounds, digoxin (also available synthetically), digitoxin, and lanatosides. The magnitude of the need for cardiotonic therapy is suggested by the estimate that more than three million cardiac sufferers in the United States routinely use the preferred digoxin as one of several available drugs.

In congestive heart failure, the heart does not function adequately as a blood pump, giving rise to either congestion of blood in the lungs or backup pressure of blood in the veins leading to the heart. When the veins become engorged, fluid accumulates in the tissues, and the swelling is known as edema or dropsy. Cardiotonic glycosides increase the force of heart muscle contraction without a concomitant increase in oxygen consumption. The heart muscle thus becomes a more efficient pump and is better able to meet the demands of the circulatory system. If heart failure is brought on by high blood pressure or hardening (loss of elasticity) of the arteries, cardiotonic glycosides are also widely used to increase contractibility and improve the tone of the heart muscle, resulting in a slower but much stronger heart beat. If the heart begins to beat irregularity, again these cardioactive compounds will convert irregularities and rapid rates to normal rhythm and rate.

The search for new medicinal plants continues as remote regions of natural habitat are explored by botanists, plant **systematists**, and ethnobotanists. Further clinical studies of chemical components of these new discoveries may yield important novel drugs for the treatment of human diseases. SEE ALSO ALKALOIDS; CANNABIS; COCA; DIOSCOREA; ECONOMIC IMPORTANCE OF PLANTS; ETHNOBOTANY; HERBALS AND HERBALISTS; OPIUM POPPY; PHARMACEUTICAL SCIENTIST; PLANT PROSPECTING; PSYCHOACTIVE PLANTS; SYSTEMATICS, PLANT.

*Walter H. Lewis*

**Bibliography**

Balick, Michael J., and Paul Alan Cox. *Plants, People, and Culture: The Science of Ethnobotany.* New York: Scientific American Library, 1996.

Kreig, Margaret G. *Green Medicine.* New York: Rand McNally, 1964.

Lewis, Walter H., and Memory P. F. Elvin-Lewis. *Medical Botany: Plants Affecting Man's Health.* New York: John Wiley & Sons, 1977.

Nigg, Herbert N., and David Seigler, eds. *Phytochemical Resources for Medicine and Agriculture.* New York: Plenum Press, 1992.

Plotkin, Mark. *Tales of a Shaman's Apprentice.* New York: Viking, 1993.

Robbers, James E., and Varro E. Tyler. *Tyler's Herbs of Choice: The Therapeutic Use of Phytochemicals.* Binghamton, NY: Haworth Herbal Press, 1998.

# Mendel, Gregor

**Austrian Natural Scientist**
**1822–1884**

Gregor Mendel elucidated the theory of particulate inheritance, which forms the basis of the current understanding of genes as the hereditary material. Born in Heinzendorf, Austria, in 1822, Johann Gregor Mendel was the fourth of five children in a family of farmers. He attended the primary school in a neighboring village, which taught elementary subjects as well as the natural sciences. Mendel showed superior abilities, and in 1833, at the advice of his teacher, his parents sent him to the secondary school in Leipnik, then to the gymnasium in Troppau. There he attempted to support himself by private tutoring, but his lack of the necessary financial support made the years that Mendel spent in school extremely stressful for him. His younger sister gave him part of her dowry and, in 1840, he enrolled in the University of Olmütz, where he studied physics, philosophy, and mathematics. In 1843 he was admitted into the Augustinian monastery in Brno, where he stayed for almost two decades. Originally, Mendel was not interested in religious life, but joining the monastery freed him from the financial concerns that plagued him and allowed him to pursue his interests in the natural sciences.

Gregor Mendel.

Under the leadership of its abbot, F. C. Napp (1792–1867), the monastery in Brno integrated higher learning and agriculture by arranging for monks to teach natural sciences at the Philosophical Institute. Napp encouraged Matthew Klácel to conduct investigations of variation and heredity on the garden's plants. Klácel, a philosopher by training, integrated natural history and Hegelian philosophy to formulate a theory of gradual development. This work eventually led to his dismissal, and he immigrated to the United States. Mendel was put in charge of the garden after Klácel's departure.

From 1844 through 1848 Mendel took theological training as well as agricultural courses at the Philosophical Institute, where he learned about artificial pollination as a method for plant improvement. After he finished his theological studies, Mendel served a brief and unsuccessful stint as parish chaplain before he was sent to a grammar school in southern Moravia as a substitute teacher. His success as a teacher qualified him for the university examination for teachers of natural sciences, which he failed because of his lack of formal education in zoology and geology. To prepare himself to retake the test, he went to the University of Vienna, where he enrolled in courses in various natural sciences and was introduced to botanical experimentation. After completing his university training he returned to Brno and was appointed substitute teacher of physics and natural history at the Brno technical school.

Mendel was an excellent teacher, and he often taught large classes. In 1856 he began botanical experiments with peas (*Pisum*), using artificial pollination to create **hybrids**. Hoping to continue his education, he once again took the university examination, but failed and suffered an emotional and physical breakdown. His second failure spelled the end of his career as a student, but he remained a substitute teacher until 1868, when he was elected abbot of the monastery. Mendel stayed in Brno, serving the monastery, performing botanical experiments, and collecting meteorological information until he died of kidney failure in 1884. At the time of his death, he was well

**hybrid** a mix of two varieties or species

known for his liberal views and his conflict with secular authorities over the setting aside of monastery land; at this time, only the local fruit growers knew him for his botanical research.

## Experiments on Inheritance

While his contemporaries knew little of his scientific work, Mendel's historical significance lies almost entirely in his experimental work with the **hybridization** of plants and his theory of inheritance. Beginning in 1856 and continuing through 1863, Mendel cultivated nearly thirty thousand plants and recorded their physical characteristics. Beginning with a hypothesis about the relationship between characteristics in parents and offspring, Mendel formulated an experimental program.

Mendel believed that heredity was particulate, that attributes were passed from parents to offspring as complete characters. His notions of heredity were contrary to the belief in blending inheritance, which was generally accepted at the time and explained the attributes of an organism as a blended combination of its parents' characters. Instead of viewing an organism's individual characteristics as composites of its predecessors, Mendel asserted that organisms inherited entire characters from either one or the other parent. To test his theory, he chose seven plant and seed characteristics, such as the shape of the seed or the color of the flower, and traced the inheritance of the characters through several generations of pea plants.

As he crossed thousands of pea plants and recorded the seven characteristics, Mendel found that certain traits were passed from parent to offspring in a lawlike fashion. Just as he had hypothesized, certain traits regularly appeared when he crossed plants with different combinations of characteristics. He used the term "dominant" in reference to those traits that were passed from the parent to the offspring and the term "recessive" in reference to those traits that were exhibited in at least one of the parents, but not in its offspring. Mendel denoted plants with dominant traits by recording two capital letters, such as AA, and those that expressed recessive traits with lower case letters, like aa. In the first generation of offspring from crosses of AA with aa, dominant traits always appeared and recessive traits never appeared.

Mendel's system of denoting dominant and recessive traits with two letters allowed him to trace dominant and recessive characters through successive generations. The crossing of AA with aa would result in the production of individuals with traits represented by Aa, with the dominant trait always appearing, but not the recessive trait. By crossing two Aa individuals, Mendel found that the dominant trait appeared three times for every one time that the recessive trait appeared. Mendel explained that the crossing of two Aa individuals resulted in the production of the following combinations:

AA  Aa  Aa  aa

Because the dominant trait always decided the characteristic, any organism with at least one A would express the dominant trait. Recessive characteristics would appear only in those individuals with aa.

Mendel's 1866 "Versuche über Pflanzenhybriden" (Attempts at Plant Hybridization) presented his entire theory of inheritance and has become one of the most significant papers in the history of biology. He explained that his results "were not easily compatible with contemporary scientific knowledge" and, as such, "publication of one such isolated experiment was

**hybridization** formation of a new individual from parents of different species or varieties

doubly dangerous, dangerous for the experimenter and for the cause he represented." In an attempt to bolster his case, Mendel experimented on several other plants and then with animals. However, after 1866 he published only one more short article on the subject.

## Rediscovery of Mendel's Work

Mendel's painstaking experimental work on plant hybridization and heredity sat virtually unnoticed for thirty-five years before three natural scientists simultaneously rediscovered it at the turn of the twentieth century. His 1865 paper, presented at the Natural Sciences Society of Brno and published in the Society's *Verhandlungen* in 1866, received little notice from his contemporaries. However, in 1900 Carl Correns, Erich von Tschermak, and Hugo DeVries, each working independently, found Mendel's paper while they were each in the process of completing similar experiments. In the hands of a new generation of natural scientists, Mendel's work was immediately and widely accepted, and he was touted as the epitome of a scientist.

Mendelism, as his work was called, was often posited in opposition with the Darwinian theory of natural selection. Many early twentieth-century Mendelians and Darwinians believed that the two theories were incompatible with one another, in part because of Darwin's reliance on the theory of **pangenesis** and because contemporary biologists, who also viewed Darwinism in conflict with DeVries's mutationism, associated Mendel's work with mutationism.

Despite the debates over the relationship between Mendelism and Darwinism, Mendel's work immediately received widespread support, and it served as the basis for work in genetics as well as plant and animal breeding. Beginning around 1900, Mendelism also provided a substantial boost to the growing science of eugenics, the genetic improvement of humans by encouraging "high-quality" individuals to have children while discouraging "low-quality" people from reproducing. By scientifically explaining inheritance, Mendelism bolstered the eugenicists' claim that "good begets good and bad begets bad." Later geneticists distanced themselves from eugenics by arguing that, while Mendelism easily explained simple traits like eye color or blood type, it did not apply to more complicated traits like intelligence or industriousness.

Beginning in the late 1930s, yet another generation of natural scientists reinterpreted Mendelism and Darwinism, and they concluded that they were mutually reinforcing scientific theories. R. A. Fisher, Sewall Wright, J. B. S. Haldane, and other so-called synthesis biologists argued that Mendelism provided the explanation for one facet of evolution, inheritance, while Darwinism explained another, selection. Viewed in this light, Mendel's work complemented Darwin's theory of natural selection, and the two have served as the principal basis for modern biological thought since the mid-twentieth century. SEE ALSO CHROMOSOMES; DARWIN, CHARLES; GENETIC MECHANISMS AND DEVELOPMENT.

*Mark A. Largent*

**pangenesis** the belief that acquired traits can be inherited by bodily influences on the cells

### Bibliography

DeVries, Hugo, Carl Correns, and Armin von Tschermak. *The Birth of Genetics.* Brooklyn, NY: Brooklyn Botanic Garden, 1950.

Iltis, Hugo, Eden Paul, and Cedar Paul. *Life of Mendel.* London: G. Allen & Unwin, 1932.

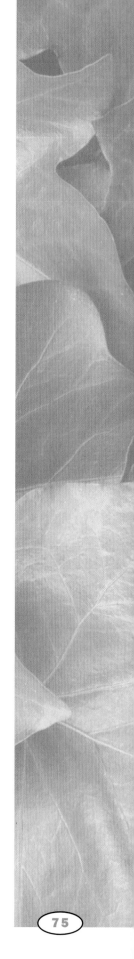

Kruta, V., and V. Orel. "Johann Gregor Mendel." In *Dictionary of Scientific Biography*, Vol. 9. New York: Charles Scribner's Sons, 1974.

Olby, Robert. *The Origins of Mendelism*. New York: Schocken Books, 1966.

# Meristems

Meristems are regions of active cell division within a plant. In general there are two types of meristems: **apical** meristems and **lateral** meristems. Apical meristems are located at the tip (or apex) of the shoot and the root, as well as at the tips of their branches. These meristems occur in all plants and are responsible for growth in length. By contrast, lateral meristems are found mainly in plants that increase significantly in diameter, such as trees and woody shrubs. Lateral meristems are located along the sides of the stem, root, and their branches; are found just inside the outer layer; and are responsible for growth in diameter.

The term *meristem* comes from the Greek word meaning "divisible," which emphasizes the fundamental role played by mitotic cell division in these tissues. Meristematic cells are those that divide repeatedly and in a self-perpetuating manner; that is, when a meristematic cell divides, one of the daughter cells remains meristematic. Meristems, however, may not be constantly active. For example, in temperate climates meristematic cells stop dividing during the winter but then begin dividing again in the spring.

## Apical Meristems

Both root and shoot apical meristems consist of a group of two types of cells: initials and their immediate derivatives. Initials are the true meristematic cells in that they divide almost continuously throughout the growing season. When an initial divides it forms two daughter cells, one a new initial and the other a derivative that soon stops dividing and eventually differentiates into part of the mature tissues of the plant. In many cases the older derivatives elongate, and it is this process that pushes the initials of the shoot apical meristem higher into the air and the initials of the root apical meristem deeper into the soil. All tissues produced by an apical meristem are called primary tissues.

In most plants the root apical meristem is covered by a protective root cap and consists of a group of relatively small, roughly spherical cells, each having a dense cytoplasm and a large nucleus but no apparent **vacuole**. The derivatives of certain apical initials give rise to additional root cap cells, thus replacing those that were lost as the root cap rubbed against soil particles. The derivatives of other initials give rise to the mature tissues of the main body of the root, such as xylem, phloem, cortex, and **epidermis**. In the center of the root apex is a cluster of cells that divides very infrequently. These cells comprise the quiescent center, whose apparent function is to serve as a source of cells should the initials become damaged.

In **angiosperms**, the shoot apical meristem is not covered by a protective cap and has additional features that distinguish it from the root apex. For example, the lateral appendages of the stem—the leaves and lateral buds—are produced at the shoot apex. Leaves arise as small protuberances (called leaf **primordia**) slightly to the side of the apical-most cells. As they

**apical** at the tip

**lateral** away from the center

**vacuole** the large fluid-filled sac that occupies most of the space in a plant cell. Use for storage and maintaining internal pressure

**epidermis** outer layer of cells

**angiosperm** a flowering plant

**primordia** the earliest and most primitive form of the developing leaf

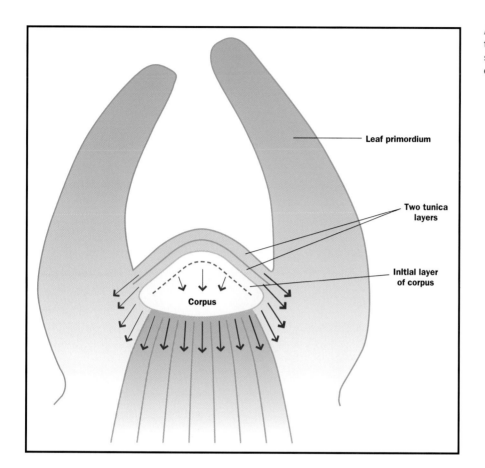

A schematic diagram of
the apical meristem,
showing the directions of
cell division.

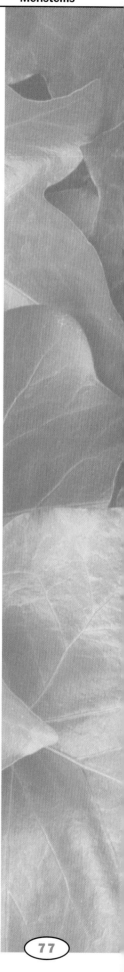

elongate, the resulting leaves cover and protect the apical meristem. Buds
develop in the angle between the stem and each leaf primordium, a location called the leaf axil. In a plant growing vegetatively, these **axillary** (or
lateral) **buds** contain meristems that can develop into branches. When the
plant reproduces sexually, the shoot apical meristem produces flowers instead of leaves. The various flower parts—petals, **sepals**, stamens, and
**carpels**—are modified leaves and are produced in a manner similar to that
of leaf primordia.

The apical meristem of most angiosperms has a tunica-corpus arrangement of cells. The tunica consists of two or more layers of cells, and the
corpus is a mass of cells underneath. Cells of the tunica and corpus give rise
to the leaves, buds, and mature tissues of the stem.

## Lateral Meristems

Two types of lateral meristems, also called cambia (singular: cambium),
are found in plants: the **vascular** cambium and the cork cambium. Each type
consists of a hollow, vertical cylinder of cells that contribute to the thickness of woody plants. As with apical meristems, lateral meristems consist of
initials and their immediate derivatives. All tissues produced by a lateral
meristem are called secondary tissues.

The vascular cambium contains two kinds of initials: fusiform initials
and ray initials, both of which have large vacuoles. Each type of initial produces derivatives toward the inside that develop into xylem cells and deriv-

**axillary bud** the bud
that forms in the angle
between the stem and
leaf

**sepals** the outermost
whorl of flower parts;
usually green and leaf-
like, they protect the
inner parts of the flower

**carpels** the innermost
whorl of flower parts,
including the egg-
bearing ovules, plus
the style and stigma
attached to the ovules

**vascular** related to
transport of nutrients

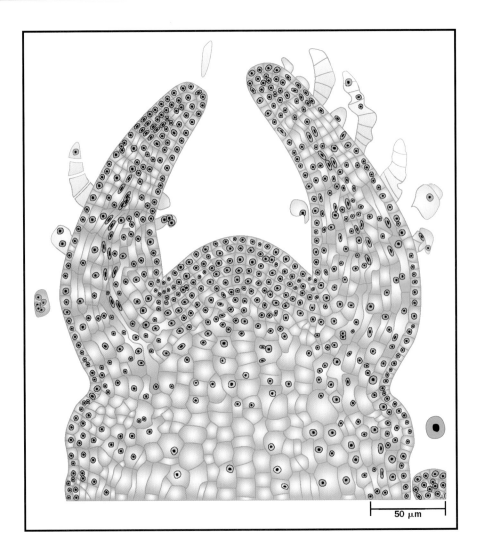

50 μm

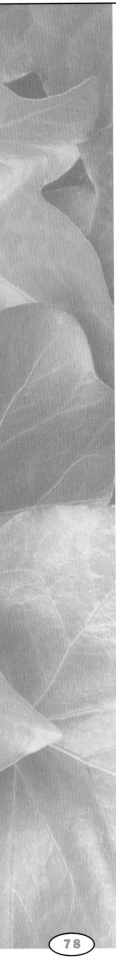

**parenchyma** one of
three plant cell types

**pathogen** disease-
causing organism

atives toward the outside that develop into phloem cells. The fusiform initials are long, tapering cells that are vertically oriented. They give rise to xylem vessel elements and phloem sieve-tube members; these cells are involved in the vertical transport of materials through the plant. The ray initials are cube-shaped cells that give rise to xylem **parenchyma** and phloem parenchyma and together constitute the vascular rays. Rays are involved in the lateral transport of materials. Both the fusiform and ray initials produce many more xylem cells than phloem cells. The accumulating xylem cells push the vascular cambium increasingly farther away from the center of the root, stem, or branch, and as a result the organ increases in diameter.

In response to this increase in thickness the epidermis and other cells exterior to the vascular cambium stretch and eventually break. Before cracks occur, a cork cambium differentiates from cells of the cortex. The cork cambium (or phellogen) produces cork cells (phellem) toward the outside and phelloderm toward the inside. Together, these three tissues constitute the periderm. Cork cells have a flattened shape, and their walls become filled with suberin, a fatty material that makes these cells an impermeable barrier to water, gases, and **pathogens**. Although the cork cambium and phelloderm are alive at maturity, cork cells are dead. The cork thus provides an effective seal that replaces the epidermis. As the plant organ con-

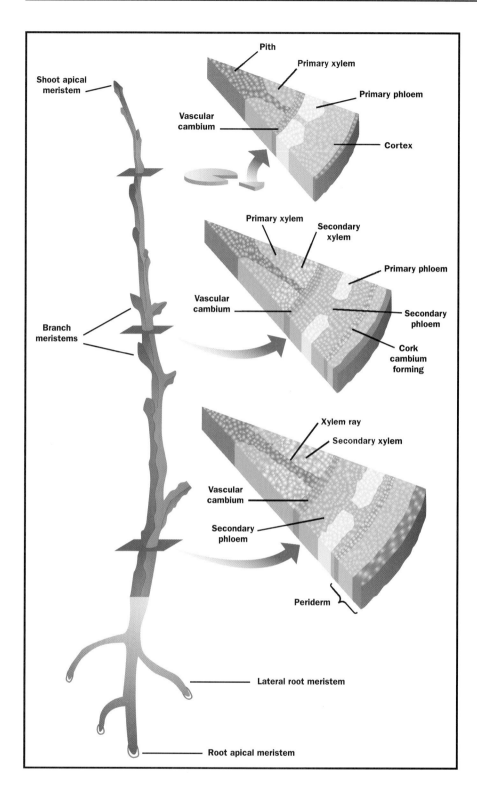

Meristem locations, with cross-sections of vascular tissues. Redrawn from Moore et al., 1998, Figure 16.1.

tinues to increase in diameter, the cork cells themselves crack, and additional cork cambia differentiate from underlying tissues as replacements. SEE ALSO ANATOMY OF PLANTS; BARK; CELLS, SPECIALIZED TYPES; DIFFERENTIATION AND DEVELOPMENT; GERMINATION AND GROWTH; TISSUES; VASCULAR TISSUES.

*Robert C. Evans*

**Bibliography**

Esau, Katherine. *Plant Anatomy*, 2nd ed. New York: John Wiley & Sons, 1965.

Mauseth, James D. *Plant Anatomy*. Menlo Park, CA: Benjamin/Cummings Publishing Co., 1988.

Moore, Randy, W. Dennis Clark, and Darrell S. Vodopich. *Botany*, 2nd ed., New York: McGraw-Hill, 1998.

Raven, Peter H., Ray F. Evert, and Susan E. Eichhorn. *Biology of Plants*, 6th ed. New York: W. H. Freeman and Company, 1999.

## Mold  *See Fungi*

# Molecular Plant Genetics

The appearance and chemical composition of all life are determined by the action of genes functioning in the context of the conditions surrounding the organism. While both genes and environment are important in determining the characteristics of plants, it is becoming clearer that genes control many more characteristics, and to a higher degree, than we had previously imagined. Hence, the study of genes and their effects on organisms, genetics, has allowed us to combat a wide range of human diseases. The burgeoning plant biotechnology industry, which promises to produce revolutionary plants and plant products in the twenty-first century, has also arisen. An intriguing tenet of modern genetics is that the cellular molecules that carry the genetic information (deoxyribonucleic acid [DNA]) and transmit this data to cells (ribonucleic acid [RNA] and proteins) are the same in plants and animals, so that geneticists speak one universal language that can be interpreted and manipulated, through science, to beneficially alter any species.

## DNA, Genes, and Chromosomes

DNA is the molecule that constitutes genes. The main component of each cell's DNA is found in its nucleus. The individual, very large DNA molecules of the nucleus are chromosomes, each of which consists of thousands of genes, and each cell of an individual plant species has the same DNA and chromosomal composition. Copies of all genes are transmitted from both parents to their offspring, accounting for inheritance, the principle wherein offspring resemble their parents.

The chemical structure of DNA allows it to store information and for that information to be incorporated into the design of developing cells and organs. DNA molecules are very long linear structures comprised of millions of repeating units. Segments, consisting typically of a few thousand of these units, constitute individual genes. Each gene carries the information that dictates the structure of a single protein. Proteins catalyze all of the chemical reactions in cells generating its components and forming the cells into recognizable tissues and organs.

The backbone of a DNA molecule consists of alternations of the 5-carbon sugar, 2-deoxyribose, and phosphate. Note that the sugars are linked at their number three position (3′, read as "three prime") to a phosphate and their number five position (5′) at the other end to another phosphate. Further, the sugars are all oriented by these links in the same di-

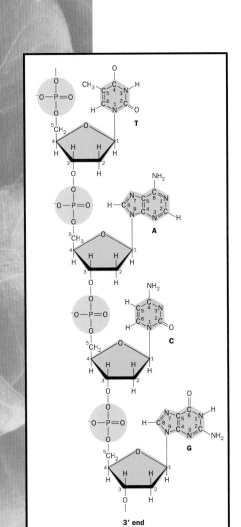

DNA sugar-phosphate backbone with linked bases.

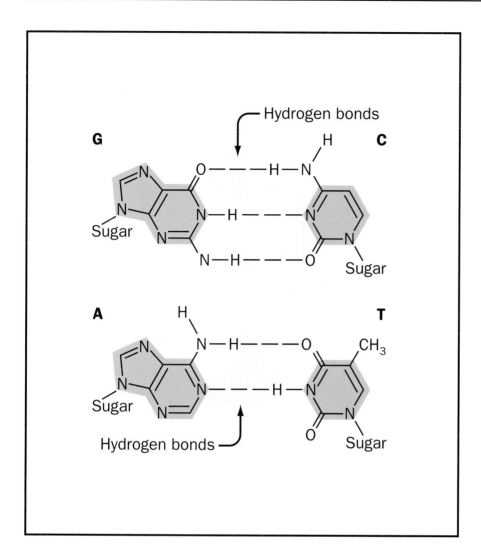

Paired bases of DNA showing the weak bond (dotted lines) that holds them together.

rection so that the backbone has direction—that is, a 5′ and a 3′ end. Connected to each sugar, at its 1′ position, is one of four nitrogenous bases: adenine, cytosine, guanine, or thymine. Each DNA backbone is actually paired for its full length with a second DNA backbone, with the chemical linkage between the two occurring via weak hydrogen bonding between the bases of the two chains. Two aspects of this pairing should be noted: 1) the two sugar-phosphate backbones have opposite orientations (they are antiparallel); and 2) any adenine of either chain is bonded (paired) with a thymine, and each guanine is paired with a cytosine. Consequently, the sequence of bases of the two chains are complementary to one another so that one can be predicted from the other. It is the sequence of bases within a gene that determines the type of protein that the gene codes for, including the protein's function in plant cells. Within a gene for a particular protein, three successive bases determine one amino acid. For example, A (abbreviation for adenine), followed by T (thymine), and then G (guanine) code for the amino acid methione (ATG is the term for this code in DNA sequence terminology), and each of the twenty possible amino acids that are incorporated into proteins have their own three-base determinants, or codons. For most amino acids, there are several three-base sequences that will code for a particular amino acid.

**enzyme** a protein that controls a reaction in a cell

## Replication

For DNA to function as a hereditary molecule, it must be duplicated (replicated) so that the daughter cells produced by cell division can receive identical copies. Replication of DNA is accomplished by a large complex of **enzymes**, within which the main replication enzyme, DNA polymerase, carries out the main synthesizing reaction. In DNA replication, the following steps are accomplished by the synthesis complex:

1. the two halves of the starting double-stranded DNA, which are wound together in a ropelike helix, are separated so that the bases are exposed;

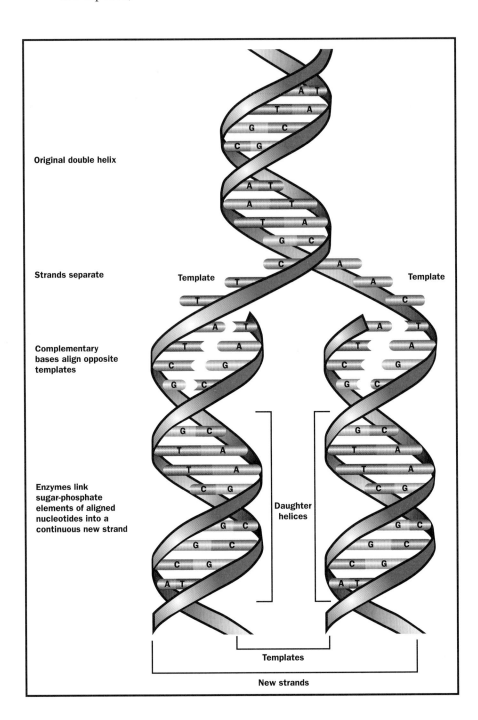

**Original double helix**

**Strands separate**

Template                                                                    Template

**Complementary bases align opposite templates**

**Enzymes link sugar-phosphate elements of aligned nucleotides into a continuous new strand**

**Daughter helices**

**Templates**

**New strands**

A DNA molecule being replicated.

2. the replication complex reads each half of the unwound DNA so that molecules complementary to each of original halves of the helix are synthesized from new subunits; and

3. these new chains are left bonded to old ones so that there are now two half-new, half-old identical DNAs. DNA replication must occur in each cell before the cell can divide and is also necessary in reproduction prior to the generation of pollen grains and ovules.

## Protein Synthesis

The process by which genes are read and the sequence used to form a **polymer** of amino acids in a protein consists of two steps. In the first transcription, a copy of the gene is made in the form of RNA. Then, via the process of translation, the RNA sequence is interpreted by the translation machinery to make the actual protein. RNA is a molecule that is similar to DNA in structure, with the following differences: 1) its sugar is ribose, also a 5-carbon molecule, but which has an OH group at the 2′ position, 2) it is usually single stranded, rather than consisting of two paired strands, and 3) it utilizes the base uracil in place of thymine, which does have similar base pairing characteristics. Hence, RNA has a similar, but not identical, sugar-phosphate backbone to DNA, and the sequences of bases in its structure can convey information in the same fashion.

In a biochemical sense, the events of transcription (DNA-dependent RNA synthesis) are similar to the steps of DNA replication. The paired halves of the DNA constituting one end of the gene are separated, and an enzyme complex is attached. Included in this complex is an enzyme called RNA polymerase that reads the DNA and builds an RNA molecule having a base sequence complementary to that of the template DNA.

Once the RNA copy, called messenger RNA (mRNA), is made in a plant nucleus, it undergoes several modifications and is then transmitted to the cytoplasm. Here, the mRNA is utilized by the process of translation that generates a protein having an amino sequence corresponding to the base sequence of the mRNA and its gene. The process of translation, or protein synthesis, takes place on ribosomes, which are composed of ribosomal RNA (rRNA) and more than one hundred proteins. The ribosome attaches to an mRNA and moves along its length, synthesizing a protein by adding the correct amino acids, in sequence, one at a time. The addition of the correct amino acid at each point is accomplished by the pairing of three bases of the mRNA with a transfer RNA, which has a three-base segment complementary to this set of bases and which was previously attached to the correct amino acid by an enzymatic reaction. Consequently, the correct functioning of transcription and translation allows the information of each gene to be interpreted and converted into a protein, which carries out a very specific metabolic reaction in the cell.

## Polyploidy

An interesting feature of plant chromosomes that is much less common in animals is polyploidy. Polyploidy occurs when the entire set of chromosomes is multiplied, relative to the normal two of each kind per cell. For example, the normal **diploid** number of corn chromosomes is

**polymer** a large molecule made from many similar parts

**diploid** having two sets of chromosomes, versus having one (haploid)

**sepals** the outermost whorl of flower parts; usually green and leaf-like, they protect the inner parts of the flower

## ARABIDOPSIS

*Arabidopsis thaliana* is a small plant that has played a large part in unraveling the molecular genetics of plants. It has an approximately two- to four-inch-wide cluster of leaves and a several-inch-tall flowering structure and is capable of producing thousands of tiny seeds within four to six weeks after germination. Because of its small size and short generation time, it has long been used for genetic research. In the 1980s it was discovered that the deoxyribonucleic acid (DNA) content of its genome was very small, and it was therefore adopted as the favorite model for basic study of molecular control of plant development and metabolism. In the 1990s more research was published on *Arabidopsis* than on any other plant. Further, as biotechnology has developed, it was realized that a model organism could form the focus for initial evaluation of key systems, and several startup biotechnology firms that have substantial *Arabidopsis* research components have been established.

A new biological discipline called genomics has recently arisen. A genome is defined simply as the entire set of chromosomes (and thus DNA) of a species. Genomics is the analysis of the entire set (or at least a very large subset) of an organism's genes. Plant genomics is made possible by two circumstances: 1) the capability to clone and determine the base sequence of the entire length of all of the chromosomes of a plant, and 2) the development

*(continued on page 85)*

twenty; that is, each cell of a normal plant contains two of each of ten different chromosomes. If this number were doubled so that there were a total of forty, with each of the ten different types being represented four times, the result would be tetraploid corn containing four of each chromosome. The common peanut is a natural tetraploid species. Polyploid strawberries have been created artificially to increase the desirable characteristics of the fruit.

## Mutations and Polymorphisms

Any change in a DNA molecule of a plant or animal is called a mutation, whether occurring in nature or induced experimentally. Changes in DNA occur in nature as a result of either environmental agents or rare but inevitable mistakes in the DNA replication process. The resulting natural variations of DNA sequence among the individuals of a species, DNA polymorphisms, fuel evolution. These polymorphisms can be analyzed through molecular techniques and can be used to determine the relationship among plants and molecular plant improvement as well as identifying individual plants. Hence, we have seen the development of DNA fingerprinting for intellectual property protection of novel genetic improvements in plant breeding—which is similar to the fingerprinting techniques used in several human criminological contexts.

Specific mutational changes in DNA may affect the function of the resulting protein, usually by reducing its efficiency or rendering it completely nonfunctional. However, in rare cases, a mutation may make the enzyme more useful for metabolism in some way. The former type of change is widely used by plant scientists to discover the roles of genes in growth and development; the latter represents the goal of protein engineering and is the basis of plant biotechnology.

## Uses of Mutants

The genetic dissection of plant growth and development is one of the outstanding uses of mutations for scientific analysis. For example, a number of mutants block aspects of flower development. One mutant was discovered whose flowers lack petals, another lacks both the male and female reproductive parts of the flower, and still another lacks **sepals** and petals. Detailed analysis of the effects of these mutants, along with the cloning and characterization of the genes themselves, has led to a partial understanding of how a plant makes flowers. It is likely that a complete picture will eventually result. Interestingly, the original flower development model was developed for the small dicot, *Arabidopsis*, which has both sexes in one flower, but the same regulators act in the crop plant corn, which has separate male and female flowers, and which are completely different in appearance from those of *Arabidopsis*.

Another experimental application of mutant analysis illustrates the use of genetics in biotechnology and the generation of transgenic plants. Plants are said to be transgenic when DNA from some external source is introduced by scientists through biotechnology. In this case, a mutation was discovered in *Arabidopsis* called "leafy." This mutation is a loss-of-function change, which results in the replacement of flowers and fruits by leaves. Hence, the normal version of this gene must promote the ability to produce flowers. Subsequently, the normal gene was cloned and inserted into different plant species by transgenic techniques. When poplar trees received the gene, the genetically modified tree seedlings germinated normally but flowered within months rather than several years later, as occurs in normal trees.

Transgenically modified plants used in agriculture are often referred to as GMOs or genetically modified organisms. An example of GMOs are Roundup-Ready soybeans, which have resistance to this effective, nonpolluting herbicide through a transgene. These beans are widely used but are somewhat controversial. The public debate over the use of GMOs in agriculture involves a number of complex political issues in addition to the public health and environmental concerns that may also be relevant for certain types of GMOs. The handling of this issue represents one of the important public policy issues of our era. Another example of a potentially beneficial GMO is rice that is altered to carry more iron in its seeds. This should dramatically improve its nutritional value and prove especially valuable in areas of the world where food is scarce and human diets are typically not well balanced.

Improvement of crop plants has been practiced by plant breeders for centuries. The molecular tools discussed above simply enhance the range of alterations that are possible for improving crops. Traditional crop breeding involves finding and evaluating potentially useful genetic variants of a species, intercrossing them so that the most optimal set of characteristics can be combined into one strain, and then evaluating a number of resulting strains for final use in actual production farming. This is a long and costly process. In addition, many of the traits, which are of interest from an agronomic perspective, are quantitative as opposed to qualitative in inheritance. That is, they are controlled by large numbers of genes, each of which has a relatively small effect on performance. When this is the case, the application of classical genetics and molecular biology is difficult, since individual genes affecting a quantitative trait are very difficult to identify or clone. However, molecular markers can be correlated with important quantitative traits of a segregating population and utilized to pinpoint the general chromosomal locations where greater-than-average effects on the quantitative traits are exerted. Loci found in this way are referred to as quantitative trait loci or QTLs. QTL approaches are being pursued in many crops as alternative means of developing improved crop varieties and understanding the genetic basis of quantitatively inherited traits. SEE ALSO BREEDING; CELL CYCLE; CHROMOSOMES; CREIGHTON, HARRIET; GENETIC ENGINEER; GENETIC ENGINEERING; GENETIC MECHANISMS AND DEVELOPMENT; MCCLINTOCK, BARBARA; MENDEL, GREGOR; POLYPLOIDY; QUANTITATIVE TRAIT LOCI; TRANSGENIC PLANTS; WARMING, JOHANNES.

*Randy Scholl*

### Bibliography

Dennis, E. *Multinational Coordinated* Arabidopsis thaliana *Genome Research Project—Progress Report: Year Four.* Arlington, VA: National Science Foundation, 1995.

Fletcher, C. "A Garden of Mutants." *Discover* 16 (1995): 54–69.

Klug, William R. and Michael R. Cummings. *Essentials of Genetics,* 2nd ed. Upper Saddle River, NJ: Prentice-Hall, 1996.

of new technologies to assay whether genes are being transcribed on a genome-wide scale. The *Arabidopsis* Genome Initiative (AGI), an international collaboration, was established in 1995 with the goal of determining the DNA base sequence of the entire *Arabidopsis* chromosome set (genome). By the time the project finished in 2000, all of the estimated twenty thousand plus genes of this plant were available for molecular and biological analyses.

Given the availability of the complete genomic sequence data, the next focus of international *Arabidopsis* cooperation is functional genomics. Functional genomics is simply the analysis of genes and their effects on the full scale of the entire genome, that is, all (or most) of the genes at once. In one of the most powerful full-genome approaches, microarrays of copies of each of a large number of genes are bound to small glass slides so they can be used to quantify the amounts of their ribonucleic acids (RNA) produced under differing conditions. For example, RNA can be isolated from plants both infected and not infected with a pathogenic fungus so that the genes that are turned on in response to the fungus can be rapidly identified. These and many other similarly large-scale analyses will allow swift determination of how plants respond to their environment and the full set of changes that occur in different stages of development.

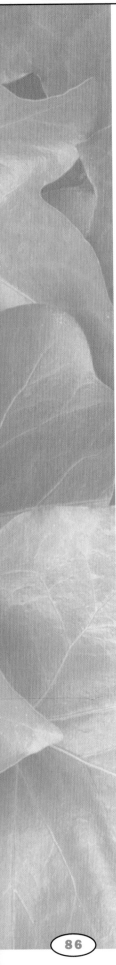

# Monocots

The monocotyledons (or, in abbreviated form, the monocots), class Liliopsida, are one of the major groups of flowering plants (angiosperms). There are about 100 families and 67,000 species of monocots, and the monocots consequently represent about one-fourth of the approximately 250,000 species of flowering plants. Some of the larger families of monocots are the grass family (Poaceae, or Gramineae), palm family (Arecaceae, or Palmae), and orchid family (Orchidaceae).

## Economic and Ecologic Importance

Many of the most important plant species grown for human consumption are in the grass family, which includes rice, corn (maize), wheat, rye, barley, teff, millet, and other species. Many species of the grass family are also grown for animal consumption or as lawn grasses; examples include timothy, fescue, and bluegrass. Another group of great economic importance is the palm family, which includes coconuts, dates, and the oil palm. In addition to these foods, the palm family provides construction materials for housing, thatching, and a variety of tools and implements in many parts of the world. The largest family of monocots, in terms of number of species, is the orchid family. Although orchids are widely grown as ornamentals, only one species, the vanilla orchid, is grown as a food plant. The flavoring agent vanilla is extracted from the podlike fruits of this species.

Apart from their obvious economic importance as sources of foods and other materials of use to humanity, various monocots are of great significance as dominant elements in a variety of habitats, such as prairies (many grasses), marshes, bogs, and other wetlands (many members of the sedge family, or Cyperaceae), and ponds and streams (various members of the frog's-bit family, Hydrocharitaceae, and related aquatic families). Members of the orchid family and the pineapple family (Bromeliaceae) are important **epiphytes** in tropical forests, where they provide food to pollinating insects and birds and habitat for insects, fungi, and other kinds of organisms in the forest canopy.

**epiphytes** plants that grow on other plants

## Anatomy

One of the distinctive characteristics of monocotyledons is the feature that gives the group its name, the presence of a single cotyledon, or seed leaf, in the embryo (as opposed to two in dicotyledons). Another important characteristic of monocots is the early death of its primary root, the initial root that emerges when a seed germinates. Thus, there is no taproot, and the entire root system of an older plant consists entirely of roots that emerged from stems. Another characteristic of monocots is the presence of scattered **vascular** bundles in the stems, as observed in cross-section, in contrast with the characteristic arrangement of the vascular bundles in a ring, as occurs in dicots and **gymnosperms**. Secondary growth, the process by which a stem or root continues to increase in girth through the development of additional cell layers, occurs in only a few monocots, such as the Dracaena. True wood (as occurs in gymnosperms and many dicots) is the result of secondary growth, and because this form of development is absent in most monocots, almost all of them are herbaceous plants.

**vascular** related to transport of nutrients

**gymnosperm** a major group of plants that includes the conifers

## COMMON MONOCOT FAMILIES

| Family | Common Name | Number of Species (approximate) | Uses |
|---|---|---|---|
| Araceae | Aroid family | 3,300 | Taro and other species cultivated for starchy tubers and rhizomes; many ornamentals |
| Arecaceae (or Palmae) | Palm family | 2,000 | Food (dates, coconuts, oil); construction of houses; numerous implements such as baskets |
| Bromeliaceae | Bromeliad family | 2,700 | Pineapples; ornamentals |
| Cyperaceae | Sedge family | 5,000 | Ecological dominants in wetlands, providing habitat and food for wildlife |
| Hydrocharitaceae | Frog's-bit family | 75 | Habitat and food for aquatic animals; several species are noxious weeds in ponds; some species grown in aquaria or ponds as ornamentals |
| Liliaceae | Lily family | 600 | Lilies, tulips, and other ornamentals |
| Orchidaceae | Orchid family | 25,000 | Vanilla; numerous ornamentals |
| Poaceae (or Gramineae) | Grass family | 11,000 | Grain for human consumption and both grain and vegetation for animal consumption; ecological dominants in prairies and other ecosystems; lawn grasses; bamboos |
| Zingiberaceae | Ginger family | 1,400 | Ginger, turmeric, and other spices; ornamentals |

Monocots nonetheless exhibit a variety of growth forms. Most are perennial herbs, often with specialized organs such as bulbs, corms, tubers, and rhizomes, which store food resources. These structures, which are specialized stems with or without specialized leaves, are seen in many perennial herbs such as crocuses, daffodils, irises, and onions. The aboveground parts of these plants die back each year when a cold or dry season approaches and are regenerated from the various belowground structures when suitable growing conditions return. Although they are often called trees, banana plants are actually large herbaceous perennials that lack wood as well as a vertical trunk. The actual stem of a banana plant extends only a short distance above the base of the plant, and what appears superficially to be the main stem is actually a tight aggregation of the lower parts of the leaves. Most monocots that are woody in texture, such as bamboos and palm trees, lack secondary growth, and their stems are relatively uniform in diameter from the base to the top of the plant. Several families of monocots are floating or rooted aquatics in fresh and salt water. These plants often have ribbonlike stems and leaves, and can be mistaken for algae if their flowers and fruits are overlooked.

Many species of monocots have leaf bases that completely encircle the stem, thus forming a sheath. The layers of an onion bulb (members of the Alliaceae family) are leaves of this type. In the leaf blades of most monocots the major strands of vascular tissue (the veins) are parallel to each other. In this manner they differ from the typically reticulate or netlike system of veins that occurs in most dicots, where the major veins branch and diverge, with many of the branches meeting. There are exceptions, and a reticulate leaf venation system occurs in some groups of monocots, such as the aroid family (Araceae), which includes skunk cabbage, Jack-in-the-pulpit, and philodendron, the latter of which is frequently grown as a houseplant. An unusual variant form of parallel leaf venation occurs in a group of monocots that includes the ginger family (Zingiberaceae) and the banana family

(Musaceae). In these families, as exemplified by the leaf of the banana plant, there is a bundle of parallel veins along the midrib of the leaf, and these diverge in succession toward the margin of the leaf, the result being a characteristic pinnate-parallel leaf venation pattern.

In most monocots, the floral parts occur in multiples of three. One example is the tulip, which has six petals (often called tepals, since there is no clear differentiation of **sepals** and petals), six stamens, and a **pistil** with three chambers or locules, representing the three **carpels**. The pollen grains of monocots also differ from those of most dicots. In monocots, each pollen grain has just one thin-walled region, the colpus, which is the area from which the pollen tube emerges when the pollen grain germinates. Most dicots, in contrast, have three such regions. This thin area of the pollen wall often takes the form of a single elongate furrow, or sulcus, that extends most of the length of the pollen grain. SEE ALSO Alliaceae; Bamboo; Dicots; Evolution of Plants; Grasses; Orchidaceae; Palms; Systematics, Plant.

*Jerrold I. Davis*

**sepals** the outermost whorl of flower parts; usually green and leaf-like, they protect the inner parts of the flower

**pistil** the female reproductive organ

**carpels** the innermost whorl of flower parts, including the egg-bearing ovules, plus the style and stigma attached to the ovules

**Bibliography**

Bailey, L. H. *Manual of Cultivated Plants.* New York: Macmillan, 1949.

Dahlgren, R. M. T., H. T. Clifford, and P. F. Yeo. *The Families of Monocotyledons.* New York: Springer-Verlag.

Heywood, V.H., ed. *Flowering Plants of the World.* Oxford: Oxford University Press, 1993.

Wilson, K. L., and D. A. Morrison, eds. *Monocots: Systematics and Evolution.* Victoria, Australia: CSIRO Publications, 2000.

## Mushroom   *See Fungi.*

# Mycorrhizae

**gymnosperm** a major group of plants that includes the conifers

Mycorrhizae are intimate, mutually beneficial associations between fungi and the roots of plants (*mycorrhiza* comes from the Greek word meaning "fungus-root"). All **gymnosperms** and approximately 80 percent of all an-

Ectotrophic mycorrhizae on host roots.

giosperms are thought to have naturally occurring mycorrhizal associations. The plant provides the fungus with carbohydrates made in photosynthesis, and the fungus provides the plant with increased amounts of mineral elements and water absorbed from the soil. The fungus also protects the root from **pathogens**.

There are two major types of mycorrhizae, the ectomycorrhizae (also called ectotropic mycorrhizae; *ecto*, meaning "outside") and the endomycorrhizae (endotropic mycorrhizae; *endo*, meaning "inside"), that are distinguished on the basis of whether or not the fungus penetrates the root cells.

## Ectomycorrhizae

In ectomycorrhizae the fungal component is usually a basidiomycete or sometimes an ascomycete. Ectomycorrhizae occur on certain groups of temperate shrubs and trees such as beeches, oaks, willows, poplars, cottonwoods, and pines. The associations are most common in vegetation experiencing seasonal growth, where they are thought to extend the growing period. In addition, ectomycorrhizae are common on trees growing in the cold, dry conditions close to the Arctic Circle and high on the slopes of mountains where they make the trees better able to survive in harsh conditions.

In an ectomycorrhizal association, the fungus forms a thick mat, called a mantle, on the outside of the young roots, and it also grows in between epidermal cells and into the cortex of the root interior. Within the root, the fungus never penetrates any of the cells but instead remains confined to the intercellular spaces where it forms a network called a Hartig net. The fungal **filaments**, called **hyphae**, also extend outward from the root where they increase the volume of soil available to be "mined" for nutrients. They also increase the surface area for the absorption of water and mineral salts, particularly phosphates but also $NH_4$, $K^+$, $Cu^{2+}$, $Zn^{2+}$, and $NO_3^-$. Once the root is colonized by the fungus, the production of root hairs slows or even ceases as the absorptive role of the root hairs is taken over by the hyphae of the ectomycorrhizal fungus.

## Endomycorrhizae

Far more common are the endomycorrhizae, which have a zygomycete as the fungal component and which actually penetrate the cell walls of the root cortex. Although the hyphae do not enter the cytoplasm of the **cortical** cells, in most cases they cause the plasma membrane to bulge inward, forming highly branched structures called arbuscules and terminal swellings called vesicles. Thus, this type of endomycorrhizae is referred to as vesicular-arbuscular mycorrhizae, or VAM. The arbuscules are in intimate contact with the cortical cells and provide an increased surface area over which carbohydrates can pass from the plant to the fungus and mineral elements from the fungus to the plant. The vesicles are thought to function as storage compartments for the fungus. As with the ectomycorrhizae, the fungal hyphae extend from the root into the soil and increase the surface area for absorption, but there is no mantle or Hartig net, and root hairs are often present. The VAM are found on almost all herbaceous angiosperms, some gymnosperms, and many ferns and mosses. Endomycorrhizae are particularly important in the tropics where the soils are typically poor in phosphates. Studies have indicated that roots associated with

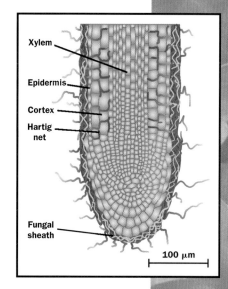

Xylem
Epidermis
Cortex
Hartig net
Fungal sheath

100 μm

Ectotrophic mycorrhizal fungi infecting a root. Redrawn from Taiz and Zeiger, 1998, Figure 5.10.

**pathogen** disease-causing organism

**filament** a threadlike extension

**hyphae** the threadlike body mass of a fungus

**cortical** relating to the cortex of a plant

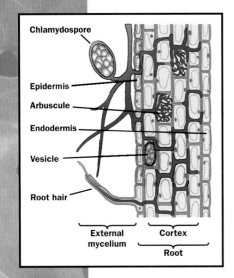

Chlamydospore

Epidermis

Arbuscule

Endodermis

Vesicle

Root hair

External mycelium | Cortex

Root

Association of vesicular-arbuscular mycorrhizal fungi with a plant root section. Redrawn from Taiz and Zeiger, 1998, Figure 5.11.

**enzyme** a protein that controls a reaction in a cell

**compound** a substance formed from two or more elements

**ecosystem** an ecological community together with its environment

mycorrhizal fungi can take up phosphate four times faster than roots without such fungi. Mycorrhizal fungi are particularly effective in utilizing highly insoluble rock phosphorus, $Ca_3(PO_4)_2$, that cannot be used by plants. The fungal hyphae make phosphates available to the plant by converting them to a soluble form.

## Other Associations

Two other types of mycorrhizae are found in the heather and orchid families. In heather (family Ericaceae), the fungus secretes **enzymes** into the soil that convert materials, particularly nitrogen-containing **compounds**, into forms that can be taken up more readily. In orchids (family Orchidaceae), the seeds contain a mycorrhizal fungus that is required for seed germination. Within the seed, the hyphae absorb stored carbohydrates and transfer them to the plant embryo.

Some plants, such as those of the mustard family (Brassicaceae) and the sedge family (Cyperaceae), lack mycorrhizae. In addition, most plants growing in flooded soils (or under hydroponics) do not form mycorrhizae nor do plants grown where conditions are extremely dry or saline. Also, plants growing in very fertile (i.e., nutrient-rich soils) have less-developed mycorrhizae compared to plants growing in nutrient-poor soils.

## Ecological Importance of Mycorrhizae

The importance of mycorrhizae in **ecosystems** became particularly apparent in the 1960s when plants grown in greenhouses were transplanted into areas such as slag heaps, landfills, and strip-mined areas in order to reclaim the land. With few exceptions, such plants did not survive in these infertile areas. Not until later was it realized that greenhouse soil is often sterilized to prevent the growth of pathogens, and the sterilization process killed the mycorrhizal fungi as well. Today, such reclamation attempts are much more successful because mycorrhizal fungi are inoculated with the plants when they are transplanted into the reclaimed areas. Similarly, attempts to grow certain species of European pines in the United States were unsuccessful until mycorrhizal fungi from their native soils were added at the time of transplanting.

Mycorrhizae are thought to have played an important role in the colonization of the land by plants some four hundred million years ago. Studies of fossil plants have shown that endomycorrhizae were prevalent at that time, and such associations may have been crucial in helping plants make the transition from the nutrient-rich sea to the nutrient-poor land. SEE ALSO ECOSYSTEM; FUNGI; INTERACTIONS, PLANT-FUNGAL; NUTRIENTS.

*Robert C. Evans*

**Bibliography**

Raven, Peter H., Ray F. Evert, and Susan E. Eichhorn. *Biology of Plants*, 6th ed. New York: W. H. Freeman and Company, 1999.

Ricklefs, Robert E. *Ecology*, 3rd ed. New York: W. H. Freeman and Company, 1990.

Salisbury, Frank B., and Cleon Ross. *Plant Physiology*, 4th ed. Belmont, CA: Wadsworth, Inc., 1992.

Taiz, Lincoln, and Eduardo Zeiger. *Plant Physiology*, 2nd ed. Sunderland, MA: Sinauer Associates, Inc., 1998.

# Native Food Crops

Native food crops are the crops of the world's ancient farming systems. The seeds of these cultivars have been passed down by native agriculturalists across generations and selected and preserved for local **ecosystems**. Native seeds, and the methods used to grow them, were developed for a wide range of temperatures, soil types, and precipitation without expensive, often ecologically destructive, chemicals. Many of these crops continue to be grown around the world today by traditional, indigenous farmers. They represent irreplaceable sources of genetic material to improve modern **hybrid** crops for nutrition as well as for disease and drought resistance. Examples of modern food crops that had their origin from native sources include corn, rice, chilies, potatoes, and wheat. Other highly nutritious crops such as quinoa and amaranth are becoming more common in Western diets, while ulloco (oo-yoo-ko), a wildly colored, high-altitude tuber (root crop) that was a staple of the Incas, is still relatively unknown outside of South America. SEE ALSO AGRICULTURE, HISTORY OF; BARK; CULTIVAR; ETHNOBOTANY; SEED PRESERVATION; SEEDS.

*Miguel L. Vasquez*

**ecosystem** an ecological community together with its environment

**hybrid** a mix of two species

## Bibliography

Foster, Nelson, and Linda S. Cordell, eds. *Chilies to Chocolate: Food the Americas Gave the World*. Tucson, AZ: University of Arizona Press, 1992.

Nabhan, Gary P. *Enduring Seeds*. San Francisco: North Point Press, 1989.

# Nitrogen Fixation

Biological nitrogen ($N_2$) fixation is the reduction of atmospheric nitrogen gas to ammonia, according to the equation:

$$N_2 + 10H^+ + 8e^- + 16ATP \rightarrow 2NH_4^+ + H_2 + 16ADP + 16P_i$$

The reaction is mediated by an oxygen-sensitive **enzyme** nitrogenase and requires energy, as indicated by the consumption of adenosine triphosphate (**ATP**). This conversion of **inert** $N_2$ gas into a form utilized by most organisms is the second most important biological process on Earth after photosynthesis. It contributes 175 million tons of nitrogen per year to the global nitrogen economy and accounts for 65 percent of the nitrogen used in agriculture. In Brazil alone, $N_2$ fixation contributes the equivalent of 2.5 million tons of fertilizer nitrogen annually to agricultural production and is essential to a country with limited natural gas reserves for fertilizer nitrogen production.

This article emphasizes **symbiotic** $N_2$ fixation in grain and pasture **legumes** in the family Fabaceae. $N_2$ fixation also occurs in leguminous and actinorhizal trees, sugarcane, and rice.

## $N_2$-Fixing Organisms and Variation in Their Rates of Fixation

The ability to fix $N_2$ is restricted to prokaryotic organisms. Within this group the ability occurs in many different species. These include **cyanobacteria** and **actinomycetes,** as well as eubacteria, including heterotrophic (e.g., *Azotobacter*), **autotrophic** (*Thiobacillus*), aerobic (*Bacillus*), **anaerobic** (*Clostridium*), and photosynthetic (*Rhodospirillum*) species.

**enzyme** a protein that controls a reaction in a cell

**ATP** adenosine triphosphate, a small, water-soluble molecule that acts as an energy currency in cells

**inert** incapable of reaction

**symbiosis** a relationship between two organisms from which each derives benefit

**legumes** beans and other members of the Fabaceae family

**cyanobacteria** photosynthetic prokaryotic bacteria formerly known as blue-green algae

**actinomycetes** common name for a group of Gram positive bacteria that are filamentous and superficially similar to fungi

**autotroph** "self-feeder;" any organism that uses sunlight or chemical energy

**anaerobic** absence of oxygen

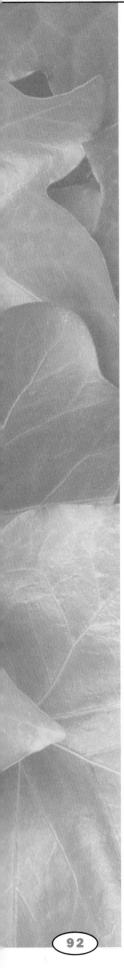

Root nodules of the broad bean *Vicia faba* formed by the nitrogen-fixing bacteria *Rhizobium*.

**symbiosis** a relationship between organisms of two different species in which at least one benefits

$N_2$-fixing organisms can live free in nature (e.g., *Azotobacter*), enter loose (associative) **symbiosis** with plants or animals (*Acetobacter* and sugarcane), or establish longer-term relationships within specialized structures provided by their host (*Rhizobium* and the legume nodule).

Some free-living organisms fix enough $N_2$ in vitro to grow without added nitrogen, but limited energy supply can limit $N_2$ fixation in nature. For instance, non-symbiotic organisms in primary successional areas of the Hawaii Volcanoes National Park were found to fix only 0.3 to 2.8 kilograms of $N_2$ per hectare per year, and non-symbiotic $N_2$ fixation in soil rarely exceeds 15 kilograms per hectare per year. Higher levels in tidal flats and rice paddies are largely due to photosynthetic bacteria and cyanobacteria.

The importance of energy supply for fixation can be seen by comparing these rates to those found in legumes, where the symbiotic bacteria are supplied with high-energy products from photosynthesis. Rates of symbiotic $N_2$ fixation in legumes vary with plant species and cultivar, growing season, and soil fertility. Some forage legumes can fix 600 kilograms per hectare per year but more common values are 100 to 300 kilograms per hectare per year. Rates for grain legumes are often lower. Inclusion of legumes in **crop rotations** is generally thought to improve soil nitrogen levels, but benefits depend on the level of $N_2$ fixed and the amount of nitrogen removed in grain or forage. A good soybean crop might fix 180 kilograms per hectare but remove 210 kilograms per hectare in the grain.

## Nodule Formation and Structure in Legumes

The most-studied symbiotic system is between $N_2$-fixing bacteria known as rhizobia and legumes such as clover and soybean. Rhizobia produce stem or root nodules on their host(s), and within these nodules receive protection from external stresses and energy for growth and $N_2$ fixation. The host receives most of the nitrogen it needs for growth. Six genera of rhizobia (*Rhizobium*, *Azorhizobium*, *Mesorhizobium*, *Bradyrhizobium*, *Sinorhizobium*, and *Allorhizobium*) are recognized.

Rhizobia use several different mechanisms to infect their host, but only infection via root hairs is described here. Infection is initiated with the attachment of suitable rhizobia to newly emerged root hairs and leads to localized hydrolysis of the root hair cell wall. Root hair curling and deformation results, with many of the root hairs taking the shape of a shepherd's crook. Hydrolysis of the cell wall allows rhizobia to enter their host, but they never really gain intracellular access. Plant-derived material is deposited about them, and as they move down the root hair toward the root cortex they remain enclosed within a plant-derived infection thread. Even within the nodule they are separated from their host by a host-derived **peribacteroid** membrane. This separation is usually seen as a mechanism to suppress plant defense responses likely to harm the bacteria.

Presence of the rhizobia causes multiplication and enlargement of root **cortical** cells and gives the nodule a characteristic shape and structure: either round as in soybean or elongated as in alfalfa or clover. Such nodules have several distinct regions. The area of active $N_2$ fixation is either pink or red in color due to the presence of hemoglobin needed for oxygen transport. In most legumes nodules are visible within six to ten days of **inoculation;** $N_2$ fixation as evidenced by improved plant growth and coloration of the nodules can occur within three weeks.

## Molecular Changes Associated with Nodulation and $N_2$ Fixation

The signs of infection are paralleled at a molecular level by signaling between host and rhizobia. Nodulation genes in *Rhizobium* are borne on extra-chromosomal (plasmid) deoxyribonucleic acid (DNA). They include both common genes found in all rhizobia and host-specific genes involved in the nodulation of specific legumes. Most are only expressed in the presence of a suitable host. Substances termed **flavonoids** present in the root exudate trigger this response, with legumes differing in the flavonoids each produced. Rhizobia also differ in their response to these **compounds**.

More than fifty nodulation genes have been identified. Some are involved in the regulation of nodulation, but most function in the synthesis of a **chitin**-like lipo-chito-oligosaccharide or nod factor. These molecules all have the same core structure (coded for by the common nodulation genes), but they vary in the side chains each carries, affecting host range.

**crop rotation** alternating crops from year to year in a particular field

**peribacteroid** a membrane surrounding individual or groups of rhizobia within the root cells of their host; in such situations the bacteria have frequently undergone some change in surface chemistry and are referred to as bacteroids

**cortical** relating to the cortex of a plant

**inoculation** use of a commercial preparation, most often but not always peat-based, used to introduce rhizobia into soils; inoculants may be seed applied or introduced directly into the soil

**flavonoids** aromatic compounds occurring in both seeds and young roots and involved in host-pathogen and host-symbiont interactions

**compound** a substance formed from two or more elements

**chitin** a cellulose-like molecule

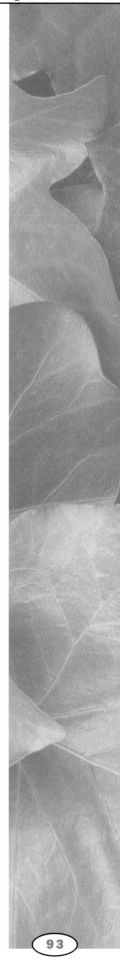

A micrograph of *Rhizobium* in the root of a bean plant.

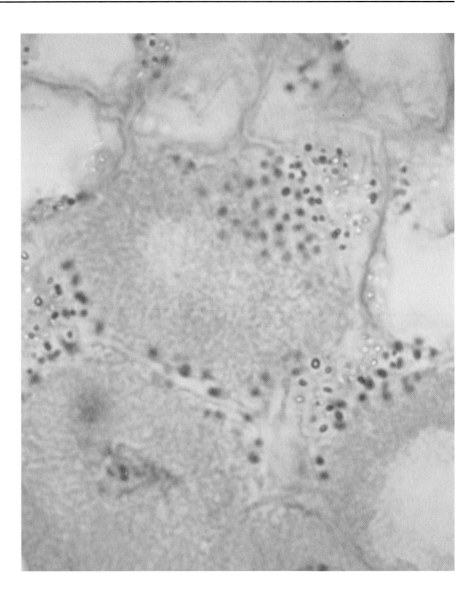

They are powerful plant hormones, which at low concentration can initiate most of the changes found during nodule development.

Interaction of host and rhizobia is also accompanied by the expression of nodule-specific proteins or nodulins. Several nodulins have now been found in actinorhizal and mycorrhizal symbiosis, and together with pea mutants that neither nodulate nor form mycorrhizal associations indicate some common elements in symbiosis.

Nodulin expression can vary temporally and spatially. Early nodulins are involved in infection or nodule development and may be expressed within six hours of inoculation. Later nodulins are involved in nodule function, carbon and nitrogen metabolism, or to $O_2$ transport. Nodule hemoglobin is an obvious example of this group.

## Specificity in Nodulation

Given the complex signaling involved, specificity in nodulation is to be expected. Each rhizobium has the ability to nodulate some, but not all, legumes. Host range can vary, with one rhizobia only nodulating a particular species of clover, for example, while another will nodulate many different legumes. A consequence of this specificity is that legumes being introduced into new areas will usually need to be inoculated with appropriate rhizobia before seeding. In the early 1900s this was often achieved by mixing seed with soil from an area where the crop had been grown before. Today, more than one hundred different inoculant preparations are needed for the different crop, tree, and pasture legumes used in agriculture and conservation. Most are grown in culture and sold commercially. The legumes for which inoculant preparations are available, and the methods used to prepare, distribute, and apply these cultures, are detailed on the Rhizobium Research Laboratory Web site (http://www.Rhizobium.umn.edu).

When properly carried out, legume inoculation should result in abundant nodulation and high levels of $N_2$ fixation. Reinoculation should not be necessary because large numbers of rhizobia will be released from nodules at the end of the growing season and establish themselves in the soil. Problems with the culture used and environmental and soil factors can limit response, especially in the lesser-developed countries. Common concerns include:

- poor-quality inoculant strains weak in $N_2$ fixation and noncompetitive or nonpersistent in soil

- inoculants with low rhizobial numbers because of problems in production or packaging or during shipment

- inappropriate use of fertilizer or pesticides injurious to the rhizobia

- soil acidity, drought, or temperature conditions that affect strain survival or nodulation and $N_2$ fixation.

Because of earlier problems in inoculant production and quality, many countries have now developed regulations governing the quality of inoculant cultures. In the United States, inoculant quality control still rests with the producer. SEE ALSO Atmosphere and Plants; Biogeochemical Cycles; Cyanobacteria; Eubacteria; Fabaceae; Fertilizer; Flavonoids; Mycorrhizae; Nutrients; Roots.

*Peter H. Graham*

### Bibliography

Graham, P. H. "Biological Dinitrogen Fixation: Symbiotic." In *Principles and Applications of Soil Microbiology*, eds. D. Sylvia et al. Upper Saddle River, NJ: Prentice-Hall, 1998.

Young, J. P. W. "Phylogenetic Classification of Nitrogen-Fixing Organisms." In *Biological Nitrogen Fixation*, eds. G. Stacey et al. New York: Chapman & Hall, 1992.

# Nutrients

Of the ninety-two naturally occurring elements, only about twenty are indispensable or essential for the growth of plants. Plants, however, absorb many more mineral elements than that from the soil in which they grow. Which of these elements are the essential ones? The best way to answer that is to withhold the element in question from the plants. If then the plants grow poorly or die while plants supplied with the element thrive, the element has been shown to be essential.

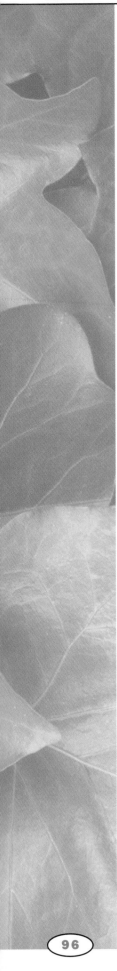

A Swiss cheese plant (*Montsera,* family Araceae), suffering from marginal chlorosis, indicating a nitrogen deficiency.

Such an experiment cannot be done with soil-grown plants. Soils contain most of the elements in the periodic table of elements. No element can be removed from soil so thoroughly as to deprive plants of that element; the chemical means for doing that would destroy the soil.

Therefore scientists devised a simplified method for growing plants, called solution culture, or hydroponics. In this technique the roots of the plants are not in soil but in water, which contains the dissolved salts of those elements considered to be essential. That way, scientists can control and monitor the chemical composition of the medium in which the plants grow.

Failure of the plants in such an experiment suggests that some essential element is missing, and by trial and error scientists then determine which element cures the deficiency. By this method most of the elements known now to be essential have been identified. Those elements needed in relatively large amounts are called macronutrients; those needed in only small or very small amounts are micronutrients.

By the latter half of the nineteenth century, all the macronutrient mineral elements (see accompanying table) and one micronutrient, iron, had been identified. But throughout the twentieth century additional elements were shown to be micronutrients. It took so long to identify them because early on the water and the nutrient salts used for supplying the macronutrient elements contained substantial impurities, some of which were micronutrients. Investigators therefore supplied, without knowing it, several micronutrients

## MINERAL ELEMENTS IN CROP PLANTS

| Element | Range of Concentrations |
|---|---|
| **Macronutrients** | |
| Nitrogen (N) | 0.5–6%* |
| Phosphorus (P) | 0.15–0.5% |
| Sulfur (S) | 0.1–1.5% |
| Potassium (K) | 0.8–8% |
| Calcium (Ca) | 0.1–6% |
| Magnesium (Mg) | 0.05–1% |
| **Micronutrients** | |
| Iron (Fe) | 20–600 ppm† |
| Manganese (Mn) | 10–600 ppm |
| Zinc (Zn) | 10–250 ppm |
| Copper (Cu) | 2–50 ppm |
| Molybdenum (Mo) | 0.1–10 ppm |
| Chlorine (Cl) | 10–80,000 ppm |
| Boron (B) | 0.2–800 ppm |
| Nickel (Ni) | 0.05–5 ppm |
| **Other Elements** | |
| Sodium (Na; essential for some plants) | 0.001–8% |
| Silicon (Si; quasi-essential for some plants) | 0.1–10% |
| Cobalt (Co; essential in all nitrogen-fixing systems) | 0.05–10 ppm |

\* Percent of dry matter.
† Micrograms per gram dry matter (or parts per million).

**SOURCE:** Data collected from various sources.

to their experimental plants. Once this was understood, plant biologists developed ever more refined methods for purifying water and nutrient salts and, little by little, several additional elements were shown to be essential.

When determining the chemical composition of plants, plant nutritionists usually dry the plant first, keeping it at about 70°C (158°F) for forty-eight hours. Fresh plant material is mostly water ($H_2O$) so that its dry weight is only around 10 to 20 percent of the initial fresh weight. Carbon and oxygen each make up about 45 percent of the dry matter, and hydrogen 6 percent. These elements can be removed by careful digestion. The inorganic nutrients together make up only about 4 percent of dry plant matter and are left in the digest.

## Essential Elements

The table above lists the elements known to be essential to plants, in addition to carbon, oxygen, and hydrogen, and also includes a quantitative indication of their prevalence in plant tissues. For the macronutrient elements, these values are expressed as percent of the dry matter, and for the micronutrients, as micrograms per gram dry matter, or parts per million. The reason for giving a range of values rather than a single one for each element is that these values differ considerably, depending on the kind of plant, the soil in which it grows, and other factors. Three of these elements, sodium, silicon, and cobalt, cannot unequivocally be called nutrients, as explained below.

Living plants use up much water in **transpiration**. Water is also their main constituent. Carbon, oxygen, and hydrogen are the elements that make up carbohydrates. Plant cells have walls composed mostly of cellulose and related carbohydrate polymers. These three elements make up a high per-

**transpiration** movement of water from soil to atmosphere through a plant

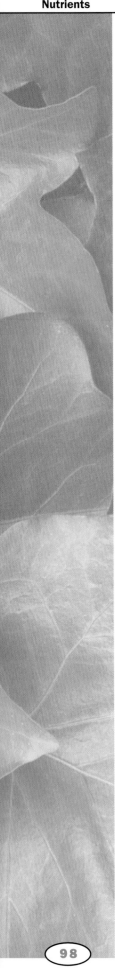

**translocate** to move, especially to move sugars from the leaf to other parts of the plant

**compound** a substance formed from two or more elements

**ATP** adenosine triphosphate, a small, water-soluble molecule that acts as an energy currency in cells

**enzyme** a protein that controls a reaction in a cell

**solute** a substance dissolved in a solution

**symbiosis** a relationship between two organisms from which each derives benefit

**legumes** beans and other members of the Fabaceae family

centage of plant dry matter because quantitatively most of it is cell wall. In addition, it is mainly in the form of sugars (i.e., carbohydrates) that carbon initially assimilated by leaves through photosynthesis is **translocated** to the rest of the plant body, including the roots.

- **Nitrogen** is a component of all amino acids, and as proteins are amino acid polymers, of all proteins. Nucleic acids and other essential **compounds** also contain nitrogen.

- **Phosphorus** is part of several compounds essential for energy transfer, of which adenosine triphosphate (**ATP**), the "energy currency" of cells, is the best known. Nucleic acids and several other classes of biochemical entities also contain phosphorus as an integral component.

- Three **sulfur**-containing amino acids and other compounds needed in metabolism account for the essentiality of sulfur.

- **Potassium** is not an integral part of any compound that can be chemically isolated from plants. However, it activates some seventy **enzymes**, and along with other **solutes** regulates the water relations of plants.

- **Calcium** is part of the middle lamella, the layer between the cell walls of adjacent cells. Another function is maintenance of the integrity of cell membranes. Calcium is also a cofactor (nonprotein part) of several enzymes. It functions to signal environmental changes in plant cells.

- **Magnesium** is a constituent of the chlorophyll molecule and activates numerous enzymes.

- **Iron** is a part of many metabolites, including those primarily involved in energy acquisition (photosynthesis), utilization (respiration), and nitrogen fixation.

- **Manganese** activates a number of enzymes and is part of the protein complex that causes the evolution of oxygen, $O_2$, in Photosystem II of photosynthesis.

- **Zinc** is a constituent of several enzymes.

- **Copper** is also a constituent of several enzymes.

- **Nickel,** the element required in the least amount, is a constituent of the enzyme urease. A deficiency of it causes an excessive accumulation of urea.

- **Boron** has several functions in plant growth; severe boron deficiency causes the growing tips of both roots and shoots to die.

- **Chlorine** (in the form of chloride ion) is required in Photosystem II of photosynthesis. Severely chlorine-deficient plants wilt, suggesting some unknown function in water relations.

- **Molybdenum** is a constituent of enzymes active in the acquisition of nitrogen.

- **Cobalt** is required by the **symbiotic** nitrogen-fixing bacteria associated with the root nodules of **legumes** and some other plants.

- **Sodium** is prominent in many soils of arid and semiarid regions, and native wild plants growing on these saline soils grow best with an ample supply of it. Crops, however, often suffer under saline con-

ditions. Plants with the C$_4$ photosynthetic pathway require sodium as a micronutrient.

- **Silicon** is essential for plants of the family Equisetaceae, the horsetails or scouring rushes. Although apparently not absolutely essential for plants in general it has nevertheless many beneficial effects; it has been called quasi-essential.

## Deficiency and Toxicity Symptoms

When some element is deficient or present in such high concentration as to be toxic, plants often have symptoms somewhat characteristic of the particular condition afflicting them. For example, yellowing of leaves, or chlorosis, often indicates a deficiency of nitrogen. Nevertheless, visual identification of deficiencies or toxicities is not a reliable procedure. For example, sulfur deficiency may result in symptoms very similar to those of nitrogen deficiency. Therefore even experts check their visual impression by analyzing the tissue to find out whether its content of the suspected element is in fact below the value deemed adequate for that particular crop or present in excess. Often, such unrelated conditions as diseases caused by fungi or bacteria may result in the development of symptoms that mimic those of nutrient disorders. SEE ALSO BIOGEOCHEMICAL CYCLES; FERTILIZER; HALOPHYTES; HYDROPONICS; NITROGEN FIXATION; SOIL, CHEMISTRY OF.

*Emanuel Epstein*

**Bibliography**

Bennett, W. F., ed. *Nutrient Deficiencies and Toxicities in Crop Plants.* St. Paul, MN: American Phytopathological Society, 1993.

Epstein, Emanuel. *Mineral Nutrition of Plants: Principles and Perspectives.* New York: John Wiley & Sons, 1971.

———. "Silicon." *Annual Review of Plant Physiology and Plant Molecular Biology* 50 (1999): 641–64.

Taiz, Lincoln, and Eduardo Zeiger. *Plant Physiology*, 2nd ed. Sunderland, MA: Sinauer Associates, 1988.

# Odum, Eugene

*American Ecologist*
*1913–*

Eugene Odum is an American ecologist who has worked to advance ecological awareness and research. Born in 1913 to an academic family, he spent most of the twentieth century promoting the ecosystem concept and warning of the impact humans have on the **ecosystems** in which we live. One of his most important accomplishments was writing *Fundamentals of Ecology* in 1953, which he wrote partly in response to the zoology department at the University of Georgia rejecting ecology as an important area of study. His book was remarkably clear and concise, and it presented the important principles of ecology in a way that helped to define the science.

*Fundamentals of Ecology* also brought the idea of an ecosystem to a wider audience at a time when the concept was just beginning to gain recognition among ecological specialists and ways to study ecosystems were just being developed. Previously, ecology had focused on natural history and on the

**ecosystem** an ecological community together with its environment

variety of species in the environment rather than on the details of physical and metabolic interactions among the species and nonliving material around them, as is done in the study of ecosystems. Odum placed the idea of the ecosystem at the beginning, as a fundamental concept of ecology. He explained that ecosystems are the largest functional unit in ecology, comprising both living and nonliving parts that exchange materials in cycles. These interactions and exchanges of nutrients could allow ecosystems to evolve as units over time. Ecosystems could be seen at many levels, from something as small as a lake to the entire Earth seen as a global ecosystem.

In emphasizing how the study of ecology needs to examine the way humans affect their ecosystems, Odum published ideas that became the focus of the environmental movement. Given the knowledge that humans were influential and often destructive components of ecosystems, it was especially important that Odum's book was clear and understandable by non-ecologists. Being at the time one of the only ecological textbooks, *Fundamentals of Ecology* was enormously important in driving the study of ecosystems.

Odum also wrote several other works while teaching and doing research at the University of Georgia. His work was funded by the Atomic Energy Commission, an institution that funded much early ecological research. He became a leading authority on ecosystem studies, defending the new discipline against its critics, and he also served as chair of a section of the International Biological Program. His leadership in the program helped guide research into landscape ecosystems, studying terrestrial and marine areas and the human influences on them. Remaining active into his late eighties by the turn of the twenty-first century, Eugene Odum still worked to promote the study of ecosystems. He has done much to encourage environmental study around the world, and especially where he works in Georgia. SEE ALSO ECOLOGY; ECOLOGY, ENERGY FLOW; ECOLOGY, HISTORY OF; ECOSYSTEM; WARMING, JOHANNES.

*Jessica P. Penney*

**Bibliography**

Golley, Frank B. *A History of the Ecosystem Concept in Ecology.* New Haven, CT: Yale University Press, 1993.

Odum, Eugene. *Fundamentals of Ecology.* First printed in 1953. Philadelphia: Saunders, 1971.

# Oils, Plant-Derived

Plant oil sources are typically the seeds or seed coats of plants. Plant breeding and genetic engineering have made available many plant oils with fatty acid compositions quite different from the typical values cited in the accompanying table.

Oils are extracted from plants by using pressure or solvents, usually the petroleum fraction hexane. Olive oil, for example, is a typical seed coat oil and is extracted by multiple pressings of the fruit pulp. The oil from the first pressing has the best quality and is termed virgin oil. Oilseeds may be extracted with pressure in a mechanical expeller but usually are cracked and pressed into flakes for extraction with hexane. The hexane is removed from the extracted crude oil by distillation.

Crude oils contain small amounts of undesirable **pigments**, phospholipids, and free fatty acids (i.e., fatty acids not chemically linked to glycerol) that make the oils dark, hazy, and smoky, respectively, on heating. Olive oil has a good flavor and is typically sold without treatment other than filtering or **centrifugation** for clarity. However, most other oils are refined. Refining involves mixing with water to wash out phospholipids (degumming), treatment with lye solutions to remove free fatty acids, bleaching with absorptive clays to remove pigments, and a vacuum steam treatment (deodorization) to remove undesirable flavors. Plant oils also contain small amounts of **sterols** and fat-soluble vitamins. These may be partly removed by deodorization and are regarded as harmless or desirable components of the oil.

Although most plant oils are used as food they are also used to make such things as paint and surface coatings, detergents, linoleum, and plastics. Some plant oils, such as castor and tung, contain special fatty acids used to make surface coatings.

Oils from plants are chiefly triglycerides, which are made up of one glycerol molecule linked to three fatty acids. The fatty acids have linear carbon chains varying in length, generally from six to twenty-two carbon atoms, with various amounts of hydrogen linked to the carbon. Carbon chains that hold all the hydrogen that they can are called saturated, and those with less hydrogen are unsaturated. Where the unsaturation occurs, the carbon chain is linked by double bonds.

Most plant oils are clear liquids at ambient temperatures rather than fats, which are plastic solids at room temperature. Butters, such as cocoa butter (chocolate fat), melt around room temperature. The solidification temperature of an oil depends on the length and saturation of its fatty acid chains. Short chains and double bonds (less saturated) decrease the solidification point. To change liquid oils, such as soybean oil, to a shortening or margarine, the oil is treated with hydrogen under pressure and a nickel catalyst. The resulting more saturated fat is said to be hydrogenated. During hydrogenation some of the double bonds are converted from their native cis form to trans isomers.

Fats and oils provide the most concentrated source of calories in the human diet, about nine calories per gram. Certain fatty acids produced in plants are nutritionally required. These essential fatty acids contain multiple double bonds and are called polyunsaturated. They come in two families called n-3 or n-6 based on the position of the first double bond counting from the tail of the fatty acid chain. SEE ALSO ECONOMIC IMPORTANCE OF PLANTS; LIPIDS; SEEDS.

*Earl G. Hammond*

**Bibliography**

Hammond, E. G. "The Raw Materials of the Fats and Oils Industry." In *Fats and Oils Processing*, ed. P. Wan. Champaign, IL: American Oil Chemists' Society, 1991.

Hegarty, Vincent. *Nutrition Food and the Environment.* St. Paul, MN: Eagen Press, 1995.

Stryer, Lubert. *Biochemistry.* New York: W. H. Freeman and Company, 1995.

Ulbricht, T. L. V., and D. A. T. Southgate. "Coronary Heart Disease: Seven Dietary Factors." *Lancet* 338 (1997): 985–92.

## HEALTHY FATS AND OILS

Animal fats contain the sterol cholesterol. The human body naturally produces all the cholesterol it needs; therefore, overconsumption of fatty foods rich in cholesterol is believed to encourage artery disease. Artery disease is also influenced by the fatty acids we consume. Fats and oils are considered healthy if they contain low proportions of saturated fatty acids with chain lengths of twelve to sixteen carbons. The animal fats lard, tallow, and milk fat and the plant oils palm, palm kernel, and coconut contain significant proportions of these less-desirable fatty acids. An atherogenicitiy index (AI) for fats and oils has been proposed to predict their tendency to cause artery disease.

$$AI = [\%12{:}0 + 4\,(\%14{:}0) + \%16{:}0] / \%\text{ all unsaturates}$$

where %12:0 represents the weight percent of a fatty acids with twelve carbons and no double bonds, and so on.

A low index value is desirable. The AI of animal fats range from 0.6 to 4. Some believe that consumption of the fatty acids with trans double bonds formed during hydrogenation also predisposes us to artery disease. Our diets should contain adequate amounts of the unsaturated n-3 and n-6 fatty acids. We should consume less than 30 percent of our total calories as fat.

**pigments** colored molecules

**centrifugation** spinning at high speed in a centrifuge to separate components

101

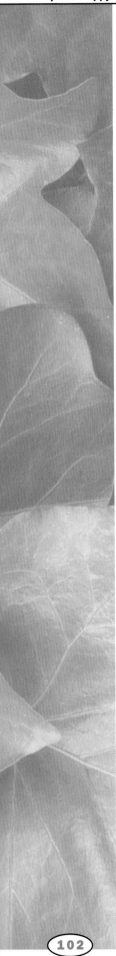

**sterol(s)** chemicals related to steroid hormones

---

**COMMON EDIBLE PLANT OILS**

| Oil Name | Plant Name | Oil-Bearing Tissue | Percentage $C_{12}$–$C_{16}$ Saturated Fatty Acids* | Atherogenicity Index† |
|---|---|---|---|---|
| Canola | Brassica campestris, Brassica napus | Seed | 6 | 0.04 |
| Cocoa butter | Theobroma cacao | Seed | 26 | 0.73 |
| Coconut | Cocos nucifera | Seed | 74 | 21.72 |
| Corn | Zea mays | Seed | 12 | 0.13 |
| Cottonseed | Gossypium hirsutum, Gossypium barbadense | Seed | 23 | 0.34 |
| Olive | Olea europea | Seed coat | 13 | 0.15 |
| Palm | Elaeis guineensis | Seed coat | 45 | 0.97 |
| Palm kernel | Elaeis guineensis | Seed | 73 | 7.12 |
| Peanut | Arachis hypogaea | Seed | 11 | 0.15 |
| Safflower | Carthamus tinctorius | Seed | 6 | 0.06 |
| Sesame | Sesamum indicum | Seed | 10 | 0.17 |
| Soybean | Glycine max | Seed | 11 | 0.13 |
| Sunflower | Helianthus annuus | Seed | 6 | 0.07 |

* Saturated fatty acids with 12 to 16 carbons are regarded as atherogenic or predisposing to artery disease.
† The atherogenicity index of Ulbrict and Southgate (1997) based on the data of Hammond (1991) is an estimate of the atherogenic effect of the various fatty acid. The smaller the index value, the more healthful the oil. Plant breeding and genetic engineering have made available many of these plant oils with fatty acid compositions greatly different from these typical values.

SOURCE: T. L. V. Ulbricht and D. A. T. Southgate, "Coronary Heart Disease: Seven Dietary Factors." *Lancet* 338 (1997): 985–92 and E. G. Hammond, "The Raw Materials of the Fats and Oils Industry." In *Fats and Oils Processing*, edited by P. Wan (Champaign, IL: American Oil Chemists' Society, 1991).

# Opium Poppy

The opium poppy (*Papaver somniferum*) was known to humans before the time of the Greeks. In many cultures the plant has been considered an important medicine, used to treat pain and dysentery. The time and place of the origin of the opium poppy is a mystery. It probably arose in central Europe during the late Bronze Age and was taken southward into the Mediterranean region. It then spread eastward into the Orient, likely transported by Arab traders in the seventh century.

The opium poppy has been widely grown in southeast Asia, as well as in Afghanistan and Turkey. One of the most infamous areas of the world for opium poppies is the Golden Triangle, the region in southeast Asia where Burma, Laos, and Thailand meet. The poppy grows best at about 1,000 meters (3,300 feet) elevation. The fields are cleared by the slash-and-burn technique, in which the native plants are cut, dried, and burned in order to have a clear hillside for crops. The opium plant is an annual, and must be grown from seed each year. Often it is grown as a second crop during the rainy season, with the seeds being planted between maize (corn) plants in October, which provide protection to the young poppy seedlings. The maize is harvested and the old stems removed, allowing the poppies full sunlight and making it easier to weed. They grow to a height of about 1 meter (3 feet) in about three months. Flowers appear in December, varying in color from pure white to deep reddish-purple. The flower withers and the fruit, a capsule, begins to develop. In a week or so the capsule turns from green to slightly gray-green, and the latex is ready to harvest. The capsule is tapped with a special knife consisting of three to five razor-sharp blades, which cut fine slits in the fruit wall, allowing the milklike latex to ooze out. This latex contains the alkaloids for which the opium poppy is so well known. By the next day, it has congealed somewhat into a dark yellowish-brown mass, which is carefully scraped off and placed in a container. The dried latex is packaged and sold or further processed in a laboratory.

Opium poppy latex contains more than twenty-five different alkaloids, of which six are important to humans. Morphine is a powerful painkiller, narcotic, and stimulant. It is strongly addicting but critical in modern medicine. Heroin is actually synthesized from morphine by the addition of two acetyl groups. It is a much stronger painkiller, but is also much more addicting. It is not used medically and has become a serious social problem because it has been badly abused. Papaverine, present in small amounts, is an important muscle relaxant. Codeine, the most extensively used opium alkaloid, is frequently found in cough medicines and decongestants. It is much less addicting than morphine or heroin, but may be sleep inducing. Narcotine speeds up respiration, but is used very little. Thebaine produces spasms similar to those caused by strychnine, and is sometimes used in the treatment of heroin addiction. SEE ALSO ALKALOIDS; MEDICINAL PLANTS; PSYCHOACTIVE PLANTS.

Edward F. Anderson

An opium poppy (*Papaver somniferum*) that was cut for its resin in a field in northwest Thailand.

**Bibliography**

Anderson, Edward F. *Plants and People of the Golden Triangle.* Portland, OR: Dioscorides Press, 1993.

Duke, J. A. "Utilization of *Papaver*." *Economic Botany* 27 (1973): 390–400.

Merlin, Mark. D. *On the Trail of the Ancient Opium Poppy.* Rutherford, NJ: Fairleigh Dickinson University Press. 1984.

White, P. T. "The Poppy." *National Geographic* 167, no. 2 (1985): 143–89.

# Orchidaceae

The plants belonging to the family Orchidaceae represent a pinnacle of evolutionary success in the plant kingdom. Represented by approximately twenty-five thousand species, they are possibly the largest family of flowering plants on Earth. Although orchids are most diverse in the tropics, they are found on every continent except Antarctica and can be found as far north as Alaska and as far south as Tierra del Fuego. Perhaps the main reason that orchids are so successful is that they have developed close relationships with insect pollinators and fungi. Their life histories are extremely complex and intricately woven together across three kingdoms of life: Plantae, Animalia, and Fungi.

Unlike other plants, orchid seeds contain no storage food for their **dormant** embryos. In order for most orchid seeds to germinate, they must be infected by fungal **hyphae**. After infection takes place, the orchid is able to take nourishment from the fungus, but it is unclear whether the fungus gets any benefit in return. This life strategy enables orchids to survive in habitats with poor soils, such as bogs, or those that lack soil altogether. Many tropical orchids are **epiphytes**, and some live completely underground, lacking chlorophyll and depending on fungi for all their nutritional needs.

**dormant** inactive, not growing

**hyphae** the threadlike body mass of a fungus

**epiphytes** plants that grow on other plants

The elaborate and intricate flowers of the *Paphiopedilum* orchid hybrid.

**pistil** the female reproductive organ

**pheromone** a chemical released by one organism to influence the behavior of another

The close association of orchids with insects was carefully studied by Charles Darwin. Through evolution, orchids have reduced their reproductive organs to one anther and one **pistil**. Moreover, orchids have fused these two organs into a single structure, the column, and have amassed all of their pollen into a single unit called a pollinium. As a consequence, most orchid flowers have only one chance to pollinate another flower. This strategy may seem risky, but when successful it delivers enough pollen to produce as many as seventy-two thousand seeds. To ensure success, orchids have evolved intricate pollination mechanisms. Some of these include explosive shotguns and glue to attach the pollinium to insects, or floral traps that force bees to take pollen with them when they escape. One of the most fascinating strategies is seen in orchids that not only mimic female wasps in morphology but also produce fragrances similar to female wasp **pheromones**. These orchids manage to fool male wasps into copulating with their flowers, thereby effecting pollination.

Only one orchid species, *Vanilla planifolia*, is of significant agricultural value, as the source of natural vanilla flavoring. Cultivation and processing of this spice is a long, labor-intensive process involving pollinating each flower by hand, drying and fermenting the fruits, and extracting the aromatic vanillin flavoring with alcohol. For this reason, natural vanilla is extremely expensive.

*Vanilla*, however, is not the only orchid of economic value. An enormous industry exists for cut flowers, corsages, and cultivation of orchids by hobbyists. Ancient texts indicate that orchids have been cultivated in China since at least 550 B.C.E. Today, the American Orchid Society alone has more than thirty thousand members, all of whom share a fascination and appreciation of these breathtakingly beautiful flowers. Unfortunately, many orchid species are threatened with extinction because of habitat destruction and over-collecting in the wild. However, all orchids are protected under international treaties. SEE ALSO Epiphytes; Horticulture; Interactions, Plant-Insect; Monocots; Pollination Biology.

*Kenneth M. Cameron*

**Bibliography**

Cameron, K., et al. "A Phylogenetic Analysis of the Orchidaceae: Evidence from *rbc*L Nucleotide Sequences." *American Journal of Botany* 86 (1999): 208–24.

Darwin, Charles. *The Various Contrivances by Which Orchids Are Fertilised by Insects.* London: John Murray, 1888.

Dressler, Robert. *The Orchids: Natural History and Classification.* Cambridge, MA: Harvard University Press, 1990.

Luer, Carlyle. *The Native Orchids of the United States and Canada Excluding Florida.* New York: New York Botanical Garden Press, 1975.

# Ornamental Plants

Ornamental plants are grown for use by the green industry and public for purposes such as landscaping for sport, and conservation. The green industries include commercial plant nurseries, flower growers, parks, and roadside and landscape plant installation and maintenance.

The primary use for these plants is not for food, fuel, fiber, or medicine. However, ornamental plants contribute significantly to the quality of life by acting as barriers to wind, providing cooling shade, reducing or eliminating erosion, cleaning the air and water of pollutants including dust and chemicals, reducing noise pollution, and providing food and habitat for wildlife while making both suburban and urban areas more beautiful. Their economic and emotional impact is significant.

Ornamental plants include perennial deciduous and evergreen shade trees, conifers, and shrubs grown in horticultural production by the commercial nursery industry. Ornamental plants also include herbaceous and woody indoor and outdoor landscape broadleaf plants, grasses, and palms produced by traditional floricultural and nursery techniques within greenhouses, shaded structures, and other environments significantly modified to favor healthy, rapid, and profitable plant growth.

Ornamentals include annual, biennial, or perennial plants. They may be field grown in native or **amended soils** and then harvested and marketed

**amended soils** soils to which fertilizers or other growth aids have been added

A number of rhododendron species and hybrids grow in the maritime climate at Broughton-in-Furness, Cumbria, England.

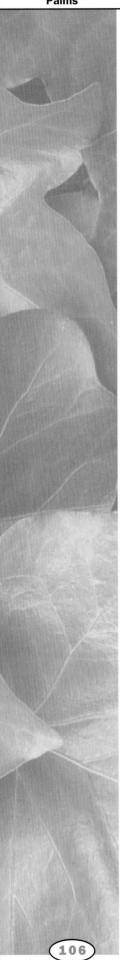

with native soils intact. This form of horticulture is generally referred to as "balled and burlapped" (B&B) plant production even though burlap may not be used in their harvest. They may also be harvested without soil and referred to as "bare root." The most popular method of growing ornamental plants is in soilless growing media within containers. Soilless growing media are most often natural organic materials such as peat or tree bark mixed with a mineral component such as sand or perlite.

Ornamental plants comprise one of the economically and environmentally most important segments of American horticulture. U.S. Department of Agriculture farm income estimates from the production of greenhouse and nursery crops were $11 billion in 1997. California, Florida, Texas, and North Carolina were the top states producing ornamental plants. SEE ALSO HORTICULTURE; HORTICULTURIST; LANDSCAPE ARCHITECT; ORCHIDACEAE; PROPAGATION.

*Richard E. Bir*

**vascular** related to transport of nutrients

# Palms

The palm family, Arecaceae, is primarily a tropical family of tree, shrub, and vining monocotyledonous plants, remarkable for the size that many attain without secondary growth (the ability to regenerate **vascular** tissue in their stems as is present in woody dicots). There are at least twenty-seven hundred species of palms, arranged in about two hundred genera. Palms have the largest leaves of any plant, and their leaves are either fan-shaped (palmate, like a hand) or featherlike (pinnate, with many individual leaflets arranged along a central axis). The stems may be solitary or clustering. In time, many palms form tall woody trunks with the leaves clustered in an aerial crown. Palm flowers are individually small, but are contained in often large flower stems (inflorescences) that appear from within the leafy crown or below the sheathing leaf bases. The majority of palms bear male

Coconut palms in Florida.

and female flowers on the same flower stem, but a number of species may produce separate male or female plants; relatively few palms produce bisexual flowers. A handful of palms grow for many years, flower and fruit once, then die. Most palms are pollinated by insects. Palm fruits range from pea-sized to nearly 18 inches wide. The fruit is either fibrous or fleshy, sometimes berrylike. Palms are important components of tropical rain forests worldwide, but many also occur in seasonally dry tropical **ecosystems**, including savannas. A few species are mangrovelike, growing in brackish estuaries near the sea. About twelve species are native to the southern United States, the majority in Florida. Coconut, African oil palm, and date palm are the three most important crop species, but many others are significant sources of food, fiber, wax, and construction material in tropical nations. SEE ALSO MONOCOTS; TREES.

**ecosystem** an ecological community together with its environment

*Alan W. Meerow*

**Bibliography**

Tomlinson, Philip B. *Structural Biology of Palms.* Oxford: Clarendon Press, 1990.

Uhl, Natalie, and John Dransfield. *Genera Palamarum.* International Palm Society, 1987.

# Palynology

Palynology is the study of plant pollen, spores, and certain microscopic planktonic organisms (collectively termed palynomorphs) in both living and fossil form. Botanists use living pollen and spores (actuopalynology) in the study of plant relationships and evolution, while geologists may use fossil pollen and spores (paleopalynology) to study past environments, **stratigraphy,** historical geology, and paleontology.

**stratigraphy** the analysis of strata (layered rock)

The oil industry is credited with demonstrating the usefulness of palynomorphs in the study of stratigraphic sequences of rocks and the potential for oil and gas exploration. Because palynomorphs are resistant to decomposition and are produced in great abundance, their recovery from rocks and sediments via special and careful chemical treatments is possible and provides scientists with information needed to describe plant life of past ages. By describing the sequence of selected palynomorphs through the rock layers of Earth, stratigraphers (scientists who study the rock layers of Earth) are able to correlate rocks of the same age and may therefore locate and correlate layers that contain oil or natural gas.

Palynomorphs found in the gut of early humans, and those found with **artifacts** found at their grave sites have been used to understand the diets and hunting or farming practices of these early people. For instance, the pollen and spores found in the feces of humans living seven thousand years ago allowed scientists to describe the changes in the diets through several generations of native people in northern Chile.

**artifacts** pots, tools, or other cultural objects

Melissopalynology is the study of pollen in honey, with the purpose of identifying the source plants used by bees in the production of honey. This is important to honey producers because honey produced by pollen and nectar from certain plants as mesquite, buckwheat, or citrus trees demand a higher price on the market than that produced by other plant sources. Some plants

Micrograph of pollen grains.

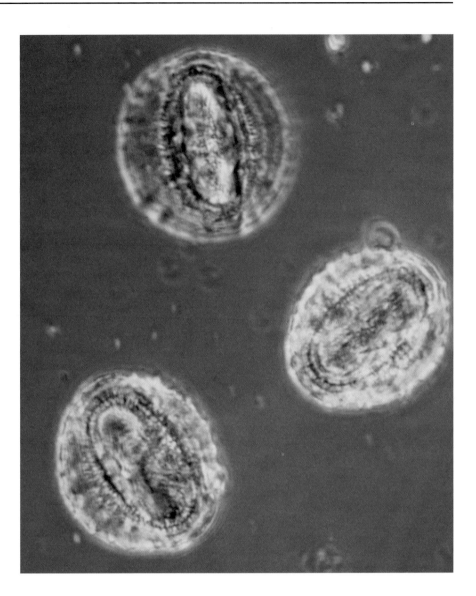

may produce nectar and pollen that is harmful to human health. A careful examination of the pollen types found in honey may identify these toxic plants, and the honey produced may be kept out of the commercial market.

Palynology is a useful tool in many applications, including a survey of atmospheric pollen and spore production and dispersal (aerobiology), in the study of human allergies, the archaeological excavation of shipwrecks, and detailed analysis of animal diets. Entomopalynology is the study of pollen found on the body or in the gut of insects. It is useful for determining insect feeding and migratory habits, especially as it involves economically important insects (e.g., the boll weevil). Forensic palynology, or the use of pollen analysis in the solving of crimes, is used by law enforcement agencies around the world. SEE ALSO DENDROCHRONOLOGY; FORENSIC BOTANY; POLLINATION BIOLOGY.

*David M. Jarzen*

**Bibliography**

Bryant, V. M., Jr., and S. A. Hall. "Archaeological Palynology in the United States: A Critique." *American Antiquity* 58 (1993): 416–21.

Hoen, P. "Glossary of Pollen and Spore Terminology." [Online] 1999. Available at http://www.biol.ruu.nl/~palaeo/glossary/glos-tin.htm.

Jarzen, D. M., and D. J. Nichols. "Pollen." In *Palynology: Principles and Applications*, Vol. 1, eds. J. Jansonius and D. C. McGregor. American Association of Stratigraphic Palynologists Foundation, 1996.

Traverse, Alfred. *Paleopalynology*. Boston: Unwin Hyman, 1988.

# Paper

Paper is a flexible web or mat of pulp fibers of plant (usually wood) origin. It is widely used for printing, packaging, and sanitary applications and also has a wide variety of specialized uses. Paper is formed from a dilute aqueous slurry of pulp fibers, fillers, and additives. Fillers are **inert** materials such as calcium carbonate, clay, and titanium dioxide that make printing papers whiter and increase opacity (the ability to read print on one side of the paper without print on the other side of the paper showing through). Additives are materials used to improve the papermaking process and modify the final product. Additives include dyes, strength agents, and sizing agents (used to make paper resistant to water penetration).

**inert** incapable of reaction

Pulp is obtained by mechanical or chemical means or by a combination of the two. The two most common pulping methods are thermomechanical pulping and kraft chemical pulping. Thermomechanical pulp accounts for about 20 percent of pulp production in North America. The process consists of introducing wood chips between two large metal discs (on the order of 2 meters in diameter) that have raised bars on their surfaces and that rotate in opposite directions. The discs are in a pressurized refiner that operates at a temperature of 130°C. The combination of mechanical action and steam forms a wood pulp. This wood pulp retains the original lignin of the wood so the paper made from it is not very strong and yellows with age. Mechanical pulp is the chief component of newsprint.

Kraft pulp is formed by cooking wood chips in a highly alkaline aqueous solution at 170°C. It accounts for about 70 percent of pulp production in North America. In this process most of the lignin is removed. The brown pulp is used in sack paper and for the production of corrugated boxes. The bleached pulp is used in white printing papers and tissue papers.

Wood fiber accounts for about 98 percent of pulp production in North America, while globally it accounts for about 92 percent of pulp production. About two-thirds of the wood comes from softwoods because their high fiber length (3 to 5 millimeters) produces strong paper. The short fibers of hardwood species (approximately 1 millimeter) are used with softwood fibers in printing papers to achieve high strength and surface smoothness. Major nonwood sources of fiber, in decreasing levels of global production, include straw (especially wheat), sugarcane residue, bamboo, reeds, and cotton linters. Hemp fibers can also be used, but their fibers are so long that they must be cut in order to make paper from them.

The paper machine continuously forms, drains water, presses, and dries the web of paper fibers, using a single continuously moving plastic screen. The pulp slurry that is applied to the wire consists of 3 to 6 kilograms of dry fiber per 1,000 kilograms of water. Water is then removed by gravity, vacuum, pressing rolls, and, finally, heat in the drier section of the machine.

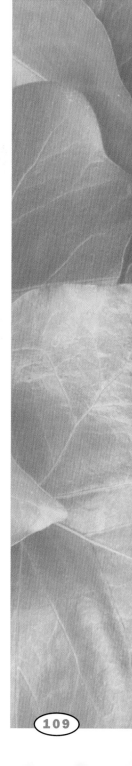

At a paper mill, wet pulp is spread onto a moving belt from where the water is drained away.

Twin wire machines form the web between two plastic screens, and cylinder machines form several layers of paper that are combined to form heavyweight boards. Paper is converted to a wide variety of products in operations that may include trimming, rewinding onto smaller rolls, cutting into sheets, coating, printing, and box making. SEE ALSO ECONOMIC IMPORTANCE OF PLANTS; FIBER AND FIBER PRODUCTS; FORESTRY; TREES; WOOD PRODUCTS.

*Christopher J. Biermann*

### Bibliography

Biermann, Christopher J. *Handbook of Pulping and Papermaking,* 2nd ed. New York: Academic Press, 1996.

Smook, Gary. *Handbook for Pulp and Paper Technologists,* 2nd ed. Atlanta: Tappi Press, 1992.

## Parasitic Plants

The parasitic mode of existence is frequently encountered among all life forms, including flowering plants. In this discussion a plant will be considered parasitic only if it produces a haustorium, the modified root that forms the **morphological** and physiological link to another plant (the host). Some plants, such as the ghostly white Indian Pipe (*Monotropa*) are often called parasites, but are more properly termed mycotrophs (Greek *mykes,* meaning "fungus," and *trophos,* meaning "feeder"). Mycotrophs, which occur in many plant families, lack chlorophyll and are nonphotosynthetic, and their

**morphology** shape and form

## PARASITIC PLANT FAMILIES

| Family | Common Name | Number of Genera (approximate) | Number of Species (approximate) | Parasitism Type | Genera Example |
|---|---|---|---|---|---|
| Balanophoraceae* | Balanophora family | 18 | 45 | Root, holoparasite | Balanophora, Corynaea, Cynomorium, Thonningia |
| Cuscutaceae† | Dodder family | 1 | 160 | Stem, hemiparasite and holoparasite | Cuscuta |
| Hydnoraceae | Hydnora family | 2 | 15 | Root, holoparasite | Hydnora, Prosopanche |
| Krameriaceae | Krameria family | 1 | 17 | Root, hemiparasite | Krameria |
| Lauraceae | Laurel family | 1 | 20 | Stem, hemiparasite | Cassytha |
| Lennoaceae | Lennoa family | 2 | 5 | Root, holoparasite | Lennoa, Pholisma |
| Santalales | Sandalwood order | | | | |
| Loranthaceae | Showy mistletoe family | 74 | 700 | Stem and root, hemiparasite | Amyema, Phthirusa, Psittacanthus, Tapinanthus |
| Misodendraceae | Feathery mistletoe family | 1 | 8 | Stem, hemiparasite | Misodendrum |
| Olacaceae | Olax family | 29 | 193 | Root, hemiparasite | Schoepfia, Ximenia |
| Opiliaceae | Opilia family | 10 | 32 | Root, hemiparasite | Agonandra, Opilia |
| Santalaceae‡ | Sandalwood family | 40 | 490 | Root, hemiparasite | Comandra, Santalum, Thesium |
| Viscaceae | Christmas mistletoe family | 7 | 350 | Stem, hemiparasite | Arceuthobium, Phoradendron, Viscum |
| Rafflesiaceae§ | Rafflesia family | 8 | 50 | Stem and root, holoparasite | Cytinus, Rafflesia |
| Scrophulariaceae‖ | Figwort family | 78 | 1940 | Root, hemiparasite and holoparasite | Agalinis, Buchnera, Castilleja, Epifagus, Euphrasia, Pedicularis, Orobanche, Rhinanthus, Striga |

\* Including Cynomoriaceae.
† Sometimes placed in Convolvulaceae (morning glory family).
‡ Including Eremolepidaceae.
§ Including Apodanthaceae, Cytinaceae, and Mitrastemonaceae.
‖ Including Orobanchaceae.

roots are associated with mycorrhizal fungi, which surround tree roots. Bromeliads such as Spanish moss (*Tillandsia*) and some orchids are also sometimes mistaken for parasites, but these plants are actually epiphytes (Greek *epi*, meaning "upon," and *phyton*, meaning "plant"). Epiphytes use the other plant simply as a support and do not derive water or nutrients directly from their tissues. In true parasitic plants, the haustorium physically penetrates the host stem or root thus connecting to the water-conducting and/or sugar-conducting tissues (xylem and phloem, respectively).

The degree of nutritional dependence on the host varies widely among parasitic plants. Some parasites are photosynthetic and can therefore produce their own food from sunlight as is done by other green plants. Such hemiparasites include root parasites such as Indian paintbrush (*Castilleja*, Scrophulariaceae) and stem parasites such as mistletoes (Loranthaceae, Viscaceae; see accompanying table). Some root hemiparasites can actually grow to maturity in the absence of a host plant, and hence are termed **facultative** hemiparasites. Others, such as the mistletoes, must attach to a host in order to complete their life cycle and are thus referred to as **obligate** hemiparasites. Hemiparasites can be considered xylem parasites in that they derive only water and dissolved minerals from their hosts. In contrast, holoparasites, being nonphotosynthetic, must also obtain the carbohydrates found in host phloem.

Parasitism has evolved in **angiosperms** at least nine independent times, but, interestingly, not in monocots (grasses, palms, lilies, etc.). There exists more than 270 genera and 4,000 species of parasitic plants worldwide. Holoparasitism has evolved at least six times independently. In two families

**facultative** capable of but not obligated to

**obligate** required, without another option

**angiosperm** a flowering plant

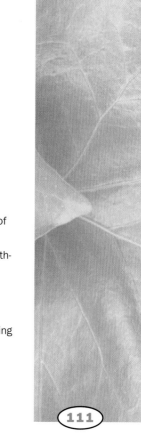

Dodder tendrils choking a pickleweed plant.

**chloroplast** the photosynthetic organelle of plants and algae

**genome** the genetic material of an organism

**pathogen** disease-causing organism

**mycelium** the vegetative body of a fungus, made up of threadlike hyphae

(Cuscutaceae and Scrophulariaceae) both hemi- and holoparasites can be found. Members of these families represent important organisms for studying the genetic changes that occur when photosynthesis is lost. For example, a root parasite of beech trees (*Fagus*) found in Eastern North America is called beechdrops (*Epifagus*). The complete deoxyribonucleic acid (DNA) sequence of the beechdrops **chloroplast genome** has been obtained and is less than half the size of a typical photosynthetic plant, mainly owing to the loss of genes specifically involved in photosynthesis.

Other members of Scrophulariaceae represent some of the most economically damaging **pathogens** of crop plants in Africa, the Middle East, and Asia. Witchweed (*Striga*) is a devastating pest on maize (corn), sorghum, and other grasses, while broomrape (*Orobanche*) parasitizes sunflowers, tomatoes, and beans. Similarly, the spaghetti-like dodder (*Cuscuta*) can become a problem weed on crops such as alfalfa. These parasites are difficult to eradicate because they produce thousands of tiny, dustlike seeds that persist in the soil and are easily moved from site to site. In North America, the genus *Arceuthobium* (dwarf mistletoe) destroys commercially important trees in the pine family (Douglas-fir, hemlock, pine, etc.). Unlike other members of its family (Viscaceae) whose seeds are bird-dispersed, dwarf mistletoes have evolved a fruit that explosively expels the sticky seed, which can reach a velocity of 27 meters per second and can travel up to 16 meters.

Although some parasitic plants are weeds, the vast majority are benign and often go unnoticed by the casual observer. Some of the most spectacularly beautiful flowers that exist in nature can be found in the showy mistletoe family (Loranthaceae). Many species produce long, tubular red flowers that are bird-pollinated. Indeed, the mistletoe bird (*Dicaeum*) effects pollination when feeding upon the nectar and aids in seed dispersal when feeding on the fruits, a good example of coevolution.

Certainly, no treatment of parasitic plants would be complete without mention of *Rafflesia*, the queen of the parasites. This holoparasite has no stems, leaves, or roots but exists within the host vine (*Tetrastigma*, Vitaceae) as a fungal-like **mycelium** until flowering. At that time, the flower emerges from the host as a small, golf-ball sized bud and continues to grow until it is the size of a cabbage. Eventually it opens as a flower that may exceed 1 meter in diameter—the largest flower in the world. The spotted red flower has five leathery petals surrounding a deep cup that exudes a stench like that of rotting flesh, thus attracting flies (the pollinators). All species of *Rafflesia* are endangered owing to habitat loss in Malaysia, Indonesia, and the Philippines. SEE ALSO ENDANGERED SPECIES; EPIPHYTES; FUNGI; INTERACTIONS, PLANT-PLANT; MYCORRHIZAE; RECORD-HOLDING PLANTS.

*Daniel L. Nickrent*

**Bibliography**

Calder, Malcolm, and Peter Bernhardt. *The Biology of Mistletoes.* New York: Academic Press, 1983.

*Parasitic Plant Connection.* [Online] Available at http://www.science.siu.edu/parasitic-plants/index.html

Kuijt, Job. *The Biology of Parasitic Flowering Plants.* Berkeley, CA: University of California Press, 1969.

Press, Malcolm C., and Jonathan D. Graves. *Parasitic Plants.* London: Chapman & Hall, 1995.

# Pathogens

A pathogen is an agent that causes disease. The agent usually is a microorganism, such as a fungus, bacterium, or virus. The most numerous and prominent pathogens of plants are the fungi, but many plant diseases are also caused by bacteria and viruses. Although the diseases caused by phytoplasmas are similar to those caused by viruses, these pathogens are actually a kind of bacterium. A few diseases are caused by viroids, agents that are similar to but are even simpler than viruses. Other pathogens include nematodes (roundworms), which attack many types of plants, and 2,500 species of **angiosperms** that live parasitically on other plants. Relatively few of the angiosperms are economically important pathogens.

**angiosperm** a flowering plant

A pathogen usually initiates disease by parasitizing a host, that is, taking its organic nutrients. However, in a few cases the host actually benefits by the presence of the parasite. Mycorrhizal fungi attack roots and live parasitically in the roots. But infected roots are much more effective than nonmycorrhizal roots in obtaining mineral nutrients, especially phosphorus. Where the level of phosphorus in the soil is low, the plants with mycorrhizal roots are much healthier. Since the parasite actually benefits the plant, it does not cause disease and is not considered a pathogen.

## Types of Pathogens

**Fungi.** Like all **eukaryotic** organisms, fungal cells have nuclei, a well-defined **endoplasmic reticulum** with ribosomes, and cell **organelles** such as mitochondria. The fungal body consists of **filamentous** strands called **hyphae** that collectively make up a mycelium. Sometimes the hyphae become compressed, forming a tissue such as that found in a mushroom fruiting body.

**eukaryotic** a cell with a nucleus (*eu* means "true" and *karyo* means "nucleus"); includes protists, plants, animals, and fungi

**endoplasmic reticulum** membrane network inside a cell

**organelle** a membrane-bound structure within a cell

**filamentous** thin and long

**hyphae** the threadlike body mass of a fungus

Fungi are classified in the kingdom Fungi, separate from all other organisms. There are many different groups within the kingdom, and most groups have prominent plant pathogens. Of particular note are the Ascomycetes, Fungi Imperfecti, and some of the Basidiomycetes. Ascomycetes produce sexual spores called ascospores that are vital in survival between hosts. They also produce asexual spores called conidia that play a major role in the spread of disease during the growing season. The Fungi Imperfecti usually are ascomycetes that have lost the ascospore (sexual) stage. Sometimes they produce ascospores but have been classified according to the conidial stage because of its importance in the disease cycle. It is valid to classify a fungus based either on its perfect (sexual) state or on its imperfect (asexual) state.

The Basidiomycetes are extremely common in nature, but only the rusts and smuts are notable plant pathogens. While most basidiomycetes produce basidiospores in a fruiting body such as a mushroom, in rusts and smuts the basidiospores are produced from a specialized, overwintering spore called a teliospore. The rust fungi are especially common and usually have a complex sexual cycle with four spore stages and two different hosts required for completion of the sexual cycle. Rusts also produce an asexual spore called a uredospore that is responsible for spread of disease during the growing season.

A fourth group of fungi, the Oomycetes, has long been recognized to be very different from other fungi in both morphology and chemistry. They

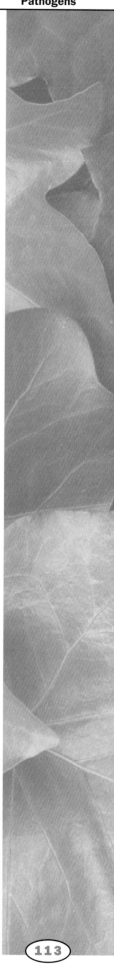

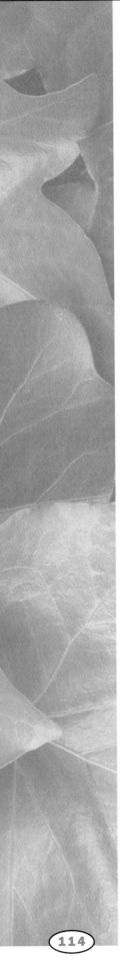

**motile** capable of movement

**flagella** threadlike extension of the cell membrane, used for movement

**macromolecules** a large molecule such as a protein, fat, nucleic acid, or carbohydrate

produce overwintering sexual spores called oospores and asexual **motile** spores (zoospores) that spread disease during the season. The current trend is to place these fungi in a kingdom other than Fungi. The Oomycetes contain the *Pythium* and *Phytophthora* species and the downy mildews, plant pathogens that are of worldwide importance. Regardless of classification, these pathogens will continue to be treated much the same as true fungi by those who work with plant diseases.

The potato late blight disease caused by *Phytophthora infestans* that resulted in famine in Ireland in 1845 and 1846 first brought the attention of the world to plant diseases. At that time many thought that fungi arose spontaneously in diseased plants and did not themselves cause disease. However, publications by the German scientist Anton de Bary beginning in 1853 convincingly demonstrated the prominent role fungi play as plant pathogens.

**Bacteria.** The plant pathogenic bacteria are rod-shaped eubacteria. They are prokaryotes, having a chromosome but no nucleus. The cytoplasm has ribosomes but no endoplasmic reticulum and no organelles. The cells have a cell wall and may or may not have **flagella**.

The first bacterium shown to cause a plant disease, fire blight of pome fruits, was reported by Thomas Burrill in Illinois in 1878. However, it was the research by Erwin F. Smith from 1890 to 1915 that demonstrated the importance of these agents as plant pathogens.

**Viruses.** Viruses are nucleoprotein **macromolecules**. They contain genetic information, either ribonucleic acid (RNA) or deoxyribonucleic acid (DNA), which is covered by protein subunits. Plant pathogenic viruses usually contain RNA rather than DNA. Since viruses are not cellular organisms, they express lifelike characteristics only when within a susceptible host cell. Additionally, since they are not cellular, they do not obtain organic nutrients directly from the host. Instead, the RNA or DNA of the virus directs the metabolic machinery of the host cell to use organic nutrients present in the cell. Various chemical reactions lead to symptom expression as well as production of new virus particles.

## DISTINGUISHING CHARACTERISTICS OF VARIOUS PATHOGENS

| Character | Fungi | Bacteria | Viruses | Phytoplasmas | Nematodes |
|---|---|---|---|---|---|
| **Body type** | Hyphae make up a mycelium (eukaryotic) | Cells with cell walls (prokaryotic) | Nucleoprotein (not cellular) | Cells with no cell walls (prokaryotic) | Worms with organ systems, males and females |
| **Inoculum** | Overwinter by ascospores, teliospores, and oospores; spread of disease by conidia, zoospores, uredospores | Cells | Virus particles | Cells | Larvae |
| **Dissemination** | Wind and splashing rain | Splashing rain | Transmission by insects, mechanically, or planting stock | Transmission by insects | Soil movement, running soil water |
| **Penetration** | Direct by appressorium and penetration peg; some through wounds or natural openings | Through natural openings (stomata) or wounds | Through wounds (insects) or planting stock | Through wounds (insects) | Direct with stylet mouthpart |
| **Host–parasite relation** | Inter- and intracellular; intercellular with haustoria | Intercellular | Intracellular in parenchyma or phloem tissue | Intracellular in phloem tissue | Intercellular with stylet inserted in host cells |

Tobacco mosaic disease was shown in the 1890s to be caused by a submicroscopic infectious agent later determined to be a virus, now called tobacco mosaic virus.

**Viroids.** A viroid is a small, infectious piece of RNA. Unlike a virus, it has no protein, but it behaves as a plant parasite much the same as a virus. In 1967, Theodor Diener and William Raymer reported on the basic characteristics of the agent causing spindle tuber of potato, and in 1971 Diener named these agents "viroids." About twenty diseases have been shown to be caused by this type of pathogen.

**Phytoplasmas.** Phytoplasmas are prokaryotic cellular organisms. They represent a separate group of bacteria, having no cell wall or flagella. Much like viruses, they are transmitted by insects and cause phloem necrosis-type diseases. These diseases, having yellows witches'-broom-type symptoms, were thought to be caused by viruses until 1967 when Yoji Doi and others in Japan showed that the disease-inducing agents are mycoplasma-like organisms. Some of these pathogens, especially the aster yellows phytoplasma, have a wide host range and attack plants in many families.

For many years these plant pathogens were identified as mycoplasma-like organisms, but they now are called phytoplasmas. Although viruses and phytoplasmas are very different biological agents, similarities in transmission and in host-parasite interactions and symptoms make it easy to understand why researchers before 1967 thought all these diseases were caused by viruses.

**Nematodes.** Plant pathogenic nematodes (roundworms) are usually found in soil. These plant pathogens have a stylet (spearlike) mouthpart that is used to penetrate and feed on roots. Although root knot nematode diseases have been well known since the 1850s, it was not until the period between

1920 and 1940 that research by many investigators showed the full significance of these agents as plant pathogens.

**Angiosperms.** Like typical flowering plants, parasitic angiosperms have stems, leaves, flowers, and seeds. They do not have true roots but produce a structure that penetrates stems and unites with the **vascular** system of the host. The leaves may or may not have **chloroplasts**, but these pathogens are completely dependent on the host for water and mineral nutrients. Dwarf mistletoe is a prominent pathogen of coniferous forest trees, and the dodders attack many crops worldwide. Leafy mistletoe, known as a popular household Christmas decoration, attacks hardwood trees but is seldom a leading pathogen.

**vascular** related to transport of nutrients

**chloroplast** the photosynthetic organelle of plants and algae

**Insects.** Insects do not merely feed on plants; they often produce **toxins** and growth substances that cause diseaselike symptoms. Some of the biological interactions are similar to those that occur with nematodes. However, there are hundreds of thousands, perhaps millions, of insect species, and their life cycles and behavior may be very complex. Although the phenomenon may be much the same, insect problems are worked on by experts (entomologists), and the insects usually are not thought of as pathogens. They are, however, major **vectors** of diseases, including those caused by viruses and phytoplasmas and some fungi and bacteria.

**toxin** a poisonous substance

**vector** carrier of disease

## How Pathogens Cause Disease

Pathogens **impede** normal growth of plants in many ways. They attack and kill seeds and seedlings (damping off diseases). They invade and kill roots, preventing absorption of water and mineral nutrients (root rots). They invade and plug xylem tissue, preventing movement of water and minerals to leaves and growing points (vascular wilts). They kill leaves, preventing photosynthesis and production of carbohydrates (leaf spots and blights, downy mildews, powdery mildews, and rusts). The phloem tissue may be invaded and killed, preventing translocation of the carbohydrate produced in photosynthesis to other parts of the plant (phloem necrosis). After the crop has been produced, pathogens may rot fruits and vegetables in transit or storage or in the marketplace (fruit and vegetable rots). A few pathogens cause disease by inducing abnormal growth, thus stunting normal growth (galls).

**impede** slow down or inhibit

**Damping Off.** Many fungi that live in the soil invade and kill seeds or seedlings. This is called damping off. Beyond the seedling stage, a plant is no longer susceptible to damping off. There is no resistance but seed treatments with fungicides usually provide effective control.

**Root Rots.** Roots may be rotted by many fungi living in the soil. The resulting lack of water and mineral nutrients stunts growth and causes a general yellowing due to lack of chlorophyll. There usually is little resistance, and chemical controls are ineffective. **Crop rotation** may hold crop losses to acceptable levels.

**crop rotation** alternating crops from year to year in a particular field

**Vascular Wilts.** Vascular wilts, diseases of the xylem tissue, are caused by fungi and bacteria. Fungi causing this disease are soilborne. They infect roots and grow through the plant, colonizing the xylem. Bacteria that cause vascular wilts are transmitted by insects or penetrate leaves through **stomatal** openings. They invade xylem tissue through pits in the xylem vessel

**stomata** openings between guard cells on the underside of leaves that allow gas exchange

Cedar-apple rust gall on a cedar tree

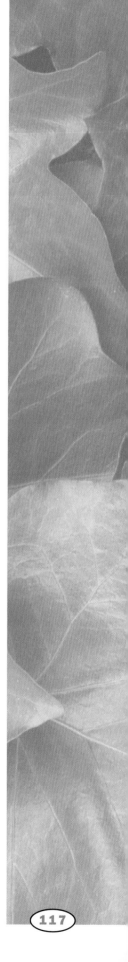

cell walls and become **systemic** in the plant. Vascular wilts caused by both fungi and bacteria reduce movement of water and mineral nutrients to stems and leaves, resulting in symptoms of wilting and yellowing. There is no chemical control but genetic resistance may be helpful. Crop rotation is important in combating vascular wilts.

**systemic** spread throughout the plant

**Leaf Diseases.** Many fungi and bacteria attack leaves, causing leaf spots and blights. The downy and powdery mildews also cover the leaves with fungal structures further reducing photosynthesis. Both of the mildews and the rusts eventually kill leaf tissue, but since all three are **obligate parasites,** they no longer can obtain nutrients after the leaves are dead. Resistance to these fungal diseases often is available, and chemical controls usually are effective. Most of the fungicides applied to crops are used to control leaf diseases. There are fewer leaf diseases caused by bacteria, and this is fortunate because genetic resistance is seldom available and chemical controls are usually ineffective.

**obligate parasite** without a free-living stage in the life cycle

**Phloem Necrosis.** Viruses and phytoplasmas are transmitted by insect vectors that feed on leaves. The vectors often feed on the phloem tissue, directly depositing the pathogen in the tissue. These agents then become systemic in the phloem tissue, killing the phloem cells (necrosis) and preventing translocation of organic nutrients throughout the plant. Typical symptoms are stunting, yellowing, mosaic (different shades of green and yellow), and mottling (blotches of different colors). There is no chemical control and often little resistance. Cultural practices such as use of healthy planting stock often limit disease incidence.

**Fruit and Vegetable Rots.** Postharvest rots by fungi and bacteria often cause serious losses. Chemical treatments help control these diseases, but more significant prevention tactics include sanitation and use of proper storage conditions, particularly reduced temperature and increased air circulation.

**Galls.** Abnormal growth is an extremely common phenomenon and can be caused by many biological agents. The most notable abnormal growth diseases of crops are crown gall, caused by the bacterium *Agrobacterium,* club

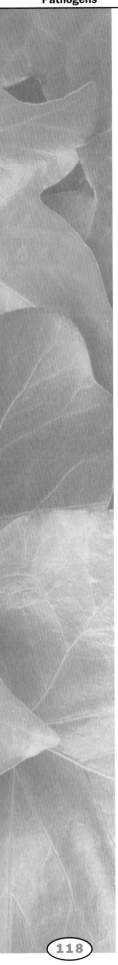

root of crucifers caused by the fungus *Plasmodiophora brassicae*, and root knot caused by the nematode *Meloidogyne*. Abnormal growth results from action of the same kinds of growth substances that are responsible for normal growth: **auxins**, cytokinins, and gibberellins.

**auxin** a plant hormone

## Recognition and Penetration

Relatively little is known of the biochemistry of recognition of a susceptible host by a pathogen. Fungal and bacterial inoculum (infectious material) is spread at random to both hosts and nonhosts. **Mucilagenous** substances on the surface of the inoculum facilitates adherence to host surfaces. Some host chemicals that serve as signals leading to penetration are known, and some pathogen chemicals that serve as elicitors in disease development have been identified. In some cases penetration occurs but growth in the host is limited, and disease does not develop. Either the agent does not produce the elicitors that lead to infection, or the host produces chemicals that prevent infection. Since viruses and phytoplasmas are brought to hosts by insect vectors, disease may result from an adaptive sequence in which the vector feeds preferentially on the hosts that are susceptible to the pathogen.

**mucilagenous** sticky or gummy

Fungi usually penetrate leaves by production of a specialized structure called an appressorium. As a fungal hypha grows over the surface of a leaf, the hyphal tip mounds up and becomes cemented to the leaf, forming an appressorium. A specialized hypha, called a penetration peg, grows from the appressorium and penetrates the leaf, largely by mechanical pressure. The penetration peg also may produce cutinase and cellulose **enzymes** that soften the tissue. The leaf **epidermis** is covered by a **cuticle** made primarily of a waxy substance called cutin, and the epidermal cell walls have a high cellulose content. Sometimes a fungus penetrates through a stoma, a hole in the lower epidermis of the leaf formed by two guard cells. Even when a fungus penetrates through a stoma, an appressorium is usually produced. Of course, the penetration peg meets no resistance.

**enzyme** a protein that controls a reaction in a cell

**epidermis** outer layer of cells

**cuticle** the waxy outer coating of a leaf or other structure, providing protection against predators, infection, and water loss

Inside the leaf, fungal hyphae grow between cells (intercellular) and through cells (intracellular) to obtain nutrients. When the leaf dies, the fungus is able to obtain nutrients from the dead cells. The fungi that are obligate parasites (downy mildews, powdery mildews, and rusts) grow intercellularly and produce haustoria (specialized hyphal structures) that penetrate the host cells. The haustoria produce enzymes and obtain nutrients from the host cells. Eventually the cells die, and these fungi are no longer able to obtain nutrients.

Bacteria that attack leaves are disseminated in splashing rain and penetrate through stomata or wounds. The bacteria are found between cells in the host and never penetrate the living cells. Nutrients leaking from the host cells provide sufficient food for the bacteria. After the death of leaves, the bacteria continue to obtain nutrients from the dead cells.

**parenchyma** one of three plant cell types

**propagate** to create more of through sexual or asexual reproduction

Viruses and phytoplasmas are usually transmitted by insects. Feeding by the insects deposits these agents into the phloem or **parenchyma** tissues. Some viruses can be transmitted by workers in the field. Handling plants causes small wounds and transmits small amounts of contaminated sap. Many viruses attack crops that are **propagated** vegetatively (by bulbs, corms, budding, etc.), and the diseases are transmitted through use of infected planting stock. Both viruses and phytoplasmas are obligate parasites and cannot obtain nutrients from tissues that have died.

Nematodes penetrate roots mechanically by use of the stylet mouth part. Once inside they insert the stylet into parenchyma cells of the cortex and obtain nutrients. Some nematodes have a long stylet and feed on plant roots while the body is outside the root. Plant pathogenic nematodes are all obligate parasites, capable of obtaining nutrients only from living host cells.

## Role of Enzymes, Toxins, and Phytoalexins

Because cutin and cellulose provide tough, protective barriers for the plant, cutinase and cellulase enzymes are necessary to the penetration of plant hosts by pathogenic fungi. They break down the cutin in the cuticle and the cellulose in the primary cell wall. Hydrolytic (digestive) enzymes also play important roles in pathogenesis. The organic food in the host is usually in the form of complex carbohydrates, fats, and proteins. To be absorbed by pathogens, they must be broken down to their simpler units: simple sugars, fatty acids, glycerol, and amino acids. Common digestive enzymes—amylases, cellulases, lipases, and proteases—produced by pathogens break down these complex foods.

The middle lamella, the area between cells in parenchyma tissue, has a high pectin content. For many diseases pathogenesis involves production of pectolytic enzymes that break down pectin. This causes dissolution and eventually death of the cells. Damping off, root rots, vascular wilts, and fruit and vegetable rots are caused by pathogens that produce large amounts of pectolytic enzymes.

Several toxins have been shown to be produced by plant pathogenic fungi and bacteria. Most of them are nonhost-specific toxins. They usually kill cells but may act on the **permeability** of the cytoplasmic membrane. Although they are involved in pathogenesis, in some cases strains of the pathogen that are unable to produce the toxin still can cause disease. In a few cases the toxin is host-specific and only affects that host at normal toxin concentrations.

**permeability** the property of being permeable, or open to the passage of other substances

Most plants are resistant to infection because of the presence of preexisting chemicals. However, there are many cases where chemicals that ward off infection are produced by the host only after the pathogen is present. These chemicals are called phytoalexins. This is a rather common phenomenon, with about three hundred chemicals from thirty different families of plants having been identified as phytoalexins. SEE ALSO AGRICULTURE, MODERN; CHESTNUT BLIGHT; DEFENSES, CHEMICAL; DUTCH ELM DISEASE; EUBACTERIA; FUNGI; HERBICIDES; HORMONES; INTERACTION, PLANT-FUNGAL; POTATO BLIGHT.

*Ira W. Deep*

### Bibliography

Agrios, George N. *Plant Pathology*, 4th ed. New York: San Diego, CA: Academic Press, 1997.

Bove, Joseph M. "Wall-less Prokaryotes of Plants." *Annual Review of Phytopathology* 22 (1984): 361–96.

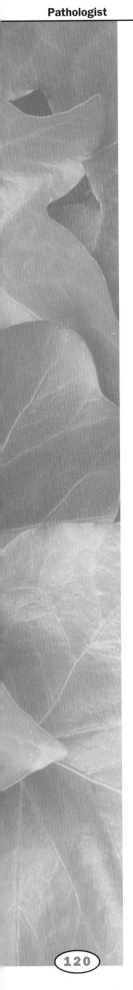

Doi, Yoji, et al. "Mycoplasma- or PLT Group-like Microorganisms Found in the Phloem Elements of Plants Infected with Mulberry Dwarf, Potato Witches'-Broom, Aster Yellows, or Paulownia Witches'-Broom." *Annual Phytopathological Society of Japan* 33 (1967): 259–66.

Diener, Theodor O. "The Viroid—A Subviral Pathogen." *American Scientist* 71 (1983): 481–89.

Schumann, Gail L. *Plant Diseases: Their Biology and Social Impact.* St. Paul, MN: American Phytopathological Society Press, 1991.

# Pathologist

Plant pathologists are scientists who work with plant diseases. Trained primarily as biologists, they have expertise both in plant science and microbiology. Whereas in medicine the pathologist is a specialist who analyzes diseased tissues, the plant pathologist is concerned with all aspects of plant disease. All plants are subject to disease, and the work of plant pathologists is central to the management of diseases.

Many plant pathologists may be compared to the general practitioner in medicine, but there are many areas of specialization that may involve the kind of crop or pathogen. Most plant pathologists who work with field crops or vegetables have rather general training in plant pathology, but virologists and nematologists require specialized training because these agents are very different from all other pathogens. Forest pathologists also need unique training, both because the forest is a very different crop and because the common pathogens are different from those that attack agricultural crops. Some plant pathologists are biochemists or molecular biologists who study diseased plants or pathogens. Epidemiologists study the spread of disease in populations and they must be well grounded in mathematics and statistics.

**physiology** the biochemical processes carried out by an organism

Most jobs taken by plant pathologists require a doctorate degree, but some directors of diagnostic labs have a master's degree. Plant pathologists must be well versed in plant **physiology** and genetics and must have knowl-

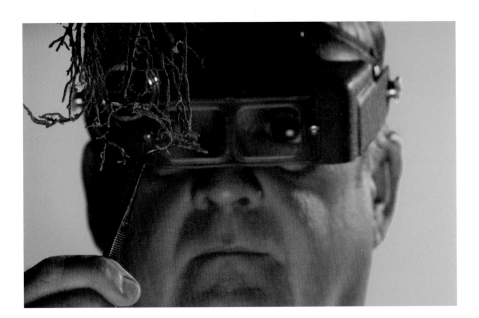

A U.S. Department of Agriculture scientist uses tweezers and magnifying goggles to examine citrus roots for fungus.

edge of all disease-causing agents. The study of the fungi is particularly important since these are the most numerous and troublesome pathogens of plants. Courses in plant pathology provide background in disease initiation and progress for each kind of pathogen. This knowledge is used when designing programs for management of disease.

Plant pathologists are employed by universities, federal and state governments, and a wide range of industries. All **land-grant universities** have plant pathologists who are responsible for resident instruction, research, and extension education. Plant pathologists conduct research at state agricultural experiment stations and the U.S. Department of Agriculture, and are employed by federal and state agencies that enforce regulations regarding pesticide use and food safety. Chemical companies employ plant pathologists for production of more effective and safer pesticides, and seed companies use their expertise to produce disease resistant varieties. Many plant pathologists work as consultants or provide service in diagnostic labs.

The complexity of two interacting living systems—the plant and the pathogen—makes plant pathology a very challenging field. An appealing feature of employment as a plant pathologist is the opportunity for work in a wide range of environments. Teaching may occur on the farm as well as in the classroom, and research may be conducted in the field or greenhouse as well as in the laboratory. Disease **specimens** may be diagnosed in the lab, but disease progress must be evaluated in the field. Plant pathologists have opportunities for research in international centers and for cooperative work with plant pathologists in other countries.

Work by the plant pathologist touches on many important contemporary issues, such as overpopulation, the safety of genetically engineered food, and the effects of pesticides on human health and the environment. But the role played by plant pathologists in the production of abundant, safe food for people of the world is of central importance. SEE ALSO PATHOGENS.

*Ira W. Deep*

**land-grant university** a state university given land by the federal government on the condition that it offer courses in agriculture

**specimen** object or organism under consideration

### Bibliography

The American Phytopathological Society. [Online] Available at http://www.apsnet.org/.

# Peat Bogs

A peat bog is a type of wetland whose soft, spongy ground is composed largely of living and decaying *Sphagnum* moss. Decayed, compacted moss is known as peat, which can be harvested to use for fuel or as a soil additive.

Peat bogs are found throughout the world where cool temperatures and adequate rainfall prevail. Estimates indicate that peatlands (bogs and fens) cover as much as 5 percent of the land surface, primarily in northern temperate and arctic regions. Canada contains approximately 130 million hectares of bogs, while the United States has approximately 7 million hectares.

Bogs are not just any type of wetland, and they require a particular sequence of events in order to form. A bog begins in a low spot where groundwater is close to or above the surface. Such a spot, sometimes called a fen, contains a wide mix of water-tolerant plants, including grasslike plants such

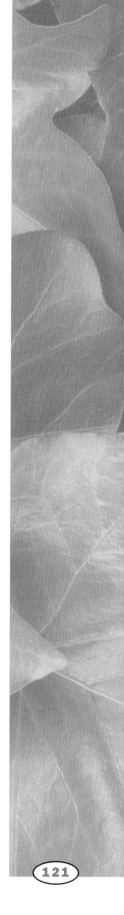

Sphagnum moss grows in a bog near Mount Kosciusko, Australia's highest point. The moss acts as a sponge, and releases the water it has absorbed in winter throughout the rest of the year.

**ions** charged particles

**pH** a measure of acidity or alkalinity; the pH scale ranges from 0 to 14, with 7 being neutral; low pH numbers indicate high acidity; high numbers indicate alkalinity

as reeds and sedges, and trees such as alders. Groundwater has a relatively high mineral content, which helps support this variety of plant types. Because water in such low spots is still, oxygen is not replenished quickly, and normal decomposition of dead plants is slowed somewhat by the low oxygen content. When plant deposition exceeds plant decay, the fen begins to fill in, and the uppermost level of the fen loses contact with groundwater. In many wetland areas, this leads to drying out of the wetland and development of a field or woodland. However, if there is sufficient rainfall and other conditions are right, the fen may be transformed into a raised bog— a self-contained wetland that grows up to and even above the surrounding terrain.

Most plants cannot survive on the low mineral content of rainwater, but the several dozen species of mosses of the genus *Sphagnum* can, and these come to dominate the bog flora. *Sphagnum* removes positive **ions** from the water such as calcium and sodium, leaving positive hydrogen ions, which are acidic. As a result, the **pH** of bog water may be as low as 3.5, about the acidity of tomato juice. As new *Sphagnum* grows atop the partially decayed growth of previous years, it compacts the layers below it into the thick, crumbly, spongelike material known as peat. Other bog plants include the carnivorous sundews (*Drosera* spp.) and acid-tolerant reeds and sedges.

Peat has been harvested as a fuel for millennia, and it is still used this way today. Fuel peat is harvested both commercially and by individuals. Because bog peat is approximately 95 percent water, it must be dried before use. Dried peat is also used as a soil additive in gardens and nurseries, and its harvest and export for this purpose is economically significant to Canada, Sweden, Ireland, and several other countries.

Like other wetlands throughout the world, bogs are threatened by human activities, including draining and filling, and harvesting of peat. Estimates indicate that 90 percent or more of former boglands has been lost in several European countries. SEE ALSO BRYOPHYTES; CARNIVOROUS PLANTS; WETLANDS.

*Richard Robinson*

**Bibliography**

Eastman John A. *The Book of Swamp and Bog: Trees, Shrubs, and Wildflowers of the Eastern Freshwater Wetlands.* Mechanicsburg, PA: Stackpole Books, 1995.

Feehan, John. *The Bogs of Ireland: An Introduction to the Natural, Cultural and Industrial Heritage of Irish Peatlands.* Dublin: The Environmental Institute, University College, 1996.

# Pharmaceutical Scientist

Pharmacists are professionals whose goals are to achieve positive outcomes from the use of medication to improve patients' quality of life. The practice of pharmacy is a vital part of the complete health care system. Due to society's many changing social and health issues, pharmacists face constant challenges, expanded responsibilities, and increasing growth in opportunities.

A pharmaceutical scientist performing research, holding calipers that grip electrical wires inside a glass container while vapors spread around the container's base.

Pharmacists are specialists in the science and clinical use of medications. They must have the knowledge about the composition of drugs, their chemical and physical properties, and their uses as well as understand the activity of the drug and how it will work in the body. Pharmacy practitioners work in community pharmacies, hospitals, nursing homes, extended care facilities, neighborhood health centers, and health maintenance organizations. A doctor of pharmacy degree (Pharm.D.) requires four years of professional study, following a minimum of two years of pre-pharmacy study.

Pharmacy practitioners may combine their professional activities with the challenge of scientific research. Many pharmacists go on to obtain postgraduate degrees in order to meet the technical demands and scientific duties required in academic pharmacy and the pharmaceutical industry. Students have the opportunity to complete advanced study (graduate work) at pharmacy schools across the United States. Graduate studies may qualify the student for a Master of Science (M.S.) or Doctor of Philosophy (Ph.D.) degree in various areas of pharmaceutical sciences (medicinal and natural products chemistry, **pharmacognosy**, pharmacology, toxicology). These research degrees require an undergraduate bachelor's or a doctor of pharmacy degree. The pharmaceutical scientists are mainly concerned with research that includes sophisticated instrumentation, analytical methods, and animal models that study all aspects of drugs and drug products.

**pharmacognosy** the study of drugs from natural products

The pharmaceutical industry offers many opportunities to pharmaceutical scientists in research, development, and manufacture of chemicals, prescription and nonprescription drugs, and other health products. Colleges and schools of pharmacy present options in teaching and in academic research. Pharmaceutical scientists may also be employed in a variety of federal and state positions including with the U.S. Public Health Service, the Department of Veterans Affairs, the Food and Drug Administration, the Centers for Disease Control, and in all branches of the armed services. In addition, they may also be engaged in highly specialized jobs such as science reporters, as experts in pharmaceutical law, or as drug enforcement agents, or they may specialize in medicinal plant cultivation and processing.

As society's health care needs have changed and expanded, there has been an increased emphasis on the use of herbal remedies as dietary supplements or the search for new prescription drugs from natural sources such as microbes and plants. As a result, an increased number of pharmaceutical scientists hold doctoral degrees in natural products chemistry, pharmacognosy, or medicinal chemistry and are involved in **biodiversity** prospecting for the discovery of new medicines. At the turn of the twenty-first century there exists a shortage of specialists in this area, and they are in great demand if they are also trained in **ethnobotany.**

**biodiversity** degree of variety of life

**ethnobotany** the study of traditional uses of plants within a culture

There are many opportunities and great potential for advancement and competitive salaries within a pharmacy science career. In 1999, starting annual salaries average between $50,000 and $65,000, depending on location. SEE ALSO ETHNOBOTANY; MEDICINAL PLANTS; PLANT PROSPECTING.

*Barbara N. Timmermann*

# Photoperiodism

Photoperiodism is an organism's response to the relative lengths of day and night (i.e., the photoperiod). We have always known that plants are tied to the seasons: each kind of plant forms flowers at about the same time each year; for example, some in spring, some in summer, some in autumn. Botanists knew that plants responded in various ways to temperature and other changes in the environment, but it was not until World War I (1914–18) that anyone tested plant responses to photoperiod. At that time Wightman W. Garner and Henry A. Allard at the U.S. Department of Agriculture in Maryland began to control various parts of the environment in their greenhouses to see if they could make a new **hybrid** tobacco bloom in summer rather than only in winter. Nothing worked until they put plants into dark cabinets for various times overnight in midsummer. Long nights caused their tobacco plants to flower, and they soon tested other species. They published their results in 1920.

**hybrid** a mix of two varieties or species

## Long-Day, Short-Day, and Day-Neutral Plants

Garner and Allard (and others) discovered that tobacco, soybeans, chrysanthemums, and several other species flowered only when the days were shorter than some maximum length and the nights were longer than some minimum length, with the exact times depending on the species. They called plants with this response "short-day plants." Such plants flower in either spring or fall. Radishes, spinach, a different species than their experimental tobacco, and other species had an opposite response: they flowered only when days were longer than some minimum length and nights were shorter than some maximum length. These are called long-day plants. These plants flower primarily in the summer. Tomato, sunflower, yet another species of tobacco, and several other species formed flowers almost independently of daylength. These are called day-neutral plants.

Later work by other investigators found a very few species, called intermediate-day plants, that flowered only when the days were neither too

Short-day plants, which flower when the days are shorter than some maximum length and the nights were longer than some minimum length, include these Autumn Days chrysanthemums.

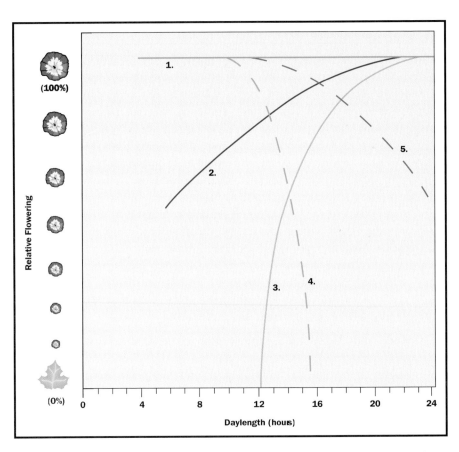

A diagram illustrating the principle of flowering responses to different daylengths. Curve 1 shows the response of a truly day-neutral plant that flowers in response to all daylengths. Such plants are rare. Curve 2 shows a day-neutral plant that flowers in response to all daylengths but is promoted in its flowering by longer days. Note that the responses of almost all plants become somewhat complex at the very short daylengths—shorter than 4 to 6 hours. Curve 3 shows a typical absolute long-day plant that requires long days to flower and remains vegetative almost indefinitely on short days. The curve that is shown might represent henbane (*Hyoscyamus niger*); unless days are longer than about 12 hours it remains vegetative. In that case, the 12 hours is the critical daylength. Other species might have other critical daylengths. Curve 4 shows a typical absolute short-day plant that remains vegetative on long days but flowers when the days reach a critical daylength. The curve is drawn to represent cocklebur (*Xanthium strumarium*), which requires at least 8.3 hours of darkness to form flowers (the critical night). Note that both henbane and cocklebur flower when days are between 12 and 15.7 hours long. (Again, other species of short-day plants can have different critical days—or critical nights.) Curve 5 shows a typical day-neutral plant that is promoted in its flowering by shorter days but will eventually flower at any daylength.

short nor too long. The opposite is also known: some plants flower on long or short but not on intermediate days. A few species have an absolute photoperiod requirement while others are promoted by some photoperiod but eventually flower without it. Although light intensity sometimes influences the response, typically plants respond not to the amount of light but only to the durations of light and dark. A short-day cocklebur plant (*Xanthium strumarium*), for example, blooms only when nights are longer than about 8.3 hours, while long-day henbane (*Hyoscyamus niger*) flowers only when the nights are shorter than about 12 hours.

Although the effective durations of light and dark are typically almost independent of temperature, temperature often influences the type of response.

Some species, for example, may require cool temperatures followed by long, warmer days (e.g., sugar beet). Some species may be day-neutral at one temperature and have a photoperiod requirement at another temperature.

Many plant responses in addition to flowering are controlled by photoperiodism. (Animal breeding times, migration times, fur color, and many other phenomena are also influenced by photoperiod.) Photoperiod influences stem lengths, dormancy and leaf fall in autumn, germination of some seeds, tuber and bulb formation, and many other plant manifestations. In flowering, it is the leaf that senses the photoperiod, so some signal must be sent from the leaf to the buds where flowers form. Although numerous attempts have failed to isolate a chemical signal for flower formation—a hormone—most researchers still feel confident that such a so-called **florigen** must exist.

**florigen** a substance that promotes flowering

## Measuring Time

The essence of photoperiodism is the measurement of time, the durations of day and night. Early experiments showed that the night was especially important for many species. Interrupting the night with even a brief period of light (seconds to an hour or two, depending on species and light intensity) stops the short-day response or promotes the long-day response. If the total of light plus dark adds up to more or less than twenty-four hours, it is the dark period that seems to be important. More recent experiments, however, show that photoperiod-sensitive plants measure the durations of both day and night. Time measurement in photoperiodism is clearly related to **circadian** leaf movements and other manifestations of the biological clock.

**circadian** "about a day"; related to a day

How do the plants *know* when it is light or dark? The pigment phytochrome, so important in many plant responses, couples the light environment to the mysterious biological clock. Phytochrome exists in two forms, both of which absorb certain wavelengths (colors) of light. One form, called $P_r$, absorbs red light, which converts it to the other form, $P_{fr}$. $P_{fr}$ absorbs longer wavelengths of light, called far red, which convert it back to $P_r$. During the day, red light predominates so most of the pigment is in the $P_{fr}$ form, signaling to the clock that it is light; the clock measures how long it is light. As it begins to get dark, the $P_{fr}$ begins to break down, and some of it is spontaneously converted to $P_r$. This drop in $P_{fr}$ level signals the clock that it is getting dark, and the clock begins to measure the length of the dark period. When the lengths of both day and night are right for the particular species, the next steps in the response to photoperiod are initiated; for example, florigen may begin to be synthesized.

Much study has gone into understanding these phenomena, and recent work has emphasized the role of specific genes in the flowering process.

## Photoperiodism and the Distribution of Plants

Photoperiodism influences the distribution of plants on Earth's surface. As expected, species that require long days for flowering (in spring or summer) occur far from the equator. Short-day species occur in the same regions but flower in late summer. Tropical short-day species also occur, growing only 5° to 20° from the equator. These species detect very small changes

in daylength (e.g., one minute per day in March and September at 20° north or south of the equator).

With respect to photoperiod, there can be many ecotypes within a species. For example, the northern ecotypes of short-day cocklebur or lambsquarters (*Chenopodium rubrum*) or the long-day alpine sorrel (*Oxyria digyna*) require longer days and shorter nights to flower than their more southern counterparts. In these examples, the different photoperiod ecotypes within a species are virtually identical in appearance but have different clock settings.

## Advantages of Photoperiodism to a Species

The ecotype differences are often clearly of advantage to the species. For example, frost comes much earlier in the year in more northern climates, and the various ecotypes of cocklebur all flower about six to eight weeks before the first killing frost in autumn, allowing time for seed ripening.

Because of photoperiodism, flowering and other responses within an ecotype population of plants are synchronized in time. This is certainly an advantage if the plants require cross pollination; it is essential that all bloom at the same time. Garner and Allard noticed that soybean plants, despite being planted at various times from early spring to early summer, all came into bloom at the same time in late summer. Photoperiodism had made the small plants, which were planted late, flower at almost the same time as the large plants, planted much earlier.

There is much to learn about the ecological importance of photoperiodism. So far, responses of only a few hundred of the approximately three hundred thousand species of flowering plants have been studied. SEE ALSO CLINES AND ECOTYPES; HORMONAL CONTROL AND DEVELOPMENT; PHYTOCHROME; RHYTHMS IN PLANT LIFE.

*Frank B. Salisbury*

**Bibliography**

Bernier, George, Jean-Marie Kinet, and Roy M. Sachs. *The Physiology of Flowering.* Boca Raton, FL: CRC Press, 1981.

Dole, J. M., and W. F. Wilkins. *Floriculture, Principles and Species.* Upper Saddle River, NJ: Prentice-Hall, 1999.

Garner, W. W., and H. A. Allard. "Effect of the Relative Length of Day and Night and Other Factors of the Environment on Growth and Reproduction in Plants." *Journal of Agricultural Research* 18 (1920): 871–920.

Halevy, Abraham H., ed. *Handbook of Flowering.* Boca Raton, FL: CRC Press, 1985.

Salisbury, Frank B., and Cleon Ross. *Plant Physiology,* 4th ed. Belmont, CA: Wadsworth Publishing Co., 1992.

Thomas, Brian, and Daphne Vince-Prue. *Photoperiodism in Plants,* 2nd ed. San Diego, CA: Academic Press, 1997.

## Photorespiration   *See Photosynthesis, Carbon Fixation and.*

# Photosynthesis, Carbon Fixation and

Virtually all life on Earth ultimately depends on the light-driven fixation of carbon dioxide ($CO_2$) according to the following equation:

$$6CO_2 + 6H_2O \rightarrow C_6H_{12}O_6 \text{ (glucose)} + 6O_2$$

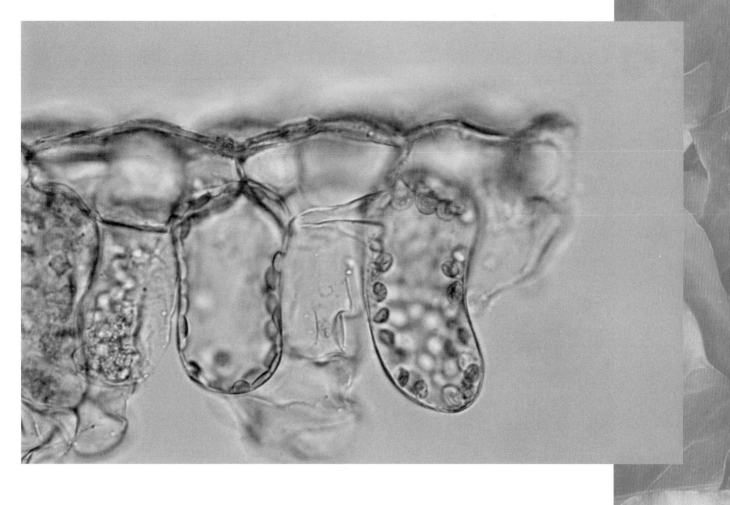

A micrograph of plant cell chloroplasts.

**chloroplast** the photosynthetic organelle of plants and algae

Photosynthesis takes place in subcellular membrane-bound compartments called **chloroplasts**. As radiotracers such as carbon-14 became available to researchers following World War II (1939–45), one application was to define the biochemistry of photosynthetic $CO_2$ fixation. Major class divisions in the plant kingdom are based on how $CO_2$ is fixed.

**C₃ Photosynthesis.** Many important biological processes are sustained by cycles that continuously consume and renew one or more key intermediates while producing some other major product. Photosynthesis is sustained by the Calvin-Benson cycle.

The $C_3$ photosynthetic mechanism is so named because the carbon atom of a molecule of $CO_2$ taken up by an illuminated leaf is first detected in the three-carbon **compound** 3-phosphoglyceric acid (PGA). The vast majority of higher plants and algae are $C_3$ species. PGA is formed when $CO_2$ combines with a 5-carbon sugar, ribulose biphosphate (RuBP). The reaction is catalyzed by the **enzyme** RuBP carboxylase/oxygenase, an abundant protein in all green tissues. This multifunctional enzyme has come to be called rubisco.

**compound** a substance formed from two or more elements

**enzyme** a protein that controls a reaction in a cell

During each turn of the Calvin-Benson cycle, two molecules of PGA (a total of six carbon atoms) undergo a complex series of enzyme-catalyzed transformations in which the carbon atoms pass through metabolite pools consisting of three-, four-, five-, six-, and seven-carbon sugar phosphates. These reactions regenerate RuBP, which then combines with $CO_2$ to form two PGAs and complete the cycle. So, of the six (2 H 3) original carbon

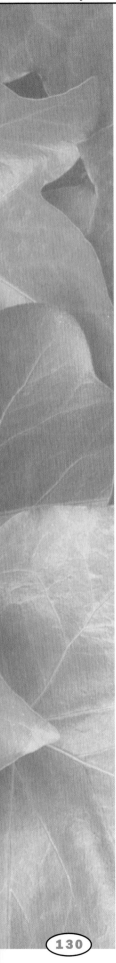

atoms in PGA, five give rise to RuBP and the one remaining appears as one of the six carbon atoms in the sugar glucose-6-phosphate (G6P). Therefore, for every six $CO_2$ molecules fixed, one G6P leaves the Calvin-Benson cycle for synthesis of starch, sucrose, cellulose, and ultimately all of the organic constituents of the plant.

In terms of pure chemistry, the conversion of $CO_2$ to carbohydrate is an example of reduction, in which a source of energy-rich electrons is required. As the term *photosynthesis* suggests, the energy for the reductive reactions of the Calvin-Benson cycle comes from visible light. An extensive membrane system in the chloroplast harbors the **pigments** (chlorophylls and carotenoids) that transfer light packets (quanta) to specialized pigment-protein sites where they energize individual electrons extracted from molecules of water ($H_2O$). The oxygen atoms in the water are released as $O_2$. Each high-energy electron consumes the energy of two quanta. Two electrons are used to convert a compound called nicotinamide adenosine dinucleotide phosphate from its oxidized form ($NADP^+$) to its reduced form ($NADPH$). The sequence of electron transport from $H_2O$ to $NADP^+$ also fuels the phosphorylation of adenosine diphosphate (ADP) to high-energy adenosine triphosphate (**ATP**). Both NADPH and ATP interact directly with the enzymes of the Calvin-Benson cycle during fixation of $CO_2$. Two molecules of NADPH and three molecules of ATP are required to fix each molecule of $CO_2$ during $C_3$ photosynthesis.

**Photorespiration.** $C_3$ plants also engage in an active $CO_2$-releasing process called photorespiration that operates concurrently with normal photosynthesis in the light. Photorespiration drains away useful energy, and is thus a wasteful process. Since the $CO_2$ formed by photorespiration is rapidly refixed by photosynthesis it is difficult to measure directly, and its existence was not suspected until the 1950s. Since then, biochemists and physiologists have elucidated the mechanism, but have not come to agreement on its purpose, if any. It is important to note that photorespiration is not the same as the ubiquitous respiratory $CO_2$ released from **mitochondria** in all **eukaryotic** cells, including animal and plant tissues.

Photorespiration starts with the formation of a two-carbon phosphoglycolic acid molecule during photosynthesis. Since this is a potent inhibitor of the Calvin-Benson cycle, its metabolism to nontoxic derivatives is essential. First, the phosphate group is removed (by action of an enzyme called a phosphatase) to yield glycolate. The following series of conversions:

2 glycolate → 2 glyoxylate → 2 glycine → serine → hydroxypyruvate → PGA

results in the formation of a Calvin-Benson cycle intermediate (PGA) that is used to make RuBP. Notice that the four glycolate carbon atoms ultimately appear as one molecule of PGA (three carbon atoms). The fourth atom of carbon is released as $CO_2$ during the glycine to serine conversion, and this is the source of $CO_2$ released in photorespiration. Additional photosynthetic energy (i.e., NADPH and ATP) is consumed during metabolism of photorespiratory PGA, refixation of $CO_2$, and reassimilation of ammonia released during the glycine→serine step. Hence, photorespiration drains energy away from productive photosynthesis.

Photorespiration can be observed by a number of means. When a stream of $CO_2$-free air is passed over a $C_3$ leaf, release of $CO_2$ by the leaf results

**pigments** colored molecules

**ATP** adenosine triphosphate, a small, water-soluble molecule that acts as an energy currency in cells

**mitochondria** cell organelles that produce ATP to power cell reactions

**eukaryotic** a cell with a nucleus (*eu* means "true" and *karyo* means "nucleus"); includes protists, plants, animals, and fungi

in an elevated concentration of this gas in the downstream flow. This release rate is highly dependent upon illumination of the leaf and will be depressed severalfold by darkening. Another method relies on the fact that the rate of photosynthetic fixation of $CO_2$ is directly dependent on the concentration of $CO_2$ at low levels of this component. Hence, sealing a leaf in a small transparent vessel under illumination will cause the concentration of $CO_2$ inside to fall until the rate of uptake equals the rate of evolution due to photorespiration. The final equilibrium concentration of $CO_2$ (called the $CO_2$ compensation point) is highly dependent on the concentration of $O_2$ in the gas and is commonly employed as a robust, although indirect, measure of photorespiration. But the most direct indicator of photorespiration is based on comparison of rates of $CO_2$ uptake at high and low levels of $O_2$ in the surrounding atmosphere. Lowering the $O_2$ concentration from the normal 21 percent to 1 to 2 percent can result in an instantaneous 30 percent increase in photosynthetic rate (see below). This response of photosynthesis to $O_2$ is attributed to photorespiration and is called the Warburg Effect for its discoverer Otto Warburg.

Although the source of phosphoglycolic acid for photorespiration was for some time a controversial subject, it is now widely accepted that it originates at the site of $CO_2$ fixation. Specifically, when RuBP binds to rubisco its structure is perturbed, rendering it vulnerable to attack by either $CO_2$ or $O_2$. Reaction of RuBP with $CO_2$ yields two PGAs while reaction with $O_2$ results in formation of one PGA molecule and one phosphoglycolic acid molecule. The probability that a bound RuBP will react with either $CO_2$ or $O_2$ is governed by the relative concentrations of these gases in the aqueous environment of the chloroplast. Hence, $CO_2$ and $O_2$ are considered to compete for the bound RuBP. This competition accounts for the increase in photorespiration at high $O_2$ concentration, and the fact that photorespiration can be almost completely suppressed by high concentrations of $CO_2$ even in the presence of $O_2$. Measurements with purified rubisco in the laboratory indicate that the rate of photorespiratory release of $CO_2$ is about 20 percent of the total rate of $CO_2$ uptake for a healthy $C_3$ leaf in air at 25°C. Photorespiration increases considerably with temperature, however. Photorespiration is most significant when temperatures are high and plants must close **stomata** to prevent water loss. Without access to fresh $CO_2$ from the atmosphere, photorespiration becomes the major reaction catalyzed by rubisco.

The role of photorespiration in plant metabolism is the subject of debate. It has been suggested to be a means of disposal of excess photosynthetic energy. Also, it may provide a way to protect the leaf from damaging effects of light that could occur if $CO_2$ levels inside the leaf were to fall below some critical threshold. Still, there may be no essential role for photorespiration. It is probably an anomaly of the rubisco mechanism that appeared on this planet before $O_2$ was present in the atmosphere. Later, as $O_2$ levels in the atmosphere rose due to photosynthesis, this vulnerability to $O_2$ affected photosynthesis and growth. Interestingly, some plants have evolved means to suppress photorespiration while retaining rubisco and the Calvin-Benson cycle.

$C_4$ **Photosynthesis.** Familiar species possessing the $C_4$ photosynthesis mechanism are maize, sorghum, sugarcane, and several common weeds. The defining feature of $CO_2$ fixation in this case is involvement of two distinct

**stomata** openings between guard cells on the underside of leaves that allow gas exchange

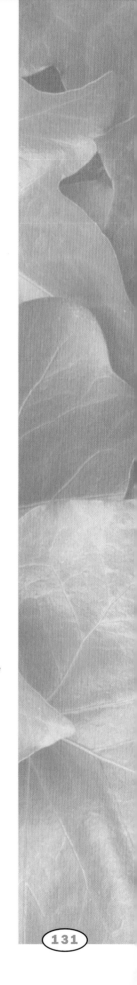

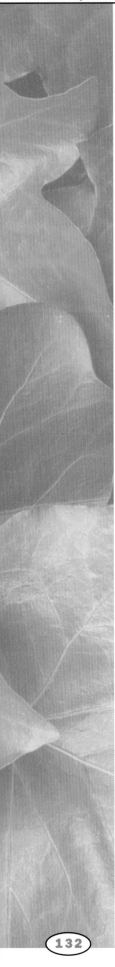

cell types that shuttle metabolites back and forth to complete a modified photosynthetic cycle. Microscopic examination of leaf sections reveals two chloroplast-containing cell types in an arrangement termed Kranz anatomy. Bundle sheath cells form a cylindrical layer one cell deep around each leaf vein. These cells are typically enlarged, thick walled, and densely packed with chloroplasts. At least two layers of loosely packed mesophyll cells separate adjacent bundle sheath strands. Although mesophyll cells resemble those observed in $C_3$ leaves, they function much differently.

When $CO_2$ enters the leaf it is first fixed in the mesophyll cells by the enzyme phosphoenolpyruvate (PEP) carboxylase. The carbon atom from $CO_2$ is first detected in the four-carbon organic acid oxaloacetic acid (OAA), hence the name $C_4$ photosynthesis. The OAA is then reduced to malic acid or converted to the amino acid aspartic acid depending on species. Malate and aspartate are transported to bundle sheath cells where they are decarboxylated, thereby releasing $CO_2$. This newly formed $CO_2$ is refixed by rubisco and metabolized by the Calvin-Benson cycle present in the bundle sheath chloroplasts. The remaining three carbon atoms derived from the malate and aspartate are transported back to the mesophyll cells as pyruvic acid to regenerate the three-carbon PEP.

The characteristic carboxylation/decarboxylation sequence of $C_4$ photosynthesis pumps $CO_2$ from mesophyll to bundle sheath cells, thereby accomplishing one desirable end. The concentration of $CO_2$ in bundle sheath cells of $C_4$ plants is severalfold higher than in leaf cells of $C_3$ species. Hence, photorespiration is virtually absent in $C_4$ leaves. Since none of the other enzyme-catalyzed reactions is sensitive to $O_2$, the Warburg effect is not observed and the $CO_2$ compensation point (a reliable indicator of photorespiratory capacity, see above) is very low for $C_4$ leaves. Somewhat more light energy is required to fix each molecule of $CO_2$ using the $C_4$ pathway since PEP regeneration requires ATP. Although 2 NADPH are consumed as in $C_3$ plants, the ATP requirement for $C_4$ photosynthesis is four to five per $CO_2$ fixed.

**Crassulacean Acid Metabolism (CAM).** The crassulacean acid metabolism (CAM) mode of photosynthesis was discovered first in plants of the family Crassulaceae but familiar species include pineapple and cacti. It is considered an adaptation to life in arid environments. CAM photosynthesis resembles $C_4$ photosynthesis in terms of the pathway of fixation of carbon. The prominent difference, however, is that CAM plants take up $CO_2$ from the atmosphere at night and synthesize malic acid via PEP carboxylase. During the daytime the leaf pores (stomata) that admit $CO_2$ close to conserve water. Malic acid is decarboxylated and the $CO_2$ is refixed by the Calvin-Benson cycle. Some of the starch accumulated during daytime is converted to PEP at night to support $CO_2$ fixation. Also, unlike $C_4$ photosynthesis, all of the CAM reactions take place in each leaf cell.

## Significance of Carbon Fixation Reactions

The choice of $CO_2$ fixation pathway has profound implications for how a plant responds to the innumerable combinations of light intensity, leaf internal $CO_2$ concentration, temperature, and water status in the natural environment. As discussed above, at normal atmospheric $CO_2$ levels photosynthesis is lower by at least 25 percent in $C_3$ plants than it would be if photorespiration were absent. The generally higher rates of photosynthesis in $C_4$ plants are attributable to both suppression of photorespiration in these species and the superior ability of PEP carboxylase to fix $CO_2$ at the very low concentrations of this gas that can occur inside leaf tissue. These differences are most pronounced at high light intensity. Photosynthesis in $C_3$ leaves attain maximal rates at light levels of about 50 percent of full sunlight. However, $C_4$ photosynthesis continues to increase with light intensity even in full sunlight. It is little wonder that the highest yielding crop species use the $C_4$ mechanism. Conversely, $C_3$ plants are capable of more efficient use of light quanta when light levels are low, as would be the case for shaded conditions. Also, high temperatures favor $C_4$ plants because the number of molecules of $H_2O$ lost to evaporation via the stomata (transpiration) per $CO_2$ fixed is much lower for these species compared to $C_3$ species. However, $C_3$ plants tend to be more competitive in cool environments. Finally, although projected increases in global atmospheric $CO_2$ levels during the twenty-first century should enhance photosynthesis in all species, associated changes in distribution of temperature and rainfall will also exert great influence on the composition and characteristics of Earth's flora. SEE ALSO ATMOSPHERE AND PLANTS; CACTUS; CALVIN, MELVIN; CHLOROPLAST; DE SAUSSURE, NICHOLAS; INGENHOUSZ, JAN; PHOTOSYNTHESIS, LIGHT REACTIONS AND.

*Richard B. Peterson*

**Bibliography**

Bassham, J. A., and M. Calvin. *The Path of Carbon in Photosynthesis.* Englewood Cliffs, NJ: Prentice-Hall, 1957.

Edwards, G., and D. Walker. *$C_3$, $C_4$: Mechanisms, and Cellular and Environmental Regulation, of Photosynthesis.* Berkeley, CA: University of California Press, 1983.

Hall, D. O., and K. K. Rao. *Photosynthesis.* Boca Raton, FL: CRC Press, 1994.

Szalai, V. A., and G. W. Brudvig. "How Plants Produce Dioxygen." *American Scientist* 86 (1998): 542–51.

Walker, D. *Energy, Plants, and Man.* East Sussex, England: Oxygraphics Ltd., 1992.

Whitmarsh, J., and Govindjee. "The Photosynthetic Process." In *Concepts in Photobiology: Photosynthesis and Photomorphogenesis,* ed. G. S. Singhal, G. Renger, S. K. Sopory, K-D Irrgang, and Govindjee. New Delhi/Dordrecht: Narosa Publishers/Kluwer Academic Publishers, 1999.

# Photosynthesis, Light Reactions and

Life requires a continuous input of energy. On Earth, the main source of energy is sunlight, which is transformed by photosynthesis into a form of chemical energy that can be used by photosynthetic and nonphotosynthetic organisms alike. Photosynthesis is the molecular process by which plants, algae, and certain bacteria use light energy to build molecules of sugar from carbon dioxide ($CO_2$) and water ($H_2O$). The sugar molecules produced by photosynthetic organisms provide the energy as well as chemical building blocks needed for their growth and reproduction. In plants and algae the photosynthetic process removes $CO_2$ from the atmosphere while releasing molecular oxygen ($O_2$) as a by-product. Some photosynthetic bacteria function like plants and algae, giving off $O_2$; other types of photosynthetic bacteria, however, use light energy to create organic **compounds** without producing $O_2$. The type of photosynthesis that releases $O_2$ emerged early in

**compound** a substance formed from two or more elements

Earth's history, more than three billion years ago, and is the source of the $O_2$ in our atmosphere. Thus photosynthetic organisms not only provide the food we eat, but also the air we breathe. In addition, ancient photosynthesis produced the building blocks for the oil, coal, and natural gas that we currently depend on for our survival.

The overall photosynthetic process can be written as:

Carbon Dioxide + Water + Light → Carbohydrate + Oxygen

and can be summarized by the following chemical equation:

$$6\ CO_2 + 6\ H_2O + \text{Light Energy} \rightarrow (CH_2O)_6 + 6\ O_2$$

However, this simple chemical equation does not reveal all the reactions that must occur inside a plant to produce carbohydrate. If you shine light on a mixture of $CO_2$ and $H_2O$, you end with what you started, $CO_2$ and $H_2O$. Add a plant, however, and you get sugar. Plants create this sugar in a series of molecular steps using a complicated machinery made up of proteins and other organic molecules.

This article describes the photosynthetic process in plants, focusing on the first stage of photosynthesis, known as the light reactions. The light reactions capture light energy and store it within two chemicals, **NADPH** (nicotinamide adenine dinucleotide phosphate) and **ATP** (adenosine triphosphate). These two molecules provide the energy needed to drive the second stage of photosynthesis, known as the Calvin-Benson cycle, in which carbohydrates (sugars) are made from $CO_2$ and $H_2O$.

To perform photosynthesis a plant must gather light energy, transport electrons between molecules, transfer protons across a membrane, and finally rearrange chemical bonds to create carbohydrates. To understand the light reactions it is helpful to focus on the path of three critical elements: energy, electrons, and protons (hydrogen **ions**). However, before considering the series of individual reactions that make up the light reactions, the molecular machinery that does all the work must be examined.

## Chloroplasts

In plants and algae, photosynthesis occurs in chloroplasts, which are small **organelles** located inside cells. The chloroplast can be thought of as a factory, providing the plant with food and energy. A typical cell in a leaf contains many chloroplasts. Fortunately chloroplasts from different plants are more similar than different. This means that if you understand how photosynthesis works in one plant, you will have a general understanding of photosynthesis in all plants. The chloroplast contains a membrane system, known as the photosynthetic membrane (or thylakoid membrane), that contains most of the proteins required for the light reactions. The Calvin-Benson cycle **enzymes** that capture $CO_2$ and produce carbohydrate are located in the water phase of the chloroplast outside the photosynthetic membrane. The photosynthetic membrane, like other cellular membranes, is composed mainly of lipid molecules arranged in a bi-layer. As will be explained, a critical feature of the photosynthetic membrane is that it forms a **vesicle** that defines an inner and an outer water space. The photosynthetic membrane is organized into stacked membranes that are interconnected by nonstacked

**NADPH** reduced form of nicotinomide adenine dinucleotide phosphate, a small, water-soluble molecule that acts as a hydrogen carrier in biochemical reactions

**ATP** adenosine triphosphate, a small, water-soluble molecule that acts as an energy currency in cells

**ions** charged particles

**organelle** a membrane-bound structure within a cell

**enzyme** a protein that controls a reaction in a cell

**vesicle** a membrane-bound cell structure with specialized contents

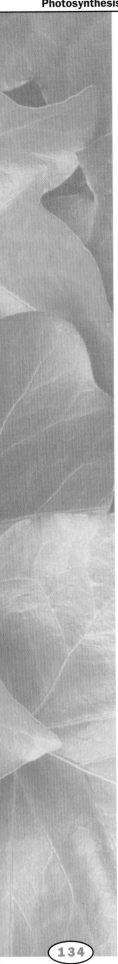

membranes. Researchers are uncertain as to why the photosynthetic membrane is organized in such a complicated structure. Fortunately, to understand the photosynthetic light reactions we can represent the shape of the photosynthetic membrane as a simple vesicle.

## Gathering Sunlight: The Antenna System

Plants capture sunlight by using pigment molecules that absorb visible light (wavelengths from 400 to 700 **nanometers**). The main light-absorbing molecule is chlorophyll, which gives plants their green color. Chlorophyll is green because it is efficient at absorbing blue light and red light, but not very efficient at absorbing green light. The chlorophyll and other light-absorbing molecules (for example, **carotenoids**, which are yellow) are bound to protein complexes embedded in the photosynthetic membrane that make up an **antenna system**. This antenna system is designed to absorb light energy and funnel it to a protein complex called a **reaction center**. The reaction center can use the energy to drive an electron uphill from one site to another within the reaction center. Each reaction center is located at the center of the antenna system, which contains two hundred to three hundred chlorophyll molecules. Before the first chemical step can take place, the light energy captured by the antenna system must be transferred to the reaction center.

To understand light absorption it is best to think of light as packets of energy known as photons. The job of the antenna system is to capture photons and change the light energy into another form of energy known as excitation energy, which is a type of electronic energy. The excitation energy can be thought of as a packet of energy that jumps from antenna molecule to antenna molecule until it is trapped by a reaction center. The antenna system is very efficient. Under optimum conditions more than 90 percent of the photons gathered by the antenna system are transferred to the reaction center. The migration of excitation energy in the antenna system is also very fast. A photon is absorbed, transferred around the antenna system, and trapped by a reaction center within a few trillionths of a second ($10^{-12}$ s).

**nanometer** one-billionth of a meter

**carotenoid** a yellow-colored molecule made by plants

**antenna system** a collection of protein complexes that harvests light energy and converts it to excitation energy that can migrate to a reaction center. The light is absorbed by pigment molecules (e.g., chlorophyll, carotenoids, phycobilin) that are attached to the protein

**reaction center** a protein complex that uses light energy to create a stable charge separation by transferring a single electron energetically uphill from a donor molecule to an acceptor molecule, both of which are located in the reaction center

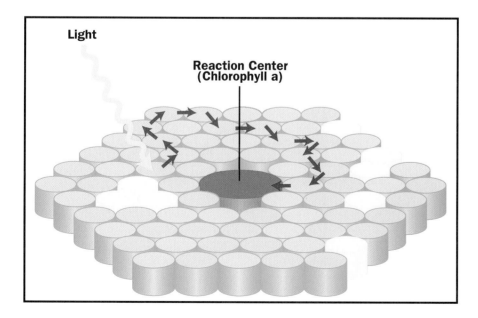

Figure 1: Antenna system with a reaction center (middle). The arrows indicate the pathway of excitation energy migration. Redrawn from Starr and Taggart, 1998, Figure 7.9.

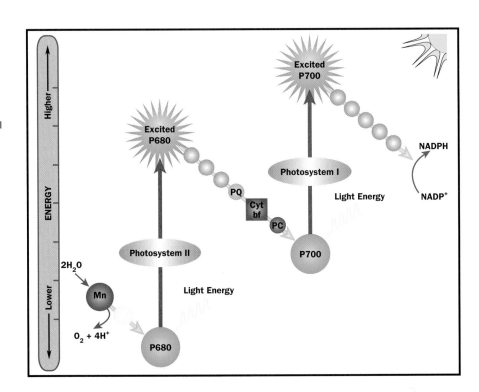

**NADP⁺** oxidized form of nicotinomide adenine dinucleotide phosphate

## Electron Transport

The excitation energy trapped by a reaction center provides the energy needed for electron transfer, which is the next step in the photosynthetic light reactions. During electron transfer, individual electrons are removed from water molecules and transferred, by an electron transport chain, to **NADP⁺**. Electron transport in photosynthesis is like electron flow in an electric circuit driven by a battery. The voltage difference across the battery pushes electrons through the circuit, and the electron current can be used to do work. In photosynthesis, light energy pushes electrons up an energy hill in the reaction centers. Subsequent electron flow in the electron transport chain is energetically downhill and can be used to do work. Figure 2 shows the electron carriers that make up the photosynthetic electron transport chain in a way that reveals the relative electronic energy on the vertical scale. This is known as the Z-scheme. Note that a negative voltage corresponds to a higher energy, so that downhill electron flow is from the top to the bottom of the figure.

The electron transport pathway includes electron transfer from one site to another within a protein, as well as electron transfer from one molecule to another (Figure 3). Most of the electron carriers are located in the photosynthetic membrane, but a few (for example, NADP⁺) are located in the water phase surrounding the membrane. It is important to keep in mind that the electron transport chain shown in the figure is repeated many times in each chloroplast. A typical chloroplast will contain more than a million electron transport chains.

Electron transfer from one molecule to another is possible because certain types of molecules can easily give up or receive electrons. Some electron carriers can give up and receive a single electron (e.g., plastocyanin), while others can accept or donate more than one electron (e.g., NADP⁺

Figure 2: Z-scheme showing the pathway of electrons from water to NADP⁺ producing oxygen and the reducing power (NADPH). Redrawn from www.life.uiuc.edu/govindjee/ZschemeG.html Mn = manganese; P680 = reaction center chlorophyll *a* of Photosystem II; PQ = plastoquinone; Cyt bf = cytochrome bf complex; PC = plastocyanin; P700 = reaction center chlorophyll of Photosystem I.

can accept two electrons). In addition, some electron carriers can take up a proton along with an electron (plastoquinone can accept two electrons and two protons), making them hydrogen (H) carriers.

When a compound gains an electron it is said to be *reduced* (**reduction**), whereas when it gives up an electron it is said to be *oxidized* (**oxidation**). In biological electron transport pathways, the electrons are always bound to a molecule (they are too reactive to hang around free), which means that an oxidation reaction is always coupled to a reduction reaction. Electrons spontaneously jump from one molecule to another because some molecules hold onto their electrons more tightly than others. This is another way of saying that energetically, electrons flow downhill. If two molecules, A and B, are close enough together, and if A is reduced and B is oxidized, an electron will jump from A to B if it is energetically downhill.

## NADPH Production

Moving an electron from water to $NADP^+$ requires an input of energy. This job is done by reaction centers, which use the light energy gathered by the antenna system to move an electron energetically uphill. As shown in Figure 3 the electron transport chain in chloroplasts uses two different types of reactions centers: Photosystem II and Photosystem I. (For historical reasons the reaction centers are not numbered according to their order in the electron transport chain, i.e., Photosystem II sends electrons to photosystem I.)

Photosystem II catalyzes two different chemical reactions. One is the oxidation of water and the other is the reduction of plastoquinone. Water oxidation is a critical reaction in photosynthesis because the electrons removed from $H_2O$ are ultimately used to reduce $CO_2$ to carbohydrate. Photosystem II performs this reaction by binding two $H_2O$ molecules and removing one electron at a time. The energy for the removal of a single electron is provided by a single photon. For Photosystem II to completely oxidize two $H_2O$ molecules and reduce two molecules of plastoquinone, it requires four photons. (Note that electron transport from $H_2O$ all the way to $NADP^+$ requires two light reactions: Photosystem II and Photosystem I. Thus eight photons are required for the release of one $O_2$ molecule.) This process creates $O_2$, which is released, and $H^+$ ions, which are used in ATP synthesis (see below).

As shown in Figure 3, electron transfer from water to $NADP^+$ requires three membrane-bound protein complexes: Photosystem II, the cytochrome *bf* complex (Cyt bf), and Photosystem I. Electrons are transferred between these large protein complexes by small mobile molecules. Because these small molecules carry electrons (or hydrogen atoms) over relatively long distances, they play a critical role in photosynthesis. This is illustrated by plastoquinone (PQ), which transfers electrons from the Photosystem II reaction center to the cytochrome *bf* complex and at the same time carries protons across the photosynthetic membrane.

Plastoquinone operates by diffusing in the photosynthetic membrane until it becomes bound to a pocket on the Photosystem II complex. The photosystem II reaction center reduces plastoquinone by adding two electrons taken from $H_2O$ and two protons taken from the outer water phase, creating $PQH_2$. The reduced plastoqinone molecule unbinds from Photosystem II and diffuses in the photosynthetic membrane until it encounters a binding site on the cytochrome *bf* complex. In a reaction sequence that is

**reduction** the addition of one or more electrons to an atom or molecule. In the case of a molecule, protons may be involved as well, resulting in hydrogen being added

**oxidation** The removal of one or more electrons from an atom or molecule. In the case of a molecule, a proton may be involved as well, resulting in hydrogen being removed

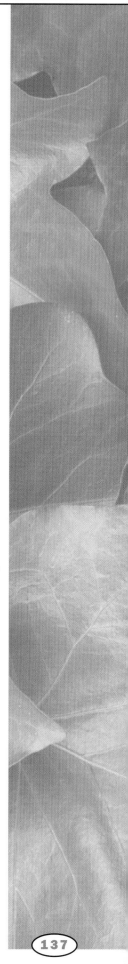

Figure 3: The electron transport chain showing the carriers in a membrane that forms a vesicle. Modified from photoscience.la.asu.edu/ photosyn/education/ photointro.html. See text for abbreviations used.

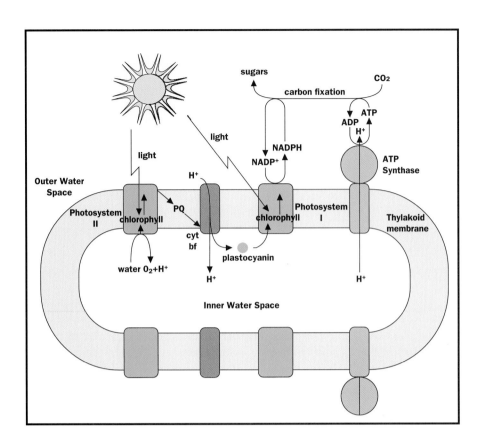

not completely understood, the cytochrome *bf* complex removes the electrons from reduced plastoquinone and releases protons into the inner water space of the photosynthetic vesicle. The cytochrome *bf* complex then gives up the electrons to another small molecule, plastocyanin (PC). The electrons are transferred to the Photosystem I reaction center by plastocyanin. The proton gradient, produced by water oxidation and oxidation of reduced plastoquinone, is used to create ATP (see below).

The Photosystem I reaction center is like Photosystem II in that it is served by a chlorophyll-containing antenna system and uses light energy to move an electron energetically uphill, but Photosystem I catalyzes different reactions: it oxidizes plastocyanin and reduces ferredoxin. Ferredoxin itself becomes oxidized, losing its electrons to another acceptor. The last step in the photosynthetic electron transport chain is reduction of $NADP^+$, producing NADPH.

## ATP Production

In plants essentially all electron flow from water follows the pathway shown in Figure 3, at least up to ferredoxin. However, once an electron reaches ferredoxin the electron pathway becomes branched, enabling a fraction of the **redox** free energy to enter other pathways, including cycling through the Photosystem I reaction center. Photosystem I cyclic electron transport provides additional energy for ATP production, which allows plants to adjust the energy flow according to their metabolic needs.

Most of the energy from the electron transfer reactions is stored as redox energy in NADPH as described above. However, some of the energy

**redox** oxidation and reduction

is stored across the membrane of the photosynthetic vesicle in the form of a **pH** gradient (or protein gradient) and an electric potential (positive inside). As previously noted, the electron transport chain concentrates protons in the inner water phase of the vesicle by the release of protons during the oxidation of water by Photosystem II and by transporting protons from the outer water phase to the inner water phase via plastoquinone (Figure 3). In addition, electron transport creates a net positive charge on the inner side and a net negative charge on the outer side of the vesicle, which gives rise to an electric potential across the membrane. The energy stored in the pH gradient and electric potential is known as the transmembrane proton electrochemical potential or the proton motive force.

The conversion of proton electrochemical energy into the chemical-free energy of ATP is accomplished by a single protein complex known as ATP synthase, which catalyzes the formation of ATP by the addition of inorganic phosphate ($P_i$) to ADP:

$$ADP + P_i \rightarrow ATP + H_2O$$

The reaction is energetically uphill and is driven by the transmembrane proton electrochemical gradient. The ATP synthase enzyme is a molecular rotary motor. Protons move through a channel in the ATP synthase pro-

**pH** a measure of acidity or alkalinity; the pH scale ranges from 0 to 14, with 7 being neutral; low pH numbers indicate high acidity; high numbers indicate alkalinity

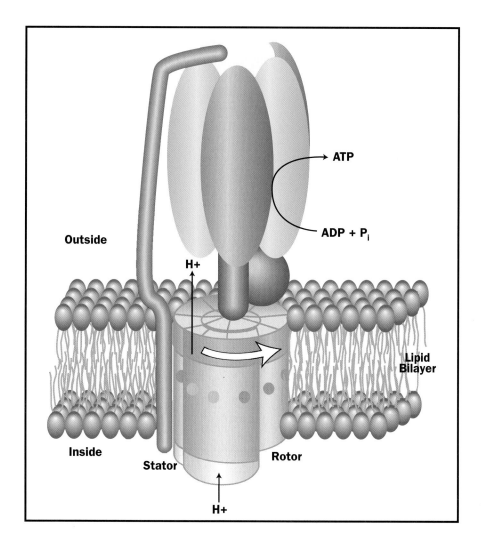

Figure 4: Rotary model of how ATP synthase catalyzes ATP. Redrawn from Fillingame, 1999, pp. 1687–88.

tein (from the inner water phase to the outer water phase of the vesicle) providing the energy for ATP synthesis. However, the protons are not involved in the chemistry of adding phosphate to ADP at the catalytic site. Although it has not been proven, it appears that proton flow drives the rotation part of the ATP synthase at rates as high as one hundred revolutions per second (Figure 4). The rotation of ATP synthase can be thought of as pushing ADP and $P_i$ together to form ATP and water.

## From the Light Reactions to the Calvin-Benson Cycle

The job of the photosynthetic light reactions is to provide energy in the form NADPH and ATP for the Calvin-Benson cycle. Although all plants depend on the Calvin-Benson cycle to make carbohydrates, the way they get the carbon dioxide to the cycle varies. The most efficient plants (soybean, for example) require two molecules of NADPH and three molecules of ATP for each molecule of $CO_2$ that is taken up, while some other types of plants (corn, for example) must use more energy to fix a single $CO_2$ molecule. During brief periods photosynthesis in plants can store nearly 30 percent of the light energy they absorb as chemical energy. However, under normal, day-to-day growing conditions the actual performance of the plant is less than one-tenth of the maximum efficiency. The factors that conspire to lower photosynthesis include limitations imposed by molecular reactions and environmental conditions that limit plant performance such as low soil moisture or high temperature. Our increasing understanding of plant **genomes** opens the door for improving plant performance under diverse environmental conditions (for example, enabling farmers to grow crops on marginal lands). A crucial step in this direction is understanding the molecular processes involved in photosynthesis. SEE ALSO CHLOROPHYLL; CHLOROPLASTS; INGENHOUSZ, JAN; PHOTOSYNTHESIS, CARBON FIXATION AND; WATER MOVEMENT.

*John Whitmarsh and Govindjee*

**genome** the genetic material of an organism

### Bibliography

Fillingame, R. H. "Molecular Rotary Motors." *Science* 286 (1999): 1687–88.

Govindjee, and W. Coleman. "How Does Photosynthesis Make Oxygen?" *Scientific American* 262 (1990): 50–58.

Hall, D. O., and K. K. Rao. *Photosynthesis*, 6th ed. Cambridge: Cambridge University Press, 1999.

Starr, Cecie, and Ralph Taggart. *Biology: The Unity and Diversity of Life.* Belmont: CA: Wadsworth Publishing Co., 1998.

Walker, D. A. *Energy, Plants and Man.* East Sussex, U.K.: Oxygraphics Limited, 1992.

Whitmarsh, J., and Govindjee. "The Photosynthetic Process." In *Concepts in Photobiology: Photosynthesis and Photomorphogenesis*, ed. G. S. Singhal, G. Renger, K-D. Irrgang, S. Sopory, and Govindjee. New Delhi/Dordrecht: Narosa Publishers/Kluwer Academic Publishers, 1999.

# Phyllotaxis

Phyllotaxis is the study of the patterns on plants. The word itself comes from the Greek *phullon*, meaning "leaf," and *taxis*, meaning "arrangement." Phyllotaxis, in the restricted sense, is the study of the relative arrangement of what is called the primordia of plants. A primordium is, for example, what will become a leaf on a stem, a scale on a pinecone or on a pineapple fruit, a seed in the head (called the **capitulum**) of a sunflower, or a floret in the capitulum of a daisy. In other words, phyllotaxis is the study of the patterns made by similar parts (such as florets, scales, and seeds) on plants and in their buds. Anatomically, phyllotactic patterns are closely related to the **vascular** systems of plants, but phyllotaxis-like patterns are even present in the brown alga *Fucus spiralis*, in which there is no vascular system. The study of phyllotaxis has brought about new ideas and considerable progress in our knowledge of the organization of vegetative shoots. Phyllotaxis was the oldest biological subject to be mathematized, well before genetics.

## Types of Phyllotaxis

In the mid-1830s naturalists noticed the spirals in the capituli of daisies and sunflowers. There are indeed two easily recognizable families of spirals, winding in opposite directions with respect to a common pole that is the center of the capitulum. They also noticed the patterns of scales making families of spirals on the pineapple fruit surface. Depending on whether the scales are rectangular or hexagonal, there are two or three such families of spirals or helices that can be easily observed. These spirals are referred to as parastichies, meaning "secondary spirals." The accompanying figure of the *Pinus pinea* shows a cross-section of an **apical** bud with five parastichies in one direction and eight in the opposite direction. Similar patterns of helices are made by the points of insertions of the leaves around stems, such as the patterns of scars made by the leaves on the trunk of a palm tree.

Apart from the spiral or helical pattern, which is the type most frequently encountered in nature, there is another main type of phyllotaxis called whorled. A pattern is whorled when $n$ primordia appear at each level of the stem, such as in horsetails (*Equisetum*), in which $n$ can take values from 6 to 20. When the $n$ primordia on a level are inserted in between those of the adjacent level, the **whorl** is said to be alternating, as in fir club moss (*Lycopodium selago*). When they are directly above those in the adjacent level, the whorl is called superposed, as in *Ruta* and *Primula*.

## Numbers in Phyllotaxis

In the case of the spirals in the capitulum of the daisy, or in the case of those in the cross-section of the young pine cone in the figure, the spirals are often conceived as logarithmic spirals. In the case of mature pinecones and stems they are helices made by scales winding around a cylinder-like form. When naturalists count the spirals they find that in 92 percent of all the observations, the numbers of spirals are terms of the Fibonacci sequence, named after Leonardo Fibonacci, the most famous mathematician of the twelfth century. It is also called the main sequence. This is the recurrent sequence 1, 1, 2, 3, 5, 8, 13, 21, 34, . . . where each term is the sum of the preceeding two. The next terms are thus 55 and 89, and the three dots (. . .) indicate that the sequence is infinite. Still more fascinating and puzzling is the fact that the number of spirals are consecutive terms of the Fibonacci sequence. For example, in the pine we have (2, 3), (5, 3), and (5, 8) phyllotaxes, in capituli the pairs found are (21, 34), (55, 34), (55, 89), and (89, 144), and on pineapples with hexagonal scales the triplets (8, 13, 21) or (13,

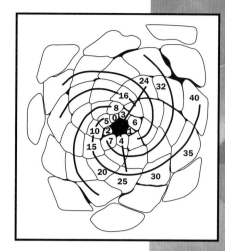

Cross-section of an apical bud of *Pinus pinea,* with five parastichies in one direction and eight in the opposite direction.

**capitulum** the head of a compound flower, such as a dandelion

**vascular** related to transport of nutrients

**apical** at the tip

**whorl** a ring

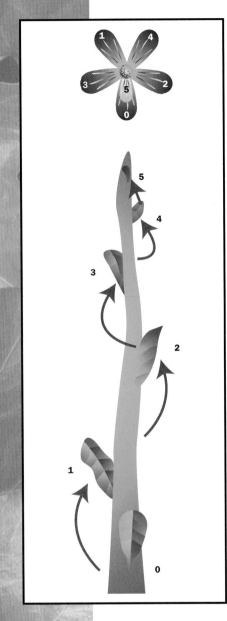

A leafy stem showing a divergence angle, between consecutively borne leaves, of 2/5 of a turn around the stem (144 degrees).

**specimen** object or organism under consideration

21, 34) are found, depending on the size of the **specimens**. The prevalence of the Fibonacci sequence in phyllotaxis is often referred to as "the mystery of phyllotaxis."

There are, of course, exceptions to the rule, but in the other cases of spiral (as opposed to whorled) phyllotaxis, the numbers obtained are consecutive terms of a Fibonacci-type sequence. This is a sequence of integers built on the same recurrence relationship as for the Fibonacci sequence, but starting with numbers different from 1 and 1, for instance: 1, 3, 4, 7, 11, 18, 29. . . . This sequence, encountered in *Araucaria* and *Echinocactus*, is present in about 1.5 percent of all observations, while the sequence 2, 2, 4, 6, 10, 16, 26 (the double Fibonacci sequence called the bijugate sequence) arises in around 6 percent of all the cases and is observed for example in *Aspidium* and *Bellis*. The phenomenon of phyllotaxis is thus essentially simple as far as those sequences are concerned, but the matter becomes complicated when on the same plant, such as *Bryophyllum* and *Anthurium*, one observes many Fibonacci-type sequences. This phenomenon is referred to as discontinuous transition. In the capituli of sunflowers and daisies, transitions are made along the same sequence. For example, we can observe in the center of the head (5, 8) phyllotaxis, followed in the middle part by (13, 8) phyllotaxis, and in the outer part by (13, 21) phyllotaxis. This is called a continuous transition. This phenomenon of growth has to do with the way crystals grow, and the daisy can be considered a living crystal.

**Stems of Leaves and the Golden Number.** Let us consider now a stem of leaves, as naturalists did in the mid-1830s. Take a point of insertion of a leaf at the bottom of the stem, and, in a helical or spiral movement around the stem, go to the next leaves above by the shortest path from one leaf to the next until a leaf is reached that is directly above the first chosen one. The leaves are then linked consecutively (1, 2, 3, 4, 5, . . .) along a helix, while in the case of the pine cone in the figure the five parastichies link the primordia by steps of five (e.g., 0, 5, 10, 15, 20, . . .). Then by making the ratio of the number of turns around the stem to the number of leaves met, excluding the first one, we obtain a fraction, such as 2/5, illustrated in the accompanying figure of the stem. In a significant number of cases the fractions obtained on various stems are 1/2, 1/3, 2/5, 3/8, 5/13, 8/21. . . . The numerators and the denominators of this sequence of fractions are consecutive terms of the Fibonacci sequence. Each fraction represents an angle $d$ between two consecutive leaves along the helix, known as the divergence angle. In the case of the pine cone the divergence is the angle between consecutively numbered primordia such as #24 and #25, and using a protractor it can be checked that $d \cong 137.5$ degrees, which is known as the Fibonacci angle.

These divergences are closely related to what is known as the golden number, denoted by the Greek letter $\tau$ (tau), where $\tau \cong 1.618$. Indeed, the value of $1/\tau^2 \cong 0.382$, which is the value the sequence of fractions approaches. For example, $5/13 \cong 0.384$ or $8/21 \cong 0.380$, and as we take fractions farther away in the sequence, such as $21/55$, we find that $21/55 \cong 0.381$ and that we are gradually approaching the value of $1/\tau^2$. Also the value of $360/\tau^2 \cong 137.5$.

**Phyllotaxis and Explanatory Modeling.** The aim of explanatory modeling is to try to reproduce the patterns from rules or mechanisms or principles—

imagined or hypothesized by the modeler—that are considered to be in action in shoot apices. The hypotheses are then transcribed into mathematical terms and their consequences are logically drawn and compared to reality. Two old hypotheses in particular have been scrutinized in different manners by the modelers. One is the chemical hypothesis that a substance such as a plant hormone produced by the primordia and the tip of the apex is at work, inhibiting the formation of primordia at some places and promoting their formation at others, thus producing the patterns. Another stresses the idea that physical-contact pressures between the primordia generate the patterns. A new hypothesis suggests that elementary rules of growth such as branching, and elementary principles such as maximization of energy, are at work producing the patterns. This model predicts the existence of a very unusual type of pattern, known as monostichy, in which all the primordia would be superimposed on the same side of the stem. This type of pattern was later discovered to exist in *Utricularia*. The same model shows the unity behind the great diversity of patterns.

Phyllotaxis is clearly a subject at the junction of botany and mathematics. Mathematics helps to organize the data, give meaning to it, interpret it, and direct attention to potentially new observations. The study of phyllotaxis has become a multidisciplinary subject, involving general comparative morphology, paleobotany, genetics, molecular biology, physics, biochemistry, the theory of evolution, **dynamical system theory**, and even **crystallography**. The patterns observed in plants can be seen to a much lesser extent in other areas of nature. SEE ALSO ANATOMY OF PLANTS; LEAVES; SHAPE AND FORM OF PLANTS; STEMS.

*Roger V. Jean*

**dynamical system theory** the mathematical theory of change within a system

**crystallography** the use of x-rays on crystals to determine molecular structure

### Bibliography

Church, A. H. *On the Relation of Phyllotaxis to Mechanical Laws.* London: Williams and Norgate, 1904.

Jean, Roger V. *Phyllotaxis: A Systemic Study in Plant Morphogenesis.* Cambridge: Cambridge University Press, 1994.

———, and Barabé Denis, eds. *Symmetry in Plants.* Singapore: World Scientific Publishing, 1998.

# Phylogeny

Before the mid-1800s, classification of organisms into groups, called **taxa**, was generally based on overall similarity of physical appearance. There was no guiding principle as to why the members of one group were more similar to each other than to the members of other groups. In 1859, Charles Darwin's *Origin of Species* was published, and Darwin's theory of evolution provided the explanation that natural groups occur because the members of the group are the descendants of a common ancestor. Based on Darwin's principles, in 1866, the German naturalist, Ernst Haeckel, coined the term *phylogeny* to describe the "science of the changes in form through which the phyla or organic **lineages** pass through the entire time of their discrete existence." Today the term phylogeny is used more widely to mean the evolutionary history or exact genealogy of a species or group of organisms. Phylogenies are based on the study of fossils, morphology, comparative anatomy, ultrastructure, biochemistry, and molecules.

**taxa** a type of organism, or a level of classification of organisms

**lineage** ancestry; the line of evolutionary descent of an organism

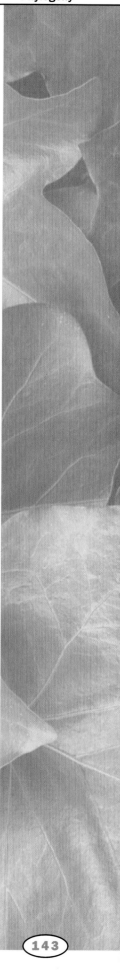

## "PRIMITIVE" VS. "ADVANCED" CHARACTERS

Fossil evidence has shown that bryophytes are the most primitive of the extant land plants. Bryophytes lack true xylem and phloem, although some mosses and liverworts have conducting tissues. Therefore, the absence of true xylem and phloem is a primitive feature. The presence of well-developed vascular tissue (xylem and phloem) in gymnosperms and angiosperms is a derived character.

Similarly, gymnosperms lack vessels in the xylem and angiosperms have vessels. The fossil record tells us that the gymnosperms came first, therefore, we know the vessels are a more recent, or derived, character. Often it is the fossil record that helps scientists polarize characters. For those plants for which we do not have an adequate fossil record, such as many of the green algae, polarizing characters and constructing a phylogeny becomes more difficult.

**monophyletic** a group that includes an ancestral species and all its descendants

## Theoretical Foundations

In his explicit phylogenetic scheme for land plants, Haeckel rejected theories of multiple origins for organisms, which he called polyphyletic. He used the term monophyly to describe a natural group of two or more taxa whose members are all descended from the nearest common ancestor. Phylogenies are based on **monophyletic** groups. The taxonomic theory of phylogenetic systematics is organized around the principles that organisms are related through descent from a common ancestor, that there are natural groups of monophyletic taxa, and that unique changes or modifications shared by members of a taxon are evidence of their evolutionary history.

Although monophyletic taxa exist in nature whether they are discovered or not, the goal of phylogenetic systematics is to reveal natural groups of taxa. The main principle of phylogenetic systematics is that natural groups are defined by uniquely shared evolutionary novelties, or homologous characters. A character is a heritable feature (one that is passed from an ancestor to its descendants) of an organism that can be described, measured, or otherwise compared to other organisms. To be considered homologous, a character must be not only heritable, but also independent from any other characters in an organism. The different forms a character may take are called the character states.

## Similarities and Phenetic Systems

Systems of classification that are based on overall similarity are called phenetic systems. Phenetic classification schemes do not distinguish between homologous characters (where taxa share a similar characteristic because they inherited it from a common ancestor) and analogous characters (where the characteristic shared by taxa was not inherited from a common ancestor). Sharing of homologous characters is evidence that taxa are evolutionarily related. For instance, the phloem that is found in carnations, roses, and lilies is a homologous similarity because all of these plants inherited the character from a common ancestor. The analogous phloemlike conducting tissue found in the giant kelps off the coast of California is functionally similar to phloem, but not inherited from the same common ancestor as the flowering plants. The evolution of analogous characters is also known as convergence or homoplasy, and often is the result of similar selection pressures in the environment on different organisms. In phylogenetic analysis, characters that are not recognized as being analogous can lead to unreliable results.

A homologous character can be an ancient retained feature, known as a plesiomorphy; while a homologous character that is the result of more recent evolutionary modifications is termed a derived character, or apomorphy. If taxa have the same apomorphy (that is, they share the same derived character), the character is termed a synapomorphy. German entomologist Willi Hennig, whose work was first translated into English in 1966, argued that only these shared, derived homologous characters (synapomorphies) could provide information about phylogeny, the evolutionary relationships of organisms. The methodology Hennig proposed to group taxa that share derived characters is now called cladistics.

## The Rise of Cladistics

Cladistic analysis is designed to find evidence about which two taxa are more closely related to each other than either is to a third. Finding this evidence requires distinguishing between primitive and derived states of a character, a process known as determining character polarity. The most widely used method for determining character polarity is the outgroup method.

The outgroup method is comparative. If a group of organisms being compared (the in-group) shares a character state with organisms outside the group (the outgroup), then the character state is considered to be plesiomorphic, and this character provides no information about relationships among the in-group taxa. For instance, as in the example above, phloem is found in carnations, roses, and lilies (the in-group). Phloem is also found, however, in pine trees (the outgroup), and, therefore, in this instance the presence of phloem is plesiomorphic. These comparisons are also relative. The presence of phloem is considered apomorphic (and informative) when used as evidence of monophyly in higher plants, because although phloem is found in all higher green plants, it is not found in the lower green plants, such as green algae or bryophytes.

In cladistics, these hierarchical relationships are shown on a branching diagram that is called a cladogram (sometimes referred to as an evolutionary tree). Taxa that share many homologues will group together more closely on a cladogram than taxa that do not. All of the taxa on each branch of a cladogram are considered to form a monophyletic group, comprising of all the descendants of a common ancestor plus that ancestor. This group is also known as a clade. Clades that are next to each other on a cladogram are known as sister clades and the taxa in the clades as sister taxa.

Cladistic methodology is based on a type of logical reasoning called parsimony. The principle of parsimony states that of two hypotheses, the one that explains the data in the simplest manner, or with the smallest number of steps, is best. Looking again at the example of presence of phloem, the hypothesis that carnations, roses, and lilies all have phloem because they inherited it from a single common ancestor requires fewer evolutionary steps and is therefore more parsimonious than the hypothesis that phloem arose two or three separate times.

## Phylogeny of the Green Plants

The concepts and practices discussed above have been used to study the phylogeny of the green plants as a whole, as well as many smaller groups of taxa. Although the presence of chlorophylls *a* and *b* was long thought to be a unifying character (synapomorphy) for the green plants, the fascinating phenomenon of **endosymbiosis** has resulted in organisms that are not green plants yet still have chlorophylls *a* and *b*. Specifically, the euglenophytes and the chloroarachniophytes, groups once considered to be green algae, carry the remains (that is, the chloroplasts) of their green algal endosymbionts, yet are themselves in very different evolutionary lineages than green algae.

For the true green algae and land plants, the whole array of characters mentioned earlier (for example, morphology, biochemistry, anatomy, and molecular comparisons) have provided some clear understanding of the basic phylogeny for this all-important group—the green plants—upon which life depends.

One of the most interesting observations provided by current phylogenies is the fact that there are two major lineages of green photosynthetic organisms: the Chlorophyta, which includes only freshwater and marine green algae, and the Streptophyta, which includes some freshwater green algae and all of the land plants. Another interesting aspect of the phylogeny of

## CHARACTER STATES

A botanist working with a particular group of flowering plants could observe that the flowers on some plants are red, whereas those on other plants are pink or white. The botanist might choose flower color as a character, with red, white, and pink as the character states.

If a character remains the same over generations with no changes, it will have only one state:

Pink—Pink—Pink—Pink—Pink

However, if the character changes in a species and the change is transmitted to descendants, there will be more than one character state:

Pink—White—White—White
\—Red—Red—Red

Choice of characters is one of the most important aspects of phylogenetic analysis. In the example above, flower color might be considered a good character if all species being examined have flowers of the same type, varying only in color. However, if the group contained species that did not ever flower, then the independence of the character flower color would be in question, because flower color would depend first on the presence or absence of flowers in general. Independence of characters is one of the main attractions of using molecular sequences for phylogenetic reconstruction. Since the early 1990s, use of sequence data from different genes has become so common in phylogenetic analysis that this methodology has its own term: molecular systematics.

**endosymbiosis** a symbiosis in which one organism lives inside the other.

## CONVERGENT EVOLUTION

The evolution of similar features in organisms that do not share a recent common ancestor is termed convergence. Convergence is often the result of similar, selective environmental pressures acting on organisms in different parts of the world. The classic botanical example of convergent evolution involves three very different groups of flowering plants—cacti, spurges, and milkweeds—growing in similar desert environments in the New World, Asia, and Africa. The harsh desert environment favors adaptive characteristics that provide the capacity for water storage (such as large, fleshy stems) and protection from extremes of heat and dryness (reduced leaves or spines). Although members of these groups of plants resemble each other in appearance, they do not have a close common ancestor.

green plants is that there was a single origin of the land plants from a green algal ancestor. Botanists are not absolutely certain which of the algae living today are the most closely related to the land plants, but they have narrowed the field to two groups.

Phylogenetic studies have also robustly established that the bryophytes (the mosses, liverworts, and hornworts) are the most primitive land plants. But, interestingly, there is still some uncertainly about which type of bryophyte is most closely related to the green algae—the hornworts or liverworts.

For the green plants, the phylogenetic history is not completely resolved, and scientists will continue using various methods of phylogenetic investigation to constantly improve and refine the understanding of the exact evolutionary history of all green plants, that is, the true phylogeny. SEE ALSO DARWIN, CHARLES; ENDOSYMBIOSIS; EVOLUTION OF PLANTS; SYSTEMATICS, MOLECULAR; SYSTEMATICS, PLANT; TAXONOMY.

*Russell L. Chapman and Debra A. Waters*

**Bibliography**

Forey, P. L., C. J. Humphries, I. L. Kitching, R. W. Scotland, D. J. Siebert, and D. M. Williams. *Cladistics: A Practical Course in Systematics.* New York: Oxford University Press, 1994.

Hennig, Willi. *Phylogenetic Systematics.* Urbana, IL: University of Illinois Press, 1966.

Lipscomb, Diana. *Basics of Cladistic Analysis.* Washington, DC: George Washington University, 1998.

Raven, Peter H., Ray F. Evert, and Susan E. Eichhorn, eds. *Biology of Plants*, 6th ed. New York: W. H. Freeman and Company, 1999.

Strickberger, Monroe W. *Evolution.* Boston: Jones and Bartlett Publishers, 2000.

Wiley, E. O. *Phylogenetics: The Theory and Practice of Phylogenetic Systematics*, 3rd ed. New York: Wiley-Interscience, 1981.

# Physiologist

**compound** a substance formed from two or more elements

**physiology** the biochemical processes carried out by an organism

A plant physiologist studies a large variety of plant processes, such as how chemicals are transported throughout the plant, how plants capture the energy from the sun, and how plants defend themselves from attack by microbes or insects. Plant physiologists also study the process of plant growth and development: how plant cells perceive their place and role within the plant, how factors such as light and gravity affect what plant cells will do, and how plant hormones signal to cells about environmental conditions. Thus, plant physiologists may study the mechanisms by which plants produce **compounds** of medicinal value or the effect of increased carbon dioxide concentrations or drought stress on plant growth. Such research can lead to identification of medicines, may serve to determine how plants respond to the proposed greenhouse effect, and may be used to create plants resistant to drought stress. Overall the study of plant **physiology** can benefit humanity by providing an increase in crop yields for farmers or the identification of more effective medicines. A plant physiologist is responsible for designing, implementing, and interpreting experiments related to plant biology. Plant physiologists also serve as teachers of plant biology to students of all ages and may help inform politicians of the role of science in our daily lives.

In order to pursue a career in plant physiology an individual should obtain a bachelor's degree in plant biology or a bachelor's degree in biology

Researchers in a seed technology laboratory examining sprouts.

with an emphasis in plants. Further specialized study, such as obtaining a master's or doctorate in plant biology, are helpful in securing employment and ensuring career advancement. Laboratory training in the methods and rationale of plant physiology is essential.

Universities, industry, botanical gardens, government agencies, and conservation organizations employ plant physiologists. The work performed by plant physiologists can be pursued in a wide variety of environments. Some physiologists pursue research purely in the laboratory. They may cultivate their plant of interest in a greenhouse or growth chamber and use these plants to study a process of interest by performing experiments within the laboratory. Other plant physiologists study plants in their native environment and spend a great deal of time outdoors. Depending on what plant process is being studied these scientists may travel the globe, studying medicinal plants in the tropical rain forest or carbon fixation in the arctic tundra.

The career of a plant physiologist is exciting because it is forever changing. Each day experiments are performed that provide new insight into how plants function and allow for discoveries of the unknown. The work may give a person the satisfaction of having contributed to a knowledge base that will forever serve to improve the quality of life on this planet. SEE ALSO PHYSIOLOGY.

*Sabine J. Rundle*

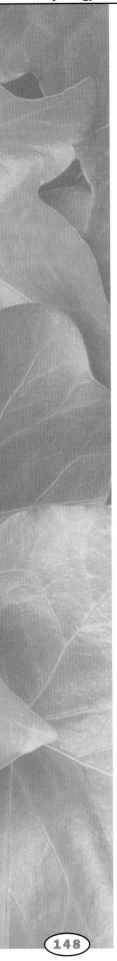

# Physiology

Plant physiology encompasses the entire range of chemical reactions carried out by plants. Like other living organisms, plants use deoxyribonucleic acid (DNA) to store genetic information and proteins to carry out cellular functions. **Enzymes** regulate both anabolism (buildup of complex **macromolecules**) and catabolism (the breaking down of macromolecules into simple molecules). Unlike animals, plants create a large variety of secondary metabolites, complex molecules with a range of specialized functions.

## Structure and Function of Macromolecules

**DNA.** Deoxyribonucleic acid (DNA) is a high-molecular-weight **polymer**, containing phosphate, four nitrogen bases, and the pentose sugar deoxyribose. There are two pyrimidine bases, cytosine and thymine, and two purine bases, adenine and guanine. These nitrogen bases are joined to long chains of alternating sugar and phosphate. The three-dimensional structure of DNA consists of a two-stranded alpha-helix with each strand consisting of a long chain of polynucleotides and the strands joined through the bases by hydrogen bonding. The two strands are precisely complementary in their base sequence, since adenine in one chain is always paired with thymine on the other (and vice versa) and, similarly, guanine is always paired with cytosine (see the accompanying figure of the structure of DNA).

DNA occurs in the chromosomal material of the nucleus, closely associated with proteins called histones. In higher plants, DNA is also present in the **chloroplasts** and mitochrondria of each cell. The sequence of DNA codes for protein synthesis in such a way that different base triplets determine, in turn, the amino acid sequence of that protein.

**RNA.** Ribonucleic acid (RNA) is similar in structure to DNA except that a different sugar, ribose, is present and the thymine of DNA is replaced by uracil. RNA also differs from DNA in being single- rather than double-stranded and it is also more labile (unstable) than DNA. The purpose of

**enzyme** a protein that controls a reaction in a cell

**macromolecule** a large molecule, such as protein, fat, nucleic acid, or carbohydrate

**polymer** a large molecule made from many similar parts

**chloroplast** the photosynthetic organelle of plants and algae

Basic structure of deoxyribonucleic acid (DNA).

Thymine    Adenine

Ribose

Phosphate

Cytosine    Guanine

**Sugar-phosphate chain**    **Sugar-phosphate chain**

RNA is to transfer the genetic information locked up in the DNA so that proteins are produced by the plant cell. In order to carry out this operation, there are three classes of RNA. Messenger RNA (mRNA) provides the exact template on which proteins of specific amino acid sequences are synthesized. Ribosomal RNA provides the site within the **cytosol** for protein formation. Transfer RNA (tRNA) makes up to 10 to 15 percent of the total cellular RNA, and serves an essential function in the decoding process of translating mRNA sequences into proteins. It carries amino acids to the ribosome, where they are linked together in the sequence dictated by mRNA. The result is a protein.

**cytosol** the fluid portion of a cell

**Proteins.** The proteins in plants, as in other organisms, are high-molecular-weight polymers of amino acids. These amino acids are arranged in a given linear order, and each protein has a specific amino acid sequence. In the simplest cases, a protein may consist of a single chain of amino acids, called a polypeptide. Several identical chains may, however, aggregate by hydrogen bonding to produce complex units with a much higher molecular weight. A polypeptide may coil up partly as an alpha-helix and thus adopt a particular three-dimensional structure. Many proteins are rounded in shape and hence are called globular proteins.

Many proteins are enzymes that catalyze particular steps in either primary or secondary metabolism. There are also many different storage proteins, found mainly in seeds, that provide a source of nitrogen in the young seedling. Perhaps the most important plant protein is ribulose 1,5-bisphosphate carboxylase, the essential catalyst for photosynthesis, which comprises up to 50 percent of the leaf protein in most green plants. Each green leaf, however, may synthesize up to one thousand different proteins, each with an assigned role in plant growth and development.

**Polysaccharides.** The chemistry of polysaccharides is, in a sense, simpler than that of the other plant macromolecules since these polymers contain only a few types of simple sugars in their structures.

The most familiar plant polysaccharides are cellulose and starch. Cellulose represents a very large percentage of the combined carbon in plants and is the most abundant organic **compound** on Earth. It is the fibrous material of the cell wall and is responsible, with lignin, for the structural rigidity of plants. Cellulose is known chemically as a beta-glucan and consists of long chains of $\beta 1 \rightarrow 4$ linked glucose units, the molecular weight varying from 100,000 to 200,000. Cellulose occurs in the plant cell as a crystalline lattice, in which long straight chains of polymer lie side by side linked by hydrogen bonding.

**compound** a substance formed from two or more elements

Starch differs from cellulose in having the linkage between the glucose units as $\alpha 1 \rightarrow 4$ and not $\beta 1 \rightarrow 4$ and also in having some branching in the chain. Starch, in fact, comprises two components, amylose and amylopectin. Amylose (approximately 20 percent of the total starch) contains about three hundred glucose units linked in a simple chain, which exists in vivo in the form of an alpha-helix. Amylopectin (approximately 80 percent) contains chains with regular branching of the main chain by secondary $\alpha 1 \rightarrow 6$ linkages. Its structure is thus randomly branched. Starch is the essential storage form of energy in the plant, and starch granules are frequently located within the chloroplast close to the site of photosynthesis.

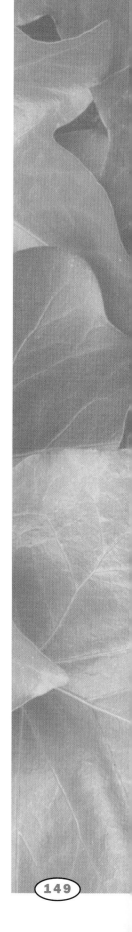

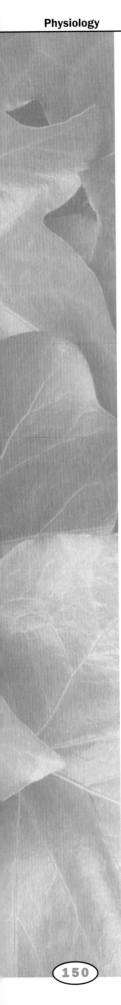

The different classes of polysaccharide fall into two groups according to whether they are easily soluble in aqueous solutions or not. Those that are soluble include starch, inulin, pectin, and the various gums and mucilages. The gums that are exuded by plants, sometimes in response to injury or infection, are almost pure polysaccharide. Their function in the plant is not entirely certain, although it may be a protective one. The less-soluble polysaccharides usually comprise the structural cell wall material and occur in close association with lignin. Besides cellulose, there are various hemicelluloses in this fraction. The hemicelluloses have a variety of sugar components and fall into three main types: xylans, glucomannans, and arabinogalactans. They are structurally complex, and other polysaccharide types may also be found with them.

## Anabolism and Catabolism: Biosynthesis and Turnover

**Anabolism.** Anabolism is the energy-requiring part of metabolism in which simpler substances are used to build more complex ones. In plants, primary metabolites are built up from very basic starting materials, namely $CO_2$, $H_2O$, nitrate ($NO^-_3$), sulfate ($SO_4^{2-}$), phosphate ($PO_4^{3-}$), and several trace metals. Each metabolite is formed by a discrete biosynthetic pathway, each step in the pathway being catalyzed by a separate enzyme.

**stomata** openings between guard cells on the underside of leaves that allow gas exchange

The most important anabolic pathway in green plants is the formation of starch from external $CO_2$ through the process of photosynthesis. Light energy is used to capture the atmospheric $CO_2$, taken in via the **stomata**, and convert it to sugar by condensing it with glycerophosphate, forming glucose 1-phosphate in the Calvin-Benson ($C_3$) cycle. In tropical plants, an additional carbon pathway is involved in photosynthesis, whereby the $CO_2$ is first captured by the plant in the form of simple organic acid such as malate. This is known as the Hatch-Slack ($C_4$) cycle, which provides a more efficient use of atmospheric $CO_2$. Regardless of the pathway, the glucose 1-phosphate is then used to produce starch. A similar end-product of carbohydrate metabolism is sucrose. Sucrose is important as an easily transportable form of energy within the plant. Starch, by contrast, is laid down mainly in the seed (e.g., of a cereal grain), and is not remobilized until that seed germinates in the following year.

Another equally important anabolic pathway in plants is that leading to protein synthesis. The starting material is usually inorganic nitrate taken in via the root from the soil and transported up the stem into the leaf. Here it is reduced to ammonia, which is immediately combined with alpha-ketoglutaric acid to yield glutamine. By a reshuffling process, glutamine is then converted to glutamic acid and by a variety of related processes the other eighteen protein amino acids are produced. These are then combined with tRNA and assembled together to yield the polypeptide chain(s) of protein.

Yet another anabolic mechanism is the formation of a lipid (an oil or fat). Lipids are produced from fatty acids, formed in turn from acetyl-coenzyme A, a product of glycolysis. Lignin, the building strength in wood and in plant stems, is produced by a pathway starting from the sugar sedoheptulose, available from the Calvin-Benson cycle. The nucleic acids and their bases are formed from protein amino acids. Purines are produced from glycine while pyrimidines are produced from aspartic acid.

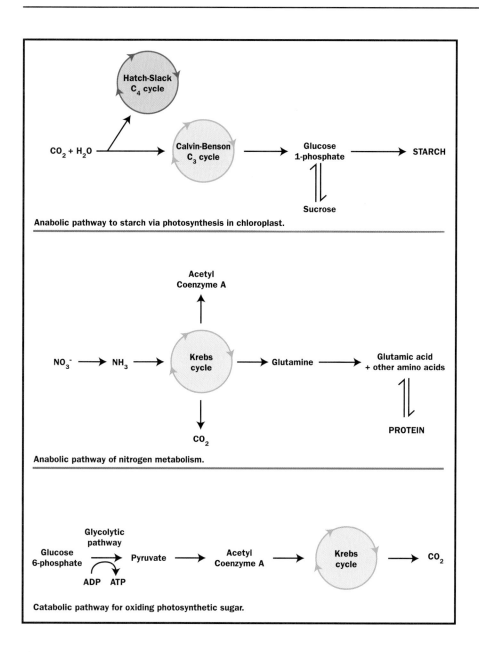

Anabolic pathway to starch via photosynthesis in chloroplast.

Anabolic pathway of nitrogen metabolism.

Catabolic pathway for oxiding photosynthetic sugar.

**Catabolism.** Catabolism includes any metabolic process involving the breakdown of complex substances into smaller products. Catabolism is thus the reverse of anabolism. No sooner is sugar available to the plant from photosynthesis than it is turned over and metabolized in order to provide the energy (e.g., in the form of adenosine triphosphate [**ATP**]) needed to drive the various processes that are taking place in the cell. Some ATP is provided in the process of glycolysis, by which glucose 1-phosphate is broken down to pyruvate and subsequently to acetyl-coenzyme A. The last stages in sugar metabolism include the entry of acetyl-coenzyme A into the Krebs tricarboxylic acid cycle. This process returns the carbon, originally taken in via photosynthesis, back into the atmosphere as respired $CO_2$, and each turn of the Krebs cycle provides more ATP for the cell.

A related pathway involving the Krebs cycle is the glyoxylate cycle, a pathway for lipid breakdown. This catabolic pathway can also become anabolic, converting the stored lipid into sugar.

**ATP** adenosine triphosphate, a small, water-soluble molecule that acts as an energy currency in cells

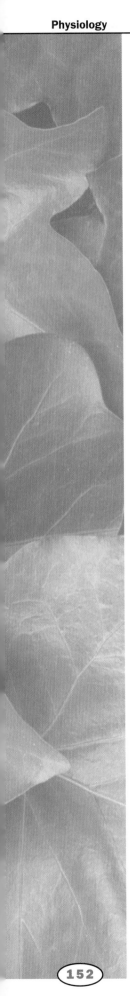

In summary, every metabolite in the plant cell is subject to both anabolism and catabolism. In other words, there is a continual turnover, with the building up and breakdown of larger molecules. In general, anabolism involves the input of energy to build molecules, while catabolism involves the release of that energy when molecules are broken down. Thus, the plant is in a continual state of flux or metabolic activity throughout its life cycle.

## Primary Metabolites vs. Secondary Metabolites

The compounds present in plants are conveniently divided into two major groups: primary and secondary metabolites. Primary metabolites are those produced by and involved in primary metabolic pathways such as respiration and photosynthesis. Secondary metabolites are clearly derived by **biosynthesis** from primary metabolites and are generally much more variable in their distribution patterns within the plant kingdom.

**biosynthesis** creation through biological pathways

Primary metabolites include the components of processes such as glycolysis, the Calvin-Benson cycle, and the Krebs cycle. Primary metabolites are virtually identical throughout the plant kingdom: they are mainly sugars, amino acids, and organic acids. As intermediates in metabolic pathways, these molecules may be present in some activated form. Glucose, for example, when taking part in metabolism, occurs in an energy-rich form as glucose 1-phosphate or as uridine diphosphoglucose. Other primary metabolites are the proteins, nucleic acids, and polysaccharides of plant cells. These have universal functions as enzymes, structural elements, storage forms of energy, and hereditary materials.

Secondary metabolites are produced by biosynthetic pathways, beginning with primary metabolites as starting materials. It has been estimated that about one hundred thousand secondary metabolites have been characterized in plants, and additional substances are continually being discovered. The amount of any secondary compound present in a plant is the result of an equilibrium between synthesis, storage, and metabolic turnover. Regulation of secondary metabolism is complex, and production may be limited to certain organs of the plant and may only take place during a single phase of the life cycle (e.g., during flowering or fruit formation).

**tannins** compounds produced by plants that usually serve protective functions; often colored and used for "tanning" and dyeing

Secondary metabolites are conveniently divided into three main chemical classes: the phenolics, the terpenoids, and the nitrogen-containing substances. The phenolics include the lignins, which are the aromatic materials of cell walls, and the anthocyanins, the colorful red to blue pigments of angiosperm flowers. Another phenolic class are the plant **tannins**, mainly present in woody plants, which have the special property of being able to bind to protein. They impart an astringent taste to plant tissues containing them and are significant flavor components in tea, wine, and other plant beverages.

**carotenoid** a colored molecule made by plants

The terpenoids are probably the most numerous of secondary substances. They are subdivided into monoterpenoids and sesquiterpenoids (essential oils); diterpenoids, including resin acids; triterpenoids (phytosterols, cardenolides, limonoids, etc.); and tetraterpenoids (**carotenoids**). The most visible terpenoids are the yellow to red carotenoid pigments present in flowers and fruits. Limonin gives lemon its characteristic taste. By contrast, volatile terpenoids give caraway and carrot their characteristic scents.

The nitrogen-based secondary metabolites are variously classified as amines, alkaloids, **cyanogenic** glycosides, and mustard oil glycosides. In general they have only limited occurrences. Alkaloids are the best known compounds of this type and are found in 20 percent of all plant families. Some alkaloids, such as morphine, because of their physiological activities in humans, have been used extensively in medicine. Other alkaloids, such as coniine from the hemlock, have been used as poisoning agents.

While the role of primary metabolites is clear, the functions of secondary substances are still uncertain. The anthocyanin and carotenoid pigments, together with the floral essential oils, are necessary to attract animals to flowers. The gibberellins, **auxins**, and cytokinins, together with abscisic acid and ethylene, control plant growth and development. Alkaloids and tannins deter animals from feeding on green tissues and thus are valuable to plants for limiting the extent of insect herbivory and animal grazing. SEE ALSO ALKALOIDS; CACAO; CARBOHYDRATES; CAROTENOIDS; CELLULOSE; COCA; DEFENSES, CHEMICAL; FLAVONOIDS; LIPIDS; OPIUM POPPY; PHOTOSYNTHESIS, CARBON FIXATION AND; PHOTOSYNTHESIS, LIGHT REACTIONS AND; PHYSIOLOGIST; PSYCHOACTIVE PLANTS; TERPENES.

*Jeffrey B. Harborne*

**cyanogenic** giving rise to cyanide

**auxin** a plant hormone

**Bibliography**

Dennis, D. T., and D. H. Turpin. *Plant Physiology, Biochemistry and Molecular Biology.* Harlow, Essex, UK: Longman Group, 1990.

Salisbury, F. B., and C. W. Ross. *Plant Physiology*, 3rd ed. Belmont, CA: Wadsworth Publishing, 1985.

Taiz L., and E. Zeiger. *Plant Physiology*, 2nd ed. Sunderland, MA: Sinauer Associates, 1998.

# Physiology, History of

The history of physiology—the discipline concerned with the functioning of plants—can be organized around the discovery of several key processes.

One of the first physiological questions to be studied scientifically was how plants obtain food. Although we now know that plants manufacture carbohydrates from carbon dioxide and water via photosynthesis, the ancient Greeks reasoned that a plant's food must come from the soil. This idea persisted until the 1600s, when Jean Baptiste van Helmont performed an experiment in which he carefully weighed a pot of soil and planted a willow seedling in it. Over a period of five years he added nothing but water to the pot, and the willow grew into a tree weighing over one hundred pounds. When he cut down the tree he found that the soil weighed the same, less about two ounces, as when he began the experiment. Thus, the soil could not be the source of the plant's food. Van Helmont concluded it could have come only from the water he added.

The idea that air could be utilized by plants was first suggested by Stephen Hales in the early 1700s. Hales noticed bubbles exuding from the cut ends of stems and reasoned that air might enter the plant through its leaves and circulate to other organs. At that time air was considered a uniform substance, and it was not until the late 1700s that Joseph Priestley found that air in a closed container could be altered by a burning candle or a living an-

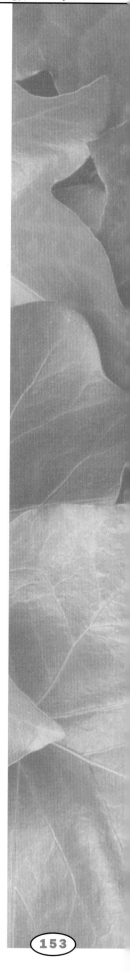

Joseph Priestley was the first to demonstrate that plants produce oxygen.

**chloroplast** the photosynthetic organelle of plants and algae

**radioisotopes** radioactive forms of an element

**transpiration** movement of water from soil to atmosphere through a plant

**osmotic** related to the movement of water across a membrane, due to differerences in concentration of dissolved substances

imal such that the flame would be extinguished and the animal would die. However, the presence of a plant in the container kept the candle burning and the animal alive. Priestley's results were the first to demonstrate that plants produce oxygen, now known to be a product of photosynthesis. Consequently, Jan Ingenhousz showed that oxygen is produced only by green parts of plants (and not roots, for example) and only in the light.

The remainder of the photosynthetic equation was elucidated largely by Nicholas de Saussure, who showed that during photosynthesis carbon dioxide is converted to organic matter, approximately equal amounts of carbon dioxide and oxygen are exchanged, and water is a reactant. In addition, Julius von Sachs, considered the founder of modern plant physiology, demonstrated that chlorophyll, located in **chloroplasts**, is involved. Thus, by the late 1800s photosynthesis could be summarized as follows:

$$6CO_2 + 6H_2O + light$$
$$\downarrow \text{ chlorophyll}$$
$$C_6H_{12}O_6 + 6O_2$$

In the 1930s C. B. van Neil suggested that the oxygen released in photosynthesis came from water rather than from carbon dioxide, and this was verified in the 1940s using **radioisotopes**. Details concerning the role of light were worked out by Robin Hill, Robert Emerson, and Daniel Arnon, and the reactions by which carbon dioxide is converted to carbohydrate were elucidated by Melvin Calvin and his colleagues in the early 1950s.

## Mineral Nutrition and the Transport of Water, Minerals, and Sugars

It had long been known that water, along with dissolved minerals, enters a plant through its roots. Sachs demonstrated that plants do not require soil and can be grown in an entirely liquid medium as long as the medium contains the minerals required for survival. This technique of hydroponics facilitated studies of the mechanisms for mineral uptake by the roots.

Another contribution of Hales was to demonstrate how water is transported in the plant. Hales established that water passes upward from the roots to the leaves, where it is lost to the atmosphere by the process of **transpiration**. But it was not until 1895 that Henry Dixon and John Joly proposed the cohesion theory to explain how transpiration causes water and dissolved minerals to be pulled upward through the xylem.

The transport of carbohydrates was found to take place by a different mechanism. In the late 1600s Marcello Malpighi noticed that when the bark was removed in a ring around a tree the portion of the bark above the ring increased in thickness while the portion below the ring did not. Because ringed trees continue to transpire, the ringing process apparently did not hinder water transport but instead prevented the transport of other substances necessary for growth. Later it was shown that bark contains phloem tissue, which transports sugars from the leaves to other plant parts. The mechanism of sugar transport, termed translocation, was a mystery until 1926, when E. Münch proposed the pressure-flow model, in which the **osmotic** entry of water into the phloem generates a hydrostatic pressure that pushes the dissolved carbohydrates both upward to the shoot tip and downward to the roots.

## Plant Hormones, Environmental Physiology, and Molecular Genetics

In the late 1800s Sachs suggested that the formation of roots and shoots was controlled by internal factors that moved through the plant. The first such factor, the plant hormone auxin, was discovered in 1928 by Fritz Went, building on experiments with phototropism by Charles and Francis Darwin, Peter Boysen-Jensen, and Arpad Paál. Went found that phototropism, the process by which stems bend toward the light, is the result of auxin migrating from the illuminated side of a **coleoptile** to the shaded side, where it stimulates growth. Over the next decades other plant hormones—most notably the gibberellins, cytokinins, ethylene, and abscisic acid—were discovered. Together with auxin, they regulate almost every aspect of plant growth and development.

In the 1950s emphasis shifted to biochemical mechanisms underlying physiological and developmental processes. Particularly important was the discovery by Harry Borthwick and Sterling Hendricks in 1952 of phytochrome, a pigment involved in a variety of developmental responses including flowering, seed germination, and stem elongation. In addition, there was a trend toward environmental physiology, a discipline in which the methods of plant physiology are applied to the problems of ecology, including plant responses to extremes of cold, salt, or drought.

The 1970s introduced the era of molecular genetics. Plant physiologists use molecular genetics to localize and identify the genes on a chromosome, understand the mechanisms by which genes are expressed, and elucidate the processes involved in coordinating the expression of genes in response to environmental signals. SEE ALSO CALVIN, MELVIN; DARWIN, CHARLES; DE SAUSSURE, NICHOLAS; GENETIC MECHANISMS AND DEVELOPMENT; HALES, STEPHEN; HORMONES; HYDROPONICS; INGENHOUSZ, JAN; PHOTOSYNTHESIS, CARBON FIXATION AND; PHOTOSYNTHESIS, LIGHT REACTIONS AND; PHYSIOLOGIST; PHYSIOLOGY; PHYTOCHROME; SACHS, JULIUS VON; TRANSLOCATION; TROPISMS; VAN HELMONT, JAN BAPTISTE; VAN NIEL, C. B.; WATER MOVEMENT.

*Robert C. Evans*

**coleoptile** the growing tip of a monocot seedling

### Bibliography

Moore, Randy, W. Dennis Clark, and Darrell S. Vodopich. *Botany*, 2nd ed. New York: McGraw-Hill, 1998.

Morton, A. G. *History of Botanical Science.* New York: Academic Press, 1981.

Salisbury, Frank B., and Cleon W. Ross. *Plant Physiology*, 4th ed. Belmont, CA: Wadsworth Publishing Co., 1992.

# Phytochrome

A plant grown in the dark appears long and spindly, is pale yellow, and has unexpanded leaves. When transferred to light, the growth rate of the stem slows, **chloroplasts** begin to develop and accumulate chlorophyll, and the primary leaves begin to expand and develop. Many of these dramatic changes are the result of activation of light receptors (photoreceptors) called phytochromes. Phytochromes are proteins with an attached pigment molecule that allows them to detect light, especially in the red

**chloroplast** the photosynthetic organelle of plants and algae

and far-red region of the spectrum. Depending on the light conditions, a phytochrome molecule may be converted to an active form or reconverted to an inactive form.

Most plants have more than one gene coding for different phytochromes, and these different products of the phytochrome gene family frequently control different responses to the light environment. Phytochromes regulate many aspects of plant growth and development by measuring the duration, intensity, and wavelengths of light. From the information gathered through phytochromes, a plant can determine the season, time of day, and whether it is growing beneath other plants versus in an open field. These photoreceptors control numerous functions throughout the life of the plant, including whether seeds germinate, how rapidly cells expand and divide, which genes are expressed, what shape and form a plant will take, and when the organism will flower and produce new seeds. SEE ALSO PHOTOPERIODISM; RHYTHMS IN PLANT LIFE.

*Timothy W. Short*

### Bibliography

Sage, Linda C. *Pigment of the Imagination: A History of Phytochrome Research*. San Diego, CA: Academic Press, 1992.

Quail, Peter H., Margaret T. Boylan, Brian M. Parks, Timothy W. Short, Yong Xu, and Doris Wagner. "Phytochromes: Photosensory Perception and Signal Transduction." *Science* 268 (1995): 675–80

# Pigments

Plant pigments are essential for photosynthesis, a process that supports all plant and animal life. They also play a key role in sensing light to regulate plant development and in establishing the communication between plants and the animals around them. Further, some plant pigments are the source of nutritional **compounds** required for or useful to the diets of humans and other animals.

**compound** a substance formed from two or more elements

The major classes of visible plant pigments are chlorophylls, carotenoids, flavonoids (including anthocyanins), and betalains. Each of these classes of pigments is composed of several individual compounds. For example, there are two major chlorophylls in higher plants, while there are hundreds of carotenoids and flavonoids that occur in nature. Phytochrome is a blue-green plant pigment that is not plentiful enough to be visible but serves as an important sensor of light, which stimulates plant growth and development.

## Pigment Occurrence and Function

All plants contain chlorophylls and carotenoids in their leaves and other green plant parts. The chlorophylls are green and central to the process of photosynthesis. They capture light energy and convert it to chemical energy to be used not only by plants but by all animals.

The carotenoids and related xanthophylls are red, orange, or yellow and occur in green plant tissues along with chlorophylls in plastids, where they capture oxidizing compounds generated during photosynthesis. Without the protection they offer, photosynthesis cannot occur, so all photosynthetic tissue contains both the visible green chlorophylls as well as the masked orange carotenoids. Carotenoids serve another function as accessory light-harvesting pigments and photoreceptors that make photosynthesis more efficient.

Animals rely on plant carotenoids as their ultimate source of all vitamin A. Some of the carotenoids, including beta-carotene, possess a chemical structure that allows them to be converted to vitamin A by animals that consume them. Some animals also derive their pigmentation from carotenoids. For example, pink flamingoes and yellow goldfish obtain their colors from dietary carotenoids.

Anthocyanins and other flavonoids, betalains, and some carotenoids serve a key role in attracting the attention of animals for pollination, dissemination of fruit, seed, and storage organs, or warning of undesirable plant flavor or antinutritional compounds. These pigments provide visual cues to animals, alerting them to maturing plant organs without chlorophyll on the background sea of green leaves, stems, and immature flowers and fruit. Anthocyanins in red roses, grapes, and potatoes; betalains in beets; and carotenoids in daylilies, oranges, and carrots are some familiar examples.

The flavonoids include the red and blue anthocyanins that attract the human and higher-animal eye. Other flavonoids are the yellow and white flavonols, flavones, aurones, and chalcones. Some of these are brilliantly colored to insects, which can detect light absorbed in the near ultraviolet range. **Tannins** are complex flavonoids that contribute to the brown or black color of leaves, seeds, bark, and wood. The betalains are red and yellow pigments that occur in several families of higher plants and serve a function similar to that of anthocyanins. SEE ALSO ANTHOCYANINS; CAROTENOIDS; CHLOROPHYLL; FLAVONOIDS; PHYTOCHROME.

*Philipp W. Simon*

**tannins** compounds produced by plants that usually serve protective functions; often colored and used for "tanning" and dyeing

**Bibliography**

Goodwin, T. W., ed. *Chemistry and Biochemistry of Plant Pigments*, 2nd ed. New York: Academic Press, 1976.

Gross, Jeana. *Pigments in Fruits.* London: Academic Press, 1987.

# Plant Community Processes

**Ecosystems** are formed from a mingling of nonliving **abiotic** components and the **biotic** community, which is composed of assemblages of living organisms. Many individuals in the biotic community are capable of capturing energy from sunlight through photosynthesis and, as a subset, form the plant community. The most prominent plants in the landscape are those with xylem and phloem forming **vascular** systems. While they are often the focus of plant community descriptions, green algae, mosses, and less-conspicuous plants also play a functional role in this ecosystem component. Heterotrophic organisms (including animals, bacteria, and fungi) feed on plants and form other subsets of the biotic community. These organisms are frequently examined along with plants in contemporary community studies. Understanding plant-plant, plant-animal, and animal-animal interactions has become a highly productive, community-level research area.

**ecosystem** an ecological community together with its environment

**abiotic** nonliving

**biotic** involving or related to life

**vascular** related to transport of nutrients

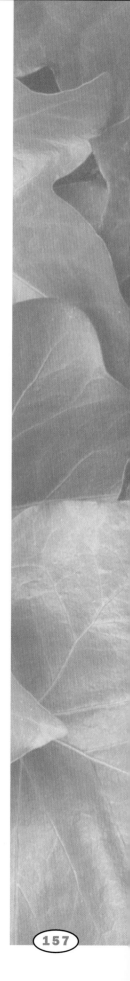

An old-growth Douglas-fir forest in the Pacific Northwest.

## Community Concept

It is possible to use the term *plant community* in two different but intertwined ways. Frequently it refers to a description of what is growing at a specific location in the landscape, such as the plant community making up the woods behind your house or the vegetation in a marshy area beside a pond. These communities are real and you can walk out into them and touch the trees or pick the flowers. Foresters refer to these real communities as stands and the term can be extended to all types of vegetation. The other reference to a plant community is more abstract. The term can be used to describe the properties of a particular assemblage of plants that appears repeatedly in many different places. People living in the eastern United States immediately draw up a picture in their mind when the phrase "oak forest" is mentioned, while those in the Midwest and Southwest know what someone is referring to when the phrases "tall prairie grassland" or "hot desert" are used respectively. Ecologists expand this familiarity into lists of probable plants and predictable appearances such the shapes of the trees, leaf types, and height of the vegetation in various types of communities. They cannot predict exactly what will be in a stand at a specific location, but they can statistically describe what would most likely be found. These descriptions expand the understanding of the meaning of the abstract community so that scientists know what someone is describing, even if they have never been there themselves.

Community types are characteristically found in geographic locations with similar climate patterns and habitat characteristics. These large-scale segments of the terrestrial landscape are referred to as biomes. The description of the overall climatic conditions, appearance, and composition of the biomes is studied in the field of **biogeography**. Many different types of plant communities exist within each biome since there are many combinations of variation in the slope, moisture availability, soil type, exposure, elevation, and other habitat characteristics within these biogeographic regions.

**biogeography** the study of the reasons for the geographic distribution of organisms

Plant communities of different types form carpets of vegetation that cover smaller segments of geographic regions, such as the drainage basin of a river or the hillsides of a mountain. This patchwork of communities, and the corridors that connect them, is referred to as the landscape mosaic. This level of organization is intermediate in scale between the biome and individual communities. Landscape elements are not only interconnected spatially, but also by functional interactions. There are properties of the landscape, which emerge from these interdependencies, that cannot be predicted from community-level studies alone, as described by Richard Forman (1995).

## Study of Communities

Plant ecologists over the years have developed many different techniques for gathering both descriptive and quantitative data from real stands, which can be used to characterize the abstract community types. *Terrestrial Plant Ecology* (1998), edited by Michael Barbour, includes an introduction to plant community sampling methodology and data analysis. John Kricher (1988 and 1993) uses a field guide approach to the understanding of the natural history of plant communities. Chapters covering community structure and function can be found in the references by Timothy Allen (1998), Manuel Molles (1999), and Robert Leo Smith and Thomas M. Smith (1998). The American roots of this discipline can be traced in *The Study of Plant Communities* (1956) by Henry J. Oosting, *Plant Communities: A Textbook of Plant Synecology* (1968) by Rexford Daubenmire, and *Plant Ecology* (1938) by John Weaver and Frederic E. Clements.

Plant community ecology can be traced back to the nineteenth century, when the Prussian biogeographer Fredrich Heinrich Alexander von Humbolt began to view vegetation as associations of plants and Johannes Eugenius Warming described various characteristics of different community types. Many other Europeans followed this line of research, notably Josias Braun-Blanquet, a central figure at the beginning of the twentieth century in what became known as the Zurich-Montpellier School of Phytosociology, where synecology (another name for community ecology) flourished.

## Community Organization

The American ecologist Frederic Clements extended the community concept to the point where obligatory plant community composition and the resulting functional interactions were thought of as unique superorgan-

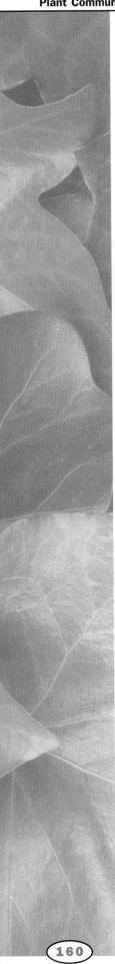

isms, with individual species being as essential to their identity as the organs are to an animal. This idea prevailed from the 1920s until after the middle of the century, when Robert Whittaker carried out several studies in mountainous regions of the United States. He clearly demonstrated that a wide variety of intermediate community compositions existed in these complex environments and that those communities functioned perfectly well. What appeared to be a superorganism, with obligatory development patterns and species composition, just happened to exist over wide areas with similar habitat conditions. This was not a completely original idea. In 1926 Henry Gleason proposed that the appearance of obligatory groupings resulted from the success of individual species having similar environmental needs occurring together by chance. This was only shortly after the superorganism concept gained its foothold on scientific thought. However, until the evidence from Whittaker's methodical study was available to support Gleason's idea, many held that interactions between individuals produced community evolution similar to that proposed for species.

**gradient** difference in concentration between two places

The community is now seen as a many-dimensioned **gradient** of possible combinations of plant species. Readily identifiable community types exist because certain groupings that are successful under conditions occurring repeatedly in the landscape are more likely to be encountered than others.

## Succession in Communities

One aspect of community organization accepted by ecologists is that the plants, animals, and microorganisms are very interconnected in function. Trees shade the forest floor and make it cooler than adjacent fields. Leaves from those trees decompose when they fall and provide nutrients for a variety of plants through their roots, which they may even reabsorb themselves. The same leaves could provide food for browsing animals while on the tree or for decomposing organisms as part of the litter on the forest floor. Fires, floods, volcanic eruptions, or human activities such as farming and forestry disrupt these interactions, but are not as disastrous to the long-term survival of the natural community as they might first appear, particularly if they do not occur with great frequency. This is because communities have self-repairing capabilities through the process of directional succession.

If the disruption to the community is limited primarily to the biological matter above the ground and at least some of the soil remains intact, as is the case with an abandoned agricultural field, pasture, or recently burnt forest, the process is called secondary succession. This is a replacement process that is facilitated by a variety of mechanisms for the replacement of vegetation. In many cases, seeds are already present in the soil as part of a seed bank; sometimes wind or animals transport them in. Often, if the disruption has not been too severe, or if the regrowth is due to a change in land use, some vegetation, including weeds, will already be growing. It will become the basis for the early stages of successional development. In other cases, such as lumbering, where the tree trunks have been harvested, or where the aboveground parts were killed by certain types of fire, branches will sprout up from living roots. This produces what is called **coppice growth**, and one or more stems will produce a new tree trunk. Because of

**coppice growth** growth of many stems from a single trunk or root, following removal of the main stem

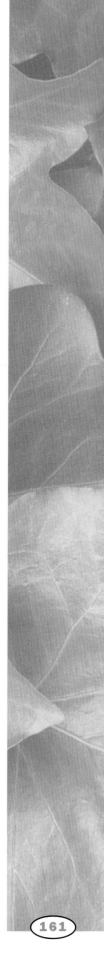

this process, the age of forest trees determined by counting rings in trunk wood may be a gross underestimate of the actual age of the organism as defined by the root tissue. Frequently more than one of these mechanisms will play a role in reestablishing plants in a disturbed area.

However, if there is no soil left at all, as is the case following a rockslide, the retreat of a glacier, or the development of vegetation on lava deposited from volcanic flows, then the process takes much longer. This is because at least some soil development is required before plants can become established in this process of primary succession. This sequential replacement on dry habitat sites is called xerarch succession, but can also occur when previously aquatic sites fill in through **sedimentation** resulting in the production of terrestrial communities called hydrarch succession. Changes under intermediate soil moisture conditions, including those for most secondary succession, occur in mesarch environments.

**sedimentation** deposit of mud, sand, shell, or other material

Different functional models exist to explain how succession proceeds. One model proposes that early species alter the environmental conditions and facilitate, or prepare the way, for species that occur in later stages. The second model suggests that some species become established early on in the process and inhibit the successful invasion by others. The third model does not involve facilitation or inhibition, but essentially holds that species that can tolerate the conditions that exist are successful in becoming established. Most likely all three processes can occur depending on conditions and timing.

Self-generating or autogenic succession leads to changes in community structure and ecosystem function. In the late 1960s, Eugene Odum described this as an overall strategy for ecosystem development. Even though general patterns of change appear to emerge, exceptions sometimes occur. There are, however, tendencies toward increases in **biodiversity** as succession progresses with slight declines as systems mature. Similarly, complexity and structure increase as succession proceeds, and increased proportional amounts of energy flow are needed to support increasing living community **biomass**; there can be a tightening of nutrient cycling as the systems age. Thirty years later, Odum (1997) updated his thoughts in light of extensive research stimulated by the original model. In addition to **systemic** changes such as these, there are also plant life cycle strategies such as high seed number production, aggressive seed dispersal, high sunlight preferences, and rapid growth amongst invasive species that appear early in succession. These are in contrast with the shade-tolerant, slower-growing, longer-lived species that play a larger role as the system matures. Fundamentally, as succession progresses, the organisms change the environment and in turn, the environment alters the relative success of individuals within the communities.

**biodiversity** degree of variety of life

**biomass** the total dry weight of an organism or group of organisms

**systemic** spread throughout the plant

## Competition Within Communities

Because plant communities are composed of organisms with similar overall climatic requirements, and because resources such as nutrients, light, and water are present in finite amounts, there is a continuing interaction between individuals that determines their success in capturing and utilizing these resources. This interaction takes various forms and is referred to as competition. Competition is one of several different types of individual

**predation** the act of preying upon; consuming for food

**mutualism** a symbiosis between two organisms in which both benefit

**obligate** required, without another option

interactions that plants can be involved in and includes forms of exploitation, such as seed **predation**, herbivory, and parasitism; cooperation, such as **mutualism,** which may or may not be obligatory; and other specialized relationships. When the individuals are of the same type, the competition is said to be intraspecific, and when they are different, the interaction is interspecific. The term symbiosis is used to describe interspecific interactions involving close and continual physical contact and may be either deleterious, as in parasitism, or highly beneficial, as in the case of **obligate** mutualism.

Competition is somewhat unique in comparison to most other relationships, where at least one of the interacting individuals benefits from the interaction when it occurs. When competition is occurring, both partners to the interaction are most likely adversely affected. The most intense competition occurs between individuals with very similar needs. Consequently, intraspecific competition generally has a greater impact on the success of a particular plant in the community than interspecific competition. However, if most individuals of one species are more successful than most of another, then there will be more of them present. Since they lack the social organization of animals, complex coordinated group competition is unlikely to be an important aspect of competition in plants; in the case of plant competition, the interaction between individuals is more likely to be significant.

## Competitive Exclusion and the Ecological Niche

The result of the interaction can affect the relative success of populations of a species and ultimately the community composition. In the 1930s, the Russian microbiologist G. F. Gause performed laboratory experiments that led to the conclusion that when populations of two different species are directly competing for a common resource in a limited environment, only one will ultimately be sustained in that space. The other will die out. This idea has come to be known as Gause's competitive exclusion principle. If this principle were to be valid in natural environments, then the number of surviving species would be greatly limited. However, this is not the case, particularly in complex plant communities.

The solution to this perplexing puzzle has been found in a process known as resource partitioning. Even some very obvious situations—where resource demand overlap between individuals clearly exists—demonstrate subtle differences in the way that the resource is exploited when examined in detail. Roots of one individual or species may penetrate to slightly different depths in the soil from another, or flowering times might be a few days different, thereby reducing competition for the services of a particular pollinator.

The entire complex of resource, habitat, physical, and other requirements that define the role of an organism within its community is called its ecological niche. The more similar the niches of two individuals or species, the greater the niche overlap. The greater the niche overlap, the greater the competition. The species composition of a community is a result of the way that individuals of different species with different niches can be packed together. Increases in the number of species within a community are accomplished by specialization, the reduction of the sizes of the niches, and efficient packing to reduce overlap. The number of niches that exist in a community is directly related to species diversity, the number of different types of organisms that can be supported.

## Competitive Interactions

The plant community is a dynamic, competitive environment. Community composition exists in steady state, a status of apparent equilibrium, for varying periods of time. A pulse disturbance such as a fire, or more chronic stresses such as disease, evolutionary change, or global warming may alter the status quo. Increased global mobility of plant seeds and fragments of tissue, as well as various pathogens and disease vectors such as insects, have increased the chances of incursion by invasive species or the introduction of new competitors, which may lead to significant alterations in community composition. Because of this flexibility and inherent resilience, communities persist over time, even though the presence of specific organisms varies.

The intense defense of resources and the aggressive forays to acquire the essentials for survival by plants are not necessarily obvious. Competition between animals can be physical combat, and plants analogously can physically grow into the space occupied by another individual and crowd it out. However, the adaptations that make plants successful as competitors are generally more indirect. Examples of this include plants with more vigorous canopy growth that intercept the available light, or the individual with the healthier and more extensive root system that is more efficient at obtaining nutrients from the soil. Sometimes, just being able to grow faster is sufficient to give a competitive advantage. Many species have evolved to produce **toxins** that inhibit the growth of other plants, a condition known as allelopathy, and this can give them a competitive edge, particularly in the case of interspecific competition where self-inhibition is limited. SEE ALSO ALLELOPATHY; BIOGEOGRAPHY; BIOME; CLEMENTS, FREDERIC; INTERACTIONS, PLANT-PLANT; ODUM, EUGENE; SYMBIOSIS.

*W. Dean Cocking*

**toxin** a poisonous substance

### Bibliography

Allen, T. F. H. "Community Ecology, The Issue at the Center." In *Ecology*. S. I. Dodson et al, eds. New York: Oxford University Press, 1998.

Barbour, Michael G., ed. *Terrestrial Plant Ecology*, 3rd ed. New York: Addison-Wesley, 1998.

Daubenmire, Rexford. *Plant Communities: A Textbook of Plant Synecology.* New York: Harper & Row Publishers, 1968.

Forman, Richard. *Land Mosaics: The Ecology of Landscapes and Regions.* Cambridge, England: Cambridge University Press, 1995.

Kricher, John, and Gordon Morrison. *A Field Guide to Eastern Forests: North America.* Boston: Houghton Mifflin Company, 1988.

———. *A Field Guide to the Ecology of Western Forests.* Boston: Houghton Mifflin Company, 1993.

Molles Jr., Manuel C. *Ecology: Concepts and Applications.* Boston: WCB/McGraw-Hill, 1999.

Odum, Eugene P. *Ecology: A Bridge Between Science and Society.* Sunderland, MA: Sinauer Associates, Inc., 1997.

Oosting, Henry J. *The Study of Plant Communities*, 2nd ed. San Francisco: W. H. Freeman and Company, 1956.

Smith, Robert L., and Thomas M. Smith. *Elements of Ecology*, 6th ed. New York: Benjamin/Cummmings, 2000

Weaver, J. E., and F. E. Clements. *Plant Ecology*, 2nd ed. New York: McGraw-Hill, 1938.

# Plant Prospecting

Plant prospecting is the seeking out of plants for the development of new foods, prescription drugs, herbal dietary supplements, flavors and fragrances, cosmetics, industrial materials, pesticides, and other profitable products. Plant prospecting includes the selection and collection of plants from terrestrial, marine, and other aquatic **ecosystems** by expeditions to diverse areas of the world, such as tropical and temperate rain forests as well as arid and semiarid lands in Latin America, Africa, Australia, and Asia.

Field studies involve collecting plant samples in the wild for identification and labeling the samples for voucher, or reference, **specimens**. The specimens are deposited in herbaria, which are collections of preserved plants. If searching for plants for drug discovery programs, one kilogram of each plant species is typically gathered for further work in the laboratory. A plant extract is produced for screening for biological activity, followed by chemical isolation and identification of the compounds responsible for activity.

Botanists follow either random or targeted approaches when choosing plants for pharmacological studies and drug discovery. The random prospecting strategy is to gather all of the available vegetation in an area supporting rich biological diversity. The more focused methods are taxonomic, ecological, and ethnobotanical. The taxonomic method emphasizes the collection of close relatives of plants already known to produce useful compounds for medicine or other uses. The ecological approach focuses on plants that offer certain clues promissory of activity, such as plants free from herbivore predation, which imply the presence of chemical defenses. Finally, ethnobotanical prospecting is done by interviewing native healers who have knowledge of the local plant's medicinal properties.

The value of plant prospecting to the pharmaceutical industry is enormous. Some extremely effective treatments in modern medicine are derived from flowering plants in nature. Many prescription drugs contain molecules derived from, or modeled after, naturally occurring molecules in **vascular** plants. Tropical rain forests, with one-half or 125,000 of the world's flow-

**ecosystem** an ecological community together with its environment

**specimen** object or organism under consideration

**vascular** related to transport of nutrients

A biologist collects plant specimens from the forest floor in Poland's Bialowieza National Park.

ering plant species, are the source of forty-seven commercial drugs, including vincristine (Oncovin), vinblastine (Velban), codeine, curare, quinine, and pilocarpine. Vincristine is the drug of choice for the treatment of childhood leukemia; vinblastine is used for the treatment of Hodgkin's disease and other neoplasms.

The potential value of the existence of undiscovered plants for use as drugs for modern medicine and other plant products of economic interest provide an incentive to conserve species-rich ecosystems throughout the world. A fear shared by many is that plant species, as well as tribal healing and conservation knowledge, will vanish before they are studied and recorded.

Because developing countries are rich in plant **biodiversity** but technology-poor, while developed countries are biodiversity-poor but technology-rich, arrangements should be made to compensate the holders of plant resources when these are used to make patentable and economic products. Efforts are underway to establish property rights of plant biodiversity, as yet-undiscovered drugs will become another powerful financial incentive to conserve tropical forests and other ecosystems. The 1992 Convention on Biological Diversity established for the first time international protocols for protecting and sharing national plant and other biological resources and specifically addressed issues of traditional knowledge. SEE ALSO HERBARIA.

*Barbara N. Timmermann*

**biodiversity** degree of variety of life

### Bibliography

Artuso, Anthony. *Drugs of Natural Origin.* New York: Haworth Press, 1997.

Grifo, Francesca, and Joshua Rosenthal, eds. *Biodiversity and Human Health.* Washington, DC: Island Press, 1997.

Rouhi, A. Maureen. "Seeking Drugs in Natural Products." *Chemical and Engineering News* 75, no. 14 (1997): 14–29.

Ten Kate, Kerry, and Sarah A. Laird. *The Commercial Use of Biodiversity.* London: Earthscan Publications Ltd., 1999.

# Plants

Plants are photosynthetic multicellular eukaryotes, well-separated evolutionarily from photosynthetic **prokaryotes** such as the **cyanobacteria**. Three **lineages** of photosynthetic eukaryotes are recognized: 1) green plants and green algae, with chlorophylls *a* and *b* and with **carotenoids**, including beta-carotene, as accessory **pigments**; 2) red algae, having chlorophylls *a* and *d*, with phycobilins as accessory pigments; and 3) brown algae, golden algae, and **diatoms**, with chlorophylls *a* and *c* and accessory pigments that include fucoxanthin.

Plants are differentiated from algae based on their exclusive multicellularity and their adaption to life on land. However, these two groups are so closely related that defining their differences is often harder than identifying their similarities. Fungi, often considered to be plantlike and historically classified with plants, are not close relatives of plants; rather, they appear to be closely related to animals, based on numerous molecular and biochemical features. Fossil evidence indicates that plants first invaded the land approximately 450 million years ago. The major groups of living land plants

**prokaryotes** single-celled organisms without nuclei, including Eubacteria and Archaea

**cyanobacteria** photosynthetic prokaryotic bacteria formerly known as blue-green algae

**lineage** ancestry; the line of evolutionary descent of an organism

**carotenoid** a colored molecule made by plants

**pigments** colored molecules

**diatoms** hard-shelled single-celled marine organisms; a type of protist

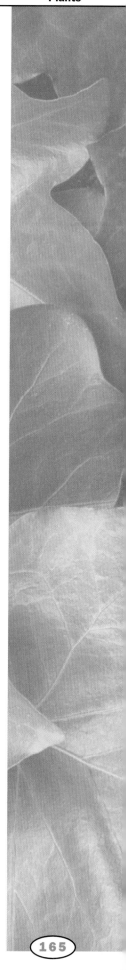

are liverworts, hornworts, and mosses (collectively termed bryophytes); ly-cophytes, ferns, and horsetails (collectively pteridophytes); and five lineages of seed plants: cycads, *Ginkgo*, gnetophytes, conifers (gymnosperms), and flowering plants (angiosperms). SEE ALSO ALGAE; ANATOMY OF PLANTS; AN-GIOSPERMS; BRYOPHYTES; ENDOSYMBIOSIS; FUNGI; GYMNOSPERMS; PIGMENTS.

*Doug Soltis and Pam Soltis*

### Bibliography

Raven, Peter H., Ray F. Evert, and Susan E. Eichhorn. *Biology of Plants*, 6th ed. New York: W. H. Freeman and Company, 1999.

# Plastids

All eukaroytic cells are divided into separate compartments, each surrounded by an independent membrane system. These compartments are called or-ganelles, and they include the nucleus, **mitochondria**, **vacuoles**, Golgi bod-ies, **endoplasmic reticulum**, and microbodies. In addition to these organelles, plant cells contain a compartment that is unique to them. This is the plastid.

## General Description of Plastids

Plastid is a term applied to an organelle that is exclusive to plant cells. Most of the **compounds** important to a plant, and to human diet, start out in the plastid. It is the place in the cell where carbohydrates, fats, and amino acids are made. As the name suggests, the plastid is plastic (i.e., changeable) in both appearance and function, and the different types of plastids can change from one type to another. The signals that trigger these changes can come from within the plant itself (e.g., developmental changes such as fruit ripen-ing or leaf senescence) or from the surrounding environment (e.g., changes in day length or light quality). Despite this plasticity, all plastids have the fol-lowing features in common: They are 5 to 10 **microns** in diameter and ap-proximately 3 microns thick, are all surrounded by a double membrane termed the envelope that encloses a water-soluble phase, the stroma, and they all contain deoxyribonucleic acid (DNA) and ribonucleic acid (RNA).

The presence of DNA is one indication that plastids used to exist as free-living organisms. Plastids would have once contained all of the genes necessary for their growth and development. Although plastid DNA (the plastid **genome**) still encodes many essential plastid components, most of the genetic information now resides in the nucleus. During evolution most of the DNA became integrated into the nucleus so that the host cell con-trolled the genes needed for division and development of plastids. This im-portant evolutionary step has consequently enabled the host cell to control most features of plastid structure and function. Thus, distinct types of plas-tids are found in different cells and tissues of the plant.

## Eoplasts

Eoplasts (*eo*, meaning "early") represent the first stage of plastid devel-opment. They are spherical and lack any obvious internal membranes of the kind seen in **chloroplasts**. They occur in young, dividing cells of a plant (i.e., the **meristematic** cells) and are functionally immature. Their presence in egg cells prior to pollination means that they are transferred through gen-

**mitochondria** cell organelles that produce ATP to power cell reactions

**vacuole** the large fluid-filled sac that occupies most of the space in a plant cell. Use for stor-age and maintaining internal pressure

**endoplasmic reticulum** membrane network inside a cell

**compound** a substance formed from two or more elements

**micron** one millionth of a meter; also called micrometer

**genome** the genetic material of an organism

**chloroplast** the photo-synthetic organelle of plants and algae

**meristematic** related to cell division at the tip

erations via maternal inheritance. This means that eoplasts can only be made from preexisting eoplasts inherited via the egg. Eoplasts are able to divide along with the cell so that their number is maintained during plant growth. Increases in eoplast numbers occur when they continue to divide after cell division is complete. This is accompanied by cell differentiation, where the cell becomes specialized, and the eoplast matures into one of the functional types of plastid described next.

## Chloroplasts

Chloroplasts are plastids found in photosynthetic tissue. This includes leaves, but also green stems, tendrils, and even fruit. Unripe tomato fruit, for example, contains chloroplasts as long as the tissue is green. On ripening, the chloroplasts change into chromoplasts and accumulate the pigments responsible for the red coloration of ripe fruit. Chloroplasts are distinguished from all other types of plastids by the presence of a complex organization of the internal membranes that form thylakoids. These form stacks of parallel membranes (called granal stacks) that contain the light-harvesting complexes involved in capturing light energy for use in photosynthesis. The chloroplast is the location of the photosynthetic processes occurring within the tissue. As well as the light-harvesting reactions, the **enzymes** responsible for carrying out the fixation of carbon dioxide, in a process called the Calvin-Benson cycle, are also located here. A mature cell of a cereal leaf, such as wheat, can contain up to two hundred chloroplasts.

**enzyme** a protein that controls a reaction in a cell

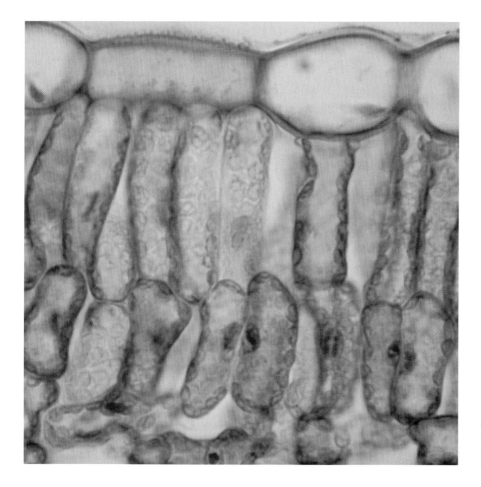

A cross-section micrograph of chloroplasts in a lilac leaf.

Chloroplasts are formed from the eoplasts present in very young leaf cells. Another route, although less common in nature, is for them to form from etioplasts, but this happens only if the leaves have been kept out of the light for several days and then transferred back into sunlight.

## Etioplasts

Etioplasts are a special type of plastid that only occurs in leaf tissue that has been kept in the dark for several days. This dark treatment causes the leaves to lose their green color, becoming pale yellow and losing their ability to photosynthesize. These leaves are described as being etiolated, hence the term etioplast. Etioplasts are characterized by containing semicrystalline structures called prolamellar bodies made up of complex arrays of membranes. When etiolated leaves are exposed to the light, the leaves turn green and the etioplasts change into chloroplasts within a very short time. The membranes of the prolamellar body are converted into the thylakoid membranes, and chlorophyll is formed together with all of the enzymes needed for photosynthesis. All of these processes are reversible. When green leaves are put back into continued darkness for several days, the chloroplasts revert once more to etioplasts.

## Chromoplasts

Chromoplasts (Greek *chromo*, meaning "color") are colored plastids found in flower petals and **sepals**, fruit, and in some roots, such as carrots. They are colored because they contain pigments. These are the carotenoids, and they produce a range of coloration including yellow, orange, and red. The purpose of this coloration is to attract pollinators and, in the case of edible fruits, animals that will aid fruit and seed dispersal. Sometimes the color may act as a warning signal to tell insects and animals that the plant is poisonous. As noted above, chromoplasts may be formed from chloroplasts as green fruit ripens and matures. Alternatively, they may be formed from the conversion of amyloplasts or by development of eoplasts.

## Leucoplasts

Leucoplasts are colorless, nonphotosynthetic plastids found in nongreen plant tissue such as roots, seeds, and storage organs (e.g., potato tubers). Their main function is to store energy-rich compounds, and types of leucoplasts include amyloplasts and elaioplasts. Amyloplasts store starch and elaioplasts contain oils and fats. In roots, amyloplasts serve two important functions. Their high starch content makes them relatively dense, and this is thought to be important in helping the root to respond to gravity (geotropism). Root amyloplasts are also very important in that they contain many of the enzymes needed for converting inorganic nitrogen taken up from the soil (as nitrate and ammonium) into organic forms, such as amino acids and proteins. Starch is a major food product and as a consequence, a lot of current research is aimed at understanding how amyloplasts work and what controls the rate of starch formation in these plastids. Similarly, the formation of oils (e.g., in oil seed rape seeds) in elaioplasts is being studied in many research and industrial laboratories throughout the world. SEE ALSO CELLS; CHLOROPLASTS; ENDOSYMBIOSIS.

*Alyson K. Tobin*

**sepals** the outermost whorl of flower parts; usually green and leaf-like, they protect the inner parts of the flower

**Bibliography**

Raven, Peter H., Ray F. Evert, and Susan E. Eichhorn. *Biology of Plants*, 6th ed. New York: W. H. Freeman and Company, 1999.

**Poaceae**  *See Grasses.*

# Poison Ivy

Poison ivy (*Toxicodendron radicans*) is a nuisance plant that grows throughout the continental United States. It grows in almost any type of soil, in both the shade and the sun. While it is most commonly found as a trailing vine, it can also form an upright shrub, and can climb trees, boulders, or walls to heights of 15 meters (50 feet). Its seeds are an important winter food for many types of birds.

Poison ivy's oil causes an itchy, blistering rash in most people who come in contact with it. All parts of the plant contain the oil, although the leaves are the most easily bruised and are therefore the most likely to cause the rash. The oil is sticky and will cling to (and be spread on) skin, clothing, tools, and animal fur. It is also spread in smoke when the plant is burned. In fact, irritation from poison ivy smoke is a major cause of temporary disability in forest fire fighters.

The active ingredient of the oil is urushiol (you-ROOSH-ee-ol). Urushiol is absorbed quickly into the skin. The itching and blistering that results is not due to direct damage done by urushiol, but by the allergic reaction mounted by the immune system. Relatively few people are actually immune to the effects of urushiol, although sensitivity varies and can change over time. Washing the oil off immediately after contact can help reduce the likelihood of developing a rash. In recent years, a clay-based lotion has been shown to help prevent the rash by binding to the urushiol before it can penetrate the skin.

Rashes last approximately two weeks. Some people find relief from the itching and blistering by applying calamine lotion or the mucilaginous sap of jewelweed (*Impatiens capensis*). Hot water can provoke a short-lived, in-

Poison ivy.

tense irritation followed by a longer period of relief. Prescription corticosteroid creams are used for severe cases.

Recognizing the plant is the best way to avoid it. The three leaflets of poison ivy are from 3 to 15 centimeters long, smooth to slightly indented at the edges, shiny and reddish in spring but becoming a glossy to dull green in summer. "Leaflets three, let it be; berries white, poisonous sight" is a handy way to remember the characteristic appearance of poison ivy.

Poison oak, which grows in California, Oregon, and Washington, has a somewhat similar appearance, while poison sumac grows as a shrub and has a compound leaf and drooping clusters of green berries (unlike other sumacs, which have upright clusters or red berries). All three plants are members of the family Anacardiaceae, many of whose members—including mango and cashew—also contain skin irritants in some plant parts. SEE ALSO DEFENSES, CHEMICAL; LIPIDS; POISONOUS PLANTS.

*Richard Robinson*

**Bibliography**

Darlington, Joan R. *Is It Poison Ivy: Field Guide to Poison Ivy, Oak, Sumac and Their Lookalikes*, 2nd ed. Durham, NH: Oyster River Press, 1999.

# Poisonous Plants

A plant or mushroom is considered poisonous or toxic if the whole organism, or any part of it, contains potentially harmful substances in high enough concentrations to cause illness or irritation if touched or swallowed. From the waxen-leaved dieffenbachia in your living room to the delicate foxglove blooming in your garden to the shoots sprouting from a forgotten potato in your refrigerator, poisonous plants are a common part of our lives. Since it is neither desirable nor practical to eliminate poisonous plants from our surroundings, we need instead to educate ourselves about their potential dangers. At the same time we need to understand that, like all plants, poisonous species have important ecological roles and many of them are also useful to us as medicines or for other purposes.

Some plants and mushrooms are extremely toxic and can quickly cause coma or death if consumed. Others, though slower acting, can also cause severe reactions. In the event of suspected poisoning by a plant or mushroom, it is imperative to seek medical attention immediately. There are poison control centers affiliated with hospitals and clinics throughout North America, where specialists can help and advise in cases of poisoning. Correct identification of the poison is essential for proper treatment. If you are seeking medical help for suspected poisoning and you do not know the plant or mushroom involved, be sure to bring along a sample, raw or cooked, for verification. Children and pets are especially vulnerable to accidental poisoning by plants and mushrooms. Of the hundreds of cases of such poisoning reported each year, however, only a very few actually result in serious illness or death.

## Why Are Plants Poisonous?

Producing toxic chemical substances is often beneficial to plants, making them less palatable and providing them with protection against plant-eating animals or insects. Milkweeds, for example, produce several types of

A baneberry bush, a perennial herb of the buttercup family (genus *Actaea*) with poisonous berries.

**toxins** that render them generally distasteful to foraging animals. A mere taste of the bitter leaves will turn away most would-be browsers, unless they are extremely hungry.

Many toxic **compounds** are secondary metabolites, which are produced as by-products of a plant's primary physiological processes. In some cases scientists do not yet understand why a particular type of plant or mushroom produces such poisons. Even within a single species, some individuals may have high concentrations of toxic compounds while others have minimal amounts. Over thousands of years, in the process of **domesticating** plants, we have learned to select and **propagate** less-toxic strains, and by these means, humans have been able to convert poisonous species into major foods. The common potato (*Solanum tuberosum*) is a good example; its wild relatives in the South American Andes are bitter and toxic due to intense concentrations of harmful **alkaloids**. Indigenous horticulturalists over many generations developed sweet and edible varieties of potato and learned how to process them to minimize these toxins. The Spanish introduced potatoes to the rest of Europe some time in the late 1500s, and, after a period of doubt and suspicion, they were adopted as a staple in many countries. Still, the domesticated potato produces harmful alkaloids in its leaves, fruits, and sprouts, and even in its tubers if they are left exposed to light and start to turn green. Many relatives of the potato, including **belladonna** (*Atropa belladonna*), black nightshade (*Solanum nigrum*), henbane (*Hyoscyamus niger*), and tobacco (*Nicotiana* spp.), contain these alkaloids and are thus quite poisonous to humans and animals.

## Important Poisonous Compounds Found in Plants and Mushrooms

**Alkaloids.** There are many different kinds of plant and mushroom toxins. Alkaloids, the major type of poisonous compound found in the potato and its relatives, are common and widely distributed in the plant kingdom, especially but not exclusively among the flowering plants or angiosperms. Alkaloids are compounds derived from amino acids and are alkaline in nature.

**toxin** a poisonous substance

**compound** a substance formed from two or more elements

**domesticate** to tame an organism to live with and to be of use to humans

**propagate** to create more of through sexual or asexual reproduction

**alkaloid** bitter secondary plant compound, often used for defense

**belladonna** the source of atropine; means "beautiful woman," and is so named because dilated pupils were thought to enhance a woman's beauty

Their molecular structure is cyclical, and they all contain nitrogen. They are generally bitter tasting, and many are similar in chemical structure to substances produced by humans and other animals to transmit nerve impulses. Consequently, when ingested, they often affect animals' nervous systems. Many alkaloids, while potentially toxic, are also valued as medicines. Some, like the caffeine found in coffee (*Coffea arabica*), tea (*Camellia sinensis*), and other beverages, are consumed by humans all over the world as stimulants. One particularly useful alkaloid-containing plant is ipecac (*Cephaelis ipecacuanha*), a plant in the coffee family. Syrup of Ipecac, made from this plant, causes vomiting when swallowed, and this makes it one of the most useful treatments for poisoning or suspected poisoning by plants or mushrooms. It is a standard item in poison control kits, but should never be used without medical advice.

**Glycosides.** Glycosides are another type of toxic compound, even more widely distributed in plants than alkaloids. These highly variable compounds consist of one or more sugar molecules combined with a non-sugar, or aglycone, component. It is the aglycone that usually determines the level of toxicity of the glycoside. For example, one class of glycosides, the **cyanogenic** glycosides, break down to produce cyanides, which in concentrated doses are violently poisonous. Cyanogenic glycosides are found in many plants, including the seed kernels of cherries, apples, plums, and apricots. They can be detected by the bitter almond smell they produce when the tissues are broken or crushed. In small amounts they are not harmful, but swallowing a cup of blended apricot pits could be fatal.

**cyanogenic** giving rise to cyanide

Like alkaloids, many glycosides have important medicinal properties. Foxglove (*Digitalis purpurea*), for example, produces digitalis and related compounds. These are cardioactive glycosides affecting the functioning of the heart. Foxglove has been used with great care as an herbal remedy by knowledgeable practitioners for centuries. In Western medicine, digitalis and its chemical relatives digoxin and digitoxin have wide application as drugs to help regulate heart function and treat heart-related illnesses. The same glycosides in foxglove that make it a useful medicine, however, can be deadly in the wrong dosage.

**Oxalates.** Other types of toxic substances include oxalates, which can interfere with calcium uptake. Calcium oxalate crystals are found in plants of the arum family, like skunk cabbage (*Lysichitum* spp., *Symplocarpus* spp.), rhubarb (*Rheum raponticum*), philodendron, and dieffenbachia. If ingested, these minute crystals cause intense burning and irritation to the tissues of the tongue and throat. The name dumbcane is sometimes used for dieffenbachia because it can make a person unable to speak by causing swelling of the tongue.

**tannins** compounds produced by plants that usually serve protective functions; often colored and used for "tanning" and dyeing

Many other classes of compounds, including **tannins**, alcohols, resins, volatile oils, and even proteins and their derivatives, can be toxic to humans and animals. Some types of toxins, phototoxins, are activated by ultraviolet light and can cause intense irritation to the skin but only if the affected area is exposed to ultraviolet light, such as in sunlight.

Perhaps the most insidious plant substances are those that are cancer-causing (carcinogenic), because their effects are more long-term and not easily traced. Some fungi, especially certain molds, such as *Aspergillus flavus*, which grows on improperly stored peanuts, are known to produce tumor-inducing substances; *Aspergillus* produces carcinogens called aflatoxins that can cause liver cancer.

Some toxins are so concentrated that only the tiniest amount can be fatal. The seeds of castor bean (*Ricinus communis*), for example, produce a high molecular weight protein called ricin, which is reputed to be one of the most toxic naturally occurring substances known. Ricin inhibits protein synthesis in the intestinal wall. It and other proteins of its type, called lectins, are violently toxic; eating one to three castor bean seeds can be fatal for a child, two to six for an adult. (Ricin injected from an umbrella tip was used to assassinate the Bulgarian dissident Georgi Markov while he waited for a bus in London in 1978.)

## Plants Poisonous to Livestock

Plant species that are poisonous to humans are also commonly poisonous to other animals. Still, it is dangerous to assume that a plant that does not harm another animal will also be edible for people. Some rabbits, for example, are known to eat belladonna, which can cause abdominal pain, vomiting, fever, hallucinations, convulsions, coma, and even death when eaten by humans. These rabbits possess an **enzyme** that allows them to break down the toxic alkaloids of belladonna into digestible ones. Also, many ruminants or range animals with multiple stomachs like cattle, sheep, and goats, have a higher capacity for ingesting toxic plants without being harmed than animals with single-stomach digestive systems, such as humans, pigs, and horses.

Livestock poisoning causes many problems and economic losses for farmers and ranchers. Usually, animals will avoid toxic plants because of their bitter, unpleasant taste. If the range is poor, however, or in winter and early spring when forage is scarce, livestock may begin feeding on poisonous plant species, and even develop a taste for them, leading to repeated poisonings or death. Malformed or stillborn young can also result from pregnant cows, mares, or ewes eating poisonous species. A usually fatal type of birth deformity in lambs, called monkeyface, was traced to ewes feeding on an alkaloid-containing plant of the lily family, false hellebore (*Veratrum californicum*), in their early pregnancy. Ensuring that pastures are not overgrazed and that animals have a good source of food, clean water, and essential vitamins and minerals is the best way to prevent livestock poisoning from toxic plants.

## Benefits to Humans of Poisonous Plants and Fungi

The benefits that people gain from poisonous plants extend well beyond the pleasure many varieties of beautiful but poisonous house and garden ornamentals, like laburnum and oleander, can bring. From the glycosides of foxglove, used as heart medicines, to the alkaloids of ipecac, used as an emetic to treat poisoning, toxic compounds and poisonous plants applied in appropriate doses provide us with many important medicines. For 80 percent of the world's people, plants are the primary source of medicine, and even in modern industrial societies, over one-quarter of prescriptions are derived at least in part from plants, many of which are potentially toxic.

Pacific yew (*Taxus brevifolia*), for example, is a small forest tree of the Pacific Northwest of North America, which has long been known to have

**enzyme** a protein that controls a reaction in a cell

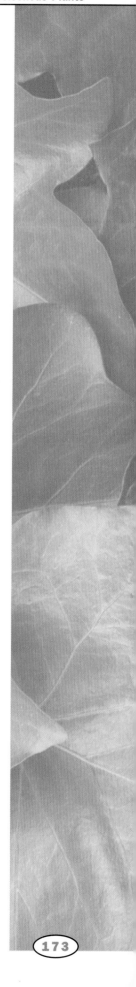

toxic foliage, seeds, and bark. In the late 1960s during a mass screening of plants sponsored by the National Cancer Institute, yew bark was found to contain a potent anticancer drug, called taxol. By the 1980s taxol had undergone extensive clinical trials and became the drug of choice for treating ovarian cancer, previously considered incurable, as well as being used for breast cancer and other forms of cancer.

Another deadly toxin that now has important medicinal applications is derived from a fungus called ergot (*Claviceps* spp.), which grows on grains like rye, wheat, and barley. For many centuries in Europe and elsewhere this fungus, a common contaminant of grain and flour, caused tremendous suffering from chronic poisoning, which produced a range of symptoms from skin ulcers to hallucinations and insanity. In modern medicine, however, ergot is used to stimulate uterine contractions during labor and to control uterine hemorrhaging.

Many other poisonous species have found important applications: strychnine (*Strychnos nux-vomica*) is used in surgery as a relaxant; belladonna's alkaloid, atropine, is used in ophthamology to dilate the pupils of the eyes; opium poppy (*Papaver somniferum*) produces the painkiller morphine; and Madagascar periwinkle (*Cantharanthus roseus*) yields two alkaloids, vincristine and vinblastine, which are used effectively as treatments for childhood leukemia and Hodgkin's disease.

Most people regularly enjoy another beneficial aspect of poisonous plants. Many spices that are used to flavor foods all over the world are actually poisonous if taken in large quantities. For example, nutmeg (*Myristica fragrans*), which grows on trees native to India, Australia, and the South Pacific, contains volatile oils that give it its distinctive aroma and flavour. Harmless in small amounts, in larger doses nutmeg can cause a series of unpleasant effects to the central nervous system, and ten grams can be enough to induce coma, and even death. Mint, black pepper, and cinnamon are further examples of common herbs and spices that are pleasant and beneficial to humans in moderation, but that can be poisonous in large amounts.

## Irritants and Allergens

There are also several types of skin irritations caused by plants. Some plants, such as stinging nettle (*Urtica* spp.) and buttercups (*Ranunculus* spp.), have chemicals in their sap or hairs that can be irritating when they come in contact with skin. Some plants contain allergens, causing irritation to the skin of those sensitized to them. Most people find, for example, that they are allergic to poison ivy, and its relatives, poison oak and poison sumac (*Toxicodendron* spp.). While not everyone reacts to these plants, most people do, especially after an initial exposure. Sometimes allergic reactions to these plants are serious enough to lead to hospitalization.

Many people also experience individual allergies to plants and mushrooms that are edible to the general population. Allergies to specific food plants, such as peanuts, lentils, or wheat, can be very serious. In some cases, these otherwise edible species are deadly poisonous allergens for those affected. Plant allergies, including hay fever, can develop at any age and may be alleviated by a program of immunization.

## Poisonous Mushrooms

Mushrooms are part of the diverse kingdom called fungi. Unlike green plants, fungi do not fuel their development, growth, and reproduction with sunlight and carbon dioxide in the process of photosynthesis. Instead, they feed off dead or living plant and animal matter. Mushrooms, which are characterized by a central stalk and rounded cap, can be easily distinguished. While some mushrooms are widely eaten, others can cause sickness if consumed, and some can be fatally toxic even in small amounts. Distinguishing between poisonous and edible mushrooms can be extremely difficult. Sometimes identification can only be verified at the microscopic level and requires the expertise of a mycologist, a person who studies fungi. Wild mushrooms should never be eaten without certain identification. As with poisonous plants, the level of toxicity in mushrooms can vary depending on genetic and environmental factors, and the same species of mushroom that can be eaten in one area may be poisonous under other conditions.

The American fly agaric (*Amanita muscaria*), a common poisonous mushroom.

The toxicity of many species of mushrooms is poorly understood, and there is no simple test for determining if a mushroom is poisonous to humans. The symptoms of mushroom poisoning generally include nausea and vomiting, cramps, diarrhea, drowsiness, hallucinations, or even coma. The effects of mushroom poisoning will vary depending on the variety and quantity of the toxins involved, and on the individual reaction of the person who eats the mushroom. The most notorious toxic mushrooms are members of the genus *Amanita*, which includes fly agaric (*A. muscaria*), panther agaric (*A. pantherina*), death cap (*A. phalloides*), and destroying angel (*A. verna, A. virosa*). The last two, especially, are the most poisonous mushroom species known. SEE ALSO ALKALOIDS; DEFENSES, CHEMICAL; FUNGI; MEDICINAL PLANTS; POISON IVY.

*Nancy J. Turner and Sarah E. Turner*

### Bibliography

Benjamin, Denis R. *Mushrooms. Poisons and Panaceas: A Handbook for Naturalists, Mycologists, and Physicians*. New York: W. H. Freeman and Company, 1995.

Cooper, Marion R., and Anthony W. Johnson. *Poisonous Plants in Britain and Their Effects on Animals and Man*. Ministry of Agriculture Fisheries and Food, Reference Book 161, London: Her Majesty's Stationery Office, 1984.

Foster, Steven. *Forest Pharmacy: Medicinal Plants of American Forests*. Durham, NC: Forest History Society, 1995.

Fuller, Thomas C., and Elizabeth McClintock. *Poisonous Plants of California*. Berkeley, CA: University of California Press, 1986.

Hardin, James W., and Jay M. Arena. *Human Poisoning from Native and Cultivated Plants*. Durham, NC: Duke University Press, 1974.

Johns, Timothy, and Isao Kubo. "A Survey of Traditional Methods Employed for the Detoxification of Plant Foods." *Journal of Ethnobiology* 8, no. 1 (1988): 81–129.

Lampe, K. F., and M. A. McCann. *AMA Handbook of Poisonous and Injurious Plants*. Chicago, IL: American Medical Association, 1985.

Turner, Nancy J., and Adam F. Szczawinski. *Common Poisonous Plants and Mushrooms of North America*. Portland, OR: Timber Press, 1991.

# Pollination Biology

Plant pollination is almost as diverse as the plant community itself. Self-pollination occurs in some plant species when the pollen (male part) produced by the anthers in a single flower comes in contact with the stigma

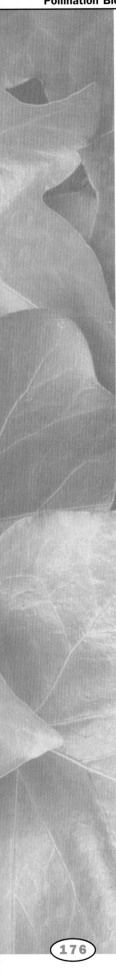

(female part) of the same flower or with the stigma of another flower on the same individual. Self-pollination does not allow much modification in the genetic makeup of the plant since the seeds produced by self-pollination create plants essentially identical to the individual producing the seed. A plant population that has all individuals identical in form, size, and growth requirements has little possibility of modifications to allow for change in its environment.

Most plant species have evolved ways to ensure an appropriate degree of interchange of genetic material between individuals in the population, and cross-pollination is the normal type of pollination. In this case flowers are only pollinated effectively if the pollen comes from another plant. Plants benefit most by being pollinated by other individuals because this broadens the genetic characteristics of individual plants. As a result, they are more adaptable to necessary changes.

Fertilization takes place when the pollen comes in contact with the stigma of a flower. Pollen reacts with the stigmatic fluids and germinates, then grows as a tube through the stigma and down the style to the ovary cavity. There the sperm unites with the ovule and develops into a seed.

There are both physical and chemical or genetic barriers to fertilization. Sometimes pollen grains are inhibited from germinating by a chemical imbalance, or germination is controlled genetically. Sometimes there is no genetic barrier but the pollen is simply not placed in the proper position in the flower. This is caused by physical restraints, such as large differences in the length of the stamens and the styles. Some species of plants have long-styled forms and short-styled forms to discourage self-pollination. The shape of the corolla and the positioning of the sexual parts (style and stamens) may also ensure that only an insect of a certain size and shape can pollinate a flower. Most of the pollination syndromes mentioned next involve these features.

## Wind Pollination

Perhaps the simplest form of pollination is that of wind pollination, which is common in many of the early spring-flowering trees in temperate areas. The oak (*Quercus* in Fagaceae), maple (*Acer* in Aceraceae), birch (*Betula* in Betulaceae), hickory (*Carya* in Juglandaceae), and many other trees in temperate forests are pollinated by wind-borne pollen. Air currents and moisture in early spring make this a suitably efficient method of pollination because the trees have not yet produced leaves, and flowers are exposed, often in slender **catkin**-type **inflorescences** that dangle with long stigmatic hairs capable of catching the pollen. The corn plant (*Zea mays* in Poaceae) is another wind-pollinated plant. Its long, silky tufts of fiber, which constitute the styles, are well suited to trapping the airborne pollen. Wind pollination is rare in the tropics, perhaps owing to the fact that trees are usually not leafless and wind-borne pollen would not be very efficient. Moreover, heavy daily rains common in the tropics would keep anthers too wet for effective wind pollination. Nevertheless, one type of airborne pollination in the tropics does exist. Understory shrubs in the Urticaceae have anthers that open explosively and throw the pollen into the air sufficiently far to effect at least self-pollination of other inflorescences on the plant.

**catkin** a flowering structure used for wind pollination

**inflorescence** an arrangement of flowers on a stalk

Bee pollinating a blossom of a kiwi fruit vine.

## Insect Pollination

Plants have coevolved with insects, and each insect pollinator group is closely associated with a particular type of plant. This is called a pollination syndrome. Without even knowing the exact insect that pollinates a plant, the type of insect that will visit the plant can be predicted because of the shape, color, size, and scent of the flower involved.

**Bees.** Most bees visit flowers that are bilaterally symmetrical (zygomorphic or not round in outline) and have a landing platform on which the bee can be properly oriented for entry. An example is the ordinary household pea plant (*Pisum sativa*) and most other members of the subfamily Papilionoideae of the **legume** family (Leguminosae). Bee flowers tend to have an aroma as well because bees have a good sense of smell. Bees are among the most prevalent of plant pollinators and are remarkably diverse in size and shape. The honeybee is the most obvious example of this pollination syndrome, and the economic importance of the honeybee to fruit and seed production is enormous. Without them and other similar bees, many of our food crops would not exist.

**legumes** beans and other members of the Fabaceae family

Bees are believed to be intelligent, and some bees return to the same plant on a regular basis (a behavior called trap lining). In such cases, the plants commonly produce just one or a few flowers each day, ensuring that all are pollinated without investing as much energy as it would in a mass-flowering species. Other species produce massive numbers of flowers so that the plant can attract large numbers of pollinators. These are two opposing strategies that accomplish the same goal: to produce seeds for reproduction.

Bees are more likely than other insects to establish a one-to-one pollination system. Many plants produce a special scent that attracts only one or a few different species of bees. This is especially common in orchids and aroids. Some flowers have evolved to produce a "style" that mimics the insect itself in appearance. Most orchids are so dependent on pollination by a single type of bee that they put all of their pollen in a single package (called pollinia) that is picked up by the bee. In the case of the *Catasetum* orchid, the sticky pollinia is forced onto the head of the bee, where it adheres until it in turn is passed onto the style of another plant. This one-chance system, though risky, ensures that all of the pollen load arrives exactly where it is most effective.

**Flies.** These are less-important pollinators, but they are essential in the pollination of some temperate and many tropical flowering plants. Flies generally visit flowers that smell foul, often with scents of decaying meat or feces. Many tropical aroids (Araceae), including such mammoth plants as *Amorphophallus*, which often produce inflorescences, are pollinated by flies. The skunk cabbage (*Symplocarpus foetidus*), another aroid and one of the earliest plants to flower in the spring (even emerging from snow banks), is pollinated by flies. Flies are seemingly less intelligent than bees and fly pollination syndromes often involve deceit and entrapment. Flies are attracted to foul-smelling plants because they anticipate finding a suitable substance, such as dung or decaying meat on which to lay their eggs. Once inside, however, the flies are unable to leave the inflorescence. In *Aristolochia* (Aristolochiaceae), the corolla tube is folded into a bend with stiff hairlike **appendages** at the base, orientated to allow the fly to enter easily. However, only after the insect has been inside long enough to ensure pollination do the appendages become loose enough to allow the fly to depart the lower part of the corolla. The tropical genus *Dracontium* (Araceae) has no real trap but instead the lower part of the spathe is white or apparently transparent, and the opening is curved so that little light enters. The not-so-intelligent fly tries repeatedly to leave through an opening that does not exist and in the process crashes against the inflorescence to deposit pollen it might be carrying from visiting other flowers.

**Moths and Butterflies.** Both have the ability to unroll their long tongues and extend them into long slender flowers. Members of the Asteraceae (Compositae), such as dandelions, sunflowers, goldenrods, and other genera, are usually visited by butterflies during daylight hours. Their moth counterparts usually fly at night and pollinate a different type of tubular flower, ones that are usually white or very pale in color, making the flowers easier to see in the dark, and flowers that produce a sweet-smelling aroma, which also makes locating them easier. Hawk moths have especially long tongues and can pollinate tropical flowers with the corolla tube up to ten

**appendages** parts that are attached to a central stalk or axis

inches long. One such flower, *Posqueria latifolia* (Rubiaceae), has a special arrangement of the stamens that causes them to be held together under tension until the anther mass is touched by the pollinator. At this point, it is released with great force and the stamens then throw a mass of pollen into the face of the pollinator. This pollen mass is carried onto the next flower, where the style is now properly positioned to accept the pollen.

**Beetles.** Although somewhat rare in temperate areas, this is quite common in the tropics. Beetles often fly at dusk, enter the inflorescence, and stay there until the following evening at dusk. Beetle pollination syndromes often involve thermogenesis, an internal heating of some part of the inflorescence caused by the rapid **oxidation** of starch. The inflorescence of *Philodendron* (Araceae) consists of a leaflike spathe that surrounds the spadix where the flowers are aggregated. The flowers of philodendron are unisexual, with the female flowers aggregated near the base and the male flowers occupying the remainder of the spadix. In most cases, it is the spadix that warms up and the temperature is commonly well above ambient temperature (that of the surrounding air). The elevated temperature is associated with the emission of a sweet scent that helps attract the beetles. Once inside the base of the spathe (the tube portion), the beetles feast on the lipid-rich **sterile** male flowers at the base of the male spadix, and they also often use this space for mating. On the following day, when the beetle is departing, the stamens release their pollen and the beetle departs covered with it. Beetles pollinate many species of palms (Arecaceae), members of the Cyclanthaceae, many Araceae, and even giant tropical water lilies such as *Victoria amazonica*. The skunk cabbage mentioned earlier under fly pollination is also thermogenic, and it is this feature that enables it to melt its way through the snow in the early spring.

**oxidation** reaction with oxygen

**sterile** unable to reproduce

**Birds and Mammals.** Although vertebrate pollinators are not as common as insect pollinators, they do exist, and include birds and mammals. Bird pollination syndromes usually involve colorful, scentless flowers that are designed to attract birds, which have excellent vision but a poor sense of smell. In the western hemisphere, hummingbirds are the most common pollinators, and their typically long tongues mean that hummingbird flowers are typically long and tubular. Many hummingbird-pollinated flowers are either red or have red-colored parts, such as bracts, which attract the bird to the inflorescence. Many tropical members of the Gesneriaceae have yellow rather than red flowers, but the leaves associated with the flowers are heavily marked with red or maroon and are clearly visible to the hummingbird pollinators.

Mammal pollination is rare but is becoming increasingly more well known among tropical animals. White-faced monkeys (*Cebus capuchinus*) are known to pollinate balsa trees (*Ochroma pyramidale* in Bombacaceae) as they search deep in the big tubular flowers for insects. Bats are more common as effective pollinators because they are skilled fliers. Because bats fly at night, the bat pollination syndrome involves pale-colored, usually large, often pendent broadly open tubular flowers, such as *Coutarea hexandra*, a tropical member of the coffee family (Rubiaceae). However, bat pollination syndromes may also involve such plants as *Inga* (Leguminosae), which have many flowers with broad tufts of stamens through which the bat can extend its tongue to forage for pollen or nectar. Some unusual mammal pollinators include gi-

raffes, who are known to pollinate *Acacia* trees with their facial hairs, and lemurs, who pollinate *Strelitzia* in Madagascar. SEE ALSO BREEDING SYSTEMS; FLOWERS; INTERACTIONS, PLANT-INSECT; INTERACTIONS, PLANT-VERTEBRATE; REPRODUCTION, FERTILIZATION AND; REPRODUCTION, SEXUAL.

*Thomas B. Croat*

**Bibliography**

Faegri, K, and L. van der Pijl. *The Principles of Pollination Ecology*. New York: Pergamon Press, 1966.

Percival, Mary S. *Floral Biology*. New York: Pergamon Press, 1965.

Real, Leslie. *Pollination Biology*. New York: Academic Press, 1983.

# Polyploidy

The analysis of plant and animal cells shows that chromosomes are present in homologous pairs, with each member of the pair carrying very similar or identical genes. In humans, for example, there are forty-six chromosomes, but these can be grouped into twenty-three pairs. This set of twenty-three unique chromosomes is known as the **haploid** number for humans, while the full complement of forty-six chromosomes (two sets of twenty-three) is known as the **diploid** number. Virtually every somatic (non-sex) cell in the body contains the diploid number, while gametes (egg and sperm) contain the haploid number. *Arabidopsis thaliana* (a well-studied model plant) has ten chromosomes in a somatic nucleus, two each of five different types. Like humans, *Arabidopsis* is diploid, with a diploid number of ten and a haploid number of five.

While some plants show this diploid pattern of chromosome number, many others show a different pattern, called polyploidy. In this pattern, near-identical chromosomes occur in numbers greater than two, and the number of chromosomes in somatic cells therefore is greater than the diploid number. For instance, the potato has forty-eight chromosomes, but analysis shows that these can be grouped into four sets of twelve, with foursomes (instead of pairs) carrying very similar genes. The potato is said to be tetraploid, which is one form of polyploidy.

Polyploidy does not have to lead to large number of chromosomes, but it often does. For instance, cultivated polyploid plants such as sugarcane are known to have as many as 150 or more chromosomes, while wild plants may have even higher numbers. Most angiosperm (flowering plant) **genomes** are thought to have incurred one or more polyploidization events. Many of the world's leading crops are polyploid.

## Chromosome Numbers

A simple **nomenclature** is widely used to provide geneticists with information about chromosome numbers in different organisms. The number of unique chromosomes making up one set is referred to as "x." For example, for humans x = 23, for *Arabidopsis thaliana* x = 5, and for potato x = 12. The number of chromosomes in the gametes of an organism is referred to as "n." For humans n = 23, and for *Arabidopsis thaliana* n = 5. In potato, n = 24, half the total number of chromosomes. Note that for diploid organisms, n = x, meaning the chromosome number of the gamete will be

**haploid** having one set of chromosomes, versus having two (diploid)

**diploid** having two sets of chromosomes, versus having one (haploid)

**genome** the genetic material of an organism

**nomenclatural** related to naming or naming conventions

equal to the number of unique chromosome types. By contrast, for polyploids, n will be some multiple of x, and the simple formula n/x reflects the number of different sets of chromosomes in the nucleus. For the potato, n/x = 2, indicating that the tetraploid potato carries twice the diploid number of chromosomes. Prefixes for other numbers of chromosomes are tri- (3), tetra-(4), penta-(5), hepta-(7), octo-(8), and so on.

During gamete formation, near-identical chromosomes (homologs) must pair up and undergo recombination (crossing over) before they are segregated into separate gametes. In diploid organisms, this pairing brings together the members of each homologous pair, so that (in *Arabidopsis*, for example), the five chromosomes from one set pair up with the five nearly identical chromosomes from the other set. In polyploid organisms, however, the number of possible pairings is larger. Scientists in fact recognize two different types of polyploidy (autopolyploidy and allopolyploidy, discussed next), based on the tendency of chromosomes from different sets to pair with one another.

## Autopolyploidy

In autopolyploid (self-polyploid) organisms, such as the potato, the multiple sets of chromosomes are very similar to one another, and a member of one set can pair with the corresponding member of any of the other sets. For the potato, this means that a single chromosome from the first set can pair with up to three other chromosomes. This can lead to multivalent pairing at **meiosis**, with one chromosome pairing with different partners along different parts of its length.

Further, because any one chromosome can have several different partners, it is impossible to establish allelic relationships. Because of the possible presence of four, six, eight, even ten or more copies of a particular chromosome, genetic analysis of autopolyploids is complex.

Examples of autopolyploids in addition to potato include alfalfa (4x), sugarcane (8-18x), sugar beet (3x), ryegrass (4x), bermuda grass (3-4x), cassava (4x), red clover (4x), Gros Michel banana (3x), apple cultivars (3x), and many ornamentals (3x). Note that many autopolyploids are **biomass** crops, grown for vegetative parts other than seeds. The multivalent pairing associated with autopolyploidy is often not conducive to seed fertility. Many autopolyploids are difficult to obtain seed from and are **propagated** by vegetative clones, such as cuttings.

## Allopolyploidy

Bread wheat (*Triticum aestivum*) is an example of allopolyploidy, in which the multiple sets of chromosomes are not composed of nearly identical chromosomes. In bread wheat, there are 42 chromosomes, divided into six sets of seven chromosomes each. These sets are denoted A, A, B, B, D, and D. While a particular member of A can pair with its homolog in the other A set, it cannot pair with any members of B or D. In effect, bread wheat has three different genomes, which are believed to have arisen from three different diploid ancestors, one each contributing the A, B, and D chromosome sets. These different ancestors are thought to have come together to form the allohexaploid genome of bread wheat. While each ancestor car-

A sugar beet plant pulled from a Minnesota sugar beet field. In autopolyploids, such as sugar beets, a member of one set of chromosomes can pair with the corresponding member of any of the other sets.

**meiosis** division of chromosomes in which the resulting cells have half the original number of chromosomes

**biomass** the total dry weight of an organism or group of organisms

**propagate** to create more of through sexual or asexual reproduction

ried many similar genes, they were not arranged in precisely the same way on each chromosome set. Since members of A are not homologous to members of B or D, pairing between the different sets during meiosis is normally not possible.

Therefore, at meiosis in normal bread wheat, there are twenty-one pairs of chromosomes formed, but A chromosomes are paired only with A, B only with B, and D only with D. Thus, despite the presence of six chromosome sets in the same nucleus, each has only one possible pairing partner, and all chromosomes pair as bivalents (one-to-one). Because of strict bivalent pairing, genetic analysis of allopolyploids is similar to that of diploids.

Examples of allopolyploids include cotton (6x), wheat (4x, 6x), oat (6x), soybean (4x), peanut (4x), canola (4x), tobacco (4x), and coffee (4x). Note that many allopolyploids are seed crops. The strict bivalent pairing associated with allopolyploidy is conducive to a high level of seed fertility.

Finally, it is significant that autopolyploidy and allopolyploidy are not mutually exclusive alternatives. Plants can contain multiple copies of some chromosomes and divergent copies of others, a state known as auto-allopolyploidy.

## Formation of Polyploids

Every plant has the potential to form an autopolyploid at every meiotic cycle, since (as in all sexually reproducing cells) the chromosome number is doubled prior to the first meiotic cycle. Normally, the chromosome number is then reduced by two rounds of chromosome separation during gamete formation. Autopolyploids may be formed when this chromosome separation fails to occur.

**hybrid** a mix of two varieties or species

**sterile** unable to reproduce

**genotype** the genetic makeup of an organism

Allopolyploids are thought to form from rare hybridization events between diploids that contain different genomes (such as AA and DD diploid wheats). Initially, the **hybrid** of such a cross, with a genetic constitution AD, would be unbalanced, since A and D chromosomes would not pair. As a result, such a hybrid would be **sterile** and would not be genetically stable over time. In rare cases, the AD hybrid may produce a gamete that fails to go through the normal reduction in chromosome number during meiosis, thereby doubling its chromosome number. Such an unreduced gamete may be of genetic constitution AADD, and both A and D chromosomes would have pairing partners, creating a genetically stable polyploid **genotype**:

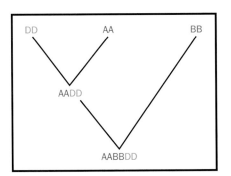

Unreduced gametes can be artificially induced by various compounds, most notably colchicine, which interferes with the action of the meiotic spindle normally responsible for separating chromosomes. Colchicine has been widely used by geneticists to create synthetic polyploid plants, both for experimental purposes and to introduce valuable genes from wild diploids into major crops. Synthetic polyploids developed by humans from wild plants have contributed to improvement of cotton, wheat, peanut, and other crops. One artifically induced polyploid, triticale (which combines the genomes of wheat and rye), shows promise as a major crop itself.

Finally, many crops that are grown for vegetative parts are bred based on crosses between genotypes of different ploidy, which produce sterile progeny. For example, many cultivated types of banana (*Musa* spp.) and Bermuda grass (*Cynodon* spp.) are triploid, made from crosses between a diploid and a tetraploid. In each of these crops, seed production is undesirable for human purposes, and the unbalanced genetic constitution of the triploids usually results in seed abortion. Each of these crops is propagated clonally by cuttings. This is a good example of how humans have applied basic research knowledge to improved quality and productivity of agricultural products.

**Occurrence in Plants, Including Economically Important Crops.** Many additional plant genomes may have once been polyploid. For example, maize has twenty chromosomes in its somatic nucleus and exhibits strict bivalent pairing—however at the deoxyribonucleic acid (DNA) level, large chromosome segments are found to be duplicated (i.e., contain largely common sets of genes in similar arrangements). In most cases, the duplicated regions no longer comprise entire chromosomes, although they may once have. Other examples of such ancient polyploids include broccoli and turnips. Hints of ancient chromosomal duplications are found in many plants and are particularly well characterized in sorghum and rice. Recent data from DNA sequencing has supported earlier suggestions from genetic mapping that even the simple genome of *Arabidopsis* may contain duplicated chromosomal segments. As large quantitites of DNA sequence information provide geneticists with new and powerful data, it is likely we will discover that many organisms that we think of as diploid are actually ancient polyploids.

**Importance in Evolution.** Because of the abundance of polyploid plants, it can be argued that the joining of two divergent genomes into a common polyploid nucleus is the single most important genetic mechanism in plant evolution. Geneticists have long debated whether the abundance of polyploid plants simply reflects plant promiscuity or if a selective advantage is conferred by polyploid formation. Plants appear to enjoy greater freedom than animals to interbreed between diverse genotypes, even between genotypes that would normally be considered to be different species. However, one could also envision that the presence of multiple copies of a gene in a plant nucleus offers flexibility to evolve. While mutation (changes in the genetic code) is necessary for evolution, most mutations disrupt the genetic information rather than improve it. In polyploids, if one copy of a gene is disrupted, other copies can still provide the required function—therefore there may be more flexibility to experiment—and allow rare favorable changes to occur.

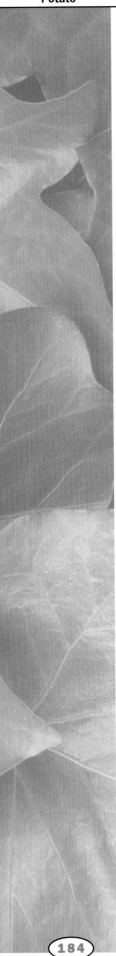

Autopolyploids may have a different type of genetic buffering. Most autopolyploids are highly heterozygous, with two, three, or more **alleles** represented at any one genetic locus. This may provide the organism with different avenues of response to the demands of different sets of environmental conditions. SEE ALSO CHROMOSOMES; COTTON; SPECIATION; WHEAT.

*Andrew H. Paterson*

**Bibliography**

Irvine, J. E. "Saccharum Species as Horticultural Classes." *Theoretical and Applied Genetics* 98 (1999): 186–94.

Jiang, C., R. Wright, K. El-Zik, and A. H. Paterson. "Polyploid Formation Created Unique Avenues for Response to Selection in *Gossypium* (Cotton)." *Proceedings of the National Academy of Sciences of the USA* 95 (1998): 4419–24.

Leitch, I., and M. Bennett. "Polyploidy in Angiosperms." *Trends in Plant Science* 2 (1997): 470–76.

Masterson, J. "Stomatal Size in Fossil Plants: Evidence for Polyploidy in the Majority of Angiosperms." *Science* 264 (1994): 421–24.

Ming, R., et al. "Alignment of the *Sorghum* and *Saccharum* Chromosomes: Comparative Genome Organization and Evolution of a Polysomic Polyploid Genus and Its Diploid Cousin." *Genetics* 150 (1998): 1663–82.

Simmonds, N. W. *Principles of Crop Improvement.* London: Longman Group, 1998.

Stebbins, G. L. "Chromosomal Variation and Evolution; Polyploidy and Chromosome Size and Number Shed Light on Evolutionary Processes in Higher Plants." *Science* 152 (1966): 1463–69.

Wendel, J. F., M. M. Goodman, and C. W. Stuber. "Mapping Data for 34 Isozyme Loci Currently Being Studied." *Maize Genetics Cooperative News Letter* 59 (1985): 90.

Wu, K. K., et al. "The Detection and Estimation of Linkage in Polyploids Using Single-Dose Restriction Fragments." *Theoretical and Applied Genetics* 83 (1992): 294–300.

Zeven, A. C. "Polyploidy and Domestication: The Origin and Survival of Polyploids in Cytotype Mixtures." In *Polyploidy, Biological Relevance*, ed. W. H. Lewis. New York: Plenum Press, 1979.

# Potato

The potato (*Solanum tubersosum*) is one of the world's most productive, nutritious, and tasty vegetables, and it is the fourth most important food worldwide regarding production (following rice, wheat, and corn). It is the most economically valuable and well-known member of the plant family Solanaceae, which contains such foods as tomatoes and peppers, and flowers such as the petunia. The edible tubers of potato are actually swollen underground stems, in contrast to the similarly appearing sweet potatoes, which have swollen roots, and are a member of the separate family Convovulaceae (morning glory family).

Early peoples in the high Andes Mountains of Bolivia and Peru, where many wild potato species grow, likely selected the potato as a food about ten thousand years ago. This is a time when many crops were believed to have been selected in Andean South America, and dried potato remains date from about seven thousand years ago from caves in Central Peru. Wild potato species have a geographic range from the southwestern United States to south-central Chile. There is much controversy regarding the number of wild potato species, from perhaps only one hundred to over two hundred.

The potato was not introduced into Europe until the late sixteenth century, where it was only slowly accepted as a food, and even then only by the poor. The potato is infected by many diseases and requires a lot of care. The fungal disease potato late blight was the cause of the devastating Irish potato famine that began in 1846. The famine killed more than one million people and stimulated the huge immigration of Irish people to continental Europe and the United States. SEE ALSO ECONOMIC IMPORTANCE OF PLANTS; POTATO BLIGHT; SOLANACEAE.

*David M. Spooner*

### Bibliography

Hawkes, J. G. *The Potato: Evolution, Biodiversity, and Genetic Resources.* Washington, DC: Smithsonian Institution Press, 1990.

Miller, J. T., and D. M. Spooner. "Collapse of Species Boundaries in the Wild Potato *Solanum brevicaule* Complex." *Plant Systematics and Evolution* 214 (1999): 103–30.

# Potato Blight

Potato blight (or potato late blight) is caused by a mildewlike fungus called *Phytophthora infestans* that can infect the potato foliage and its tubers. Although *P. infestans* is best known as a **pathogen** of the potato, this fungus also attacks the tomato and a number of other plants belonging to the family Solanaceae.

**pathogen** disease-causing organism

## History

This disease first came to the attention of the world in the 1840s, when it suddenly appeared in Europe and caused the disastrous Irish potato famine. From Europe, the fungus spread all over the world. At first it was thought that the blight was simply due to rainy, cool weather, which caused the potato foliage to turn black and die. In 1863, a German scientist, Anton deBary, proved that *P. infestans* was the cause of the disease, and through his pioneering work, deBary established the base for a new science: plant pathology.

**sporulate(s)** to produce or release spores

In 1884 in France, a fungicide spray containing copper sulphate and lime, called Bordeaux mixture, was discovered to be an effective means of controlling potato blight when applied to the foliage. This was the first time a plant disease was controlled by protective spraying. During the past fifty years hundreds of chemical fungicides have been developed for the control of potato blight. In the early twenty-first century, the potato crop receives more chemicals annually than any other food plant that we grow. The annual losses due to potato late blight, including both the direct losses in yield and the expense of chemical control, amount to billions of dollars a year.

## The Disease

*P. infestans* passes the winter in infected seed tubers kept in potato storages or in the soil of the potato field to be planted. As the new potato crop becomes established during a cool, wet season, the fungus emerges, **sporulates**, and attacks both the foliage and the tubers. If this favorable weather continues, the potato plants can be completely destroyed.

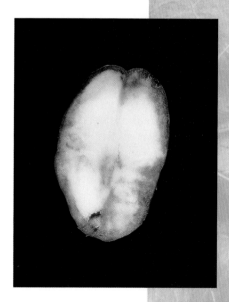

A potato diseased with potato late blight.

Unfortunately, almost all commercial potato varieties are susceptible to blight and must be protected by spraying with chemical fungicides. Although the potato has emerged as one of the four major food crops in the world during the last few centuries (rice, wheat, and corn being the others), the need for expensive protective spraying has tended to confine its major impact to the more prosperous, industrialized countries of the world. It is urgent that we initiate and support a long-term program to enable the potato to continue and expand its contribution to the nutrition of a growing world population.

An obvious solution for this disease problem, which has caused so much expense and uncertainty in world potato production, is to incorporate a durable late blight resistance in commercially acceptable potato varieties. A high level of this blight resistance has been found in a number of wild potato species in Mexico, which is now recognized as the place of origin of *P. infestans*. These resistant wild potatoes have evolved there, surviving for thousands of years, in a climate favorable for an annual battle with the blight fungus.

Research programs in many countries are now trying to develop commercially acceptable potato varieties with this durable resistance. These resistant potato varieties will not only save the farmer the cost of applying the expensive fungicides, but will provide them with greater security in the production of a good crop of potatoes. Perhaps even more important, for the first time the potato would be available as a basic food crop to many millions of subsistence farmers in developing countries. Today these farmers cannot grow the potato because they do not have the resources needed for the purchase of expensive chemicals used for the control of potato blight.

Today there is an increasing global concern over the quality of the environment. A substantial reduction in the use of agricultural chemicals is considered to be an important step if we are to make progress in improving the environment. The worldwide use of blight-resistant potato varieties would be an important contribution to this program. SEE ALSO BREEDING; ECONOMIC IMPORTANCE OF PLANTS; GENETIC ENGINEERING; INTERACTIONS, PLANT-FUNGAL; PATHOGENS; POTATO.

*John S. Niederhauser*

# Propagation

Plant propagation simply means "making more plants." Reproducing plants from seeds is called sexual propagation. If plant parts other than seeds are used to reproduce a plant, the method is known as asexual propagation. Many ornamental trees, flowering shrubs, foliage plants, and turf grasses are propagated by asexual means. Asexual propagation of plants is generally accomplished by one of three methods: cuttings, grafting, and tissue culture or micropropagation.

## Asexual Propagation

Asexual propagation is easy to accomplish, inexpensive, and often requires no special equipment. Asexual techniques are used because larger plants can be produced in a shorter period of time. If a plant does not form **viable** seeds, or if the seeds are difficult to germinate, asexual methods may

**viable** able to live or to function

Plantlets of a Mother-of-Thousands plant can be detached and potted separately.

be the only way to reproduce the species. Asexual propagation produces clones, and, consequently, all new plants will resemble the parent plant, a benefit for growers who want to multiply and sell a unique plant.

Since the newly propagated clones are genetically identical, they respond to the environment in similar ways. This uniformity makes culture and production easy. However, it can be a problem if a pest or disease attacks the crop. Asexually propagated clones may all be vulnerable to the attackers, which could wipe out the crop.

**Cuttings.** Asexual plant propagation using cuttings involves removing certain plant parts and allowing each cut part to become a new plant. Common plant parts used as cuttings include stems, leaves, leaf buds, and roots. When exposed to proper environmental conditions and appropriate cultural practices, cuttings form a root system and new foliage. New roots or shoots are termed **adventitious** growth.

Stem cuttings are one of the easiest and least-expensive methods of plant propagation. Most species will make roots in several weeks. Rooted cuttings are then easily grown to marketable size. Stem cuttings can be classified into groups according to the nature of the plant wood used: hardwood and softwood.

Hardwood stem cuttings are taken from mature **dormant** branches in late fall or early winter. If the species is deciduous, cuttings should be leafless. A 15- to 20-centimeter section of stem with at least three buds is used.

**adventitious** arising from secondary buds

**dormant** inactive, not growing

187

**succulent** fleshy and moist

**node** branching site on a stem

**petiole** the stalk of a leaf, by which it attaches to the stem

**axillary bud** the bud that forms in the angle between the stem and leaf

**suckers** naturally occurring adventitious shoots

The base of the cutting is cut at a slant to expose a larger area for rooting and to create a distinction between the cutting top and base. For evergreen species, leaves on the lower half of the cutting are stripped off. Then the base is dipped in a root-promoting hormone, either a powder or liquid. The cutting is inserted (about one-half its length) into a moist rooting medium composed of peat mixed with vermiculite or sand. Cuttings should be kept moist at a temperature favorable for optimum growth and development, depending on the plant species. Adequate light is necessary for root formation, but cuttings should never be placed in direct sunlight. Sometimes protected trays of hardwood cuttings are kept outside through mild winters, and they root as temperatures rise in the spring.

Stem cuttings of softwood generally root more easily than hardwood but require more attention and equipment. Softwood cuttings are usually 7.5 to 13 centimeters long with two or more nodes. They are usually made in late spring, using the **succulent** mature spring growth of deciduous or evergreen plants. Mature shoots, but not old woody stems, are desirable. A slanted base cut is made just below a **node,** and leaves on the lower half of the cutting are removed. Bases are treated with rooting stimulant before being placed into loose rooting mix. Softwood cuttings require high humidity, which can be achieved through the use of plastic tents, misting systems, and/or fogging. Temperature should be closely observed during rooting. Most species root best between temperatures of 25°C and 30°C at the base, with cooler temperatures for foliage. Having the base warmer than the tip promotes root growth before new top growth begins. Roots form in two to five weeks.

Leaf cuttings are another method of asexual propagation. In this process, an entire leaf (leaf blade plus **petiole**), the leaf blade only, or just a portion of the blade can be used to produce another plant. Cut surfaces may be treated with rooting hormones. High relative humidity and warm soil temperature will speed adventitious root formation. The soil mix should be loose but damp. Using the leaves allows the reproduction of more new plants than is possible with stem cuttings: sometimes more than one new plant forms from each leaf. Many leaves can fill a shallow tray. On one greenhouse table hundreds of plants can be reproduced.

Leaf-bud cuttings are basically the same as leaf cuttings, except the leaf is left attached to a short piece of stem with its healthy **axillary bud.** The cut stem surface can be treated with root-promoting compound. The cuttings are inserted in a rooting medium with the bud about 1.4 centimeters below the surface. High humidity and optimum temperature will speed rooting.

Root cuttings when buried and kept warm will produce adventitious shoots. Root cuttings consist of roots less than 1 centimeter in diameter cut into short lengths, 2.5 to 8 centimeters long. These are placed horizontally on the rooting media and covered with a 1.3 centimeter layer of fine soil or sand. The rooting medium is kept moist; it is important not to let it dry out. After the cuttings have developed adventitious roots and shoots, they can be transplanted for further growth. Plants that naturally form **suckers** at the base are good candidates for cloning through root cuttings.

**Grafting.** The process of joining plants together in such a way that they will unite and grow as one plant is commonly referred to as grafting. The

Workers prepare graft clones of cacao leaves. The tips are dipped into an enzyme and planted for rooting. Through cloning, all of the cacao on this Ecuadoran plantation is of the same variety and will be used for chocolate production.

part that becomes the upper portion or top of the graft is termed the scion, and the lower portion is called the rootstock or stock. The general process of joining plants is referred to as grafting. When the scion part is just a bud, the operation is called budding. Grafting is a method of plant propagation that is thousands of years old, and there are many methods. All of them involve fastening fresh woody stems together, excluding light, preventing the stems from drying out, and training the new growth.

The advantages of grafting and budding are numerous. Many common fruits such as apples, pears, peaches, and walnuts cannot be satisfactorily propagated by cuttings. In order to meet market demands, the grower is

forced to use grafting and budding as a means of reproduction. In other instances, certain rootstocks have desirable characteristics such as resistance to soil diseases, dwarfism (reduced plant size), cold hardiness, and vigor. Through grafting it is possible to combine desirable qualities that are found in these rootstocks with desirable flowering and fruit qualities that are found on different scion varieties. Some stocks, by imparting a dwarf quality to the scion, reduce tree size. This allows smaller trees to be planted closer together in orchards, increasing crop yield per unit of space.

Grafting also enables the agriculturalist to change the variety of established plants. This technique is often beneficial in apple orchards. An older variety may be in ill health or no longer in demand. As long as the new scion wood is compatible, the established variety can serve as a rootstock and a new variety can be grafted onto old trees without digging up the entire orchard.

**hybrid** a mix of two varieties or species

The fruits of grafted plants are always of the scion variety: they are not combinations or **hybrids** of the scion and stock varieties. When closely related plants are grafted, most will continue their growth as a single plant. When the scion and rootstock unite and continue to grow as one plant, producing for many years, the graft is said to be compatible. When unrelated plants are grafted, the usual result is failure; the graft is incompatible. Certain combinations of scion and rootstock might grow and continue in a normal manner for several weeks only to have the scion die. Trees that are advertised as being "fruit salad" trees have five or six different scion varieties grafted onto one stock. Typically several of these scions are incompatible and will die off.

**Tissue Culture or Micropropagation.** If they are kept under a proper environment, plants can reproduce themselves even from very small parts. When the removed part is not much more than a few cells, the process is called tissue culture or micropropagation. The small section that is removed is termed the explant. It may be taken from the roots, leaves, stem, or growing tips. In tissue culture, the explant is put into nutrient solution in a test tube, petri dish, or other container and kept in a clean, bright environment. The artificial medium contains all the nutrients, food, and hormones to help the explant create new cells. Roots or shoots may emerge within a few weeks. Each rooted explant can then be divided, and each smaller portion cultured again, rapidly multiplying the number of plants.

The advantages of tissue culture or micropropagation include the following:

- All the plants produced through tissue culture are clones of the parent plant.

- Because the explants and lab containers are so small, micropropagation can yield many thousands of plants in one laboratory or greenhouse.

- Many clones can be multiplied relatively quickly.

**meristematic** related to cell division at the tip

- The smallest part of the growing tip (not much more than a few cells) is often free from viruses that may be present throughout the rest of the plant. By cloning this very small **meristematic** portion, a worker can reproduce the plant virus-free.

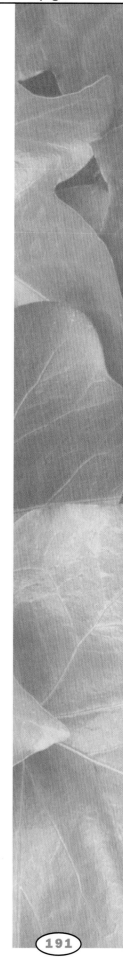

- Shipping many plants in small sterile containers is easier and safer than shipping larger plants with soil and watering problems.

- Many countries have laws that do not allow soil from other countries to cross their borders. Because these little plants in plastic containers do not have any soil, trade between these countries is not restricted.

Disadvantages or problems associated with tissue culture include the high cost of laboratory setup, the skill needed by workers, and the cost of environmental controls. Problems can also result from the lack of one of the important requirements for performing tissue culture or micropropagation successfully: a super-clean work area, correct medium, and proper environment. Laboratories or companies specializing in tissue culture often have very sophisticated equipment to ensure clean conditions. It is most important to keep bacteria and fungal spores away from the explant and nutrient medium. The explant surface is washed with a weak bleach solution to remove pathogens (bacteria or fungal spores that can spread in the container). Washing hands, cleaning tools, and surfaces with alcohol, and working quickly will prevent the contamination of containers and nutrient medium. Special nutrient mixes can be purchased from a commercial source or created from ingredients in a lab. The mix contains sugar, which supplies carbon to the tiny explant while it is unable to use the $CO_2$ in the air for photosynthesis. Also required are vitamins and nutrients that a healthy plant absorbs through its roots. Hormones stimulate cell division and the formation of roots and shoots. Light is necessary for the plant to develop roots and shoots. Temperatures must be in the range of 20 to 27°C.

There are four stages of the tissue culture or micropropagation procedure:

1. establishment and stabilization, when the small explant is inserted into the container (onto the medium) and survives the initial transplant;

2. shoot multiplication, when each explant expands into a cluster of microshoots and each cluster is divided and re-cultured to increase numbers;

3. pretransplant or in-vitro rooting, when the explant is transferred to another media mix that stimulates roots to form inside the container (in vitro means "in glass"); and

4. transplanting, acclimation, and more rooting, when the explant is transplanted into a clean potting mix and moved into a warm bright greenhouse where it will begin independent photosynthesis and establishment. SEE ALSO HORTICULTURE; REPRODUCTION, ASEXUAL; REPRODUCTION, SEXUAL; TISSUE CULTURE.

*Elizabeth L. Davison*

**Bibliography**

Bowes, Bryan G. *A Color Atlas of Plant Propagation and Conservation.* New York: New York Botanical Garden Press, 1999.

Dirr, Michael A., and Charles W. Heuser, Jr. *The Reference Manual of Woody Plant Propagation.* Athens, GA: Varsity Press, 1987.

Hartmann, T. Hudson, Dale E. Kester, Fred T. Davies, Jr., and Robert L. Geneve. *Plant Propagation: Principles and Practices,* 6th ed. Upper Saddle River, NJ: Prentice-Hall, Inc., 1997.

Thompson, Peter. *Creative Propagation: A Grower's Guide.* Portland, OR: Timber Press, 1992.

# Psychoactive Plants

**compound** a substance formed from two or more elements

Compounds in some plants can have an overwhelming effect on the central nervous system. Plants containing those **compounds** are thus known as mind-altering (active) or psychoactive plants. Their effects may be separated into hallucinogenic, stimulating, or depressing properties depending on the plant used and the present compounds, which are usually secondary metabolites. A few plants, however, have major multiple effects based on one or more compounds present, such as tobacco containing nicotine, which can be both stimulating and depressing.

Three points are worth keeping in mind about these plants. First, psychoactive drugs have been used in many cultures throughout human history. Their use has often been highly ritualized (especially true for hallucinogens) and incorporated into religions or mystical ceremonies in such a way that the novice is guided and protected by more experienced members of the ritual. Such practices have tended to minimize the potential for abuse inherent in psychoactive drugs. Second, variations in the concentrations of the active ingredients in plants make the dosing of psychoactive drugs more art than science for even the most experienced user. Last, most of the substances discussed are illegal to possess or use in the United States or Canada.

## Plants Having Hallucinogenic Effects

Most hallucinogens are plant secondary metabolic compounds. In amounts that are nontoxic, hallucinogens produce changes in perception, thought, and mood without causing major disturbances of the autonomic nervous system (the system regulating the activity of the heart, smooth muscles, and glands). The psychic changes and abnormal states of consciousness induced by hallucinogens differ from ordinary experiences. Hallucinogenic users forsake the familiar world and, in full consciousness, embrace a dreamlike world operating under different standards, strange dimensions, and in different times. These compounds are a means of escaping from reality as it is commonly understood. They are not physically addicting, although dependency may develop. A few examples are provided to illustrate these properties.

**Peyote.** The aboveground part of the cactus peyote (*Lophophora williamsii,* family Cactaceae) is chewed or a decoction (boiled in water) is drunk. Ingestion produces nausea, chills, and vomiting, and in most users anxiety and a dislocation of visual perspective. These symptoms are followed by a clarity and intensity of thought, the motion of brilliant-colored visions, and an exaggerated sensitivity to sound and other sense impressions. Activity is centered around the alkaloid mescaline.

**Nutmeg and Mace.** Powdered nutmeg or mace (*Myristica fragrans,* family Myristicaceae) is taken orally in hot water or sniffed. Unpleasant side ef-

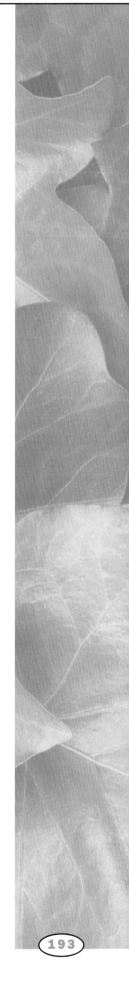

The lush foliage of an *Ayahuasca* vine in the Amazon Basin in Peru. Its leaves are used in a purging and hallucinogenic beverage.

fects almost always occur, and include headache, dizziness, nausea, sickening hangovers, and tachycardia (rapid heart beat). There are feelings of detachment, visual and auditory hallucinations, and sensations of floating or flying and separation of limbs from the body. The latter typifies the more toxic hallucinogens, and the volatile oils elemicin and myristicin are thought to be involved.

*Ayahuasca.* The bark of the woody vine *Ayahuasca* (*Banisteriopsis caapi*, family Malpighiaceae) often together with leaves of certain *Psychotria* spp., is boiled and the decoction drunk in many parts of tropical South America as a major hallucinogenic beverage. Shortly after ingesting, vomiting occurs, feelings of cold and spiral-flying sensations associated with nausea take place, and visions of blue-masked specters (often assuming grotesque forms) and alarming animals (e.g., boa constrictors) are seen. During this time, hearing is distorted and the individual becomes acutely sensitive. Later, motor coordination is reduced to staggering, the body is hot and sweaty, and salivation and spitting are continuous. If sufficient active compounds have been absorbed, the sensation of flying occurs while observing beautiful and often spectacular sights, a time when exultation sweeps the body, and all physical discomforts are forgotten. Objects and scenes are vividly colored in bright but natural colors. Very few participants reach the ultimate in psychoactive experience, reported telepathic sensitivity. The active ingredients include N,N-dimethyltryptamine (DMT) and the alkaloids harmine, harmaline, and others.

*Ololioqui.* The morning glories *Ololioqui* (*Ipomoea violacea* and *Rivea corymbosa*, family Convolvulaceae) are associated with Aztec and other Mexican Indian divinations and human sacrifices. Ingesting infusions and decoctions from powdered seeds induces delirium, hypnotic effects, and heightened visual perception. D-lysergic acid amide is the active hallucinogen.

*Angel's trumpet and jimsonweed.* Ingesting or smoking the seeds, flowers, and leaves of Angel's trumpet and jimsonweed (*Brugmansia* spp. and *Datura* spp., respectively; family Solanaceae) will severely intoxicate the user,

resulting in fever, flushing, dilated pupils, fast heart rate and pulse, and sometimes aggressive and violent behavior. In addition, a state of confused delirium may occur, which can be dangerous to the individual if not restrained. The usual hallucinations appear as a parade of material objects, sports cars and flowers, for example, in their simple colors. The vision-inducing hallucinogens are tropane alkaloids, particularly scopolamine.

**Marijuana.** Smoked or ingested, the resin from floral and leaf glands of marijuana (*Cannabis sativa*, family Cannabaceae) can cause visionary hallucinations that are often pleasant, with sexual overtones. Its most universal effect is as an euphoric, the user having a feeling of well-being and exaltation. Dangers resulting from heavy smoking exist to bronchial tracts and lungs, and prolonged use can cause personality changes that may lead to a marked deterioration in what is normally considered good mental health. The active compound is one or more resinous tetrahydrocannabinols.

## Plants Having Stimulating Effects

Stimulants have long been enjoyed by humans, for they give a sense of well-being and exhilaration, self-confidence, and power, and they alleviate fatigue and drowsiness. For most, depending on the dose, there is a price to be paid for their use: increased agitation, apprehension, and anxiety, mild mania (flight of ideas), as well as increased tolerance and often dependency. All of the stimulants described next have these positive and negative effects, except tobacco.

**Coca.** Native to and widely cultivated in the Andes of South America, the coca plant (*Erythoxylum coca*, family Erythroxylaceae) has a long history of use as a stimulant and hunger depressant. Stimulation is due to the tropane alkaloid cocaine found in leaves that are chewed or ingested as a beverage. Cocaine is readily extracted from leaves and the pure compound can be sniffed, smoked, or injected. Addiction to cocaine as a recreational drug is widespread.

**Chat or Khat.** Widely found native of the highlands of northeastern Africa and the adjacent Arabian peninsula, chat or khat (*Catha edulis*, family Celastraceae) is also cultivated in these regions. Chat leaves are chewed fresh, giving varying degrees of exhilaration and stimulation. The active ingredient is the alkaloid cathinone, and to lesser degrees norephedrine and norpseudoephedrine derived by enzymatic reduction from the unstable cathinone. Dependency on chat is common.

**Coffee, Tea, Chocolate, and Holly.** Coffee (*Coffea arabica*, family Rubiaceae), tea (*Camellia sinensis*, Theaceae), chocolate (*Theobroma cacao*, Sterculiaceae), and holly (*Ilex paraguariensis*, Aquifoliaceae) are stimulating beverages common throughout the world. All possess one or more of the xanthine alkaloids: caffeine, theobromine, and theophylline. Of the three, caffeine is the most stimulating.

**Tobacco.** Tobacco (*Nicotiana tabacum*, family Solanaceae) leaves are smoked or chewed to act as a stimulant, depressant, or tranquilizer. Tobacco with the addictive alkaloid nicotine is perhaps the most physiologically damaging substance generally used by humans. Its use is a direct cause of lung and other cancers, coronary artery disease, and emphysema.

## Plants Having Depressant Effects

By depressing the central nervous system, a number of secondary metabolites produce the effects of euphoria and well-being with sedation, including calming and tranquilizing, followed by sleep. Coma ending with death from respiratory failure can result as drug doses increase to higher levels. When controlled, all are enormously useful in medicine, but all are subject to major abuse and often lead to addiction.

**Kava.** Kava (*Piper methysticum*, family Piperaceae) roots and rhizomes are chewed or grated and prepared in cold water, which, when ingested, produce euphoria. This is the common depressant of the South Pacific region. Larger doses can result in impaired vision, lack of muscle coordination, and hypnosis. The active compounds are pyrones.

**Opium Poppy.** The opium poppy (*Papaver somniferum*, family Papaveraceae) has been long in cultivation and is probably native to western Asia. Unripe fruit capsules are incised after the petals fall and the milky exudate is air dried and molded into a gummy substance known as opium. Opium contains many compounds, but the alkaloids morphine and codeine are its most important depressants. From morphine, the **illicit** drug heroin is produced. Morphine effectively reduces pain and is a strong hypnotic, whereas codeine is widely used as a sedative to allay coughing. All are addictive with serious withdrawal symptoms. SEE ALSO ALKALOIDS; CANNABIS; COCA; ETHNOBOTANY; MEDICINAL PLANTS; OPIUM POPPY; TOBACCO.

*Walter H. Lewis*

**illicit** illegal

### Bibliography

Lewis, Walter H., and Memory P. F. Elvin-Lewis. *Medical Botany: Plants Affecting Man's Health.* New York: John Wiley & Sons, 1977.

Ott, Jonathan. *Pharmacotheon: Entheogenic Drugs, Their Plant Sources and History.* Kennewick, WA: Natural Products Co., 1993.

Schultes, Richard Evans, and Albert Hofmann. *The Botany and Chemistry of Hallucinogens.* Springfield, IL: Charles C. Thomas, 1980

# Quantitative Trait Loci

Quantitative traits are characteristics such as plant height or seed size, which can vary over a large range of possible values. The chromosomal regions controlling variation in a quantitative trait are known as quantitative trait loci.

The set of hereditary material transmitted from parent to offspring is known as the genome. It consists of molecules of deoxyribonucleic acid (DNA) arranged on chromosomes. Genetic markers are neutral DNA sequences that have no effect on an individual's physical appearance but are identifiable in the laboratory. Using statistical methods, the location of markers within an organism's genome can be estimated. The linear ordering of markers literally acts as a road map across the organism's genetic composition. This information allows a plant breeder to associate (link) an inherited observable characteristic such as seed size with a marker. This makes it possible to identify progeny possessing that characteristic (even before it shows) by determining whether the individual has that particular genetic

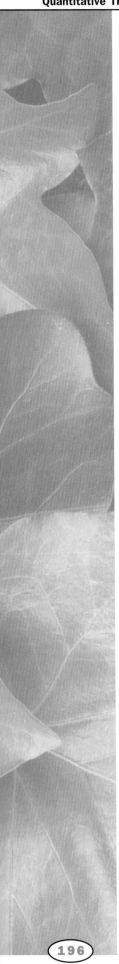

marker. In plant breeding applications, the location of specific regions of a genome responsible for controlling quantitative variation of a trait, such as seed size, is of increasing concern to those interested in crop performance.

Quantitative traits may be affected by many loci. A statistical representation (mathematical equation) of the quantitative trait describes the genetic variation in each region of the genome. Quantitative trait loci (QTL) analysis provides information for selectively manipulating genetic components of a trait. The basis of QTL detection, regardless of the crop to which it is applied, is the identification of associations between genetically determined phenotypes (physical characteristics) and genetic markers (genetic characteristics).

The emergence of high-resolution molecular marker technologies is likely to facilitate large-scale QTL analyses. QTL studies provide a first step in understanding the genetics that underlie the expression of quantitative traits. The hope for future research is that the foundation and knowledge gained from QTL research will aid our understanding of the biological function of genes, thus continuing the long history between the fields of genetics and statistics. SEE ALSO BREEDER; REEDING; GENETIC ENGINEER; MOLECULAR PLANT GENETICS.

*R. W. Doerge*

**Bibliography**

Doerge, R. W., Zhao Bang Zeng, and Bruce S. Weir. "Statistical Issues in the Search for Genes Affecting Quantitative Traits in Experimental Populations." *Statistical Science* 12, no. 3 (1997): 195–219.

Thoday, J. M. "Location of Polygenes." *Nature* 191 (1961): 368–70.

# Photo and
# Illustration Credits

*The illustrations and tables featured in* Plant Sciences *were created by GGS Information Services. The photographs appearing in the text were reproduced by permission of the following sources:*

## Volume 1

Ted Spiegel/Corbis: **2, 17, 96;** JLM Visuals: **4, 107;** Bojan Brecelj/Corbis: **6;** Tom Bean/ Corbis: **9, 49;** Thomas Del Brase/The Stock Market: **11;** Chinch Gryniewicz; Ecoscene/ Corbis: **13;** Charles O'Rear/Corbis: **19;** Steve Raymer/Corbis: **21;** Alex Rakoey/Custom Medical Stock Photo, Inc.: **28;** Wolfgang Kaehler/Corbis: **30, 100;** Field Mark Publications: **44;** Lester V. Bergman/Corbis: **50, 158;** Julie Meech; Ecoscene/Corbis: **53;** Raymond Gehman/Corbis: **55;** Dr. Kari Lounatmaa; Science Photo Library/Photo Researchers, Inc: **57;** Roger Tidman/Corbis: **58;** The Purcell Team/Corbis: **60;** David Muench/Corbis: **63, 114;** Adrian Arbib/ Corbis: **67;** Barry Griffiths; National Audubon Society Collection/Photo Researchers, Inc.: **76;** Kopp Illustration, 81; Prof. Jim Watson; Science Photo Library/ Photo Researchers, Inc: **85;** Michael S. Yamashita/Corbis: **87;** Pallava Bagla/Corbis: **88;** Bettmann/Corbis: **90, 116;** Richard T. Nowitz/Corbis: **92, 94;** UPI/Corbis– Bettmann: **109;** Owen Franken/Corbis: **112;** Bill Lisenby/Corbis: **119;** Hans & Cassady: **124, 136;** Fritz Polking; Frank Lane Picture Agency/Corbis: **128;** Ron Watts/Corbis: **130;** UPI/Bettmann Newsphotos: **131;** David Spears; Science Pictures Limited/Corbis: **138, 143;** Dr. Dennis Kunkel/Phototake NYC: **141;** Dr. Jeremy Burgess/Photo Researchers, Inc.: **146, 155;** Andrew Brown; Ecoscene/ Corbis: **148;** Richard Cummins/Corbis: **162.**

## Volume 2

Arne Hodalic/Corbis: **2;** Gregory G. Dimijian/Photo Researchers, Inc.: **5;** Michael & Patricia Fogden/Corbis: **9;** Dean Conger/ Corbis: **11, 76;** Joseph Sohm; ChromoSohm, Inc./Corbis: **16;** Darrell Gulin/Corbis: **18, 61;** Galen Rowell/Corbis: **23;** Courtesy of the Library of Congress: **24, 40, 143;** Charles O'Rear/Corbis: **26, 157;** Liba Taylor/Corbis: **29;** Richard Hamilton Smith/Corbis: **31, 32;** Bojan Brecelj/Corbis: **35;** Lester V. Bergman/ Corbis: **39, 119, 166, 175;** Robert Estall/ Corbis: **48;** William A. Bake/Corbis: **52;** Rosemary Mayer/Photo Researchers, Inc.: **54;** George Lepp/Corbis: **56;** Michael S. Yamashita/Corbis: **58, 114;** Raymond Gehman/Corbis: **62, 93;** Wayne Lawler; Ecoscene/Corbis: **64;** Dr. William M. Harlow/Photo Researchers, Inc.: **66;** William Boyce/Corbis: **74;** David Spears; Science Pictures Limited/Corbis: **82;** Roger Tidman/ Corbis: **84;** Hans & Cassady: **86;** Roger Ressmeyer/Corbis: **103;** Susan Middleton and David Liitschwager/Corbis: **107;** Robin Foster/Conservation International: **108;** John Durham/Photo Researchers, Inc.: **112;** Jaime Razuri; AFP/Corbis: **116;** Courtesy of Linda E. Graham: **122, 125;** Buddy Mays/Corbis: **136;** Michael Freeman/Corbis: **142;** Field Mark Publications: **146, 186;** David Cumming; Eye Ubiquitous/Corbis: **149;** Bob Krist/Corbis: **152;** Gunter Marx/Corbis: **154;** Jim Sugar Photography/Corbis: **156;** Courtesy of Dr. Orson K. Miller, Jr.: **162, 163, 164;** Lowell Georgia/Corbis: **167, 170;** William James Warren/Corbis: **169;** Patrick Johns/Corbis: **178;** Eric and David Hosking/Corbis: **180;** Thomas Bettge,

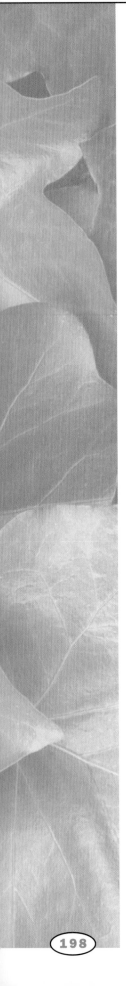

National Center for Atmospheric Research/ University Corporation for Atmospheric Research/National Science Foundation: **182, 183**; Philip Gould/Corbis: **184**; Roy Morsch/ The Stock Market: **188**; Tom Bean/Corbis: **190**; Archive Photos, Inc.: **194**; JLM Visuals: **199, 200**.

## Volume 3

Courtesy of the Library of Congress: **1, 30, 61, 73**; JLM Visuals: **3, 49, 106**; Corbis: **4**; Anthony Cooper; Ecoscene/Corbis: **9**; Photo Researchers, Inc.: **11**; Archive Photos, Inc.: **12**; Ed Young/Corbis: **23, 147**; Kansas Division of Travel and Tourism: **26**; Asa Thoresen/Photo Researchers, Inc.: **28**; Ted Streshinsky/Corbis: **32**; Michael S. Yamashita/Corbis: **35**; Patrick Johns/Corbis: **38, 96, 104, 125, 187**; Cumego/Corbis/ Bettmann: **39**; David Spears; Science Pictures Limited/Corbis: **41, 54, 114, 129**; W. Wayne Lockwood, M.D./Corbis: **42**; Field Mark Publications: **44, 57, 71, 169, 171, 175**; Michael & Patricia Fogden/Corbis: **46**; Phil Schermeister/Corbis: **52**; Judyth Platt; Ecoscene/Corbis: **59**; Courtesy of Hunt Institute for Botanical Documentation, Carnegie Mellon University, Pittsburgh, PA: **62**; UPI/Bettmann: **66**; Eric Crichton/Corbis: **72**; Biophoto Associates; National Audubon Society Collection/Photo Researchers, Inc.: **88**; Adam Hart-Davis/Photo Researchers, Inc.: **92**; Lester V. Bergman/Corbis: **94, 108, 167**; Patrick Field; Eye Ubiquitous/Corbis: **103**; Michael Boys/Corbis: **105**; Sally A. Morgan; Ecoscene/Corbis: **110**; Kevin Schafer/Corbis: **112**; Jim Zipp; National Audubon Society Collection/Photo Researchers, Inc.: **117**; Richard T. Nowitz/ Corbis: **120**; Wayne Lawler; Ecoscene/ Corbis: **122**; Bob Krist/Corbis: **123**; Tom and

Pat Lesson/Photo Researchers, Inc.: **158**; Raymond Gehman/Corbis: **164**; George Lepp/Corbis: **177**; Richard Hamilton Smith/Corbis: **181**; Nigel Cattlin; Holt Studios International/Photo Researchers, Inc.: **185**; Owen Franken/Corbis: **189**; Alison Wright/Corbis: **193**.

## Volume 4

Kevin Schafer/Corbis: **2, 42**; Wolfgang Kaehler/Corbis: **5, 7**; E. S. Ross: **9**; Galen Rowell/Corbis: **14, 127**; David Spears; Science Pictures Limited/Corbis: **17, 20, 79, 120, 161, 172**; Robert Pickett/Corbis: **19, 101**; Dr. Jeremy Burgess/Photo Researchers, Inc.: **21, 159**; Biophoto Associates/Photo Researchers, Inc.: **22, 142**; JLM Visuals: **25, 26, 40, 140, 155, 169**; Owen Franken/ Corbis: **27**; Philip Gould/Corbis: **30, 70**; Corbis: **39, 152**; Steve Raymer/Corbis: **49**; Mark Gibson/Corbis: **57**; James Lee Sikkema: **58**; Field Mark Publications: **62, 130, 167**; Wayne Lawler/Corbis: **63**; Richard T. Nowitz/Corbis: **66**; Photo Researchers, Inc.: **68**; Karen Tweedy-Holmes/Corbis: **73**; Lester V. Bergman/Corbis: **77, 147**; Craig Aurness/Corbis: **83**; John Holmes; Frank Lane Picture Agency/Corbis: **86**; Archivo Iconografico, S.A./Corbis: **92**; Paul Almasy/Corbis: **98**; Tiziana and Gianni Baldizzone/Corbis: **105**; Darrell Gulin/ Corbis: **108**; Lynda Richardson/Corbis: **110**; Courtesy of Thomas L. Rost and Deborah K. Canington: **112, 113, 114**; Laure Communi- cations: **115**; Archive Photos, Inc.: **116**; Jim Sugar Photography/Corbis: **132**; Hugh Clark; Frank Lane Picture Agency/Corbis: **136, 137**; Ron Boardman; Frank Lane Picture Agency/ Corbis: **148**; Richard Hamilton Smith/Corbis: **165**; Joseph Sohm; ChromoSohm, Inc./ Corbis: **175**; Dave G. Houser/Corbis: **176**.

# Glossary

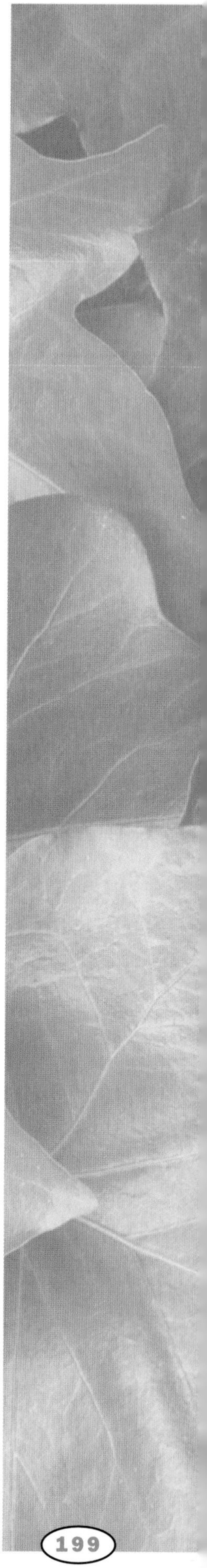

**abiotic** nonliving

**abrade** to wear away through contact

**abrasive** tending to wear away through contact

**abscission** dropping off or separating

**accession** a plant that has been acquired and catalogued

**achene** a small, dry, thin-walled type of fruit

**actinomycetes** common name for a group of Gram-positive bacteria that are filamentous and superficially similar to fungi

**addictive** capable of causing addiction or chemical dependence

**adhesion** sticking to the surface of

**adventitious** arising from secondary buds, or arising in an unusual position

**aeration** the introduction of air

**albuminous** gelatinous, or composed of the protein albumin

**alkali** chemically basic; the opposite of acidic

**alkalinization** increase in basicity or reduction in acidity

**alkaloid** bitter secondary plant compound, often used for defense

**allele** one form of a gene

**allelopathy** harmful action by one plant against another

**allopolyploidy** a polyploid organism formed by hybridization between two different species or varieties (*allo* = other)

**alluvial plain** broad area formed by the deposit of river sediment at its outlet

**amended soils** soils to which fertilizers or other growth aids have been added

**amendment** additive

**anaerobic** without oxygen

**analgesic** pain-relieving

**analog** a structure or thing, especially a chemical, similar to something else

**angiosperm** a flowering plant

**anomalous** unusual or out of place

**anoxic** without oxygen

**antenna system** a collection of protein complexes that harvests light energy and converts it to excitation energy that can migrate to a reaction center; the light is absorbed by pigment molecules (e.g., chlorophyll, carotenoids, phycobilin) that are attached to the protein

**anthropogenic** human-made; related to or produced by the influence of humans on nature

**antibodies** proteins produced to fight infection

**antioxidant** a substance that prevents damage from oxygen or other reactive substances

**apical meristem** region of dividing cells at the tips of growing plants

**apical** at the tip

**apomixis** asexual reproduction that may mimic sexual reproduction

**appendages** parts that are attached to a central stalk or axis

**arable** able to be cultivated for crops

**Arcto-Tertiary geoflora** the fossil flora discovered in Arctic areas dating back to the Tertiary period; this group contains magnolias (*Magnolia*), tulip trees (*Liriodendron*), maples (*Acer*), beech (*Fagus*), black gum (*Nyssa*), sweet gum (*Liquidambar*), dawn redwood (*Metasequoia*), cypress (*Taxodium*), and many other species

**artifacts** pots, tools, or other cultural objects

**assayer** one who performs chemical tests to determine the composition of a substance

**ATP** adenosine triphosphate, a small, water-soluble molecule that acts as an energy currency in cells

**attractant** something that attracts

**autotroph** "self-feeder"; any organism that uses sunlight or chemical energy

**auxin** a plant hormone

**avian** related to birds

**axil** the angle or crotch where a leaf stalk meets the stem

**axillary bud** the bud that forms in the angle between the stem and leaf

**basipetal** toward the base

**belladonna** the source of atropine; means "beautiful woman," and is so named because dilated pupils were thought to enhance a woman's beauty

**binomial** two-part

**biodirected assays** tests that examine some biological property

**biodiversity** degree of variety of life

**biogeography** the study of the reasons for the geographic distribution of organisms

**biomass** the total dry weight of an organism or group of organisms

**biosphere** the region of the Earth in which life exists

**biosynthesis** creation through biological pathways

**biota** the sum total of living organisms in a region of a given size

**biotic** involving or related to life

**bryologist** someone who studies bryophytes, a division of nonflowering plants

**campanulate** bell-shaped

**capitulum** the head of a compound flower, such as a dandelion

**cardiotonic** changing the contraction properties of the heart

**carotenoid** a yellow-colored molecule made by plants

**carpels** the innermost whorl of flower parts, including the egg-bearing ovules, plus the style and stigma attached to the ovules

**catastrophism** the geologic doctrine that sudden, violent changes mark the geologic history of Earth

**cation** positively charged particle

**catkin** a flowering structure used for wind pollination

**centrifugation** spinning at high speed in a centrifuge to separate components

**chitin** a cellulose-like molecule found in the cell wall of many fungi and arthropods

**chloroplast** the photosynthetic organelle of plants and algae

**circadian** "about a day"; related to a day

**circumscription** the definition of the boundaries surrounding an object or an idea

**cisterna** a fluid-containing sac or space

**clade** a group of organisms composed of an ancestor and all of its descendants

**cladode** a modified stem having the appearance and function of a leaf

**coalescing roots** roots that grow together

**coleoptile** the growing tip of a monocot seedling

**collenchyma** one of three cell types in ground tissue

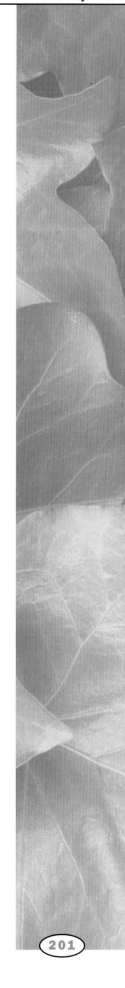

**colonize** to inhabit a new area

**colony** a group of organisms inhabiting a particular area, especially organisms descended from a common ancestor

**commensalism** a symbiotic association in which one organism benefits while the other is unaffected

**commodities** goods that are traded, especially agricultural goods

**community** a group of organisms of different species living in a region

**compaction** compacting of soil, leading to the loss of air spaces

**complex hybrid** hybridized plant having more than two parent plants

**compound** a substance formed from two or more elements

**concentration gradient** a difference in concentration between two areas

**continental drift** the movement of continental land masses due to plate tectonics

**contractile** capable of contracting

**convective uplift** the movement of air upwards due to heating from the sun

**coppice growth** the growth of many stems from a single trunk or root, following the removal of the main stem

**cortical** relating to the cortex of a plant

**covalent** held together by electron-sharing bonds

**crassulacean acid metabolism** water-conserving strategy used by several types of plants

**crop rotation** alternating crops from year to year in a particular field

**cultivation** growth of plants, or turning the soil for growth of crop plants

**crystallography** the use of x-rays on crystals to determine molecular structure

**cuticle** the waxy outer coating of a leaf or other structure, which provides protection against predators, infection, and water loss

**cyanide heap leach gold mining** a technique used to extract gold by treating ore with cyanide

**cyanobacteria** photosynthetic prokaryotic bacteria formerly known as blue-green algae

**cyanogenic** giving rise to cyanide

**cytologist** a scientist who studies cells

**cytology** the microscopic study of cells and cell structure

**cytosol** the fluid portion of a cell

**cytostatic** inhibiting cell division

**deductive** reasoning from facts to conclusion

**dendrochronologist** a scientist who uses tree rings to determine climate or other features of the past

**dermatophytes** fungi that cause skin diseases

**desertification** degradation of dry lands, reducing productivity

**desiccation** drying out

**detritus** material from decaying organisms

**diatoms** hard-shelled, single-celled marine organisms; a type of algae

**dictyosome** any one of the membranous or vesicular structures making up the Golgi apparatus

**dioicous** having male and female sexual parts on different plants

**diploid** having two sets of chromosomes, versus having one set (haploid)

**dissipate** to reduce by spreading out or scattering

**distal** further away from

**diurnal** daily, or by day

**domestication** the taming of an organism to live with and be of use to humans

**dormant** inactive, not growing

**drupe** a fruit with a leathery or stone-like seed

**dynamical system theory** the mathematical theory of change within a system

**ecophysiological** related to how an organism's physiology affects its function in an ecosystem

**ecosystem** an ecological community and its environment

**elater** an elongated, thickened filament

**empirical formula** the simplest whole number ratio of atoms in a compound

**emulsifier** a chemical used to suspend oils in water

**encroachment** moving in on

**endemic** belonging or native to a particular area or country

**endophyte** a fungus that lives within a plant

**endoplasmic reticulum** the membrane network inside a cell

**endosperm** the nutritive tissue in a seed, formed by the fertilization of a diploid egg tissue by a sperm from pollen

**endosporic** the formation of a gametophyte inside the spore wall

**endosymbiosis** a symbiosis in which one organism lives inside the other

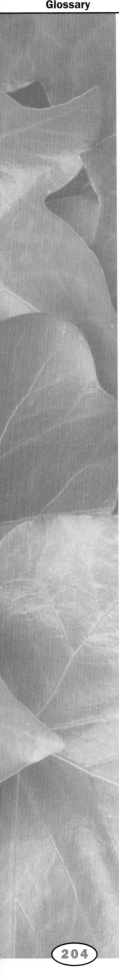

**Enlightenment** eighteenth-century philosophical movement stressing rational critique of previously accepted doctrines in all areas of thought

**entomologist** a scientist who studies insects

**enzyme** a protein that controls a reaction in a cell

**ephemeral** short-lived

**epicuticle** the waxy outer covering of a plant, produced by the epidermis

**epidermis** outer layer of cells

**epiphytes** plants that grow on other plants

**escarpment** a steep slope or cliff resulting from erosion

**ethnobotanist** a scientist who interacts with native peoples to learn more about the plants of a region

**ethnobotany** the study of traditional uses of plants within a culture

**euglossine bees** a group of bees that pollinate orchids and other rain-forest plants

**eukaryotic** a cell with a nucleus (*eu* means "true" and *karyo* means "nucleus"); includes protists, plants, animals, and fungi

**extrafloral** outside the flower

**exudation** the release of a liquid substance; oozing

**facultative** capable of but not obligated to

**fertigation** application of small amounts of fertilizer while irrigating

**filament** a threadlike extension

**filamentous** thin and long

**flagella** threadlike extension of the cell membrane, used for movement

**flavonoids** aromatic compounds occurring in both seeds and young roots and involved in host-pathogen and host-symbiont interactions

**florigen** a substance that promotes flowering

**floristic** related to plants

**follicle** sac or pouch

**forbs** broad-leaved, herbaceous plants

**free radicals** toxic molecular fragments

**frugivous** feeding on fruits

**gametangia** structure where gametes are formed

**gametophyte** the haploid organism in the life cycle

**gel electrophoresis** a technique for separating molecules based on size and electrical charge

**genera** plural of genus; a taxonomic level above species

**genome** the genetic material of an organism

**genotype** the genetic makeup of an organism

**germplasm** hereditary material, especially stored seed or other embryonic forms

**globose** rounded and swollen; globe-shaped

**gradient** difference in concentration between two places

**green manure** crop planted to be plowed under to nourish the soil, especially with nitrogen

**gymnosperm** a major group of plants that includes the conifers

**gynoecium** the female reproductive organs as a whole

**gypsipherous** containing the mineral gypsum

**hallucinogenic** capable of inducing hallucinations

**haploid** having one set of chromosomes, versus having two (diploid)

**haustorial** related to a haustorium, or food-absorbing organ

**hemiterpene** a half terpene

**herbivore** an organism that feeds on plant parts

**heterocyclic** a chemical ring structure composed of more than one type of atom, for instance carbon and nitrogen

**heterosporous** bearing spores of two types, large megaspores and small microspores

**heterostylous** having styles (female flower parts) of different lengths, to aid cross-pollination

**heterotroph** an organism that derives its energy from consuming other organisms or their body parts

**holistic** including all the parts or factors that relate to an object or idea

**homeotic** relating to or being a gene that produces a shift in structural development

**homology** a similarity in structure between anatomical parts due to descent from a common ancestor

**humus** the organic material in soil formed from decaying organisms

**hybrid** a mix of two varieties or species

**hybridization** formation of a new individual from parents of different species or varieties

**hydrological cycle** the movement of water through the biosphere

**hydrophobic** water repellent

**hydroponic** growing without soil, in a watery medium

**hydroxyl** the chemical group -OH

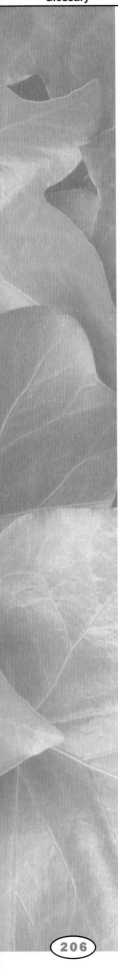

**hyphae** the threadlike body mass of a fungus

**illicit** illegal

**impede** to slow down or inhibit

**inert** incapable of reaction

**inflorescence** a group of flowers or arrangement of flowers in a flower head

**infrastructure** roads, phone lines, and other utilities that allow commerce

**insectivorous** insect-eating

**intercalary** inserted; between

**interspecific hybridization** hybridization between two species

**intertidal** between the lines of high and low tide

**intracellular bacteria** bacteria that live inside other cells

**intraspecific taxa** levels of classification below the species level

**intuiting** using intuition

**ionic** present as a charged particle

**ions** charged particles

**irreversible** unable to be reversed

**juxtaposition** contrast brought on by close positioning

**lacerate** cut

**Lamarckian inheritance** the hypothesis that acquired characteristics can be inherited

**lamellae** thin layers or plate-like structure

**land-grant university** a state university given land by the federal government on the condition that it offer courses in agriculture

**landrace** a variety of a cultivated plant, occurring in a particular region

**lateral** to the side of

**legume** beans and other members of the Fabaceae family

**lignified** composed of lignin, a tough and resistant plant compound

**lineage** ancestry; the line of evolutionary descent of an organism

**loci** (singular: locus) sites or locations

**lodging** falling over while still growing

**lytic** breaking apart by the action of enzymes

**macromolecule** a large molecule such as a protein, fat, nucleic acid, or carbohydrate

**macroscopic** large, visible

**medulla** middle part

**megaphylls** large leaves having many veins or a highly branched vein system

**meiosis** the division of chromosomes in which the resulting cells have half the original number of chromosomes

**meristem** the growing tip of a plant

**mesic** of medium wetness

**microfibrils** microscopic fibers in a cell

**micron** one millionth of a meter; also called micrometer

**microphylls** small leaves having a single unbranched vein

**mitigation** reduction of amount or effect

**mitochondria** cell organelles that produce adenosine triphosphate (ATP) to power cell reactions

**mitosis** the part of the cell cycle in which chromosomes are separated to give each daughter cell an identical chromosome set

**molecular systematics** the analysis of DNA and other molecules to determine evolutionary relationships

**monoculture** a large stand of a single crop species

**monomer** a single unit of a multi-unit structure

**monophyletic** a group that includes an ancestral species and all its descendants

**montane** growing in a mountainous region

**morphology** shape and form

**motile** capable of movement

**mucilaginous** sticky or gummy

**murein** a peptidoglycan, a molecule made up of sugar derivatives and amino acids

**mutualism** a symbiosis between two organisms in which both benefit

**mycelium** the vegetative body of a fungus, made up of threadlike hyphae

**NADP⁺** oxidized form of nicotinamide adenine dinucleotide phosphate

**NADPH** reduced form of nicotinamide adenine dinucleotide phosphate, a small, water-soluble molecule that acts as a hydrogen carrier in biochemical reactions

**nanometer** one billionth of a meter

**nectaries** organs in flowers that secrete nectar

**negative feedback** a process by which an increase in some variable causes a response that leads to a decrease in that variable

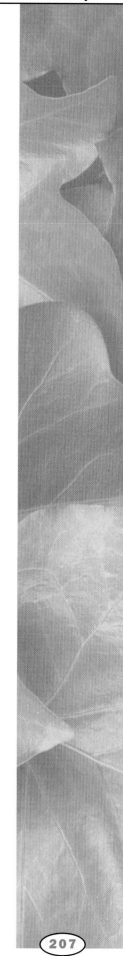

**neuromuscular junction** the place on the muscle surface where the muscle receives stimulus from the nervous system

**neurotransmitter** a chemical that passes messages between nerve cells

**node** branching site on a stem

**nomenclature** a naming system

**nonmotile** not moving

**nonpolar** not directed along the root-shoot axis, or not marked by separation of charge (unlike water and other polar substances)

**nonsecretory** not involved in secretion, or the release of materials

**Northern Blot** a technique for separating RNA molecules by electrophoresis and then identifying a target fragment with a DNA probe

**nucleolar** related to the nucleolus, a distinct region in the nucleus

**nurseryman** a worker in a plant nursery

**obligate** required, without another option

**obligate parasite** a parasite without a free-living stage in the life cycle

**odorant** a molecule with an odor

**organelle** a membrane-bound structure within a cell

**osmosis** the movement of water across a membrane to a region of high solute concentration

**oviposition** egg-laying

**oxidation** reaction with oxygen, or loss of electrons in a chemical reaction

**paleobotany** the study of ancient plants and plant communities

**pangenesis** the belief that acquired traits can be inherited by bodily influences on the reproductive cells

**panicle** a type of inflorescence (flower cluster) that is loosely packed and irregularly branched

**paraphyletic group** a taxonomic group that excludes one or more descendants of a common ancestor

**parenchyma** one of three types of cells found in ground tissue

**pastoralists** farming people who keep animal flocks

**pathogen** disease-causing organism

**pedicel** a plant stalk that supports a fruiting or spore-bearing organ

**pentamerous** composed of five parts

**percolate** to move through, as a fluid through a solid

**peribacteroid** a membrane surrounding individual or groups of rhizobia bacteria within the root cells of their host; in such situations the bacteria have frequently undergone some change in surface chemistry and are referred to as bacteroids

**pericycle** cell layer between the conducting tissue and the endodermis

**permeability** the property of being permeable, or open to the passage of other substances

**petiole** the stalk of a leaf, by which it attaches to the stem

**pH** a measure of acidity or alkalinity; the pH scale ranges from 0 to 14, with 7 being neutral. Low pH numbers indicate high acidity while high numbers indicate alkalinity

**pharmacognosy** the study of drugs derived from natural products

**pharmacopeia** a group of medicines

**phenology** seasonal or other time-related aspects of an organism's life

**pheromone** a chemical released by one organism to influence the behavior of another

**photooxidize** to react with oxygen under the influence of sunlight

**photoperiod** the period in which an organism is exposed to light or is sensitive to light exposure, causing flowering or other light-sensitive changes

**photoprotectant** molecules that protect against damage by sunlight

**phylogenetic** related to phylogeny, the evolutionary development of a species

**physiology** the biochemical processes carried out by an organism

**phytogeographer** a scientist who studies the distribution of plants

**pigments** colored molecules

**pistil** the female reproductive organ of a flower

**plasmodesmata** cell-cell junctions that allow passage of small molecules between cells

**polyculture** mixed species

**polyhedral** in the form of a polyhedron, a solid whose sides are polygons

**polymer** a large molecule made from many similar parts

**polynomial** "many-named"; a name composed of several individual parts

**polyploidy** having multiple sets of chromosomes

**polysaccharide** a linked chain of many sugar molecules

**population** a group of organisms of a single species that exist in the same region and interbreed

**porosity** openness

**positive feedback** a process by which an increase in some variable causes a response that leads to a further increase in that variable

**precipitation** rainfall; or the process of a substance separating from a solution

**pre-Columbian** before Columbus

**precursor** a substance from which another is made

**predation** the act of preying upon; consuming for food

**primordial** primitive or early

**progenitor** parent or ancestor

**prokaryotes** single-celled organisms without nuclei, including Eubacteria and Archaea

**propagate** to create more of through sexual or asexual reproduction

**protist** a usually single-celled organism with a cell nucleus, of the kingdom Protista

**protoplasmic** related to the protoplasm, cell material within the cell wall

**protoplast** the portion of a cell within the cell wall

**psychoactive** causing an effect on the brain

**pubescence** covered with short hairs

**pyruvic acid** a three-carbon compound that forms an important intermediate in many cellular processes

**quadruple hybrid** hybridized plant with four parents

**quantitative** numerical, especially as derived from measurement

**quid** a wad for chewing

**quinone** chemical compound found in plants, often used in making dyes

**radii** distance across, especially across a circle (singular = radius)

**radioisotopes** radioactive forms of an element

**rambling habit** growing without obvious intended direction

**reaction center** a protein complex that uses light energy to create a stable charge separation by transferring a single electron energetically uphill from a donor molecule to an acceptor molecule, both of which are located in the reaction center

**redox** oxidation and reduction

**regurgitant** material brought up from the stomach

**Renaissance** a period of artistic and intellectual expansion in Europe from the fourteenth to the sixteenth century

**salinization** increase in salt content

**samara** a winged seed

**saprophytes** plants that feed on decaying parts of other plants

**saturated** containing as much dissolved substance as possible

**sclerenchyma** one of three cell types in ground tissue

**sedimentation** deposit of mud, sand, shell, or other material

**semidwarf** a variety that is intermediate in size between dwarf and full-size varieties

**senescent** aging or dying

**sepals** the outermost whorl of flower parts; usually green and leaf-like, they protect the inner parts of the flower

**sequester** to remove from circulation; lock up

**serology** the study of serum, the liquid, noncellular portion of blood

**seta** a stiff hair or bristle

**silage** livestock food produced by fermentation in a silo

**siliceous** composed of silica, a mineral

**silicified** composed of silicate minerals

**soil horizon** distinct layers of soil

**solute** a substance dissolved in a solution

**Southern blot** a technique for separating DNA fragments by electrophoresis and then identifying a target fragment with a DNA probe

**spasticity** abnormal muscle activity caused by damage to the nerve pathways controlling movement

**speciation** the creation of new species

**specimen** an object or organism under consideration

**speciose** marked by many species

**sporophyte** the diploid, spore-producing individual in the plant life cycle

**sporulate** to produce or release spores

**sterile** not capable or involved in reproduction, or unable to support life

**sterols** chemicals related to steroid hormones

**stolons** underground stems that may sprout and form new individuals

**stomata** openings between guard cells on the underside of leaves that allow gas exchange

**stratification** layering, or separation in space

**stratigraphic geology** the study of rock layers

**stratigraphy** the analysis of strata (layered rock)

**strobili** cone-like reproductive structures

**subalpine** a region less cold or elevated than alpine (mountaintop)

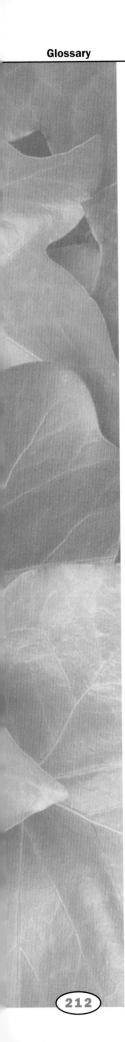

**substrate** the physical structure to which an organism attaches, or a molecule acted on by enzymes

**succession** the pattern of changes in plant species that occurs after a soil disturbance

**succulent** fleshy, moist

**suckers** naturally occuring adventitious shoots

**suffrutescent** a shrub-like plant with a woody base

**sulfate** a negatively charged particle combining sulfur and oxygen

**surfaced** smoothed for examination

**susceptibility** vulnerability

**suture** line of attachment

**swidden agriculture** the practice of farming an area until the soil has been depleted and then moving on

**symbiont** one member of a symbiotic association

**symbiosis** a relationship between organisms of two different species in which at least one benefits

**systematists** scientists who study systematics, the classification of species to reflect evolutionary relationships

**systemic** spread throughout the plant

**tannins** compounds produced by plants that usually serve protective functions, often colored and used for "tanning" and dyeing

**taxa** a type of organism, or a level of classification of organisms

**tensile forces** forces causing tension, or pulling apart; the opposite of compression

**tepal** an undifferentiated sepal or petal

**Tertiary period** geologic period from sixty-five to five million years ago

**tetraploid** having four sets of chromosomes; a form of polyploidy

**thallus** simple, flattened, nonleafy plant body

**tilth** soil structure characterized by open air spaces and high water storage capacity due to high levels of organic matter

**tonoplast** the membrane of the vacuole

**topographic** related to the shape or contours of the land

**totipotent** capable of forming entire plants from individual cells

**toxin** a poisonous substance

**tracheid** a type of xylem cell that conducts water from root to shoot

**transcription factors** proteins that bind to a specific DNA sequence called the promoter to regulate the expression of a nearby gene

**translocate** to move materials from one region to another

**translucent** allowing the passage of light

**transmutation** to change from one form to another

**transpiration** movement of water from soil to atmosphere through a plant

**transverse** across, or side to side

**tribe** a group of closely related genera

**trophic** related to feeding

**turgor pressure** the outward pressure exerted on the cell wall by the fluid within

**twining** twisting around while climbing

**ultrastructural** the level of structure visible with the electron microscope; very small details of structure

**uniformitarian** the geologic doctrine that formative processes on earth have proceeded at the same rate through time since earth's beginning

**uplift** raising up of rock layers, a geologic process caused by plate tectonics

**urbanization** increase in size or number of cities

**vacuole** the large fluid-filled sac that occupies most of the space in a plant cell. Used for storage and maintaining internal pressure

**vascular plants** plants with specialized transport cells; plants other than bryophytes

**vascular** related to the transport of nutrients, or related to blood vessels

**vector** a carrier, usually one that is not affected by the thing carried

**vernal** related to the spring season

**vesicle** a membrane-bound cell structure with specialized contents

**viable** able to live or to function

**volatile** easily released as a gas

**volatilization** the release of a gaseous substance

**water table** the level of water in the soil

**whorl** a ring

**wort** an old English term for plant; also an intermediate liquid in beer making

**xenobiotics** biomolecules from outside the plant, especially molecules that are potentially harmful

**xeromorphic** a form adapted for dry conditions

**xerophytes** plants adapted for growth in dry areas

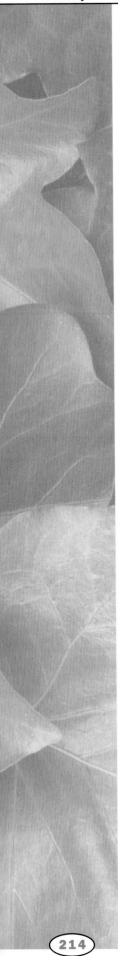

**zonation** division into zones having different properties

**zoospore** a swimming spore

**zygote** the egg immediately after it has been fertilized; the one-cell stage of a new individual

# Topic Outline

Tobacco
Transgenic Plants
Vavilov, N. I.
Vegetables
Weeds
Wheat
Wine and Beer Industry

## ANATOMY

Anatomy of Plants
Bark
Botanical and Scientific Illustrator
Cell Walls
Cells
Cells, Specialized Types
Cork
Differentiation and Development
Fiber and Fiber Products
Flowers
Fruits
Inflorescence
Leaves
Meristems
Mycorrhizae
Phyllotaxis
Plants
Roots
Seeds
Shape and Form of Plants
Stems
Tissues
Tree Architecture
Trichomes
Vascular Tissues
Vegetables
Wood Anatomy

## BIOCHEMISTRY/PHYSIOLOGY

Alcoholic Beverage Industry
Alkaloids
Anthocyanins
Biofuels
Biogeochemical Cycles
Bioremediation
Carbohydrates
Carbon Cycle
Cells
Cellulose
Chlorophyll
Chloroplasts

Cytokinins
Defenses, Chemical
Ecology, Energy Flow
Fertilizer
Flavonoids
Flavor and Fragrance Chemist
Halophytes
Herbicides
Hormones
Lipids
Medicinal Plants
Nitrogen Fixation
Nutrients
Oils, Plant-Derived
Pharmaceutical Scientist
Photoperiodism
Photosynthesis, Carbon Fixation
Photosynthesis, Light Reactions
Physiologist
Pigments
Poisonous Plants
Psychoactive Plants
Soil, Chemistry of
Terpenes
Translocation
Vacuoles
Water Movement

## BIODIVERSITY

Agricultural Ecosystems
Aquatic Ecosystems
Biodiversity
Biogeography
Biome
Botanical Gardens and Arboreta
Chapparal
Clines and Ecotypes
Coastal Ecosystems
Coniferous Forests
Curator of a Botanical Garden
Curator of an Herbarium
Deciduous Forests
Deforestation
Desertification
Deserts
Ecology
Ethnobotany
Global Warning
Herbaria
Human Impacts
Invasive Species

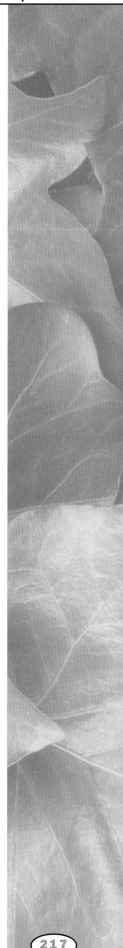

Plant Prospecting
Rain Forest Canopy
Rain Forests
Savanna
Taxonomist
Tundra
Wetlands

## BIOMES

Aquatic Ecosystems
Atmosphere and Plants
Biodiversity
Biogeography
Biome
Cacti
Chapparal
Coastal Ecosystems
Coniferous Forests
Deciduous Forests
Deforestation
Desertification
Deserts
Ecology
Ecosystem
Global Warning
Grasslands
Human Impacts
Invasive Species
Peat Bogs
Plant Prospecting
Rain Forest Canopy
Rain Forests
Savanna
Tundra
Wetlands

## CAREERS

Agriculture, Modern
Agriculture, Organic
Agronomist
Alcoholic Beverage Industry
Arborist
Botanical and Scientific Illustrator
Breeder
Breeding
College Professor
Curator of a Botanical Garden
Curator of an Herbarium
Flavor and Fragrance Chemist
Food Scientist
Forester

Forestry
Genetic Engineer
Genetic Engineering
Horticulture
Horticulturist
Landscape Architect
Pathologist
Pharmaceutical Scientist
Physiologist
Plant Prospecting
Taxonomist
Turf Management

## CELL BIOLOGY

Algae
Biogeochemical Cycles
Cell Cycle
Cell Walls
Cells
Cells, Specialized Types
Cellulose
Chloroplasts
Cork
Differentiation and Development
Embryogenesis
Fiber and Fiber Products
Germination
Germination and Growth
Leaves
Meristems
Molecular Plant Genetics
Mycorrhizae
Nitrogen Fixation
Physiologist
Plastids
Reproduction, Fertilization
Roots
Seeds
Stems
Tissues
Translocation
Trichomes
Tropisms and Nastic Movements
Vacuoles
Vascular Tissues
Water Movement
Wood Anatomy

## DESERTS

Biome
Cacti

## EVOLUTION

## FOODS

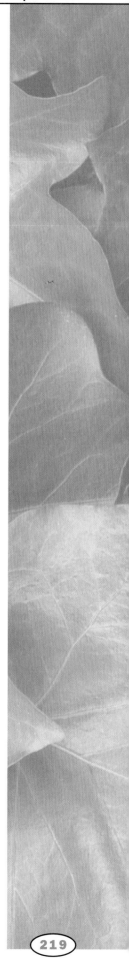

Fruits
Fruits, Seedless
Grains
Herbs and Spices
Leaves
Native Food Crops
Oils, Plant-Derived
Rice
Roots
Seeds
Solanaceae
Soybeans
Stems
Sugar
Tea
Wheat

## GARDENING

Alliaceae
Compost
Flowers
Fruits
Herbicides
Horticulture
Invasive Species
Landscape Architect
Ornamental Plants
Vegetables

## GENETICS

Breeder
Breeding
Breeding Systems
Cell Cycle
Chromosomes
Fruits, Seedless
Genetic Engineer
Genetic Engineering
Genetic Mechanisms and Development
Green Revolution
Hormonal Control and Development
Molecular Plant Genetics
Polyploidy
Quantitative Trait Loci
Reproduction, Alternation of Generations
Reproduction, Asexual
Reproduction, Fertilization
Reproduction, Sexual
Transgenic Plants

## HISTORY OF BOTANY

Agriculture, History of
Bessey, Charles
Borlaug, Norman
Britton, Nathaniel
Brongniart, Adolphe-Theodore
Burbank, Luther
Calvin, Melvin
Carver, George W.
Clements, Frederic
Cordus, Valerius
Creighton, Harriet
Darwin, Charles
de Candolle, Augustin
de Saussure, Nicholas
Ecology, History of
Evolution of Plants, History of
Gray, Asa
Green Revolution
Hales, Stephen
Herbals and Herbalists
Hooker, Joseph Dalton
Humboldt, Alexander von
Ingenhousz, Jan
Linneaus, Carolus
McClintock, Barbara
Mendel, Gregor
Odum, Eugene
Physiology, History of
Sachs, Julius von
Taxonomy, History of
Torrey, John
Van Helmont, Jean Baptiste
van Niel, C. B.
Vavilov, N. I.
Warming, Johannes

## HORMONES

Differentiation and Development
Genetic Mechanisms and Development
Herbicides
Hormonal Control and Development
Hormones
Meristems
Photoperiodism
Physiologist
Rhythms in Plant Life
Senescence
Shape and Form of Plants
Tropisms and Nastic Movements

## HORTICULTURE

Alliaceae
Asteraceae
Bonsai
Botanical Gardens and Arboreta
Breeder
Breeding
Cacti
Curator of a Botanical Garden
Horticulture
Horticulturist
Hybrids and Hybridization
Hydroponics
Landscape Architect
Ornamental Plants
Polyploidy
Propagation
Turf Management

## INDIVIDUAL PLANTS AND PLANT FAMILIES

Alliaceae
Asteraceae
Bamboo
Cacao
Cacti
Cannabis
Coca
Coffee
Corn
Cotton
Dioscorea
Fabaceae
Ginkgo
Grasses
Kudzu
Opium Poppy
Orchidaceae
Palms
Poison Ivy
Potato
Rice
Rosaceae
Sequoia
Solanaceae
Soybeans
Tobacco
Wheat

## LIFE CYCLE

Breeder
Breeding Systems
Cell Cycle
Differentiation and Development
Embryogenesis
Flowers
Fruits
Gametophyte
Genetic Mechanisms and Development
Germination
Germination and Growth
Hormonal Control and Development
Meristems
Pollination Biology
Reproduction, Alternation of Generations
Reproduction, Asexual
Reproduction, Fertilization
Reproduction, Sexual
Rhythms in Plant Life
Seed Dispersal
Seed Preservation
Seeds
Senescence
Sporophyte
Tissue Culture

## NUTRITION

Acid Rain
Biogeochemical Cycles
Carbon Cycle
Carnivorous Plants
Compost
Decomposers
Ecology, Fire
Epiphytes
Fertilizer
Germination and Growth
Hydroponics
Mycorrhizae
Nitrogen Fixation
Nutrients
Peat Bogs
Physiologist
Roots
Soil, Chemistry of
Soil, Physical Characteristics
Translocation
Water Movement

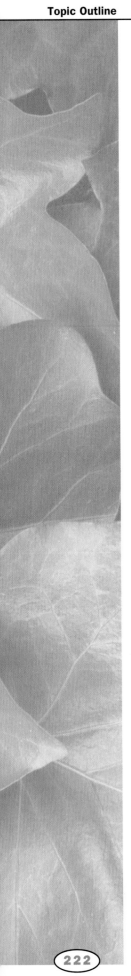

## PHOTOSYNTHESIS

Algae
Atmosphere and Plants
Biofuels
Carbohydrates
Carbon Cycle
Carotenoids
Chlorophyll
Chloroplasts
Flavonoids
Global Warming
Leaves
Photosynthesis, Carbon Fixation
Photosynthesis, Light Reactions
Physiologist
Pigments
Plastids
Translocation

## RAIN FORESTS

Atmosphere and Plants
Biodiversity
Deforestation
Endangered Species
Global Warning
Forestry
Human Impacts
Plant Prospecting
Rain Forest Canopy
Rain Forests
Wood Products

## REPRODUCTION

Breeder
Breeding
Breeding Systems
Cell Cycle
Chromosomes
Embryogenesis
Flowers
Fruits
Fruits, Seedless
Gametophyte
Genetic Engineer
Hybrids and Hybridization
Invasive Species
Pollination Biology
Propagation
Reproduction, Alternation of Generations
Reproduction, Asexual

Reproduction, Fertilization
Reproduction, Sexual
Seed Dispersal
Seed Preservation
Seeds
Sporophyte
Tissue Culture

## TREES AND FORESTS

Acid Rain
Allelopathy
Arborist
Atmosphere and Plants
Bark
Biodiversity
Biome
Botanical Gardens and Arboreta
Carbon Cycle
Chestnut Blight
Coffee
Coniferous Forests
Curator of a Botanical Garden
Deciduous Forests
Deforestation
Dendrochronology
Dutch Elm Disease
Ecology, Fire
Forester
Forestry
Interactions, Plant-Fungal
Landscape Architect
Mycorrhizae
Paper
Plant Prospecting
Propagation
Rain Forest Canopy
Rain Forests
Savanna
Shape and Form of Plants
Tree Architecture
Wood Products

## WATER RELATIONS

Acid Rain
Aquatic Ecosystems
Atmosphere and Plants
Bark
Cacti
Desertification
Deserts

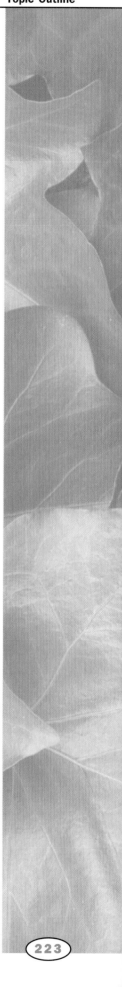

# Volume 3 Index

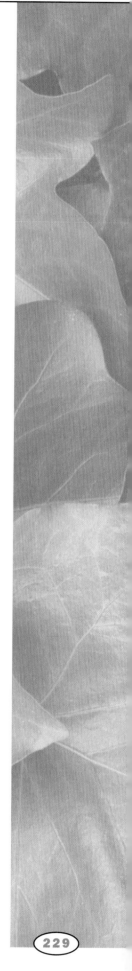

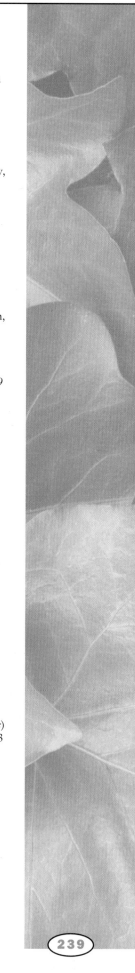

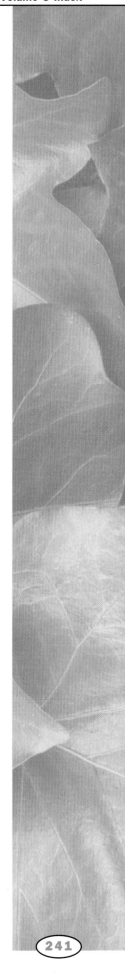